Lecture Notes in Computer Science 13180

More information about this subseries at https://link.springer.com/bookseries/7410

Xianfeng Zhao · Alessandro Piva ·
Pedro Comesaña-Alfaro (Eds.)

Digital Forensics and Watermarking

20th International Workshop, IWDW 2021
Beijing, China, November 20–22, 2021
Revised Selected Papers

Springer

Editors
Xianfeng Zhao 🆔
Institute of Information Engineering
Chinese Academy of Sciences
Beijing, China

Alessandro Piva 🆔
University of Florence
Florence, Italy

Pedro Comesaña-Alfaro 🆔
University of Vigo
Vigo, Spain

ISSN 0302-9743   ISSN 1611-3349 (electronic)
Lecture Notes in Computer Science
ISBN 978-3-030-95397-3   ISBN 978-3-030-95398-0 (eBook)
https://doi.org/10.1007/978-3-030-95398-0

LNCS Sublibrary: SL4 – Security and Cryptology

This Springer imprint is published by the registered company Springer Nature Switzerland AG
The registered company address is: Gewerbestrasse 11, 6330 Cham, Switzerland

Preface

The International Workshop on Digital-forensics and Watermarking (IWDW) is a premier forum for researchers and practitioners working on novel research, development and application of digital watermarking, data hiding, and forensics techniques for multimedia security. The 20th International Workshop on Digital-forensics and Watermarking (IWDW 2021) was organized by the State Key Laboratory of Information Security at the Institute of Information Engineering, Chinese Academy of Sciences. It was held in Beijing, China, during November 20–22, 2021. Although IWDW 2021 was held with the aid of an online conference system due to the persistent COVID-19 epidemic situation, it was very successful and as significant as the previous editions. More than 200 people attended the workshop online.

IWDW aims at promoting research and development in both new and traditional areas of multimedia security. The organizer of IWDW 2021 continued updating the topics of interest in the Call for Papers to reflect the new advances. For example, the word "steganology" has been formally adopted as a collective term for both "steganography" and "steganalysis" which make up the two aspects of one subject, and the topic of theoretical steganology has been added in to encourage research in basic theories. IWDW 2021 received 32 valid submissions. Each of them was assigned to at least two members of the Technical Program Committee for review. Finally, the decisions were made on a highly competitive basis. Only 18 submissions were accepted according to the average score ranking. The accepted papers cover many important topics in current research in multimedia security, and the presentations were organized into three sessions including "Forensics and Security Analysis", "Watermarking", and "Steganology". In addition, there were two invited keynotes: "Digital images steganography using adversarial embedding" by Tomas Pevny and "When provably secure steganography meets deep generative models" by Kejiang Chen which reported the new advances in AI-based steganology and theoretical steganology, respectively.

We would like to thank all of the authors, committee members, reviewers, keynote speakers, session chairs, volunteers, and attendees. It is the participation of them all that once again made a wonderful and special IWDW. And we appreciate the generous support from the organizer and sponsors. Finally, we hope that readers will enjoy this volume and find it rewarding in providing inspiration and possibilities for future work.

December 2021

Xianfeng Zhao
Alessandro Piva
Pedro Comesaña-Alfaro

Organization

General Chairs

Yun-Qing Shi — New Jersey Institute of Technology, USA
Hyoung Joong Kim — Korea University, South Korea

Technical Program Chairs

Xianfeng Zhao — Chinese Academy of Sciences, China
Alessandro Piva — University of Florence, Italy
Pedro Comesaña-Alfaro — University of Vigo, Spain

Program Committee

Mauro Barni — University of Siena, Italy
Patrick Bas — University of Lille, France
François Cayre — Grenoble-INP, GIPSA-Lab, France
Marc Chaumont — University of Montpellier, France
Dinu Coltuc — Valahia University of Targoviste, Romania
Isao Echizen — National Institute of Informatics, Japan
Anthony T. S. Ho — University of Surrey, UK
Yongjian Hu — South China University of Technology, China
Yongfeng Huang — Tsinghua University, China
Guang Hua — Wuhan University, China
Jiwu Huang — Shenzhen University, China
Xiangui Kang — Sun Yat-sen University, China
Sang-ug Kang — Sangmyung University, South Korea
Suah Kim — Korea University, South Korea
Christian Kraetzer — Otto-von-Guericke University Magdeburg, Germany
Minoru Kuribayashi — Okayama University, Japan
Chang-Tsun Li — Deakin University, Australia
Xiaolong Li — Beijing Jiaotong University, China
Qingzhong Liu — Sam Houston State University, USA
Wojciech Mazurczyk — Warsaw University of Technology, Poland
Jiangqun Ni — Sun Yat-sen University, China
Akira Nishimura — Tokyo University of Information Sciences, Japan
Fernando Pérez-González — University of Vigo, Spain

Sponsors

 Chinese Academy of Sciences

 State Key Laboratory of Information Security

 New Jersey Institute of Technology

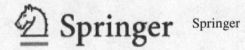 Springer

Contents

Forensics and Security Analysis

A Multi-level Feature Enhancement Network for Image Splicing Localization

Zeyu Zhang[1,2], Yun Cao[1,2], and Xianfeng Zhao[1,2(✉)]

[1] State Key Laboratory of Information Security, Institute of Information Engineering, Chinese Academy of Sciences, Beijing 100195, China
{zhangzeyu,caoyun,zhaoxianfeng}@iie.ac.cn
[2] School of Cyber Security, University of Chinese Academy of Sciences, Beijing 100195, China

Abstract. Most current neural network-based splicing localization methods are based on subtle telltales from inter-pixel differences. But for recompressed and downsampled data, these artifacts are weakened. In this paper, we propose a novel multi-level feature enhancement network (MFENet) to enhance the features. Tampering with an image not only destroys the consistency of the inherent high-frequency noise in host images, but also is performed post-processing operations to weaken this discrepancy. Therefore, based on the high-pass filtered image residuals, we combine the detection evidence of post-processing operations to complete splicing forensic task. For the purpose of enhancing the distinguishability of features in the residual domain, we use bilinear pooling to fuse low-level manipulation features and residuals. In order to improve the consistency between the ground truth and the splicing localization result, we integrate global attention modules to minimize the intra-class variance by measuring the similarity of features. Finally, we propose a multi-scale training generation strategy to train our network, which provides local and global information for the input and pays more attention to the overall localization during gradient feedback. The experimental results show that our method achieves better performance than other state-of-the-art methods.

Keywords: Splicing localization · Post-processing operations · Manipulation

1 Introduction

Due to the accessibility of user-friendly editing software such as Photoshop and GIMP, anyone can easily create convincing tampered pictures. These fakes have a significant impact on our lives: from the private, the social, to the legal [9]. It is serious security task to detect the authenticity of the image and localize the tamped regions. In this paper, we focus on a challenging task, image splicing localization task. Image splicing means a particular region of one image (called donor image) is cut and paste to the another image (called the host image).

X. Zhao et al. (Eds.): IWDW 2021, LNCS 13180, pp. 3–16, 2022.
https://doi.org/10.1007/978-3-030-95398-0_1

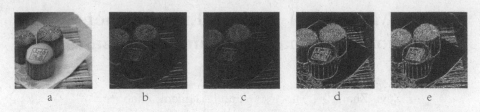

Fig. 1. Example of feature maps. (a) Original image; (b) low-level statistical feature map under the green channel; (c) Manipulation feature map under the green channel; (d) Feature map after bilinear and max pooling; (e) Feature map after bilinear and mean pooling. (Color figure online)

Traditional approaches utilize the internal inconsistency caused by tampering to achieve splicing localization, for example the low-level statistics, semantic content and noise-print. In [5,8,20], different tampering traces are used to design detectors. The photo-response non-uniformity (PRNU) [5] noise pattern is used to localize splicing area, as noise-print in the host image is different from that of the donor image. In addition, the sample correlation in the interpolation process of the color filter array (CFA) [8] will be changed due to tampering. In order to capture the discrepancies in high-order statistical, Markov feature [20] is proposed. However, these model-based splicing localization methods [7,14,15,22] may undergo expensive computational cost while producing high dimensional features, and performance will decrease for post-processed images.

Recently, splicing localization approaches based on deep learning have become popular. These methods could be classified into two categories. One type of method is non-end-to-end. First, the image is classified through a neural network, and then the pixel classification is obtained based on statistical method. Based on the statistics of the tampering probability of the image block where the pixel is located, the pixel-level classification result is obtained. In [12], they also merge the location map obtained by copy-move forgery detector to further improve the accuracy of pixel classification. In [17], morphological calculations are performed. These methods undergo additional and expensive computational cost to obtain the better results. The second type of method are end-to-end, learning directly from ground truth. As current deep learning methods show great success in semantic segmentation or object detection task, these methods are leveraged to perform forensic tasks. Salloum et al. [18] proposed a splicing localization framework based on multi-task fully convolutional network, learning jointly from tampering edge and region. Zhou et al. [23] proposed a two-stream network based on Faster R-CNN to localize spliced regions. Most current neural network-based splicing localization methods are based on statistics between adjacent pixels to learn high-level features. But the data in social networks is usually recompressed and downsampled, and the extracted artifacts will be weakened, resulting in a decrease in the accuracy of detection.

In this paper, we propose a novel multi-level feature enhancement network (MFENet). MFENet are multi-task network based on multi-level features. To classify the candidate region is spliced or not, the network combines the two evidences of the inconsistency of high-frequency noise and the detection of post-processing manipulation. In the splicing localization process, we first merge these two tampering traces to enhance statistical artifacts in post-processing data. Then, we use hierarchical special layers to extract different types of features, and concatenate multi-level features to enhance the splicing traces. In order to further optimize the extracted latent features, we integrate global attention modules in the MFENet, where the global attention reduces the intra-class differences by measuring the similarity of high-level features. Finally, we propose a multi-scale training generation strategy to provide local and global splicing area for the input and calculate the loss of generated masks at different scales. Our main contributions are as follows:

- By considering the prerequisite of image splicing task is the combination of detection evidence of post-processing manipulation and inconsistency of high-frequency noise, we propose MFENet to solve this problem.
- We combine multi-level features to enhance the splicing traces and integrate global attention module in the network to further optimize latent features.
- We propose a newly multi-scale training generation strategy to provide multi-scale information for the network and feed back the multi-scale loss to the network.

The rest of the paper is structured as follows: In Sect. 2, a brief review of related methods is introduced. In Sect. 3, We present the MFENet setup considered in this paper and introduce the main notations. In Sect. 4, experiments are conducted to demonstrate the effectiveness the proposed method. In Sect. 5, we conclude the paper with some final remarks.

2   Preliminary

Learning to tampered traces in the image residuals has become a common approach. We introduce a classic way. In order to learn prediction error and suppress the image's content, constrained convolution [3] is proposed by constraining the weights of convolution to satisfy $\mathbf{W}_k(0,0) = -1$ and $\sum_{m,n \neq 0,0} \mathbf{W}_k(m,n) = 1$, where $\mathbf{W}_k(i,j)$ is the weight of the kth filter at position (i,j). This serves to suppress an image's content, as they are not contained in prediction errors largely. Because extracted features produce correspond to prediction error fields, they are used as low-level forensic traces. This method is also used jointly with other types of convolution to enhance artifact. Wu et al. [21] leverage various convolutions to extract features, and feed concatenated features into the network to learn high-level features of manipulation traces.

We found that the low-level feature extracted by the training convolutional neural network based on constrained convolution are composed of spliced region and other image's content, as shown in Fig. 1(c). We call this feature as manipulation feature, and call this network as CONS-NET in this paper. In our network, we use high-pass filters composed of three first-order filters to extract low-level statistics, as shown in Fig. 1(b). The weight of these filters are utilized to initialize the convolution, we call this convolution as HP convolution. Multi-order filters are deprecated because feeding filtered feature into network will affect final spliced segmentation close to coarse edge. In order to further enhance artifact, manipulation feature is fused with extracted low-level statistics by bilinear pooling. Highlight the area that the jump effect from the pixel in the host image to the pixel in the donor image, as shown in Fig. 1(d)(e).

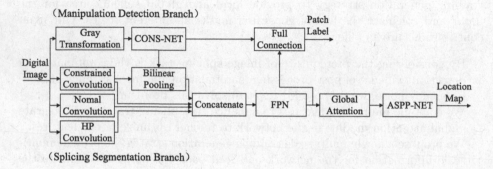

Fig. 2. Block diagram of classification and localization process.

3   Proposed Method

As shown in Fig. 2, we proposed MFENet framework is composed of two branches: manipulation detection and splicing segmentation, one of which performs image patch classification task, and the other performs pixel-level classification task. As tampering not only destroys the low-level statistical consistency, but also performs post-processing operations to make it more visually realistic, we employ CONS-NET as manipulation detection network and combine these two tampered traces for classification. For pixel-level classification task, we first use bilinear pooling to fuse the manipulation feature extracted by trained constrained convolution and the residuals extracted by HP convolution to further reflect abnormal relationships of neighbourhood pixels. Then, enhanced features are concatenated with features extracted by HP convolution [11], constrained convolution [3], normal convolution to enhance splicing artifact. Next, we use tuned Feature Pyramid Networks (FPN) to learn high-level representation of multi-level features and integrate global attention to optimize extracted latent feature. Finally, Atrous Spatial Pyramid Pooling Network (ASPP-NET) is constructed to generate location map. See Fig. 3 for more details of the MFENet.

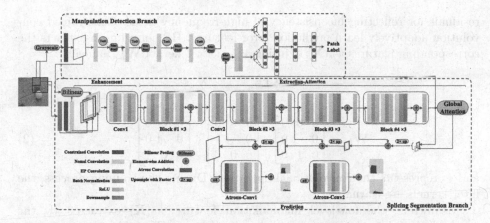

Fig. 3. The overview of our proposed MFENet.

3.1 Manipulation Detection

In the manipulation detection branch, we employ CONS-NET as a post-processing manipulation detection network. In the network, the constrained convolution is adopted at the beginning to adaptively learn manipulation traces. The resulting manipulation feature corresponds to the prediction error and suppresses the image's content. The feature is further represented through deeper layers to detect the post-processing manipulation. In order to complete the splicing detection task, we use a fully connected network to connect the extracted feature with high-level feature extracted in the splicing segmentation branch to detect whether the image patch are spliced or not.

3.2 Splicing Segmentation

As shown in Fig. 3, the splicing segmentation branch consists of three main blocks, namely, the enhancement block, the extraction-attention block and the prediction block. The enhancement block involves a hierarchically combined input layers for enhancing the splicing traces. The following extraction block, composed of 4 ResNet block, is designed to extract high-level features that are suitable for distinguishing spliced image, with the assistance of global attention modules. Eventually, the prediction block outputs the final splicing segmentation result. We are ready to explain the aforementioned three main blocks.

Enhancement Block. Several pre-designed input layers are incorporated to extract different types of features, which include HP convolution [11], constrained convolution [3] and normal convolution. HP convolution is designed to get image residuals for reflecting inconsistency of high-frequency noise. Constrained convolution adaptively learn prediction error features. HP convolution extracts the corresponding features $\Phi_h(\mathbf{X})$ by using a $5 \times 5 \times 3$ kernel $\mathbf{W}_h$, namely,

$$\Phi_h(\mathbf{X}) = \mathbf{W}_h \otimes \mathbf{X} \tag{1}$$

where

$$\mathbf{W}_h = \begin{bmatrix} 0 & 0 & 0 \\ 0 & -1 & 0 \\ 0 & 1 & 0 \end{bmatrix}; \begin{bmatrix} 0 & 0 & 0 \\ 0 & -1 & 1 \\ 0 & 0 & 0 \end{bmatrix}; \begin{bmatrix} 0 & 0 & 0 \\ 0 & -1 & 0 \\ 0 & 0 & 1 \end{bmatrix}, \tag{2}$$

and $\otimes$ represents the convolutional operation. During the training process, the filter kernels are learnable.

Meanwhile, the low-level manipulation feature $\Phi_k(\mathbf{X})$ extracted by the manipulation detection branch is adopt to fuse $\Phi_h(\mathbf{X})$, this feature can be extracted by

$$\Phi_k(\mathbf{X}) = \mathbf{W}_k \otimes \mathbf{X} \tag{3}$$

where $\mathbf{W}_k$ is trained constrained kernel. During the training process, the weight of $\mathbf{W}_k$ satisfy

$$\sum_{m,n \neq 0,0} \mathbf{W}_k(m,n) = 1$$
$$\mathbf{W}_k(0,0) = -1 \tag{4}$$

where $\mathbf{W}_k(i,j)$ is the weight of the kth at position (i,j). To further enhance artifact in residual domain, bilinear operation is performed to fuse $\Phi_h(\mathbf{X})$ and $\Phi_k(\mathbf{X})$, which is defined as:

$$bilinear\,(f_A, f_B) = f_A^T(l,X) f_B(l,X) \tag{5}$$

where $f_A(l,X)$ and $f_B(l,X)$ denotes two features of the image X in position l, $f_A(l,X) \in R^{T \times M}$ and $f_B(l,X) \in R^{T \times N}$. So, we have:

$$\Phi_{b1} = bilinear\,(Max(\Phi_h), Max(\Phi_k))$$
$$\Phi_{b2} = bilinear\,(Mean(\Phi_h), Mean(\Phi_k)) \tag{6}$$

where Max denotes elements wise maximum, Max denotes element-wise mean, and Φ_{b1} and Φ_{b2} denotes fused features.

We also use normal convolution and concatenate extracted features to enhance splicing artifacts. Next, we use two standard convolutions to initially process the enhanced features.

Extraction-Attention Block. For the extraction-attention block, we use tuned FPN as backbone network and global attention to improve the internal consistency of element of high-level features. The network contains 4 blocks and every block is constructed based on ResNet. All blocks are repeated 3 times, and downsample operation is performed in the last 3 blocks. After getting high-level feature, there are still other image's content. In order to reduce the number of misclassified pixels, global attention is utilized to minimize the intraclass variance. Practically, let $\Phi(\mathbf{X})$ be high-level feature map, when using X as the input. 1×1 Patches $\{\mathbf{P}_i\}_{i=1}^{K}$ are extracted. For each patch, we compute its intra-cosine similarities.

$$S_{i,j} = \left\langle \frac{\mathbf{P}_i}{\|\mathbf{P}_i\|}, \frac{\mathbf{P}_j}{\|\mathbf{P}_j\|} \right\rangle \tag{7}$$

Upon computing all $S_{i,j}$'s, then a similarity threshold ξ is set to select the similar patches for $\mathbf{P}_i$ by looping through all the blocks. Let $\mathcal{N} = \{n_1, \ldots, n_C\}$ record all the indexes of these similar patches. Then we have

$$\mathcal{N} = \{k \mid S_{i,j} \geq \xi\} \tag{8}$$

We then update each $\mathbf{P}_i$ via the average of its corresponding similar patches:

$$\mathbf{P}_i^* = \frac{1}{C} \sum_{j \in \mathcal{N}} \mathbf{P}_j \tag{9}$$

Therefore, the intra-class similarity is increase by updating $\mathbf{P}_i^*$ along with the training processes.

Prediction Block. In the prediction block, we upsample the tuned high-level features through the nearest interpolation algorithm. And add the feature obtained from each block to the upsampled feature. We construct Atrous Spatial Pyramid Pooling Network (ASPP-NET) to capture the information of different scales provided by the feature. ASPP-NET is consist of four parallel atrous blocks, where every block contains atrous convolution with different sampling rates. These atrous convolution can focus on tampered regions of different scales by different field-of-views. In every block, each atrous convolution is followed by convolution, batch normalization and ReLU function. Final, the feature obtained by every block are fused to generate the final masks.

3.3   Fused Loss Function

We use the negative log likelihood loss (NLLLoss) loss and CrossEntropyLoss to supervise the training of our network, as the tasks of our network are to detect tampered/pristine and locate the spliced region. More specifically, for a pair of label and predicted label $(y, \hat{y})$, the CrossEntropyLoss be defined as:

$$\Phi_{\text{dec}} = -\frac{1}{n} \sum_{i=1}^{n} y_i \log(\hat{y}_i) \tag{10}$$

where y_i (similarly for $\hat{y}_i$) denotes the ith element of y. Usually, for a pair of ground-truth and predicted spliced masks (GT, M) the NLLLoss can be defined as:

$$\Phi_{seg}(GT, M) = \frac{1}{HW} \sum_{i=1}^{H} \sum_{j=1}^{W} (\lambda GT(i,j) \log M(i,j)$$
$$+ \gamma(1 - GT(i,j)) \log(1 - M(i,j)) \tag{11}$$

where $GT(i,j)$ (similarly for $M(i,j)$) denotes the (i,j)th element of GT with a size of $H \times W$, λ and γ are hyper parameters that determines whether the network focuses more on the spliced area or the original area. We train the network based on multi-scale training-generation way, so the splicing Segmentation loss is consist of two pair of ground-truth and predicted spliced masks with a size of 32×32 and 64×64, respectively. The proposed splicing segmentation task loss is defined as:

$$\Phi = \alpha\Phi_{seg}\ (GT_{64}, M_{64}) + \beta\Phi_{seg}\ (GT_{32}, M_{32}) + \Phi_{dec} \tag{12}$$

where α and β are predefined parameters set as 5 and 1 respectively.

4   Experiments

4.1   Preparation

Implementation Details. The proposed network is implemented using the PyTorch framework. Adadelta is adopted as the optimizer. We set the batch size to 32. In the training process, the hyper parameter λ and γ are set as 20 and 1 respectively, based on analyzing the proportion of the spliced area in the ground truth mask. The network is trained on two TESLA P100 PCIe GPUs.

Datasets Setup. We compare our method with other states-of-the-art method on NC2016 dataset [1], DSO-1 dataset [4] and Columbia dataset [16]. For each dataset, we randomly split dataset into three categories with training (65%), validation (10%) and testing (25%) as Cun et al. [6]. Then, we extract the grayscale-color image pairs in training set. For multi-scale training way, we cropped images to size of 128×128 and 256×256 overlappingly. These patches with different sizes are resized to a size of 128×128 when they are fed into the network. Thus, we have more than 10k training patches on each dataset which is enough for training classification network and segmentation network. Similarly, we obtain validation and test set.

Initialization Parameter Setup. In order to detect the post-processing manipulation, we use the pre-trained weight of CONS-NET to initialize parameters of the manipulation detection branch. Based on CASIA v2.0 dataset, we build a dataset consisting of 120000 grayscale images to train the network, where 22000 images are authentic and the rest are added five post-processing operation as shown in Table 1. For different manipulations technologies (median filtering,

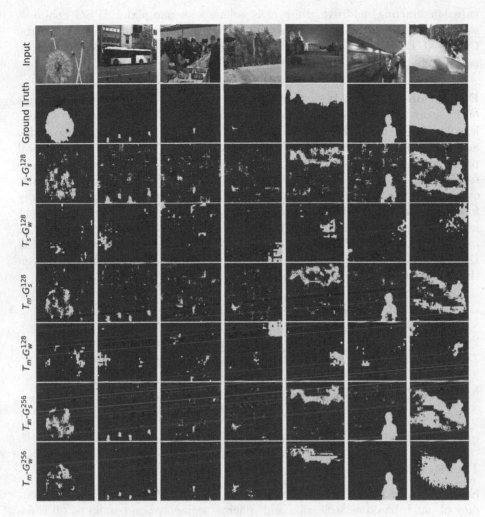

Fig. 4. Evaluation on NC2016 dataset.

Table 1. Post-processing operation and editing parameters.

Post-processing operation	Editing parameter
Resampling	Scaling = 1.4, 1.6, 1.8, 2
Median filtering	Size of Kernel = 3, 5, 7, 9
Gaussian blurring	Size of Kernel = 3, 5, 7, 9
JPEG compression	Quantization factor = 60, 61, $\cdots$, 89, 90
Additive white gaussian noise	Noise factor = 1.4, 1.6, 1.8, 2

gaussian blurring, additive white gaussian noise, resampling, JPEG compression), different editing parameters are arbitrarily selected. Finally, we use the CONS-NET weight with the highest detection accuracy to initialize the network parameters and be frozen during the subsequent training process.

Evaluation Metrics. We compare our method with seven relevant methods on F1 score and Matthews Correlation Coefficient (MCC), including three deep learning based methods: Salloum et al. [18] learn to predict the spliced edge and mask from Fully Convolutional Network; Bappy et al. [2] use the local patch to classify the tampered region; Cun et al. [6] use the local feature to segment the spliced area and add Conditional Random Fields(CRF) to optimize output result, and four traditional methods: CFA2 [7] utilize Color Filet Array for forgery detection. NOI1 [15] assume that the splicing region will have different local image noise variance. BLK [14] classify the spliced region by detecting the periodic artifacts in JPEG compression. DCT [22] detect inconsistent of JPEG Discrete Cosine Transform coefficients histogram. We also use AUC score on three datasets in Table 3.

Table 2. Comparison of classification/segmentation accuracy.

	NC2016 dataset	DSO-1 dataset	Columbia dataset
Bappy et al. [2]	95.9%/89.5%	68.6%/53.8%	85.0%/78.0%
Cun et al. [6]	**97.8%**/89.6%	**83.7%**/75.1%	**89.7%**/83.9%
Ours	96.0%/**98.1%**	64.8%/**81.2%**	84.4%/**89.5%**

4.2 Evaluation

Evaluation of Patch Classification and Segmentation. We list the accuracy of patch-based classification and splicing segmentation results on all three datasets for model evaluation. As shown in Table 2, our method gain better results than other methods in spliced segmentation. Classification accuracy is slightly lower than Bappy et al. [2]. As shown in Fig. 5, our method get better significantly segmentation results than others. For Columbia dataset, there are 180 images, and the background and the content of spliced region are often totally different, so the edge of the spliced region is easy to recognize. However, comparing with the images which spliced region rarely shown in training set (Third and fourth columns from the right of Fig. 5), our method gain better results. In NC2016 dataset, some tampered images are tamper with post-processing techniques. Our network trained based on post-processing images makes the splicing segmentation task simple. Because neural network need to inference from manipulation feature and low level feature. We list the results on NC2016 dataset in Table 3 and Fig. 4, our method is significantly better than other states-of-the-art methods on several evaluation metrics.

Table 3. Comparison on three datasets. F1, MCC score are calculated for each image firstly and then calculate the average value while AUC is calculated amount all the pixels.

Metrics	Methods	NC2016	DSO-1	Columbia
F1	Salloum et al. [18]	0.5707	0.4795	0.6117
	Bappy et al. [2]	0.6242	0.3102	0.5270
	Cun et al. [6]	0.7900	0.5006	0.6482
	Ours	**0.8188**	**0.7591**	**0.9120**
MCC	Salloum et al. [18]	0.5703	0.4074	0.4792
	Bappy et al. [2]	0.6257	0.1882	0.5074
	Cun et al. [6]	0.7847	0.4379	0.6403
	Ours	**0.8240**	**0.7429**	**0.8910**
AUC	CFA2 [7]	0.57	0.51	0.54
	NOI1 [15]	0.47	0.55	0.51
	BLK [14]	0.51	0.29	0.29
	DCT [22]	0.51	0.37	0.62
	Bappy et al. [2]	0.68	0.65	0.62
	Cun et al. [6]	0.99	0.83	0.67
	Ours	**0.99**	**0.95**	**0.94**

Table 4. The effectiveness evaluation of the proposed multi-scale training-generation strategy in terms of F_1-score and MCC on NC2016 dataset. T_s denotes single-scale training way, T_m denotes multi-scale training way. In G_s^{128}, subscript s denotes that the mask is generated by sliding window way. In the sliding window-based generation method, the stride is half the size of the generated mask, and we take the minimum operation for the overlapping part. Subscript w denotes that the mask is generated by feeding the resized whole image into network. The superscript denotes the size of the generated mask.

Metrics	F1	MCC
T_s-G_s^{128}	0.5406	0.5633
T_s-G_w^{128}	0.2671	0.2547
T_m-G_s^{128}	0.6377	0.6544
T_m-G_w^{128}	0.3485	0.3454
T_m-G_s^{256}	0.7099	0.7219
T_m-G_w^{256}	**0.8188**	**0.8240**

Effectiveness Evaluation of Multi-scale Training-Generation Strategy.
To verify the effectiveness of multi-scale training-generation strategy, ablation experiments are done on NC2016 dataset. As shown in the third to sixth rows of Fig. 4, using images with single scale to train the network and generate small-

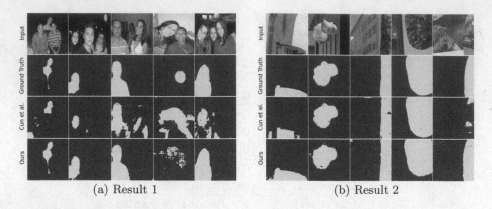

(a) Result 1   (b) Result 2

Fig. 5. Results on DSO-1 dataset (Left) and Columbia dataset (Right).

scale images can only capture coarse edges, and there are many incorrectly classified pixels. As shown in the last row of Fig. 4 and Table 4, the best results are obtained by training with multi-scale patches and feeding the resized whole image to generate large-scale location map. The multi-scale training-generation strategy increases the image receptive field without expanding the network depth to provide more information to the network. Small-scale patch focuses on the splicing edge, and large-scale patch focuses on the splicing area.

Generalization Performance Evaluation. We compare the generalization performance of our method with several state-of-the-art deep learning based methods in Shi [19], Huh [10], Salloum [18], Li [13] and Rao [17]. Following Shi [19] and Salloum [18], we train our method on CASIA v2.0 dataset while conduct cross-dataset evaluation on DSO-1 dataset. Since we fed an image with a size of 512×512 into network to obtain predicted mask, where these image with the larger scale did not appear in the training process, we finally took the object with the largest connected component as the final result. As illustrated in Table 5 and Fig. 6, the proposed method outperforms Huh [10] and Salloum [18] and Rao [17] in terms of F_1-score.

Table 5. The generalization performance comparison of the proposed method with other deep learning based methods in terms of F_1-score on DSO-1 dataset.

Method	Proposed	Salloum [18]	Huh [10]	Shi [19]	Rao [17]	Li [13]
F_1	**0.6897**	0.4790	0.5200	0.5800	0.5813	0.2304

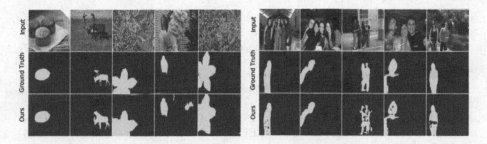

Fig. 6. Results on CASIA v2.0 dataset (Left) and DSO-1 dataset (Right). Note that, we train our network on CASIA v2.0 dataset and test on DSO-1 dataset.

5   Conclusion

In this paper, we propose a multi-level feature enhancement network (MFENet) to address the problem of image splicing detection and localization. Our MFENet combines low-level statistical inconsistency and detection evidence of post processing manipulation to patch classification/segmentation. In addition, we propose a multi-scale training-generation strategy to train MFENet. Experiments demonstrate that our method is superior other state-of-the-art algorithms. We also evaluate the effectiveness of multi-scale training-generation strategy by ablation experiments, and evaluate the generalization performance of our network through cross-dataset evaluation.

Acknowledgments. The authors would like to thank the anonymous reviewers for their valuable suggestions. This work was supported by National Key Technology Research and Development Program under 2020AAA0140000, 2019QY2202 and 2019QY(Y)0207.

References

1. NIST: Nimble media forensics challenge datasets (2016). https://www.nist.gov/itl/iad/mig/media-forensics-challenge
2. Bappy, J.H., Roy-Chowdhury, A.K., Bunk, J., Nataraj, L., Manjunath, B.: Exploiting spatial structure for localizing manipulated image regions. In: Proceedings of the IEEE International Conference on Computer Vision, pp. 4970–4979 (2017)
3. Bayar, B., Stamm, M.C.: Constrained convolutional neural networks: a new approach towards general purpose image manipulation detection. IEEE Trans. Inf. Forensics Secur. **13**(11), 2691–2706 (2018)
4. Carvalho, T., Riess, C., Angelopoulou, E., Pedrini, H., Rocha, A.: Exposing digital image forgeries by illumination color classification. IEEE Trans. Inf. Forensics Secur. **8**(7), 1182–1194 (2013)
5. Chen, M., Fridrich, J., Goljan, M., Lukas, J.: Determining image origin and integrity using sensor noise. IEEE Trans. Inf. Forensics Secur. **3**(1), 74–90 (2008)

6. Cun, X., Pun, C.-M.: Image splicing localization via semi-global network and fully connected conditional random fields. In: Leal-Taixé, L., Roth, S. (eds.) ECCV 2018. LNCS, vol. 11130, pp. 252–266. Springer, Cham (2019). https://doi.org/10.1007/978-3-030-11012-3_22

7. Dirik, A.E., Memon, N.: Image tamper detection based on demosaicing artifacts. In: 2009 16th IEEE International Conference on Image Processing (ICIP), pp. 1497–1500. IEEE (2009)

8. Ferrara, P., Bianchi, T., De Rosa, A., Piva, A.: Image forgery localization via fine-grained analysis of CFA artifacts. IEEE Trans. Inf. Forensics Secur. **7**(5), 1566–1577 (2012)

9. Ghosh, A., Zhong, Z., E Boult, T., Singh, M.: SpliceRadar: a learned method for blind image forensics. In: Proceedings of the IEEE/CVF Conference on Computer Vision and Pattern Recognition (CVPR) Workshops, June 2019

10. Huh, M., Liu, A., Owens, A., Efros, A.A.: Fighting fake news: image splice detection via learned self-consistency. In: Ferrari, V., Hebert, M., Sminchisescu, C., Weiss, Y. (eds.) ECCV 2018. LNCS, vol. 11215, pp. 106–124. Springer, Cham (2018). https://doi.org/10.1007/978-3-030-01252-6_7

11. Li, H., Huang, J.: Localization of deep inpainting using high-pass fully convolutional network. In: Proceedings of the IEEE/CVF International Conference on Computer Vision, pp. 8301–8310 (2019)

12. Li, H., Luo, W., Qiu, X., Huang, J.: Image forgery localization via integrating tampering possibility maps. IEEE Trans. Inf. Forensics Secur. **12**(5), 1240–1252 (2017)

13. Li, H., Yang, C., Lin, F., Jiang, B.: Constrained R-CNN: a general image manipulation detection model. In: IEEE ICME (2020)

14. Li, W., Yuan, Y., Yu, N.: Passive detection of doctored JPEG image via block artifact grid extraction. Sig. Process. **89**(9), 1821–1829 (2009)

15. Mahdian, B., Saic, S.: Using noise inconsistencies for blind image forensics. Image Vis. Comput. **27**(10), 1497–1503 (2009)

16. Ng, T.T., Hsu, J., Chang, S.F.: Columbia image splicing detection evaluation dataset (2009)

17. Rao, Y., Ni, J., Zhao, H.: Deep learning local descriptor for image splicing detection and localization. IEEE Access **8**, 25611–25625 (2020)

18. Salloum, R., Ren, Y., Jay Kuo, C.C.: Image splicing localization using a multi-task fully convolutional network (MFCN). J. Vis. Commun. Image Represent. **51**, 201–209 (2018)

19. Shi, Z., Shen, X., Kang, H., Lv, Y.: Image manipulation detection and localization based on the dual-domain convolutional neural networks. IEEE Access **6**, 76437–76453 (2018)

20. Singh, A., Singh, G., Singh, K.: A Markov based image forgery detection approach by analyzing CFA artifacts. Multimedia Tools Appl. **77**, 28949–28968 (2018)

21. Wu, Y., AbdAlmageed, W., Natarajan, P.: ManTra-Net: manipulation tracing network for detection and localization of image forgeries with anomalous features. In: Proceedings of the IEEE/CVF Conference on Computer Vision and Pattern Recognition (CVPR), June 2019

22. Ye, S., Sun, Q., Chang, E.: Detecting digital image forgeries by measuring inconsistencies of blocking artifact. In: 2007 IEEE International Conference on Multimedia and Expo, pp. 12–15. IEEE (2007)

23. Zhou, P., Han, X., Morariu, V., Davis, L.: Learning rich features for image manipulation detection. In: Proceedings of the IEEE Conference on Computer Vision and Pattern Recognition (CVPR), June 2018

MSA-CNN: Face Morphing Detection via a Multiple Scales Attention Convolutional Neural Network

Le-Bing Zhang[1], Juan Cai[1(✉)], Fei Peng[2], and Min Long[3]

[1] Huaihua University, Huaihua 418000, China
hhxycj@hhtc.edu.cn
[2] Hunan University, Changsha 410082, China
[3] Changsha University of Science and Technology, Changsha 410114, China

Abstract. Face morphing attack is becoming a serious threat to the existing face recognition systems. Some different approaches for morphing attack detection have been put forward. However, there are few methods concentrated on detecting the morphing artifacts, which often appear in morphed facial images. In this work, we propose a multiple scales attention convolutional neural network (MSA-CNN), a novel approach that can effectively detect the morphing artifacts in face morphing attacks. It utilizes the attention mechanism to continuously pay attention to the morphing artifacts in multiple scales and finally realizes face morphing detection. Experimental results and analysis show that it can effectively locate the region of morphing artifacts, and outperforms the existing deep learning-based blind face morphing detection frameworks.

Keywords: Face morphing detection · Morphing artifacts · Attention convolutional neural network · Multiple scales

1 Introduction

Face recognition system (FRS) is widely used in our daily identity verification due to its high accuracy and non-contact characteristics. An example is the automatic border control (ABC) system. It can conveniently verify a person's identity with his electronic machine readable travel document (eMRTD) [1], which contains a facial reference image. However, a latest identity theft method called face morphing attack can easily deceive the FRS of the ABC [2]. It utilizes morphing techniques to create a morphed facial image from two persons' facial images, where the appearance and biological information are similar to that of both individuals to deceive the FRS. An example of a morphed facial image is shown in Fig. 1.

This research was supported by National Natural Science Foundation of China under grant nos. 62072055 and U1936115. It was also supported by Scientific Research Foundation of Hunan Provincial Education Department under grant nos. 20K098 and 19C1468, and co-funded by Key Laboratory of Intelligent Control Technology for Wuling-Mountain Ecological Agriculture under grant no. ZNKZN2019.

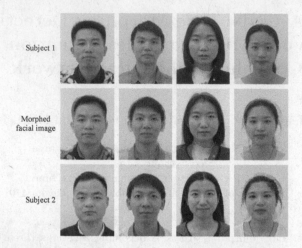

Subject 1

Morphed
facial image

Subject 2

Fig. 1. Some examples of the morphed facial images generated from two subjects.

In many countries, the submitted facial image is provided by the applicant in digital or printed form to apply for an eMRTD. Therefore, an attacker (e.g. a wanted criminal) could generate a morphed facial image by morphing his facial image with that of an accomplice (no guilty), and then the accomplice could obtain an eMRTD by submitting the morphed facial image. Since the morphed facial image is similar enough to the attacker, the attacker can use the eMRTD with the accomplice's identity to pass through the ABC. This will seriously affect the security of society. Subsequently, the vulnerability of FRS to face morphing attack [2–12] and some face morphing detection schemes [3,13–25] have been proposed to improve the security of FRS.

Although the existing face morphing detection methods achieve good performances, there still have some problems in detecting morphing artifacts which are common in morphed facial images. Morphing artifacts are shadow-like semi-transparent areas formed due to various reasons in the process of face morphing. It often appears in the region of the neck, hair, ears, pupils, nostrils, and other positions of a morphed facial image [7,21]. However, in the state-of-the-art researches of face morphing detection, the important forensic clue—morphing artifacts are ignored, and few methods can verify its effectiveness against morphing artifacts.

As a solution to such problems, we propose a novel multiple scales attention convolutional neural network (MSA-CNN). It mimics the human perception by selectively focusing on salient parts, and pays attention to the morphing artifacts in the morphed facial image for face morphing detection. The main contributions of this paper are as follows.

- We propose a multiple scales attention CNN (MSA-CNN) which can accurately locate the morphing artifacts region and effectively realize face morphing detection. To our knowledge, this is the first work to utilize a learning-based approach to investigate morphing artifacts as an important forensic clue for face morphing detection.

- To accurately detect the morphing artifacts by MSA-CNN, we propose attention-based recurrent network architecture. With this special architecture, the potential morphing artifact of a morphed facial image can be located, and a more accurate morphing artifacts region image is recurrently formed on a finer scale. The designed recurrent network architecture can accurately locate the morphing artifacts region and effectively realize face morphing detection.
- We verify the effectiveness of the proposed MSA-CNN for morphing artifacts detection and location by feature visualization. Compared with the existing deep learning architecture used in face morphing detection, it can achieve better performance and more explanatory in the effectiveness of morphing artifacts location.

The rest of the paper is organized as follows. The related work is introduced in Sect. 2; the proposed MSA-CNN is described in Sect. 3. Experimental results and analysis are provided in Sect. 4. Finally, some conclusions are drawn in Sect. 5.

2   Related Work

Currently, the research on face morphing attack is mainly focused on two aspects: the vulnerability of FRS on face morphing attack and face morphing detection methods.

2.1   Vulnerability of FRS on Face Morphing Attack

Ferrera et al. first investigated face morphing attacks in [2]. By using a morphed facial image, an attacker can successfully deceive an FRS. However, these morphed facial images are manually generated, which is time-consuming and not suitable for a large-scale generation to verify the vulnerability of FRS. Subsequently, Makrushin et al. proposed a landmark-based automatic morphed facial image generation method [3] and successfully fooled commercial-off-the-shelf FRS Luxand FaceSDK 6.1 [26] and human observers. Robertson et al. proved that it is possible to forge an eMRTD by morphed facial images in a real scenario [4]. Meanwhile, Gomez-Barrero et al. confirmed that some other biometric recognition systems are also vulnerable to morphing attacks (e.g. fingerprint and iris recognition systems) [5]. Furthermore, Some evaluation metrics were proposed to evaluate the vulnerability of the biometric systems on morphing attacks [6,7]. At the same time, Wandzik et al. investigated the vulnerability of deep learning-based FRS to landmark-based morphing attacks [8].

Recently, Damer et al. [9,10] proposed face morphing methods based on generative adversarial networks (GAN). However, there is still a certain discrepancy to the standard ID photo in the size and ratio of the facial region. Subsequently, some high-quality and high-resolution GAN-based face morphing methods were proposed [11, 12]. Although GAN-based morphed facial images are more realistic than landmark-based morphed facial images, for existing face morphing detectors, GAN-based morphed facial images are more deceptive than landmark-based ones.

2.2   Face Morphing Detection

The existing face morphing detection methods can be divided into two categories: blind face morphing detection methods and non-blind face morphing detection methods, depending on whether the auxiliary image is used or not. Most face morphing detection methods belong to the first category.

1) Blind face morphing detection methods

Blind face morphing detection methods detect whether a facial image has undergone a face morphing attack by using a single facial image. Considering the texture discrepancy between morphed facial images and real facial images, Raghavendra et al. [13] proposed a face morphing detection method based on texture descriptors. It utilized binarized statistical image features (BSIF) [27] to represent the texture discrepancy, and good detection performance can be achieved. As the generated morphed facial image is usually restored in JPEG format, some JPEG compression feature-based face morphing detection methods were proposed in [3, 14–16]. From the perspective of image source identification [28], some sensor pattern noise-based methods were proposed [17–19].

With the powerful feature extraction capabilities of deep learning, Raghavendra et al. [29] proposed a face morphing detection method based on CNN. It combined the intermediate features of VGG19 [30] and AlexNet [31] to detect both digital and print-scanned morphed facial images. Recently, Seibold et al. [20] proposed a deep learning-based face morphing detection approach. Three widely-used network architectures, such as AlexNet, GoogLeNet [32], and VGG19 were investigated, and it is found that the pre-trained VGG19 can achieve the best performance among these network architectures. Ferrera et al. [21] evaluated four typical network architectures, such as AlexNet, VGG, and ResNet [33] for face morphing detection in both digital and printing/scanning scenarios.

2) Non-blind face morphing detection methods

Different from blind face morphing detection, non-blind face morphing detection is carried out by using an extra auxiliary image. With an auxiliary image captured from FRS and a morphed image stored in the eMRTD, Ferrara et al. [22] proposed a face de-morphing method for restoring the morphing attack accomplice's facial image by face morphing inverse operation. Subsequently, Peng et al. [23] proposed a face de-morphing generative adversarial network (FD-GAN) to restore the morphing accomplice's facial image. Scherhag et al. [24] proposed a non-blind face morphing detection algorithm combining the deep face recognition features of a facial image captured from FRS and the facial image stored in the eMRTD. However, it cannot restore the morphing attack

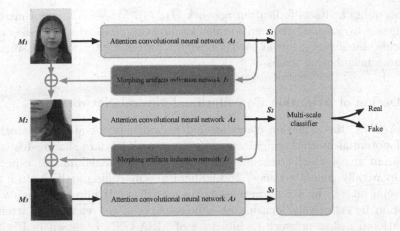

Fig. 2. The overview of MSA-CNN. The network modules with the same color indicate that they have the same network structure.

accomplice's facial image. Recently, Chaudhary et al. [25] proposed a face morphing detection method combining pre-processing and deep learning. It performs discrete wavelet transform on facial images, and uses a Siamese Inception ResNet v1 [34] for face morphing detection.

From the above analysis, face morphing detection is an open issue in biometrics security, and some works have been done to detect face morphing attacks. However, they ignore the important forensics clue—morphing artifacts in morphed facial images, and few methods can effectively prove its effectiveness in morphing artifacts detection. Especially, for deep learning-based blind face morphing detection, most of them focus on the direct or combined use of the typical networks, which lacks a reasonable explanation in feature selection. To solve these defects, a deep learning-based blind face morphing detection method named MSA-CNN is proposed in this paper.

3   The Proposed MSA-CNN

3.1   Overview of MSA-CNN

Inspired by the application of attention mechanism [35–39] and the recent success of fine-grained image recognition [39], MSA-CNN utilizes a recurrent network architecture. The overview of MSA-CNN is illustrated in Fig. 2. The inputs are recurrent from a full-size image in M_1 to fine-scale regions in M_2 and M_3, where M_2 and M_3 takes the input as the attended morphing artifacts regions from M_1 and M_2, respectively. MSA-CNN contains three parts: attention convolutional neural network, morphing artifacts indication network, and a multi-scale classifier. First, images at different scales are fed into attention convolutional neural networks (A_1 to A_3) to extract feature representation of potential morphing artifacts area. Second, networks is proceeded to predict a probability by multi-scale classifier on each scale (S_1 to S_3) and locate the morphing artifacts region by a morphing artifacts indication network (I_1, I_2). MSA-CNN is optimized to convergence by learning the multi-scale classification loss, which consists of an intra-scale classification loss at each scale and a pairwise inter-scale classification loss across neighboring scales.

3.2   Design of Attention Convolutional Neural Network

In MSA-CNN, the attention convolutional neural network aims to detect the area of potential morphing artifacts. Morphing artifacts are shadow-like semi-transparent areas, which commonly appear in morphed facial images, especially in automatically generated ones. To highlight the morphing artifacts in a morphed facial image, the attention mechanism is utilized. It mimics human visual perception by selectively focusing on salient parts of the view. The attention convolutional neural network architecture of MSA-CNN is shown in Fig. 3. It consists of ResNet18 [33] as the backbone network and convolutional block attention module (CBAM) [38]. CBAM is a lightweight and general module. It consists of channel and spatial attention modules, which is focused on "what" and "where" is the meaningful informative part, respectively. Thus, by combining with ResNet18 and CBAM, the designed attention convolutional neural network is not only lightweight but also can detect the potential area of morphing artifacts in morphed facial images.

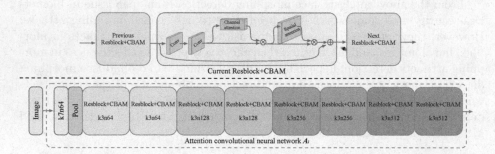

Fig. 3. The network structure of MSA-CNN's attention convolutional neural network. Where k is the kernel size, n is the number of feature maps.

3.3   Design of Morphing Artifacts Indication Network

In MSA-CNN, the morphing artifacts indication network is used to locate the most probable morphing artifact region for the next finer scale. It uses two-stacked fully-connected layers to predict the morphing artifacts region by searching the highest response value of morphing artifacts in the last layer of the proposed attention convolutional neural network. The prediction of the morphing artifacts region is represented as a square with a set of box coordinates, which is expressed as

$$[t_x, t_y, t_l] = f(W * M), \tag{1}$$

where M represents an input image, W represents the overall parameters of attention convolutional neural network mentioned above, $*$ denotes a set of operations of convolution, pooling and activation, the extracted deep representations are denoted as $W * M$, $f(\cdot)$ represents morphing artifacts indication network, t_x and t_y denotes the square's center coordinates in terms of x and y axis, respectively, and t_l denotes the half of the square's side length.

Once the location of a potential morphing artifacts region is predicted, the morphing artifacts region is cropped and zoomed to a finer scale with higher resolution to extract more fine-grained features. To ensure the morphing artifacts indication network can be optimized in training, the cropping operation is approximated by a variant of two-dimension boxcar function as a cropping mask, and it can be conducted by an element-wise multiplication between the original image at coarser scales and a cropping mask. The cropping operation is formulated as

$$M^c = M \odot C(t_x, t_y, t_l), \tag{2}$$

where M represents the original image at a coarse scale, $\odot$ represents element-wise multiplication, M^c represents the cropped region, and $C(\cdot)$ represents a cropping mask with a specific form, which is defined as

$$C(\cdot) = [g(x - t_{tl\_x}) - g(x - t_{br\_x})] \cdot [g(y - t_{tl\_y}) - g(y - t_{br\_y})], \tag{3}$$

where $g(\cdot)$ is a logistic function with large index k, t_{tl_x}, t_{br_x}, t_{tl_y}, and t_{br_y} represent the coordinates of the top-left (tl) and bottom-right (br) corners of the predict morphing artifacts region. They are defined as

$$g(x) = 1/(1 + exp^{-kx}), \tag{4}$$

$$t_{tl\_x} = t_x - t_l, t_{tl\_y} = t_y - t_l, t_{br\_x} = t_x + t_l, t_{br\_y} = t_y + t_l. \tag{5}$$

To adaptively zoom the cropped morphing artifacts region to a larger size, a bilinear interpolation is used to calculate the fine-grained morphing artifacts region M^a from the nearest four points in M^c with a linear map. The bilinear interpolation is expressed as

$$M^a_{(i,j)} = \sum_{\alpha,\beta=0}^{1} |1 - \alpha - \{i/\lambda\}||1 - \beta - \{j/\lambda\}|M^c_{(m,n)}, \tag{6}$$

where λ is a up-sampling factor, and it equals the value of enlarged size divided by t_l, $m = [i/\lambda] + \alpha$, $n = [j/\lambda] + \beta$, $[\cdot]$ represents the integral part, and $\{\cdot\}$ represents the fractional part.

3.4 Design of Multi-scale Classifier and Multi-scale Classification Loss

In MSA-CNN, multi-scale classifier can help the morphing artifacts indication network to accurately locate the position of morphing artifacts, and detect the

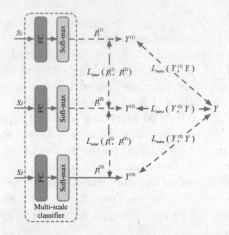

Fig. 4. The network structure of multi-scale classifier. The input and output are drawn with the solid line. Loss functions are drawn with the dash line. Blue dash lines represent intra-scale classification loss. Red dash lines represent inter-scale classification loss. (Color figure online)

face morphing attacks. It is composed of three single-scale classifiers, and each of which is composed of a fully-connected layer (FC) layer and a softmax layer. Multi-scale classification loss are designed to optimize MSA-CNN, and it is composed of intra-scale and pairwise inter-scale classification loss. The structure of multi-scale classifier is shown in Fig. 4, and the multi-scale classification loss for an image sample X is defined as

$$L(X) = \sum_{s=1}^{3} L_{intra}(Y^{(s)}, Y) + \sum_{s=1}^{2} L_{inter}(p_t^{(s)}, p_t^{(s+1)}), \tag{7}$$

where s denotes each scale, $Y^{(s)}$ and Y denotes the predicted label from a specific scale and the ground truth label, respectively. L_{intra} represents intra-scale classification loss, which predominantly optimizes the parameters of attention convolutional neural network for ensuring sufficient discrimination ability on each scale, $p_t^{(s)}$ denotes the prediction probability on the category labels t on scale s, and L_{inter} represents pairwise inter-scale classification loss, which is defined as

$$L_{inter}(p_t^{(s)}, p_t^{(s+1)}) = max\{0, p_t^{(s)} - p_t^{(s+1)} + margin\}. \tag{8}$$

It can enforce the network to achieve a more confident prediction on a finer-scale. Therefore, MSA-CNN can enable networks to take the predicted potential morphing artifacts area from coarse-scale as a reference, and gradually achieves the most discriminative morphing artifacts region.

Table 1. The morphing factor in four protocols

Evaluation protocol	Pixel fusion factor α	Position fusion factor β
Protocol I	0.5	0.5
Protocol II	0.5	0.1–0.9
Protocol III	0.1–0.9	0.5
Protocol IV	0.1–0.9	0.1–0.9

Table 2. The summary of the FM-database V2

Image size	subset	# Subject (Male, Female)	*Protocol I*		*Protocol II*		*Protocol III*		*Protocol IV*	
			# Bona fide	# Morphed	# Bona fide	# Morphed	# Bona fide	# Morphed	# Bona fide	# Morphed
360 × 480	Training set	50 (30, 20)	1121	1121	1121	1125	1121	1125	1121	1134
	Development set	25 (15, 10)	564	299	564	567	564	571	564	567
	Testing set	25 (15, 10)	566	296	566	567	566	570	566	567

4 Experiments and Analysis

4.1 Database and Evaluation Metrics

Although there are some works on face morphing database [40, 41], due to some biometric privacy reasons, we could not available to obtain these databases. Therefore, a face morphing database (FM-database V2) is built by ourselves by supplementing more subjects based on FM-database [23]. Here, FM-database V2, which contains 7,824 morphed facial images (successfully attack the commercial FRS Megvii Face++ Compare API [42]) and 2251 bona fide facial images, is used to evaluate the effectiveness of MSA-CNN.

To ensure the disjoint nature of the database, the morphed facial images are independently generated in training, development, and testing set. In each subset, the morphed facial images are automatically generated according to the workflow proposed in [3]. As the different morphing factors have impacts on the detection performance of FRS [2, 4, 8], four evaluation protocols in different morphing factors are designed for FM-database V2 to evaluate the impact of two morphing factors on face morphing detection. The morphing factors of four evaluation protocols are listed in Table 1, and the details of FM-database V2 are listed in Table 2.

For quantitative performance evaluation, two standardized ISO metrics [43]: APCER and BPCER are selected. The classification threshold is set by choosing the threshold with the equal error rate (EER) on the development set, and average classification error rate (ACER) of the testing set is used for evaluating the detection performance. *APCER*, *BPCER* and *ACER* are defined as

$$APCER = n_{mcr}/n_m, \tag{9}$$

$$BPCER = n_{rcm}/n_r, \tag{10}$$

$$ACER = (APCER + BPCER)/2, \tag{11}$$

where n_{mcr} represents the number of morphed facial images which are misclassified as the bona fide facial images, n_{rcm} represents the number of bona fide facial images which are misclassified as morphed facial images, n_m and n_r represent the number of the morphed facial images and the number of the bona fide facial images, respectively.

4.2 Implementation Details

There are two main networks in MSA-CNN: attention convolutional neural network and morphing artifacts indication network. The attention convolutional neural network is used to extract the morphing artifacts features of a suspected image (at a certain scale), and the morphing artifacts indication network is used to locate the artifact area and zoom it for further morphing artifacts feature extraction on a fine-scale. In addition, the multi-scale classification loss of MSA-CNN consists of two parts: intra-scale classification loss and inter-scale classification loss, which are used to optimize attention convolutional neural network and morphing artifacts indication network, respectively. In the MSA-CNN training stage, the two networks are trained alternately. That is, the parameters of the morphing artifacts indication network are fixed, and optimize the attention convolutional neural network by intra-scale classification loss. After that, the parameters of the attention convolutional neural network are kept unchanged, and the inter-scale classification loss is used to optimize the morphing artifacts indication network. The learning process of two networks is iterative, until two types of losses no longer change.

Here, all input facial images are resized to $448 \times 448 \times 3$, and morphing artifacts indication region are resized to $224 \times 224 \times 3$. The MSA-CNN is implemented using the deep learning toolbox PyTorch 1.3.1 [44] and runs on two NVIDIA Tesla PH402 SKU 200 GPUs. For index k in Eq. (4) and the *margin* in Eq. (8), they are empirically set as $k = 10$ and *margin* $= 0.02$, respectively.

4.3 Experiment Results

Considering the proposed method is a deep learning-based blind face morphing detection method, and the latest deep learning-based blind face morphing detection methods are focus on the direct or combined use of the typical CNNs (AlexNet, GoogLeNet, VGG19, and so on), which belongs to the same network architecture—traditional convolutional neural network architecture (denoted as T-CNN). Combining with the motivation of this work—morphing artifacts as an important forensics clue for face morphing detection, in the experiment, we compare the detection performance of different types of network architectures and analyze the influence of different network architectures on morphing artifacts detection to evaluate the effectiveness of the proposed MSA-CNN.

Here, three different network architectures are compared, and they are T-CNN, which attention mechanism and recurrent network architecture are neither used; attention convolutional neural network architecture (denoted as A-CNN), which introduces attention mechanism into the convolutional neural network;

multiple scales attention convolutional neural network architecture (denoted as MSA-CNN), which combines attention mechanism with recurrent network architecture. For T-CNN, typical VGG19 [30] and ResNet18 [33] with better performance are considered. For A-CNN, besides ResNet18 [33], CBAM [38] with attention mechanism both in space and channel is also utilized. For MSA-CNN, besides ResNet18 [33] and CBAM [38], a recurrent network architecture is constructed by the proposed morphing artifacts indication network. The face morphing detection performance of different network architectures is shown in Table 3.

Table 3. The performance of different network architectures (%)

Network architecture	Protocol I			Protocol II			Protocol III			Protocol IV		
	APCER	BPCER	ACER	APCER	BPCER	ACER	APCER	BPCER	ACER	APCER	BPCER	ACER
T-CNN (VGG19)	13.03	0	6.51	11.79	0.17	5.98	16.41	1.22	8.81	17.79	**1.75**	9.77
T-CNN (ResNet18)	10.47	0	5.23	6.17	0	3.08	10.53	13.43	11.98	17.11	27.92	22.51
A-CNN (ResNet18+CBAM)	2.36	2.83	2.59	3.35	1.94	2.64	16.14	2.12	9.13	15.52	14.66	15.09
MSA-CNN (scale 2)	1.82	3.04	2.43	2.29	0	1.14	11.57	**0.7**	6.13	18.57	1.94	10.25
MSA-CNN (scale 3)	**1.35**	0.17	**0.76**	**0.35**	0.88	**0.61**	**7.71**	4.24	**5.97**	**10.69**	4.61	**7.68**

As seen from Table 3, it can be found that the $ACER$ of MAS-CNN outperforms the other network architectures in four evaluation protocols of FM-database V2. Especially in $Protocol\ II$, the ACER of MAS-CNN is 0.61%, which is 77.18% lower than that of the second-best network architecture (A-CNN). For three different network architectures, MSA-CNN has the best performance, followed by A-CNN, and T-CNN has the worst performance. This is also consistent with our design expectations. Since the A-CNN can pay more attention to the key features (morphing artifacts feature) of the image, its performance is better than that of T-CNN. MAS-CNN utilizes morphing artifacts indication network to locate and refine the region of interest (morphing artifacts region) of the image in multiple scales. Thus, the best performance can be achieved. Furthermore, it can be also found that the performance of MSA-CNN can be improved as the scale increases.

To illustrate the effectiveness of morphing artifact detection, Grad-CAM [45] is applied to different network architectures, such as T-CNN (including VGG19 [30] and ResNet18 [33]), A-CNN, and MSA-CNN. Grad-CAM is a CNN visualization method that provides a way to explain what particular parts of the image influence the whole model's decision. By observing the region which the network has considered as important for a morphed facial image, it can reflect whether this network can effectively detect the morphing artifacts. The visualization results are illustrated in Fig. 5.

From Fig. 5, it can be found that MSA-CNN can effectively focus on the morphing artifacts region of a morphed facial image (corresponding with the red rectangle region of the input morphed facial image). To further understand why MSA-CNN selects these regions, the cropped region image (M_3) is replaced by the original input (morphed facial) image at scale 3 for the trained MSA-CNN model, and the results are shown in the last row of Fig. 5 (represents as

Fig. 5. The Grad-CAM visualization results.

MSA-CNN*). It indicates that MSA-CNN can not only capture the morphing artifacts area of the morphed facial image, but also automatically select the most probable morphing artifacts region. Furthermore, from Fig. 5, it also can be found that VGG19 extracts some facial features, and little attention is paid to the morphing artifacts area. It means that VGG19 may detect the morphed facial image by other features rather than morphing artifacts. Compared with ResNet18, A-CNN can better pay attention to morphing artifacts in morphed facial images.

The Grad-CAM visualization results show that MSA-CNN has better performance in locating the morphing artifacts region than that of the other network architectures. It means that MSA-CNN can well learn the morphing artifacts and select the artifacts as an important feature for face morphing detection.

5   Conclusion

In this paper, an MSA-CNN is proposed for face morphing detection. To the best of our knowledge, it is the first interpretable work for deep learning-based blind face morphing detection by detecting the morphing artifacts. An attention-based recurrent network architecture is specially designed to effectively locate the most probable morphing artifacts regions in the morphed facial images. It utilizes the attention convolutional neural network to extract the feature of the potential morphing artifacts area, and combines the multi-scale classifier with the morphing artifacts indication network to locate and refine the morphing artifacts region to achieve the multi-scale morphing artifacts detection. Experimental results demonstrate that the proposed MSA-CNN can achieve fairly good performance and visually illustrate its effectiveness in detecting morphing artifacts. Our future work will be focused on the research of more interpretable deep learning methods from the perspective of other morphing clues and detecting the morphed facial image generated by GAN.

References

1. The International Civil Aviation Organization: Machine readable travel documents - part 9: deployment of biometric identification and electronic storage of data in emrtds. Tech. rep. (2006)
2. Ferrara, M., Franco, A., Maltoni, D.: The magic passport. In: IEEE International Joint Conference on Biometrics (IJCB), pp. 1–7 (2014)
3. Andrey Makrushin, T.N., Dittmann, J.: Automatic generation and detection of visually faultless facial morphs. In: International Joint Conference on Computer Vision, Imaging and Computer Graphics Theory and Applications (VISIGRAPP), pp. 39–50 (2017)
4. Robertson, D.J., Kramer, R.S.S., Burton, A.M.: Fraudulent id using face morphs: experiments on human and automatic recognition. PLoS ONE 12(3), 1–12 (2017)
5. Gomez-Barrero, M., Rathgeb, C., Scherhag, U., Busch, C.: Is your biometric system robust to morphing attacks? In: International Workshop on Biometrics and Forensics (IWBF), pp. 1–6 (2017)
6. Scherhag, U., Raghavendra, R., Raja, K.B., Gomez-Barrero, M., Rathgeb, C., Busch, C.: On the vulnerability of face recognition systems towards morphed face attacks. In: International Workshop on Biometrics and Forensics (IWBF), pp. 1–6 (2017)
7. Scherhag, U., et al.: Biometric systems under morphing attacks: Assessment of morphing techniques and vulnerability reporting. In: International Conference of the Biometrics Special Interest Group (BIOSIG), pp. 1–7 (2017)
8. Wandzik, L., Vicente-Garcia, R., Kaeding, G., Chen, X.: CNNs under attack: on the vulnerability of deep neural networks based face recognition to image morphing. In: International Workshop on Digital Forensics and Watermarking (IWDW), pp. 121–135 (2017)
9. Damer, N., Saladie, A.M., Braun, A., Kuijper, A.: Morgan: recognition vulnerability and attack detectability of face morphing attacks created by generative adversarial network. In: IEEE International Conference on Biometrics Theory, Applications and Systems (BTAS), pp. 1–10 (2018)
10. Damer, N., Boutros, F., Saladi, A.M., Kirchbuchner, F., Kuijper, A.: Realistic dreams: Cascaded enhancement of gan-generated images with an example in face morphing attacks. In: 2019 IEEE 10th International Conference on Biometrics Theory, Applications and Systems (BTAS). pp. 1–10 (2019)
11. Venkatesh, S., Zhang, H., Ramachandra, R., Raja, K., Damer, N., Busch, C.: Can GAN generated morphs threaten face recognition systems equally as landmark based morphs?-vulnerability and detection. In: 2020 8th International Workshop on Biometrics and Forensics (IWBF). pp. 1–6. IEEE (2020)

12. Zhang, H., Venkatesh, S., Ramachandra, R., Raja, K., Damer, N., Busch, C.: Mip-gangenerating strong and high quality morphing attacks using identity prior driven GAN. IEEE Trans. Biomet. Behav. Ident. Sci. **3**(3), 365–383 (2021)

13. Raghavendra, R., Raja, K.B., Busch, C.: Detecting morphed face images. In: IEEE International Conference on Biometrics Theory, Applications and Systems (BTAS), pp. 1–7 (2016)

14. Hildebrandt, M., Neubert, T., Makrushin, A., Dittmann, J.: Benchmarking face morphing forgery detection: application of stirtrace for impact simulation of different processing steps. In: International Workshop on Biometrics and Forensics (IWBF), pp. 1–6 (2017)

15. Kraetzer, C., Makrushin, A., Neubert, T., Hildebrandt, M., Dittmann, J.: Modeling attacks on photo-id documents and applying media forensics for the detection of facial morphing. In: ACM Workshop on Information Hiding and Multimedia Security, pp. 21–32 (2017)

16. Neubert, T.: Face morphing detection: an approach based on image degradation analysis. In: International Workshop on Digital Forensics and Watermarking (IWDW), pp. 93–106 (2017)

17. Zhang, L., Peng, F., Long, M.: Face morphing detection using Fourier spectrum of sensor pattern noise. In: IEEE International Conference on Multimedia and Expo (ICME), pp. 1–6 (2018)

18. Debiasi, L., Scherhag, U., Rathgeb, C., Uhl, A., Busch, C.: PRNU-based detection of morphed face images. In: International Workshop on Biometrics and Forensics (IWBF), pp. 1–7 (2018)

19. Scherhag, U., Debiasi, L., Rathgeb, C., Busch, C., Uhl, A.: Detection of face morphing attacks based on PRNU analysis. IEEE Trans. Biomet. Behav. Ident. Sci. (TBIOM) **1**(4), 302–317 (2019)

20. Seibold, C., Wojciech Samek, A.H., Eisert, P.: Detection of face morphing attacks by deep learning. In: International Workshop on Digital Forensics and Watermarking (IWDW), pp. 107–120 (2017)

21. Scherhag, U., Rathgeb, C., Merkle, J., Breithaupt, R., Busch, C.: Face recognition systems under morphing attacks: a survey. IEEE Access **7**, 23012–23026 (2019)

22. Ferrara, M., Franco, A., Maltoni, D.: Face demorphing. IEEE Trans. Inf. Forensics Secur. **13**(4), 1008–1017 (2018)

23. Peng, F., Zhang, L.B., Long, M.: FD-GAN: face de-morphing generative adversarial network for restoring accomplices facial image. IEEE Access **7**, 75122–75131 (2019)

24. Scherhag, U., Rathgeb, C., Merkle, J., Busch, C.: Deep face representations for differential morphing attack detection. Trans. Inf. Forensics Secur. (TIFS) **15**, 3625–3639 (2020)

25. Chaudhary, B., Aghdaie, P., Soleymani, S., Dawson, J., Nasrabadi, N.M.: Differential morph face detection using discriminative wavelet sub-bands. In: Proceedings of the IEEE/CVF Conference on Computer Vision and Pattern Recognition, pp. 1425–1434 (2021)

26. Luxand FaceSDK. https://www.luxand.com/facesdk/. Accessed 11 Apr 2015

27. Kannala, J., Rahtu, E.: BSIF: binarized statistical image features. In: International Conference on Pattern Recognition (ICPR2012), pp. 1363–1366. IEEE (2012)

28. Zhang, L.B., Peng, F., Long, M.: Identifying source camera using guided image estimation and block weighted average. J. Vis. Commun. Image Represent. **48**, 471–479 (2017)

29. Raghavendra, R., Raja, K.B., Venkatesh, S., Busch, C.: Transferable deep-CNN features for detecting digital and print-scanned morphed face images. In: IEEE Conference on Computer Vision and Pattern Recognition Workshops (CVPRW), pp. 1822–1830 (2017)

30. Simonyan, K., Zisserman, A.: Very deep convolutional networks for large-scale image recognition (2014). http://arxiv.org/abs/1409.1556

31. Krizhevsky, A., Sutskever, I., Hinton, G.E.: ImageNet classification with deep convolutional neural networks. Adv. Neural Inf. Process. Syst. **25**, 1097–1105 (2012)

32. Szegedy, C., et al.: Going deeper with convolutions. In: IEEE Conference on Computer Vision and Pattern Recognition (CVPR), pp. 1–9 (2015)

33. He, K., Zhang, X., Ren, S., Sun, J.: Deep residual learning for image recognition. In: IEEE Conference on Computer Vision and Pattern Recognition (CVPR), pp. 770–778 (2016)

34. Szegedy, C., Ioffe, S., Vanhoucke, V., Alemi, A.A.: Inception-v4, inception-resNet and the impact of residual connections on learning. In: Thirty-first AAAI Conference on Artificial Intelligence (2017)

35. Vaswani, A., et al.: Attention is all you need. In: Advances in Neural Information Processing Systems (NIPS), pp. 5998–6008 (2017)

36. Wang, F., et al.: Residual attention network for image classification. In: IEEE Conference on Computer Vision and Pattern Recognition (CVPR), pp. 6450–6458 (2017)

37. Chen, L., et al.: SCA-CNN: spatial and channel-wise attention in convolutional networks for image captioning. In: IEEE Conference on Computer Vision and Pattern Recognition (CVPR), pp. 6298–6306 (2017)

38. Woo, S., Park, J., Lee, J.Y., Kweon, I.S.: CBAM: convolutional block attention module. In: Proceedings of the European Conference on Computer Vision (ECCV), pp. 3–19 (2018)

39. Fu, J., Zheng, H., Mei, T.: Look closer to see better: recurrent attention convolutional neural network for fine-grained image recognition. In: IEEE Conference on Computer Vision and Pattern Recognition (CVPR), pp. 4438–4446 (2017)

40. Raja, K., et al.: Morphing attack detection - database, evaluation platform and benchmarking. IEEE Trans. Inf. Forensics Secur. **99**, 1–1 (2020)

41. Scherhag, U., Rathgeb, C., Busch, C.: Performance variation of morphed face image detection algorithms across different datasets. In: 2018 International Workshop on Biometrics and Forensics (IWBF), pp. 1–6 (2018)

42. Face++ compare API. https://www.faceplusplus.com/face-comparing/. Accessed 15 May 2017

43. Information technology - biometric presentation attack detection - part 3: testing and reporting. Tech. rep. (2017)

44. Pytorch. https://www.http://pytorch.org/. Accessed 23 Apr 2019

45. Selvaraju, R.R., Cogswell, M., Das, A., Vedantam, R., Parikh, D., Batra, D.: Gradcam: visual explanations from deep networks via gradient-based localization. In: IEEE International Conference on Computer Vision (ICCV), pp. 618–626 (2017)

Double-Stream Segmentation Network with Temporal Self-attention for Deepfake Video Detection

Beibei Liu[1], Yifei Gao[1], Yongjian Hu[1(✉)], Jingjing Guo[2], and Yufei Wang[3]

[1] South China University of Technology, Guangzhou, China
{eebbliu,eeyjhu}@scut.edu.cn
[2] Institute of Forensic Science, Ministry of Public Security, Beijing, China
guojingjing@cifs.gov.cn
[3] China-Singapore International Joint Research Institute, Guangzhou, China
w.yf05@mail.scut.edu.cn

Abstract. As deep learning technology develops rapidly, the adverse impact of counterfeiting with deep learning is expanding. It has become a hot research topic to explore ways of detecting deepfakes, i.e., fake images or videos generated with deep learning methods. The results reported in the literature show that many existing detection methods deteriorate severely in cross-dataset tests. To solve this problem, we propose a novel network that embodies three key features: 1) double-stream feature extraction module to reveal artifacts simultaneously from the original image space and the noise residual space; 2) temporal self-attention module to infer the authenticity of the current frame from the temporal context; 3) tampering region segmentation module that is based on fully convolutional network and predicts the tampered face area in each frame. We also propose a modified IoU (Intersection-over-Union) measurement of the predicted tampering region against the face region, upon which the authenticity of a frame is determined. We conduct comprehensive comparative experiments on five major datasets and demonstrate the superiority of our proposed model, particularly in the challenging cross-dataset settings.

Keywords: Deepfake video detection · Image segmentation network · Temporal self-attention map · Double-stream feature extraction

1 Introduction

Powered by the fast developing engine of information technology, there are a wide range of off-the-shelf tools available for people to synthesize fake portraits. The impact of deepfakes, a coined term referring to the lifelike images and videos generated with deep learning algorithms, has stretched far beyond what people expected. Deepfakes can be easily exploited by offenders for purposes of deception, threatening, defamation, political intrigue and even terrorism attack.

X. Zhao et al. (Eds.): IWDW 2021, LNCS 13180, pp. 32–46, 2022.
https://doi.org/10.1007/978-3-030-95398-0_3

To eliminate such risks, worldwide scientists have reported efforts to establish various methods to identify deepfakes. For deepfake portrait images, fabricating artifacts can be revealed by the abnormality of color statistics, facial features, frequency spectrum and etc. For deepfake videos, the detection is mostly conducted on a frame basis. The investigation result of each frame image is aggregated in certain manner to reach a final judgement of the whole video. Besides the artifacts extracted from individual frames, the temporal artifacts across a series of frames are also studied, such as abnormal eye movements, inconsistent head behaviors and lighting conditions. Briefly, the detection methods can be categorized into two types, i.e., handcrafted feature-based ones and deep neural network-based ones. Handcrafted features tend to fail on elaborate deepfake images or videos, as the differences between real and fake ones are too subtle to characterize. Deep neural networks are found effective in discriminating between real and deepfake videos without explicit interpretation of the features extracted. However, many proposed deep learning models for deepfake detection suffer the problem of poor generalization ability. The half total error rates (HTERs) and accuracies deteriorate severely in cross-dataset tests compared with those obtained in intra-dataset tests [6,9,15].

Most deepfake detection methods model this problem as a binary classification task. The image goes through many layers of convolutional operations and typically comes to a fully connected layer at the end, outputting a final value that indicates whether the image is authentic or fake. We argue that such traditional binary classification framework may not be optimal for deepfake video for the following reasons. First, the majority of deepfake videos are created by tampering with a real source video, probably in the face region so as to alter the identity of the character. Therefore the most discriminating deepfake features tend to be localized rather than global. The existing classification networks are adept at pulling together global statistical features from different levels but would easily miss the more subtle local features. Second, labeling the frame images as a whole forces the networks to learn the differences between the entire authentic frame and the entire fake frame. Since the frames are partially manipulated or, in other word, a mixture of authentic and deepfake regions, the characteristics of the two types may counteract each other and cause misjudgments. Based on these considerations, we propose to model the deepfake detection as an image segmentation problem, where the goal is to identify the fake region from the authentic region in the frame image. The benefit of this approach is that more subtle and local features would be extracted and most importantly, the differences between the two contrary regions in a single image would reinforce rather than undermine the discrimination. Once the authentic and fake regions of a frame image is identified with the segmentation process, there could be various ways of making a final judgement about the authenticity of the whole videos.

To further enhance the detection performance, we take two extra measures. First, we utilize a double-stream structure for the image segmentation network, with the intent of capturing deepfake features from different perspectives. The original image provides the network with artifacts like strong contrast difference and unnatural object boundaries, while the noise residual image helps to expose inconsistency in noise space [31]. Second, it is known that the consecutive frames of a video are not completely independent images, but instead, are highly correlated with each other. Most deepfake videos are generated on a frame basis. No measure is taken to ensure the consistency between sequential frames after manipulation. This process would inevitably introduce temporal artifacts. The extraction of deepfake features should therefore not be confined to the spatial and frequency domains. There are many possible ways of modeling the temporal information of a video, such as resorting to recurrent networks. Inspired by the successful application in natural language processing, in this work we employ the self-attention mechanism, which has been proved in Transformer model [28] and BERT model [7] as an efficient approach of computing the representation of a sequence by relating different positions in it.

We conduct extensive experiments on five widely used datasets. The comparative results demonstrate that our proposed network is superior to the classic baselines as well as some latest studies. We achieve satisfying performance, especially on the most challenging cross-dataset scenario. The contributions of this work are threefold, as briefly listed below:

- Unlike the traditional practice of applying a binary classifier, we solve the deepfake detection problem from the perspective of image segmentation, which encourages a localized and detailed feature extraction.
- We employ the efficient self-attention mechanism to provide additional temporal clues to boost the detection accuracies.
- Our proposed network, equipped with double-stream feature extraction, temporal self-attention mechanism and segmentation based discrimination, achieves satisfying detection performances, especially on the more challenging cross-dataset scenarios.

2   Related Works

Manipulating portraits of people has been around for a long time. But it is not until recently that the technique has caused worldwide concern. The quality of the manipulated portraits is substantially improved by some latest approaches, such as Face2Face [27], FaceSwap [29] and DeepFakes [16]. While some techniques require a pair of source and target portraits for composition, the Generative Adversarial Networks (GANs) based approaches are able to generate fake faces from even random noise, such as DCGAN [22], PGGAN [13] and StyleGAN [14]. Deepfake videos can be generated by fabricating a series of images. Figure 1 shows some deepfake examples from a wildly used dataset, FaceForensic++ [23].

Faces are the major targets of deepfake images and videos, which motivates many detection approaches to derive hand-crafted biological features of human faces. Yang et al.[30] propose to estimate head poses from facial landmarks and identify fake videos with the inconsistency of head poses. Matern et al. [21] use the reflection of eyes to detect deepfake images since eyes tend to be the most difficult part to synthesize. The inherent gestures and emotions of a person,

Fig. 1. Deepfake examples from FaceForensics++ dataset. The fake images are shown in the first row while their corresponding ground-truth tampering masks are given in the second row.

which are believed to be difficult to manipulate, are utilized in [3] and [2] to determine whether the character in a video is him/herself or impersonated by someone else.

Deep neural network based detection methods are more prevalent than hand-crafted feature based methods. Various DNN-based models have been used to extract features from the spatial, frequency and temporal domains, such as VGG-19 [24], Inception [25], Xception [5], MesoNet and its variants [1] and ShallowNet [26]. Models for detecting traditional image manipulation traces have also found good applications in detecting deepfake traces [4]. [6] introduce spatial attention mechanism to their detection model. For deepfake video detection, recurrent networks are used to trace the discontinuity between video frames [11]. To detect complex videos where only partial faces are swapped, Li et al.[17] design the Shape Multiple Instance Learning model which also employs the attention mechanism.

3   Proposed Method

The overall architecture of our network is illustrated in Fig. 2. The proposed deepfake video detection network is composed of three modules: 1) Module A, the double-stream feature extraction module that extracts features from the RGB image and its corresponding noise residual. 2) Module B, the temporal self-attention module that computes multiple self-attention maps. 3) Module C, the fully convolutional network (FCN) based segmentation prediction module that calculates a pixelwise segmentation mask.

Note that while the temporal self-attention maps of Module B could boost the overall detection performance, Module A and Module C can work independently without Module B. We therefore first introduce Module A and C, with Module B following.

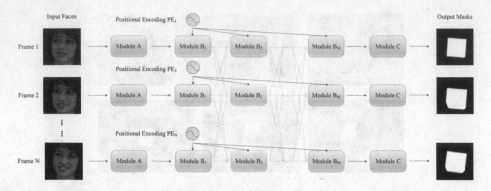

Fig. 2. Overall architecture of the proposed deepfake video detection network. The full version consists of three modules: Module A is for double-stream feature extraction, Module B is for multiple self-attention map computation, and Module C is for pixelwise segmentation prediction.

3.1   Double-Stream Fully Convolutional Network

The Module A and C constitute a Double-stream Fully Convolutional Network (DFCN) which is illustrated in Fig. 3. DFCN outputs a pixelwise segmentation map for each frame based on the artifacts learned from the RGB channels and noise features. No temporal information is exploited in this network.

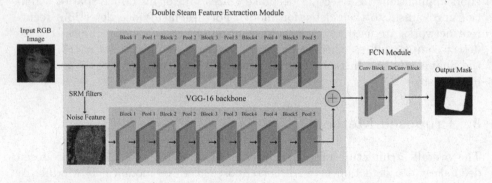

Fig. 3. The structure of Double-stream Fully Convolutional Network, a partial version of our proposed detection model which is composed of Module A and C.

Double-Stream Feature Extraction. VGG-16 [24] is exploited as the backbone feature extraction network. The RGB stream accepts the color channels of the input image, which is an ordinary practice in deepfake detection. However, many deepfake images look so real that we believe the RGB images alone are not sufficient to characterize all the subtle deepfake artifacts. Inspired by the success of noise model in image forensics [31], we introduce a noise stream to provide additional evidence. We adopt three filter kernels of the steganalysis rich model (SRM) [8] and apply them to the input RGB images. The adopted SRM filters are illustrated in Fig. 4. It is expected that the resulting noise features can suppress the image content and manifest the inconsistency between the tampered region and authentic region. The RGB images and the corresponding noise features go through the same network structures, which are excerpted from the first 5 blocks of VGG-16 Net. The output feature maps of the two streams are fused into a single one by pixelwise addition.

$$
\frac{1}{4}\begin{bmatrix} 0 & 0 & 0 & 0 & 0 \\ 0 & -1 & 2 & -1 & 0 \\ 0 & 2 & -4 & 2 & 0 \\ 0 & -1 & 2 & -1 & 0 \\ 0 & 0 & 0 & 0 & 0 \end{bmatrix} \quad
\frac{1}{12}\begin{bmatrix} -1 & 2 & -2 & 2 & -1 \\ 2 & -6 & 8 & -6 & 2 \\ -2 & 8 & -12 & 8 & -2 \\ 2 & -6 & 8 & -6 & 2 \\ -1 & 2 & -2 & 2 & -2 \end{bmatrix} \quad
\frac{1}{2}\begin{bmatrix} 0 & 0 & 0 & 0 & 0 \\ 0 & 0 & 0 & 0 & 0 \\ 0 & 1 & -2 & 1 & 0 \\ 0 & 0 & 0 & 0 & 0 \\ 0 & 0 & 0 & 0 & 0 \end{bmatrix}
$$

Fig. 4. The parameters of the three adopted SRM filters.

FCN-Based Segmentation Prediction. One major difference between our proposed method and existing methods is that we seek to make a pixelwise discrimination first, rather than make a judgement on the whole image directly. To this end, we consider the problem as an image segmentation task where two types of region in the image need to be isolated. Among the many image segmentation approaches, we employ the fully convolutional network (FCN) [20] which allows an end-to-end training and can be easily integrated into our detection model. As is shown in Fig. 3, we follow the practice in [20] and transform the last three fully connected layers of VGG 16 into convolutional layers. To obtain a segmentation map of the same size of the input image, a deconvolutional layer is employed to bilinearly up-sample the coarse outputs to pixel-dense outputs. The resulting binary mask differentiates between the authentic region and deepfake region.

Image-Level Decision. The mask obtained with the DFCN implicates the region that is suspected of being fabricated and based on which we can make an image-level decision about the authenticity. Though it seems intuitive to judge by the area of the fake region, false alarm can not be effectively reduced. Most deepfake images and videos consider the faces as the major tampering targets. As is shown in Fig. 5(a), (b) and (c), the ground truth tampered region mostly falls within the face region, while the predicted tampered region may seep into the innocent background region. In view of this, we employ an intersection over union (IoU) based metric for image-level judgement which is defined in [12] as follows:

$$\text{faceIoU} = \frac{(S_1 \cap S_2)}{((S_1 \cup S_2) + p \times (S_1 \cup S_2 - S_1))} \qquad (1)$$

S_1 is the face region identified by face detection algorithm, and S_2 is the tampered region predicted by our proposed network (either the DFCN or the TDFCN version). S_1 and S_2 are denoted respectively with green and blue boundaries in Fig. 5(d). The red boundary indicates the ground-truth tampered region S_3, which is not available in real application and therefore not taken into account in the metric. The metric of Eq. (1) measures how well the predicted tampered region overlap the face region. The term $p \times (S_1 \cup S_2 - S_1)$ in the denominator penalizes the case that a large portion of the tampered region falls outside the face, which is probably a false alarm prediction. p denotes the penalty factor. The value of Eq. (1) is compared with a pre-defined threshold to determine the authenticity of the image.

Fig. 5. Example of tampering prediction. (a) An input image in which the face region is detected and indicated by a green boundary. (b) The label image used in segmentation training, where the white box indicates the ground-truth tampered region. (c) The output mask image of the segmentation network, showing the predicted tampered region. (d) Illustration of the three types of region: the green face region S_1, the blue predicted tampered region S_2 and the red ground truth tampered region S_3. (Color figure online)

3.2 Temporal Double-Stream Fully Convolutional Network

The DFCN of Sect. 3.1 accepts one frame image as input and outputs the judgement by its own features, not using any auxiliary information from its neighboring frames. We implement a temporal self-attention module that can be inserted between the double-stream feature extraction stage and the FCN-based segmentation stage, as is shown in Fig. 2. We refer to this architecture as TDFCN for short, contrasting to the DFCN model that involves no temporal information. A video is divided into clips, each containing N frames. The N frames go through the double-stream feature extraction module and result in a group of features, which are fed into the temporal self-attention module. This module calculates an attention map that conveys the impact of one frame on its neighboring frames.

The input features are multiplied by the coefficients in the attention map to obtain the output features, on which the FCN based segmentation module is applied.

Temporal Self-attention Module. As illustrated in Fig. 6, for each frame, the input feature IF_i to the self-attention module is the fusion of its double-stream features. A latent layer f_L is applied to the input feature and the latent feature $LF_i = f_L(IF_i)$ is obtained. To incorporate the temporal information of the relative positions of each frame, we follow the practice in [28] and adopt the sine and cosine functions as the positional encodings. The latent feature with positional information is $LF_i' = LF_i + PE_i$, where the positional encoding vector is calculated as:

$$\begin{cases} PE_{i,2k} = sin(\frac{i}{10000^{2k/d_K}}) \\ PE_{i,2k+1} = cos(\frac{i}{10000^{2k/d_K}}) \end{cases} \tag{2}$$

k is the dimension index, d_K denotes the length of latent feature and is set to 256 in this work. Two latent layers are then parallelly applied on LF_i', obtaining $Q_i = f_Q(LF_i')$ and $K_i = f_K(LF_i')$. All the latent layers, such as the f_L, f_Q and f_K, are learnt from training data.

The self-attention map $AM(i,j)$, with $i, j = 1, \ldots, N$, characterizes the pairwise attentional coefficients within the current group of N frames, which is calculated as follows:

$$AM_{(i,j)} = \frac{e^{-Q_i K_j / \sqrt{d_K}}}{\sum\limits_{j=1}^{N} e^{-Q_i K_j / \sqrt{d_K}}} \tag{3}$$

The output feature is obtained as a linear combination of the original input features weighted by the attention map, which is calculated as follows:

$$OF_i = \sum_{j=1}^{N} AM_{(i,j)} IF_j \tag{4}$$

Multi-layer Self-attention. The input and the output of the self-attention module introduced above share the same dimensions, which enables the implementation of multi-layer self-attention. As is shown in Fig. 2, the output features of the previous self-attention module could be taken as the input features that are fed into the next self-attention module. Suppose M self-attention modules are concatenated serially, the calculation of the final output feature is given as:

$$OF = AM_M \cdot (AM_{M-1} \cdot (\ldots (AM_1 \cdot IF))) = \prod_{m=M}^{1} AM_i \cdot IF = MAM \cdot IF \tag{5}$$

where $MAM = \prod_{m=M}^{1} AM_i$ is the overall attention map obtained with the M layers of self-attention modules. Though multiple self-attention modules means more latent layers to be learnt, it is expected that the temporal relation between frames can be characterized more precisely, so as to further enhance the detection performance.

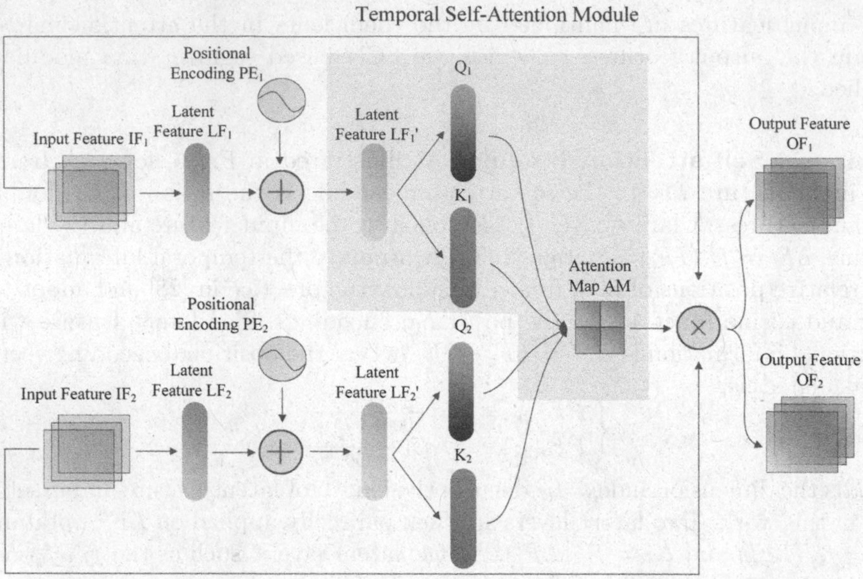

Temporal Self-Attention Module

Fig. 6. Illustration of the Temporal Self-attention Module

4   Experiments

4.1   Experimental Settings

We evaluate the proposed model on five commonly used public deepfakes datasets, namely TIMIT [16], FaceForensics++ (FF++) (C0 & C23) [23], Fake Face in the Wild (FFW) [15], DeepFakeDetection (DFD) (C23) [10] and Celeb-DF [19]. Among them, TIMIT, FFW and Celeb-DF are only used for cross-dataset testing while FF++ (C0 & C23) and DFD (C23) are adopted for both training and testing, which are split into training set, validation set and test set at the ratio of 7:2:1 based on person identities [9]. Since FFW only contains fake videos, we supplement it with 50 real videos randomly selected from FF++ (C0 & C23) for balance. We evaluate the detection performance of both intra-dataset and cross-dataset tests in terms of Half Total Error Rate (HTER) and Area Under the Curve (AUC).

We employ the face detector Dlib to extract faces from all the video frames. Centered around the extracted face, we delimit a region that is k times larger to include part of the background. The region is then resized to 256×256 pixels before being fed into the deepfake detection models. Based on our previous study, the factor k is empirically set to 1.3.

We conduct a comparison with a range of deepfake detection models that are derived from different assumptions and have different structures. The models involved in our experiments are listed below:

– MesoInception: A network with Inception blocks, which is representative of the early efforts to identify deepfake images and videos [1].
– MISLnet: A network with a constrained layer, originally applied in traditional image manipulation detection [4].
– ShallowNet: A network aiming at detecting both GANs-generated faces and human-created faces [26].
– Xception: A common classification network [5] that is shown to perform well in deepfake detection [23].
– Artifact: A ResNet-50 network trained with real faces and fake faces that are processed by random Gaussian Blurring [18].
– S-MIL-Vb and S-MIL-Fb: A network trained with multiple instance learning. S-MIL-Vb is tested on the basis of videos while S-MIL-Fb is tested on the basis of individual frames [17].
– FFD_VGG16 and FFD_Xception: A network that utilizes an attention mechanism to facilitate the identification of forged face region. FFD_VGG16 employs VGG16 as the backbone network while FFD_Xception uses Xception as the backbone network [6].
– FCN: A fully convolutional network that is originally for image segmentation [20] and is adapted to the task of deepfake face detection in [12].
– DFCN: The partial version of our proposed model that contains a double stream feature extraction module followed with a FCN module.
– TDFCN: The complete version of our proposed model that equips the fundamental DFCN with temporal self-attention module(s) to extract temporal manipulation artifacts.

4.2 Experimental Results

The models listed above are trained on FF++ (C0 & C23) and DFD (C23). The testing results on all five datasets mentioned are given by Table 1 and Table 2.

When trained on FF++ (C0 & C23), our models (either DFCN or TDFCN) lose marginally in intra-data testing where FFD_Xception performs the best. We conjecture that it is contributed to the spatial attentional map used in the FFD model, which inspires us to integrate both spatial and temporal attention mechanism in future work. However, our methods achieve the best performance on TIMIT and Celeb-DF datasets in terms of both HTER (Half Total Error Rate) and AUC (Area under Curve) metrics, and win one of the metrics on DFD (C23) and FFW datasets. When trained on DFD (C23), the advantage on cross-dataset of our methods is reasserted. It is found in Table 2 that our methods obtain the best HTER and AUC metrics in TIMIT, FF++ (C23), FFW and Celeb-DF datasets. Though the MISLnet shows a slightly higher AUC on FF++ (C0) dataset, its performance is mediocre on the other datasets. Still, our models remain competitive for most of the testing, which validates the effectiveness of the measures employed in this paper, i.e., the double-stream feature extraction and the temporal attention mechanism.

Table 1. Test results of models trained on FF++ (C0 & C23) dataset (%)

Test dataset	FF++ (C0) (intra)		FF++ (C23) (intra)		TIMIT (cross)		DFD (C23) (cross)		FFW (cross)		Celeb-DF (cross)	
Model	HTER	AUC	HTER	AUC	HTER	AUC	HTER	AUC	HTER	AUC	HTER	AUC
MesoInception	3.0	99.7	8.1	98.5	22.2	92.9	28.1	84.7	28.3	91.6	44.9	59.3
MISLnet	0.7	**100.0**	1.9	99.9	24.2	91.1	25.0	88.4	19.0	96.0	45.7	60.6
ShallowNet	1.7	99.9	4.3	99.6	25.5	87.5	28.2	85.5	18.9	95.1	47.6	62.1
Xception	0.9	**100.0**	1.7	99.9	21.4	92.2	26.6	87.0	20.4	96.2	46.8	65.9
Artifact	7.4	97.8	18.0	89.5	30.1	78.6	40.4	64.6	25.1	82.3	41.5	61.1
S-MIL-Vb	1.0	**100.0**	2.5	99.9	13.1	93.1	17.0	89.3	12.2	96.1	50.0	64.2
S-MIL-Fb	2.8	95.5	4.0	99.0	33.8	70.7	**12.7**	93.4	15.8	92.4	46.6	64.1
FFD_VGG-16	1.2	**100.0**	2.7	99.8	28.9	85.5	27.2	84.2	20.5	96.0	47.6	61.9
FFD_Xception	**0.4**	**100.0**	**0.8**	**100.0**	31.5	88.2	28.1	82.2	19.9	**97.6**	49.2	72.9
FCN	1.6	**100.0**	1.5	99.7	18.1	89.1	20.0	86.4	11.3	95.3	41.7	69.4
DFCN	1.8	**100.0**	1.6	**100.0**	13.8	92.5	19.2	90.8	11.0	94.1	38.9	71.8
TDFCN	1.8	**100.0**	1.9	**100.0**	**11.6**	**94.4**	14.6	**96.6**	**9.5**	96.3	**35.7**	**75.8**

Table 2. Test results of models trained on DFD (C23) dataset (%)

Test dataset	DFD (C23) (intra)		TIMIT (cross)		FF++ (C0) (cross)		FF++ (C23) (cross)		FFW (cross)		Celeb-DF (cross)	
Model	HTER	AUC	HTER	AUC	HTER	AUC	HTER	AUC	HTER	AUC	HTER	AUC
MesoInception	7.1	98.5	35.8	86.6	21.5	93.2	25.7	83.3	30.4	78.2	48.0	53.9
MISLnet	3.2	99.6	18.8	90.4	5.5	**98.9**	15.0	94.6	16.5	92.4	39.6	66.7
ShallowNet	5.3	98.7	27.5	89.6	19.3	90.3	21.4	87.5	20.5	87.9	39.5	66.9
Xception	2.3	99.8	21.0	90.1	14.6	95.1	18.6	89.0	23.0	85.2	40.7	65.1
Artifact	39.5	46.8	36.2	83.0	37.5	87.2	38.5	82.3	38.6	81.4	45.8	59.3
S-MIL-Vb	3.6	99.8	30.1	89.4	22.5	93.0	21.5	90.4	26.7	93.2	40.7	67.8
S-MIL-Fb	6.2	98.3	34.4	81.0	25.3	91.3	26.3	84.6	25.9	84.7	43.8	64.3
FFD_VGG-16	3.2	99.8	34.8	85.9	19.6	92.5	24.1	84.7	22.1	86.4	37.2	69.5
FFD_Xception	1.4	99.8	28.8	88.6	28.7	96.6	29.7	88.3	30.5	85.7	37.7	69.2
FCN	**1.0**	99.9	17.1	89.3	6.8	97.5	12.1	95.0	19.5	89.2	28.6	79.6
DFCN	3.1	99.8	15.9	89.3	7.3	97.3	10.5	95.4	16.2	90.6	26.5	81.5
TDFCN	2.3	**100.0**	**12.3**	**94.6**	**4.8**	98.3	**6.9**	**97.6**	**13.0**	**93.5**	**25.4**	**86.5**

4.3　Ablation Study

The effect of the double-stream module and the temporal self-attentional module can be validated from the last two rows of Table 1 and Table 2. The HTERs and AUCs obtained with DFCN are generally superior to those obtained with FCN, except for a few cases where DFCN is fractionally behind. When it comes to TDFCN, the performances are further boosted. Figure 7 shows two examples of how the temporal self-attention module improves the detection results. The first column gives two input frames and the second column gives their corresponding ground-truth tampering labels. The third column presents the detected results obtained with DFCN model, in which miss alarm regions are evident. The results obtained with TDFCN model, as given in the last column, show that the miss alarm regions are successfully removed, which is attributed to the utilization of temporal self-attention module.

We also report ablation study on the number of temporal self-attention layers to evaluate its impact on the detection performances. We conduct the same intra-dataset and cross-dataset experiments with the number of temporal self-attention layers set as 0, 1, 3, 5 and 10 respectively. The results are shown in

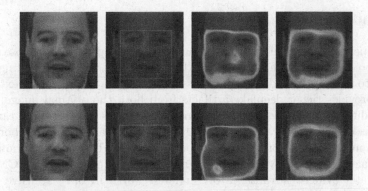

Fig. 7. Illustration of the impact of temporal self-attention module on detection. From left to right shows the input images, the ground-truth tampered regions, the predictions of DFCN and the predictions of TDFCN.

Table 3 and Table 4. The first rows in Table 3 and Table 4 correspond to cases when the number of self-attention layers is set to 0, which is effectively equivalent to the DFCN model with no temporal information involved. It is found that the performances are generally enhanced with the increase of self-attention layers. Specifically, when trained on FF++ (C0 & C23), using 5 layers of self-attention map is optimal, and when trained on DFD (C23), using 10 layers of self-attention map could further boost the performance. In view of the trade-off between performance and complexity, we employ 5 layers of self attention as the default configuration.

Table 3. Ablation results with different numbers of temporal self-attention layers when trained on FF++ (C0 & C23) (%)

Test dataset	FF++ (C0) (intra)		FF++ (C23) (intra)		TIMIT (cross)		DFD (C23) (cross)		FFW (cross)		Celeb-DF (cross)	
Number of blocks	HTER	AUC	HTER	AUC	HTER	AUC	HTER	AUC	HTER	AUC	HTER	AUC
0	1.8	**100.0**	1.6	**100.0**	13.8	92.5	19.2	90.8	11.0	94.1	38.9	71.8
1	**0.7**	**100.0**	1.1	**100.0**	10.2	89.8	18.3	92.4	11.2	94.5	34.2	75.1
3	1.7	**100.0**	**1.0**	**100.0**	**9.7**	93.9	16.8	94.0	12.3	95.5	36.7	73.5
5	1.8	**100.0**	1.9	**100.0**	11.6	**94.4**	**14.6**	**96.6**	**9.5**	**96.3**	35.7	**75.8**
10	2.4	**100.0**	2.0	**100.0**	11.2	94.0	15.1	93.4	10.4	95.4	**34.9**	74.9

Table 4. Ablation results with different numbers of temporal self-attention layers when trained on DFD (C23) (%)

Test dataset	DFD (C23) (intra)		TIMIT (cross)		FF++ (C0) (cross)		FF++ (C23) (cross)		FFW (cross)		Celeb-DF (cross)	
Number of blocks	HTER	AUC	HTER	AUC	HTER	AUC	HTER	AUC	HTER	AUC	HTER	AUC
0	3.1	99.8	15.9	89.3	7.3	97.3	10.5	95.4	16.2	90.6	26.5	81.5
1	2.5	**100.0**	15.1	89.6	7.5	95.0	9.8	94.4	12.8	91.5	26.0	80.3
3	**2.2**	**100.0**	13.5	91.8	7.0	97.5	8.6	95.6	**10.9**	94.1	24.3	83.2
5	2.3	**100.0**	12.3	**94.6**	4.8	98.3	6.9	97.6	13.0	93.5	25.4	**86.5**
10	2.4	**100.0**	10.7	93.4	**4.7**	**98.5**	**6.3**	**97.7**	13.2	**94.3**	23.5	85.6

5   Conclusion

In this paper, we investigate the detection of deepfake videos. We propose an end-to-end detection model that integrates three modules, each contributing a crucial part to the improved detection results. The double-stream feature extraction module provides richer deepfake artifacts from both the original image and its noise residual. The image segmentation module isolates the suspected tampered region based on the extracted features. Most importantly, the temporal self-attention module incorporates the temporal relations between the frames into the deepfake features. In virtue of these measures, our proposed TDFCN model demonstrates evident advantages over related works in our extensive experiments. In particular, our method significantly improves the detection results in cross-dataset scenarios, which is a constructive and meaningful step towards practical applications.

Funding Information. This work is supported by the National Key Research and Development Project under Grant 2018YFC0807306 and Grant 2019QY2202, China-Singapore International Joint Research Institute under Grant 206-A018001 and Science and Technology Foundation of Guangzhou Huangpu Development District under Grant 2019GH16.

References

1. Afchar, D., Nozick, V., Yamagishi, J., Echizen, I.: MesoNet: a compact facial video forgery detection network. In: 2018 IEEE International Workshop on Information Forensics and Security (WIFS), pp. 1–7. IEEE (2018)
2. Agarwal, S., Farid, H., El-Gaaly, T., Lim, S.-N.: Detecting deep-fake videos from appearance and behavior. In: 2020 IEEE International Workshop on Information Forensics and Security (WIFS), pp. 1–6. IEEE (2020)
3. Agarwal, S., Farid, H., Gu, Y., He, M., Nagano, K., Li, H: Protecting world leaders against deep fakes. In: CVPR Workshops, pp. 38–45 (2019)
4. Bayar, B., Stamm, M.C.: Constrained convolutional neural networks: a new approach towards general purpose image manipulation detection. IEEE Trans. Inf. Forensics Secur. **13**(11), 2691–2706 (2018)
5. Chollet, F.: Xception: deep learning with depthwise separable convolutions. In: Proceedings of the IEEE Conference on Computer Vision and Pattern Recognition, pp. 1251–1258 (2017)
6. Dang, H., Liu, F., Stehouwer, J., Liu, X., Jain, A.K.: On the detection of digital face manipulation. In: Proceedings of the IEEE/CVF Conference on Computer Vision and Pattern Recognition, pp. 5781–5790 (2020)
7. Devlin, J., Chang, M.-W., Lee, K., Toutanova, K.: BERT: pre-training of deep bidirectional transformers for language understanding. arXiv preprint arXiv:1810.04805 (2018)
8. Fridrich, J., Kodovsky, J.: Rich models for steganalysis of digital images. IEEE Trans. Inf. Forensics Secur. **7**, 868–882 (2012)
9. Gao, Y., Hu, Y., Yu, Z., Lin, Y., Liu, B.: Evaluation and comparison of five popular fake face detection networks. J. Appl. Sci. Electron. Inf. Eng. **37**, 590–608 (2019)

10. Google and JigSaw. DeepFakes detection dataset by Google & JigSaw. [EB/OL] (2019). https://ai.googleblog.com/2019/09/contributing-data-to-deepfake-detection.html. Accessed 4 Apr 2020
11. Güera, D., Delp, E.J.: DeepFake video detection using recurrent neural networks. In: 2018 15th IEEE International Conference on Advanced Video and Signal Based Surveillance (AVSS), pp. 1–6. IEEE (2018)
12. Hu, Y., Gao, Y., Liu, B., Liao, G.: Deepfake videos detection based on image segmentation with deep neural networks. J. Electron. Inf. Technol. **43**, 162–170 (2021)
13. Karras, T., Aila, T., Laine, S., Lehtinen, J.: Progressive growing of GANs for improved quality, stability, and variation (2018)
14. Karras, T., Laine, S., Aila, T.: A style-based generator architecture for generative adversarial networks (2019)
15. Khodabakhsh, A., Ramachandra, R., Raja, K., Wasnik, P., Busch, C.: Fake face detection methods: can they be generalized? In: 2018 International Conference of the Biometrics Special Interest Group (BIOSIG), pp. 1–6. IEEE (2018)
16. Korshunov, P., Marcel, S.: DeepFakes: a new threat to face recognition? assessment and detection. arXiv preprint arXiv:1812.08685 (2018)
17. Li, X., et al.: Sharp multiple instance learning for DeepFake video detection. In: Proceedings of the 28th ACM International Conference on Multimedia, pp. 1864–1872 (2020)
18. Li, Y., Lyu, S.: Exposing DeepFake videos by detecting face warping artifacts. In: CVPR Workshops, pp. 46–52 (2019)
19. Li, Y., Yang, X., Sun, P., Qi, H., Lyu, S.: Celeb-DF: a large-scale challenging dataset for DeepFake forensics (2020)
20. Long, J., Shelhamer, E., Darrell, T.: Fully convolutional networks for semantic segmentation. In: Proceedings of the IEEE Conference on Computer Vision and Pattern Recognition, pp. 3431–3440 (2015)
21. Matern, F., Riess, C., Stamminger, M.: Exploiting visual artifacts to expose Deep-Fakes and face manipulations. In: 2019 IEEE Winter Applications of Computer Vision Workshops (WACVW), pp. 83–92. IEEE (2019)
22. Radford, A., Metz, L., Chintala, S.: Unsupervised representation learning with deep convolutional generative adversarial networks (2015)
23. Rossler, A., Cozzolino, D., Verdoliva, L., Riess, C., Thies, J., Nießner, M.: Face-Forensics++: learning to detect manipulated facial images. In: Proceedings of the IEEE/CVF International Conference on Computer Vision, pp. 1–11 (2019)
24. Simonyan, K., Zisserman, A.: Very deep convolutional networks for large-scale image recognition. Computer Science (2014)
25. Szegedy, C., Vanhoucke, V., Ioffe, S., Shlens, J., Wojna, Z.: Rethinking the inception architecture for computer vision. In: Proceedings of the IEEE Conference on Computer Vision and Pattern Recognition, pp. 2818–2826 (2016)
26. Tariq, S., Lee, S., Kim, H., Shin, Y., Woo, S.S.: Detecting both machine and human created fake face images in the wild. In: Proceedings of the 2nd International Workshop on Multimedia Privacy and Security, pp. 81–87 (2018)
27. Thies, J., Zollhofer, M., Stamminger, M., Theobalt, C., Nießner, M.: Face2Face: real-time face capture and reenactment of RGB videos. In: Proceedings of the IEEE Conference on Computer Vision and Pattern Recognition, pp. 2387–2395 (2016)
28. Vaswani, A., et al.: Attention is all you need. In: NIPS (2017)
29. Wang, S.-Y., Wang, O., Owens, A., Zhang, R., Efros, A.A.: Detecting photoshopped faces by scripting photoshop. In: Proceedings of the IEEE/CVF International Conference on Computer Vision, pp. 10072–10081 (2019)

30. Yang, X., Li, Y., Lyu, S.: Exposing deep fakes using inconsistent head poses. In: 2019 IEEE International Conference on Acoustics, Speech and Signal Processing (ICASSP), ICASSP 2019, pp. 8261–8265. IEEE (2019)
31. Zhou, P., Han, X., Morariu, V.I., Davis, L.S.: Learning rich features for image manipulation detection. In: Proceedings of the IEEE Conference on Computer Vision and Pattern Recognition, pp. 1053–1061 (2018)

Exposing Deepfake Videos with Spatial, Frequency and Multi-scale Temporal Artifacts

Yongjian Hu, Hongjie Zhao, Zeqiong Yu, Beibei Liu[(⊠)], and Xiangyu Yu

South China University of Technology, Guangzhou, China
{eeyjhu,eebbliu,yuxy}@scut.edu.cn, eehjzhao@mail.scut.edu.cn

Abstract. The deepfake technique replaces the face in a source video with a fake face which is generated using deep learning tools such as generative adversarial networks (GANs). Even the facial expression can be well synchronized, making it difficult to identify the fake videos. Using features from multiple domains has been proved effective in the literature. It is also known that the temporal information is particularly critical in detecting deepfake videos, since the face-swapping of a video is implemented frame by frame. In this paper, we argue that the temporal differences between authentic and fake videos are complex and can not be adequately depicted from a single time scale. To obtain a complete picture of the temporal deepfake traces, we design a detection model with a short-term feature extraction module and a long-term feature extraction module. The short-term module captures the gradient information of adjacent frames, which is incorporated with the frequency and spatial information to make a multi-domain feature set. The long-term module then reveals the artifacts from a longer period of context. The proposed algorithm is tested on several popular databases, namely FaceForensics++, DeepfakeDetection (DFD), TIMIT-DF and FFW. Experimental results have validated the effectiveness of our algorithm through improved detection performance compared with related works.

Keywords: Deepfake video detection · Multi-domain features · Multi-scale temporal features · Cross-dataset performance

1 Introduction

In recent years, deepfake technology has developed rapidly and many deepfake videos have been widely disseminated on the Internet, posing potential hazards to law enforcement, social stability and public safety. Most current deepfake video detection algorithms perform well when the test set and training set belong to the same data domain. However, in practice, the different properties of videos which are generated with different methods and parameters can not be ignored, which explains why the performances of most algorithms deteriorate in cross-dataset testing. As pointed out in [1], most existing networks for deepfake detection tend to capture the texture patterns specific to a certain tampering method. Networks devised for a single type of features can be easily overfitted to the training datasets and work poorly on other datasets. To increase the generalization ability of deepfake detection, it is desired to characterize the deepfake artifacts from multiple rather than single aspects. It has been proved effective in deepfake detection to combine features from spatial domain, frequency domain and temporal domain.

In addition to the spatial domain which is the most intuitive source for deepfake detection, it is also recognized that frequency domain contains remarkable artifacts. To generate images with deep neural networks, it is common to adopt an up-sampling module to achieve a high-resolution outcome from a low-resolution version, which is essentially a deconvolution operation. Due to the uneven overlap of the deconvolution, "checkerboard" effect can be found in the synthesized images [2]. Farid et al. [3] pointed out that a specific image interpolation algorithm can cause the periodic phenomenon of local peaks in the discrete Fourier transform spectrum. Frank et al. [4] studied the Discrete Cosine Transform (DCT) coefficients of GAN-generated images and revealed evident difference between natural images and synthesized images. The magnitude of DCT coefficients of natural images decrease smoothly from low frequencies to high frequencies while grid-like patterns are observed in the DCT spectrum of GAN-generated images. Apart from DCT spectra, image noise is also considered as a useful carrier of high-frequency tampering artifacts. With a two-stream network, Han et al. [5] proved the effectiveness of combining ordinary spatial features from RGB values and the high frequency noise features from the noise images.

Instead of deepfake images, this work aims at detecting deepfake videos, and temporal information is believed to be most important in exposing deepfake videos. We follow the multi-domain detection strategy, but with an emphasis on the utilization of temporal artifacts. Deepfake techniques are ineffective in ensuring temporal coherence between consecutive frames and suffer from jitter problem when synthesizing fake videos. However, the temporal artifacts of deepfake videos are incurred by various factors. It is therefore inadequate to characterize the temporal artifacts in a single manner. Motivated by the approach of [6], we propose to employ two temporal feature extraction modules, with the attempt to capture both the short-term and long-term artifacts of a deepfake videos. It is worth noting that in [7], Yang et al. has adopted a similar idea that they managed to characterize the texture artifacts of deepfake images at multiple scales, using a model named multi-scale texture difference network (MTD-Net). Based on the promising results of [7], we can reasonably expect that extracting multi-scale temporal features could benefit the detection of deepfake videos.

The rest of the paper is organized as follows. Section 2 provides the overall framework of the proposed network and the detail of each individual module. The experimental results are presented in Sect. 3, where we conduct comprehensive evaluations and demonstrate improved generalization ability compared to related works. The conclusion is given in Sect. 4.

2 Proposed Method

2.1 Overall Framework

The framework of our proposed algorithm is illustrated in Fig. 1. For each frame image, the face region is first detected and cut out as a 256×256 input image. The detection network consists of two stages with the first stage containing three branches. The first branch extracts spatial domain features of a video frame from its RGB channels through an Xception network. The second branch operates on the YUV channels and extracts frequency domain features from the DCT coefficients with a MobileNet backbone. The third branch uses a short-term block to extract the gradient maps of adjacent frames, which are fed to a VGG16 network to extract higher semantic temporal features. The spatial domain features F_{RGB}, the frequency domain features F_{DCT}, and the short-term temporal features F_{grad} are concatenated into multi-domain features. The long-term temporal block (LTB) in the second stage captures the discriminating artifacts based on the multi-domain features of the frames in a certain time period. Our approach ensures that the final decision is based on both instantaneous glitch and gradual deviation of the feature set.

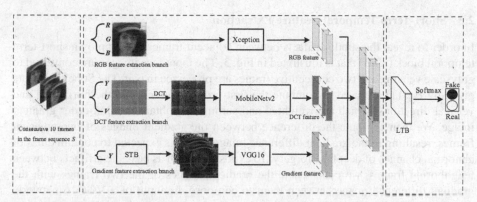

Fig. 1. The diagram of the proposed deepfake video detection network.

2.2 DCT Feature Extraction

The input face image is first converted to the YUV color space and decomposed to three channel images, I_Y, I_U and I_V, respectively. Each channel image is then divided into non-overlapping blocks on which 2-D DCT is performed. A MobileNetv2 is employed to extract frequency features from the DCT coefficients of I_Y, I_U and I_V.

It is worth noting that we observe different detection performance between different block division approaches. Instead of the common practice that divides the image into blocks of equal size, we find that irregular division leads to improved performance in cross-dataset detection. As illustrated in Fig. 2, we divide the image into blocks of different sizes, with the center block being the largest one. We conjecture that compared with the no-division and equal-division approaches, the irregular division can better differentiate between the most questionable and the most reliable areas in the image, which is confirmed by our experiments.

Fig. 2. The irregular division of an image and the corresponding DCT coefficients.

2.3 Short-Term Temporal Feature Extraction

In order to reveal the subtle artifacts between adjacent frames, we employ a short-term temporal block (STB) that is illustrated in Fig. 3. The input face images are converted to grayscale version, and two consecutive frames are processed in pair. The Sobel operators given by Eq. (1) are used to compute the first-order differences in the horizontal and vertical directions, which are weighted and summed to obtain the first-order gradient image. We then compute the difference between the gradient images of two adjacent frames, resulting in the gradient difference image which is expected to contain clues of abnormal changes of deepfake forgery. To expose as much as possible artifacts between neighboring frames, we concatenate the gradient images of the two frames with the gradient difference image between them to compose the input of a VGG16 network. Finally, we obtain a $1 \times 1 \times 512$-dimensional short-term temporal feature from the second last fully connected layer of the VGG16 network.

$$G_x = \begin{bmatrix} -1 & 0 & +1 \\ -2 & 0 & +2 \\ -1 & 0 & +1 \end{bmatrix}, \quad G_y = \begin{bmatrix} +1 & +2 & +1 \\ 0 & 0 & 0 \\ -1 & -2 & -1 \end{bmatrix} \tag{1}$$

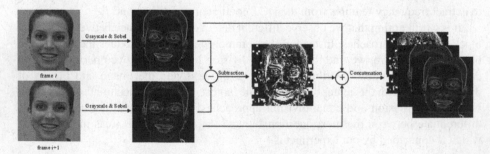

Fig. 3. Illustration of the short-term temporal block (STB)

2.4 Long-Term Temporal Feature Extraction

We use the t-SNE method [8] to obtain a 2-D visualization of the concatenated feature sets, which includes the $1 \times 1 \times 2048$ dimensional color features, the $1 \times 1 \times 1280$ dimensional DCT features, and the $1 \times 1 \times 512$ dimensional gradient features. Figure 4 shows how the features of authentic and fake frames of the DFD, FF++ and TIMIT databases are scattered. We observe that the three types of features extracted from the three branches can not differentiate well between the authentic and fake video frames, especially when models are trained and tested on different datasets. We are thus motivated to introduce a second stage to our detection network, which is designed to capture the long-term temporal artifacts of deepfake videos.

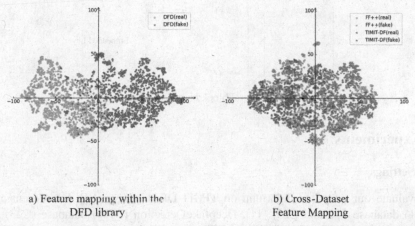

a) Feature mapping within the
DFD library

b) Cross-Dataset
Feature Mapping

Fig. 4. 2-D visualization of the concatenated three-branch features. The model is trained on DFD dataset.

The Long-term Temporal Block (LTB) in our proposed network is based on the bi-directional gated recurrent neural network (GRU) [9], which captures the feature context in a certain time period containing t frames. The LTB consists of two GRU layers that process the input sequences sequentially in the opposite directions, i.e., one delivers information in the forward temporal direction and the other in the reverse temporal direction, as shown in Fig. 5. The input of the LTB module is the feature of a single frame among the t consecutive frames, and the time step node learns the feature context not only from the 1st frame 1 to the t-th frame but also from the i-th frame to the t-th frame. Finally, the output nodes of each t time step are stitched together and fed into a 2-channel fully connected layer, and the Softmax activation function is used to output the binary classification results.

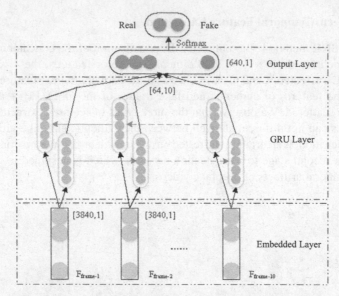

Fig. 5. Long-term temporal block based on bi-directional GRU

3   Experiments

3.1   Settings

We evaluate our proposed algorithm on TIMIT-DF database [10], FaceForensics++ (FF++) database (C0 and C23) [11], DeepfakeDetection (DFD) database (C23) and FFW database [12]. The TIMIT-DF and FFW are used for cross-dataset testing. Since the FFW dataset lacks real videos, we supplement it with 50 real videos randomly selected from the FF++ test set. The DFD (C23) database and the FF++ (C0 and C23) database are divided into training set, validation set and test set according to the ratio of 7:2:1. It is known that if the training, validation and test sets contain duplicate data, the training would cause severe overfitting of the source domain, resulting in degradation of generalization performance of the algorithm. To avoid such a problem, we partition the dataset by person IDs, which ensures that the same person could only appear in one of the training, validation and test sets.

The proposed algorithm detects the authenticity of a video clip that contains t frames, where t is the hyperparameter to be determined. To verify the effect of this hyperparameter on the performance of the model, we conduct experiments setting t to 5, 10 and 15 respectively. We evaluate the detection performance of both intra-dataset and cross-dataset tests in terms of Half Total Error Rate (HTER) and Area Under the Curve (AUC). The results are shown in Table 1. It can be seen that the model achieves optimal performance when the video clip length is set to 10 frames. Increasing the length to 15 frames does not bring in further improvement but causes performance degradation instead. We therefore choose 10 as the default value of t in our experiments.

Table 1. The impact of the video clip length t on detection performance (%)

Training set	DFD (C23)					
Testing set	DFD (C23)		FF++ (C0&C23)		TIMIT-DF	
Performance metric	HTER	AUC	HTER	AUC	HTER	AUC
5 frames	3.27	99.35	22.36	84.87	12.84	89.58
10 frames	**1.70**	**99.79**	**15.35**	**91.22**	**9.50**	**92.69**
15 frames	2.03	99.49	18.02	89.59	10.79	90.88

3.2 Ablation Study

The proposed detection network involves features from spatial, frequency and time domains. In particular, the temporal features are extracted on two scales, i.e. the short-term and long-term. To demonstrate the efficacy of the individual feature module, we conduct a series of experiments with different combinations of the feature modules. The results in terms of HTERs and AUCs are given in Table 2 and Table 3 respectively, and the ROC curves are presented in Fig. 6. The terms RGB, DCT, STB denote the features extracted with the three branches of the first stage, and LTB denotes the long-term temporal domain block of the second stage. To evaluate the performance without LTB, we apply a fully connected layer for binary classification to the concatenated features of the three branches.

Table 2. HTER results of ablation experiments

Training set				DFD (C23)			
Testing set				DFD (C23)	FF++	TIMIT-DF	FFW
RGB	DCT	STB	LTB	HTER	HTER	HTER	HTER
√				4.38	19.75	20.60	28.43
	√			12.06	22.75	23.67	20.53
		√		13.47	30.05	42.58	26.22
√	√	√		3.36	17.03	14.09	25.84
√	√		√	2.16	**14.26**	12.76	19.67
√	√	√	√	**1.70**	15.35	**9.50**	**16.06**

It is not surprising to find that among the three individual branches, the spatial domain features extracted from the original RGB channels are the most effective. Since the visual information of a frame image is mainly delivered by the pixel values, the major visual artifact can be exposed in the spatial domain. It is also found that the frequency domain features achieve a better cross-dataset performance than the spatial domain features on the FFW dataset. The HTER on FFW obtained with frequency domains is 20.53%, lower

Table 3. AUC results of ablation experiments

Training set				DFD (C23)			
Testing set				DFD (C23)	FF++	TIMIT-DF	FFW
RGB	DCT	STB	LTB	AUC	AUC	AUC	AUC
√				96.43	89.59	84.93	82.34
	√			92.84	81.73	84.44	84.02
		√		94.10	76.80	61.07	82.59
√	√	√		97.79	88.74	89.25	83.67
√	√		√	99.41	**92.68**	90.76	88.60
√	√	√	√	**99.79**	91.22	**92.69**	**90.45**

than the 28.43% obtained with the spatial features. The fourth rows of Table 2 and Table 3 demonstrate that by combining the three types of features, the detection performances can generally be improved, which supports the idea of extracting artifacts from multiple domains.

Most importantly, the efficacy of employing two-scale temporal feature extraction modules, which is one of the major contributions of this work, is evident from the last three rows of Table 2 and Table 3. Using the STB and LTB simultaneously leads to generally lower HTERs and higher AUCs than using the two modules alone, though the results of the full set combination on FF++ dataset lose marginally to the network without STB. Underpinned by these results, we envisage that it is possible to achieve even higher detection accuracies with more elaborately designed short-term temporal feature extraction module.

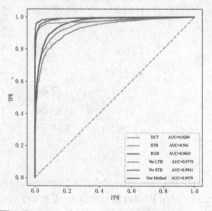

Fig. 6. ROC curves of ablation experiments

3.3 Comparison with Related Works

We compare the performance of our proposed network with several recently published deepfake detection algorithms, which includes MesoInception [13], MISLnet [14], ShallowNet [15], Xception [16], S-MIL-Vb and S-MIL-Fb [17] and FFD_Vgg16 [18]. We train the networks on DFD (C23) and FF++ (C0&C23) respectively, and the obtained HTER results are given in Table 4 and Table 5, including both intra-dataset and cross-dataset results.

As can be seen from Table 4, when trained on DFD (C23) database, the proposed algorithm performs best in the intra-database test, with an HTER of 1.70%. The cross-dataset results on the TIMIT-DF and FFW databases, being 9.50% and 16.06% respectively, also exceed those of other methods. In the cross-database tests on FF++ (C0) and FF++ (C23), our algorithm underperforms the best performing MISLnet. But when FF++ (C0&C23) is used as the training database, our algorithm outperforms the MIS-Lnet on both the intra-database and cross-database tests. As observed in Table 5, among the models trained on FF++ (C0&C23), our algorithm outperforms the other algorithms overall, except for S-MIL-Vb. However, the S-MIL-Vb algorithm performs poorly in the training results of the DFD database with diverse scenes and variable number of people in the video. Overall, compared with the other algorithms, the proposed algorithm is among the best and works stably across various experiment settings.

Table 4. HTER results obtained by training the models with DFD (C23) database (%)

Training set	DFD (C23)				
Testing set	DFD (C23)	FF++ (C0)	FF++ (C23)	TIMIT-DF	FFW
MesoInception [13]	7.26	21.54	25.76	35.88	31.08
MISLnet [14]	3.26	**5.75**	**16.21**	18.73	17.89
ShallowNet [15]	5.84	19.34	21.44	27.45	20.52
Xception [16]	4.38	18.84	22.31	20.60	28.43
S-MIL-Vb [17]	3.66	22.51	21.88	30.56	26.77
S-MIL-Fb [17]	6.29	25.39	26.34	34.43	26.09
FFD_Vgg16 [18]	3.22	19.63	24.19	34.86	22.14
Ours	**1.70**	12.46	18.62	**9.50**	**16.06**

Table 5. HTER results obtained by training the models with FF++ (C0&C23) database (%)

Training set	FF++ (C0&C23)				
Testing set	FF++ (C0)	FF++ (C23)	DFD(C23)	TIMIT-DF	FFW
MesoInception [13]	3.08	8.14	28.11	22.29	28.30
MISLnet [14]	**0.72**	1.98	25.06	24.26	19.02
ShallowNet [15]	1.76	4.37	28.27	25.55	18.92
Xception [16]	0.95	**1.88**	26.61	21.46	20.44
S-MIL-Vb [17]	1.09	2.58	17.23	**13.14**	12.26
S-MIL-Fb [17]	2.85	4.03	**12.75**	33.84	15.89
FFD_Vgg16 [18]	1.25	2.77	27.48	28.97	20.54
Ours	0.79	1.94	17.45	25.24	**8.57**

4   Conclusion

The detection of deepfake video has been studied widely in recent years. Though the intra-dataset detection results have been continually promoted, the insufficient generalization ability has remained a major challenge. In this paper, we try to find out whether the deepfake detection could benefit from a gamut of features that covers various type of information. To this end, we design a detection network in which spatial domain, frequency domain and short-term temporal domain features are first extracted through three branches and then fused together. A long-term temporal block is then applied to extract a higher-level temporal inconsistency in the video clip. Ablation study and comparative experiments verify the effectiveness of our proposed network, especially in cross-dataset evaluation. Moreover, the proposed idea of extracting temporal features at the two scales of short-term and long-term is proved advantageous to the detection. It is expected that the detection performance can be further increased with more temporal scales involved, which is our future work.

Funding Statement. This work is supported by the National Key Research and Development Project under Grant 2019QY2202, China-Singapore International Joint Research Institute under Grant 206-A018001 and Science and Technology Foundation of Guangzhou Huangpu Development District under Grant 2019GH16.

References

1. Luo, Y., Zhang, Y., Yan, J., et al.: Generalizing face forgery detection with high-frequency features. In: Proceedings of the IEEE/CVF Conference on Computer Vision and Pattern Recognition, pp. 16317–16326 (2021)
2. Odena, A., Dumoulin, V., Olah, C.: Deconvolution and checkerboard artifacts. Distill **1**(10), e3 (2016)
3. Popescu, A.C., Farid, H.: Exposing digital forgeries in color filter array interpolated images. IEEE Trans. Sig. Process. **53**(10), 3948–3959 (2005)

4. Frank, J., Eisenhofer, T., Schönherr, L., et al.: Leveraging frequency analysis for deep fake image recognition. In: International Conference on Machine Learning, pp. 3247–3258. PMLR (2020)
5. Han, B., Han, X., Zhang, H., et al.: Fighting fake news: two stream network for deepfake detection via learnable SRM. IEEE Trans. Biom. Behav. Identity Sci. **3**(3), 320–331 (2021)
6. Wang, Z., et al.: Deep spatial gradient and temporal depth learning for face anti-spoofing. In: Proceedings of the IEEE/CVF Conference on Computer Vision and Pattern Recognition (2020)
7. Yang, J., Li, A., Xiao, S., et al.: MTD-Net: learning to detect deepfakes images by multi-scale texture difference. IEEE Trans. Inf. Forensics Secur. **16**, 4234–4245 (2021)
8. Van der Maaten, L., Hinton, G.: Visualizing data using t-SNE. J. Mach. Learn. Res. **9**(11), 2579–2605 (2008)
9. Chung, J., Gulcehre, C., Cho, K., Bengio, Y.: Empirical evaluation of gated recurrent neural networks on sequence modeling. arXiv preprint arXiv:1412.3555 (2014)
10. Korshunov, P., Marcel, S.: Deepfakes: a new threat to face recognition? Assessment and detection. arXiv preprint arXiv:1812.08685 (2018)
11. Rossler, A., Cozzolino, D., Verdoliva, L., et al.: FaceForensics++: learning to detect manipulated facial images. In: Proceedings of the IEEE/CVF International Conference on Computer Vision, pp. 1–11 (2019)
12. Khodabakhsh, A., Ramachandra, R., Raja, K., et al.: Fake face detection methods: can they be generalized? In: 2018 International Conference of the Biometrics Special Interest Group (BIOSIG), pp. 1–6. IEEE (2018)
13. Afchar, D., Nozick, V., Yamagishi, J., et al.: MesoNet: a compact facial video forgery detection network. In: 2018 IEEE International Workshop on Information Forensics and Security (WIFS), pp. 1–7. IEEE (2018)
14. Bayar, B., Stamm, M.C.: Constrained convolutional neural networks: a new approach towards general purpose image manipulation detection. IEEE Trans. Inf. Forensics Secur. **13**(11), 2691–2706 (2018)
15. Tariq, S., Lee, S., Kim, H., et al.: Detecting both machine and human created fake face images in the wild. In: Proceedings of the 2nd International Workshop on Multimedia Privacy and Security, pp. 81–87 (2018)
16. Chollet, F.: Xception: deep learning with depthwise separable convolutions. In: Proceedings of the IEEE Conference on Computer Vision and Pattern Recognition, pp. 1251–1258 (2017)
17. Li, X., Lang, Y., Chen, Y., et al.: Sharp multiple instance learning for deepfake video detection. In: Proceedings of the 28th ACM International Conference on Multimedia, pp. 1864–1872 (2020)
18. Dang, H., Liu, F., Stehouwer, J., et al.: On the detection of digital face manipulation. In: Proceedings of the IEEE/CVF Conference on Computer Vision and Pattern Recognition, pp. 5781–5790 (2020)

On the Security of Encrypted JPEG Image with Adaptive Key Generated by Invariant Characteristic

Yuan Yuan[1,2], Hongjie He[2], and Fan Chen[1(✉)]

[1] School of Computing and Artificial Intelligence, Southwest Jiaotong University, Chengdu 611756, China
ytuanyuan@my.swjtu.edu.cn, fchen@swjtu.edu.cn
[2] School of Information Science and Technology, Southwest Jiaotong University, Chengdu 611756, China
hjhe@swjtu.edu.cn

Abstract. Recently, a JPEG encryption scheme with adaptive key is proposed to improve the security of encrypted images. However, it still has a security risk under chosen plaintext attack (CPA) since the adaptive key is generated by invariant characteristic of the number of AC codes (ACCs) in minimum coded units (MCUs) (NAM). This paper analyzes the possibility of ACCs encryption being attacked by the CPA from three stages: (1) the adaptive key can be forged from the NAM of encrypted image; (2) the diversity of run-length sequence in minimum coded units (MCUs) can realize the estimation of MCUs permutation sequence; (3) the plaintext images can be constructed with the unique ACCs in the same run-length to estimate ACCs permutation sequence. Therefore, this paper constructs plaintext images with same NAM and run-length sequence as encrypted image to achieve CPA attack. The estimation of the permutation sequences is based on the analyses of last two phases. Experimental results show that the higher the correct rate of MCUs permutation sequence, the higher the correct rate of ACCs permutation sequence. Texture images or images with higher quality factors are more likely to be completely attacked by the proposed CPA.

Keywords: JPEG image encryption · Permutation encryption · Security analysis · Adaptive key · Invariant characteristic

1 Introduction

JPEG image [11] is the most commonly used image format for transmission and storage in the network. To protect the privacy of JPEG images, researchers are committed to using encryption schemes to increase the security of JPEG images. To not affect the format of JPEG, the existing encryption schemes often use permutation or stream cipher to encrypt JPEG images [7]. JPEG image

This work was supported in part by the National Natural Science Foundation of China (NSFC) under Grant U1936113 and 61872303.

encryption can occur in the quantization stage and entropy coding stage of the JPEG compression process. Therefore, the main encrypted parts in JPEG images are: quantized DC/AC coefficients encryption [12,14,21], DC codes (DCCs) encryption [1,4,5,12,16–21] , AC codes (ACCs) encryption [1,3–5,12,16–21]. Next, the encryption schemes of these parts will be analyzed separately.

(1) Quantized DC/AC coefficients encryption [12,14,21]. This part is mainly encrypted by permutation. The DC coefficients is encode with differential value. The correlation of DC coefficients becomes worse after permutation, resulting in an increase in file size [12,14]. In AC coefficients permutation, the file size will change if the run-length of AC coefficients is changed [12, 14,21]. In addition, the encryption of AC coefficients can also be realized by sign flip [5]. The sign flip has low time complexity, but it is easy to be attacked by replacement attacks [19].

(2) The DCCs encryption [1,4,5,12,16–21]. This part mainly includes stream cipher encryption [12,17,18,20,21] and permutation encryption [1,4,15,16]. The reference [12,17,18,20,21] performed stream cipher encryption. This encryption scheme can keep the file size of the encrypted images unchanged, but the DC may overflow when it is decoded. This leads to inconsistent visual effects of encrypted images in different software. In addition, the [18] and [16] put some entropy coding block of the original image into APPn (reserved for application segments in JPEG image format). Once the data in APPn is deleted by Imgur, Facebook and Sina Weibo [4], the original image cannot be completely restored. In [1], DCCs is scrambled globally. The [15] performs area scrambling on DCCs. The encryption schemes in [1,15] will not increase the file size, but the problem of DC coefficient overflow may also occur due to the poor correlation of the DCCs after scrambling. In addition, the DC encryption scheme of the [15] cannot resist the sketch attack [13]. References [3,4] solved the problem of DC coefficients overflow caused by scrambling DCCs. These two algorithms scrambled consecutive DCCs with the same sign, and then and then iteratively group and swap them.

(3) The ACCs encryption [1,3–5,12,16–21]. This part mainly includes stream cipher encryption [17,18,20,21] and permutation encryption [1,3,4,12,20]. The references [17,18,20,21] encrypt ACCs with stream ciphers, and this encryption scheme does not change the file size. However, if an encryption scheme only has stream cipher encryption such as [17] is unable to resist the sketch attack [9,10]. In [18], the appended bits of ACCs is subjected to a stream cipher encryption. The [18] put some of the minimum coded units (MCUs) into APPn, it meets the conditions of resisting sketch attacks. However, the security of the [16,18] are related to the number of MCUs put into APPn. The more MCUs put into APPn, the safer it is. To solve the problem of the [16], the [21] proposed a full entropy coding encryption scheme. This encryption scheme not only performs stream cipher operations on the entire image, but also performs scrambling operations on non-zero AC coefficients and continuous zero coefficients in the MCUs. The [21] has higher security than [16], but its file growth is larger due to it changed of the run

length of non-zero AC coefficients. The [15, 20] performed a scrambling on the ACCs within the block, and did not produce file growth. The references [1, 4, 8, 12, 15, 20] encrypt MCUs with scrambling, this method does not produce file growth and can resist sketch attacks. In addition, the [3, 4] also scrambled the same run-length ACCs in the entire image, which further increased the security of ACCs without increasing the file size.

In the above algorithms, the receiver and the sender share a users key to encrypt or decrypt a large number of images. It makes the cost of key management and transmission low. The first type algorithms is that different images have same encryption key [1, 4, 5, 12, 17–19, 21]. The second type algorithms is that different images have different encryption key [3, 4, 8]. The encryption key is generated by image characteristic and users key [3, 4, 8]. Compared with the first type algorithms, the second type algorithms improves the ability of encrypted images to resist ciphertext-only attacks and known plaintext attacks. However, these algorithms [3, 4] may not be able to resist chosen plaintext attack (CPA) since the invariant characteristic (the number of ACCs in MCUs, NAM) is used to generate encryption key. Therefore, this paper focus to explore whether [4] can resist the CPA. The main contributions of this paper include: (1) analyzed the basis of CPA attack in the three stages of ACCs encryption [4]; (2) To achieve the information leakage, the CPA on a JPEG encrypted image with certain NAM characteristic is realized by constructing plaintext image with same run-length and NAM as encrypted image.

The rest of the paper is organized as follows: Sect. 2 analyzes the basis of attacking ACCs encryption of He et al. [4]; Sect. 3 proposes a CPA scheme; Experimental results are presented in Sect. 4; Sect. 5 is the concluding remarks and our feature directions.

2   The Basis of CPA for Hes ACCs Encryption

This paper will focus on the analysis of ACCs encryption since only ACCs also reveal the original image. Therefore, the following introduction and analysis are based on ACCs. The original JPEG image O with n MCUs, each MCU contains one DC coefficient and 63 AC coefficients. The AC coeds (ACCs) is obtained from encoding the AC coefficients with $(r/s, v)$ format, where v is the non-zero coefficient, r is the number of zero coefficients before v, s is the code size of v. The run-length sequence of i-th MCU in the O is,

$$R_i = \{r_{i,j} | 1 \le j \le p_i\}, \tag{1}$$

where p_i is the number of ACCs. The number of run-length is equal to the number of ACCs.

In He et al. [4], the process of constructing the encryption key is shown in Fig. 1. The NAM characteristic C of original image is input into the SHA-512 hash function to generate a 512 bits hash value.

$$C = \{c_\varpi | 0 \le \varpi \le 63\}, \tag{2}$$

where c_ϖ is the number of MCUs with the number of ACCs is ϖ. The 512 bits hash value is combined with users initial key to generate adaptive encryption key key_{en}, the specific process can refer to [4].

The ACCs encryption including two steps: ACCs permutation with same run-length, MCUs permutation excluding DCCs. In the first step, the permutation sequence Ω^1 is generated by,

$$\Omega^1 = \{\Omega^1_\varepsilon | 0 \leq \varepsilon \leq 63\}, \tag{3}$$

where Ω^1_ε is a sets of random numbers, and the length of it is the number of ACCs with run-length of ε. In the second step, the permutation sequence Ω^2 also generated by key_{en}, and the length of it is n.

Whether to find a CPA attack strategy to attack the ACCs encryption of [12] include three stages: (1) how to construct plaintext images with same adaptive encryption key as original image; (2) how to attack MCUs permutation sequence Ω^2; (3) how to attack ACCs permutation with same run-length sequence Ω^1. In the following, the three stages are discussed separately.

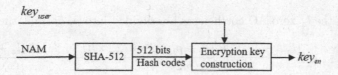

Fig. 1. The process of ACCs encryption. (a) ACCs of original image; (b) ACCs of ACCs permutation. (c) ACCs of MCUs permutation (encrypted image).

2.1 Basis of Same Adaptive Encryption Key

The permutation unit of ACCs encryption in the [12] is ACCs or MCUs, which will not affect the number of ACCs in the entire image. The specific process of ACCs encryption can refer to Fig. 2. After the first step of encryption, only the value of ACCs is changed, but its quantity is not changed. After the second step of encryption, only the position of the MCUs has changed, but the number of ACCs in the MCUs will not be affected. At this time, the NAM is same is same in the encryption image and original image. It can be seen Fig. 1, the adaptive encryption key is same when the NAM is same. In the CPA, the prerequisite to ensure that the Ω^1 and Ω^2 can be estimated correctly is constructing plaintext images with the same NAM as encrypted image.

2.2 Basis of Attacking MCUs Permutation

Attacks on the MCUs permutation should be established on the basis of not affecting the attacks of ACCs permutation. This limits the constructed plaintext images and encrypted image must have the same number ACCs in same run-length. Therefore, the run-length of encrypted image can be directly regarded as the run-length of constructed plaintext images.

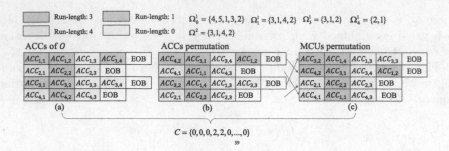

Fig. 2. The construction of the adaptive encryption key.

The study found that the run-length sequence R in different MCUs is mostly different. The i-th MCU have p_i ACC, and the number of zero AC coefficients is,

$$l_z = \sum_{j=1}^{p_i} r_{i,j}. \tag{4}$$

Then, if the l_z zero AC coefficients are divided into p_i groups, there are

$$\Psi = c_{l_z+p_i-1}^{p_i-1} = \frac{(l_z + p_i - 1) \times (l_z + p_i - 2) \times \ldots \times (l_z + 1)}{(p_i - 1)!} = \frac{(l_z + p_i - 1)!}{(p_i - 1)! l_z!} \tag{5}$$

possibilities. In the Eq. (5), the larger l_z and smaller p_i will cause larger Ψ. In other words, when a MCU has large last non-zero AC coefficient postion and small non-zero AC coefficients, the MCU is more diversified. This laid the foundation for using run-length sequence to estimate Ω^2.

2.3 Basis of Attacking ACCs Permutation with Same Run-Length

To estimate the sequence Ω^1 of ACCs permutation correctly, the ACCs with the same run-length need to be different. Attacking the Ω^1 can learn form the core idea of CPA for spatial pixel permutation [6].

The core idea is to expand intensity L of pixel value to x numbers, so that the combination value of x plaintext images at the same position is different. For example, the L is 3, x is 2 and the position is 8. The expanded matrix is $P = \{00, 01, 02, 10, 11, 12, 20, 21\}$. The value of each position in the P is a combination of 2 pixel values. The value of each position is unique in P. Split P into 2 matrices to construct 2 plaintext images. The first plaintext image is $P_1 = \{0, 0, 0, 01, 1, 1, 2, 2\}$, the second plaintext image is $P_2 = \{0, 1, 2, 0, 1, 2, 0, 1\}$. The constructed encrypted images C_1 and C_2 is generated by encrypting P_1 and P_2. The pixels permutation sequence can be estimated 100% through comparing the pixel value combination of C_1, C_2 and P_1, P_2.

The existing CPA scheme cannot be used in JPEG image directly since the particularity of it. Attacking the ACCs permutation with same run-length can achieved by constructing x plaintext images, where x ACCs combination in the same run-length and same position is different. In the previous section, it has been mentioned that the run-length of the encrypted image should be preserved. The uniqueness of ACCs combination falls on the uniqueness of the non-zero AC coefficient values combination. The intensity of AC coefficients can be known according to the JPEG coding rule, which makes CPA possible.

In general, there are corresponding solutions to the three key problems, which makes it possible for ACCs encryption [4] to be attacked by CPA.

3   The Proposed CPA

The framework of the proposed CPA scheme is shown in Fig. 3. Under the condition of CPA, only the encrypted image to be attacked and the encryption process with an unknown encryption key can be accessed. Plaintext images with the same encryption key as the encrypted image can be constructed according to the MCUII of encrypted image. The corresponding encrypted images of these plaintext images can be obtained by encrypted black box. The permutation sequence Ω^1 and Ω^2 generated by the encryption key can be estimated by comparing encrypted images and plaintext images. The decrypted ACCs image can obtained by decrypting the encrypted image by Ω^1 and Ω^2, and set DCCs to '00'. Next, each part will be introduced separately.

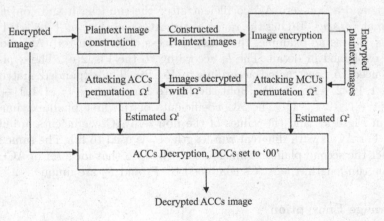

Fig. 3. The framework of proposed CPA scheme.

3.1   Plaintext Image Construction

The most important thing of the proposed CPA is how to construct a plaintext image. According to the analysis in the previous section, the plaintext images need to construct with same run-length and same number of ACCs as the encrypted image. In addition, it is also necessary to ensure that in the constructed x plaintext images, the combination of x ACCs with the same run-length and the same position is unique. The number of the plaintext images x that need to be constructed is related to the intensity of the AC coefficients and the length of the longest ACCs sequence of the same run-length,

$$x = \lceil log_\kappa l_0 \rceil. \tag{6}$$

where l_0 is the length of ACCs with run-length 0. Only l_0 is used since the run-length 0 is the most in JPEG image. The intensity of AC coefficients κ is related to the QFs. The higher QFs, the larger κ and smaller x. Therefore, the QF of the constructed plaintext images in this paper is 100. According to the DCT transformation equation, the AC coefficients of position $(1, 1)$ is,

$$F(1,1) = \frac{1}{4} \sum_{\lambda_1=0}^{7} \sum_{\lambda_2=0}^{7} (f(\lambda_1,\lambda_2)cos(\frac{(2\lambda_2+1)\pi}{16})cos(\frac{(2\lambda_1+1)\pi}{16})) \tag{7}$$

where the range of $f(\lambda_1,\lambda_2)$ is $-128 \leq f(\lambda_1,\lambda_2) \leq 127$. It can be seen that $-400 \leq F(-924,924) \leq 396$. That is, the intensity of AC coefficients is $924 - (-924) = 1848$.

Next, add a non-zero AC coefficient after the run-length and convert it to the format $(r/s,v)$. Taking the range of the AC coefficient as $\{-2,-1,1\}$, that is, the κ is 3 as an example, the filling process of the non-zero AC coefficient will be explained in detail. The l_0 according to the Fig. 2(c). The 2 plaintext images need to constructed according to Eq. (6). The expanded matrix $P = \{11, 1-1, 1-2, -11, -1-1\}$. Split the P into 2 matrixs: $P_1 = \{1,1,1,-1,-1\}$, $P_1 = \{1,-1,-2,1,-1\}$. The AC coefficients of the first plaintext image are shown in Fig. 4(a), and the values of the non-zero AC coefficients are filled by the P_1. For ACCs with different run-length, P_1 is used to fill. The same way to construct the second plaintext image. It can be seen that for a set of ACCs with the same run-length, the ACCs combined by P_1 and P_2 are unique.

3.2   Image Encryption

The encrypted constructed images C_1 and C_2 are obtained by encrypting P_1 and P_2.

3.3   Attacking MCUs Permutation Ω^2

When attacking Ω^2, only one pair of plaintext-ciphertext image is needed because the run-length of MCUs in x constructed images is same. The MCUs

Fig. 4 (a):

(1/1, 1)	(1/1, 1)	(0/1, 1)	(0/1, 1)	EOB
(3/1, 1)	(1/1, 1)	(0/1, 1)	(1/1, -1)	EOB
(4/1, 1)	(3/1, 1)	(0/1, -1)	EOB	
(4/1, 1)	(3/1, 1)	(0/1, -1)	EOB	

Fig. 4 (b):

(1/1, 1)	(1/1, -1)	(0/1, 1)	(0/1, -1)	EOB
(3/1, 1)	(1/2, -2)	(0/2, -2)	(1/1, 1)	EOB
(4/1, 1)	(3/1, -1)	(0/1, 1)	EOB	
(4/1, -1)	(3/2, -2)	(0/1, -1)	EOB	

(a)   (b)

Fig. 4. The construced plaintext images. (a) The first plaintext image; (b) The second plaintext image.

of plaintext image and ciphertext image are classified according to the number of run-length p and the sequence of run-length R. When there is one MCUs in each sets, the Ω^2 can be estimated correctly. For example, the encrypted image of Fig. 4(a) is shown in the Fig. 5(a). The first MCU of Fig. 4(a) is a class, the second MCU of Fig. 4(a) is a class, the third and fourth MCU is a class. The first and third MCU of Fig. 5(a) is a class, the second MCU of Fig. 4(a) is a class, the fourth MCUs is a class. Comparing the classes of P_1 and C_1, the $\Omega^2 = \{3, 1, 4, 2\}$ can be inferred.

Fig. 5 (a):

(4/1, 1)	(3/1, 1)	(0/1, 1)	EOB	
(1/1, 1)	(1/1, -1)	(0/1, -1)	(0/1, -1)	EOB
(4/1, 1)	(3/1, 1)	(0/1, 1)	EOB	
(3/1, 1)	(1/1, 1)	(0/1, 1)	(1/1, 1)	EOB

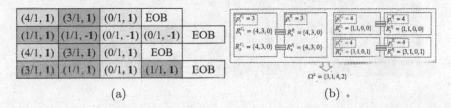

(a)   (b)

Fig. 5. The construced plaintext images. (a) The ciphertext image of Fig. 4(a); (b) The process of estimating Ω^2

3.4 Attacking ACCs Permutation Ω^1

When attacking Ω^1, the method is same as [6]. It is estimated by comparing the uniqueness of ACCs combination of P_1, P_2 and C_1, C_2 with the same run and the same position.

3.5 ACCs Decrypted Image Generation

After getting the Ω^1 and Ω^2, the ACCs decrypted image can be obtained by decrypting the encrypted image to be attacked, and setting DCCs to '00'.

4   Experimental Result

The four images shown in the Fig. 6 with 512×512 pixels are used as test images, which can be converted to JPEG images with different QFs by the JPEG toolbox [2]. The number of ACCs with run-length of 0 for this images do not exceed 512×512. Therefore, the 2 plaintext is needed when attacking one of this images according to Eq. (6).

The decrypted images when only ACCs are decrypted and DCCs is set to '00' are shown in Fig. 7, 8, 9 and 10. When the DCCs are set to '00', the best result of decryption is that the outline of the original image can be seen. It is because ACCs only contain the detailed information of the image. It can be seen that image with the higher texture or QFs (Fig. 8, Fig. 9 and Fig. 11), the better visual effect of decrypted image. And vice versa. It depends on whether there are MCUs with the same run-length sequence in the image. The more MCUs with the same run-length sequence in the image, the higher error of the Ω^2 estimation. This will directly affect the estimation accuracy of Ω^1. Next, the main content are analysis of attacking Ω^1 and Ω^2.

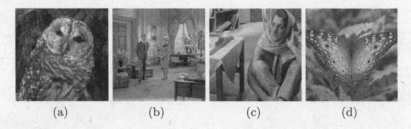

(a)   (b)   (c)   (d)

Fig. 6. Test images. (a) Owl; (b) Couple; (c) Barbara; (d) Butterfly.

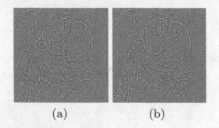   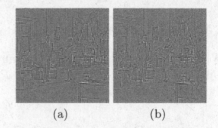

(a)   (b)   (a)   (b)

Fig. 7. The decrypted images of Owl. (a) QF = 95; (b) QF = 90.   **Fig. 8.** The decrypted images of Couple. (a) QF = 95; (b) QF = 90.

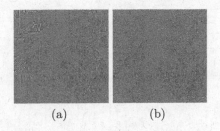

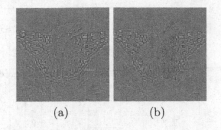

(a)　　　　　(b)　　　　　　　　(a)　　　　　(b)

Fig. 9. The decrypted images of Barbara. (a) QF = 95; (b) QF = 90.

Fig. 10. The decrypted images of Butterfly. (a) QF = 95; (b) QF = 90.

4.1　Analysis of Attacking Ω^2

The correct number of values in is estimated to be different for different images or images with different QFs. The number of estimated errors of Ω^2 with 4096 values was shown in the Table 1. It can be seen that the number of estimated errors of Ω^2 is smaller when the image have higher texture or QFs. The run-length sequence is compared between the plaintext image and encrypted image when estimating Ω^2. Therefore, the accuracy of Ω^2 is depended on whether there are MCUs with same R in the encrypted image to be attacking. As mentioned in Sect. 2.2, when the position where the position of last non-zero AC coefficient is larger and the number of non-zero AC coefficients is smaller, the run-length in MCUs have diversity. This is the characteristic of the image with higher texture or QFs.

The number of estimated errors of Ω^2 is not greater than the number of MCUs with same R. Taking the Barbara and Couple image with QF is 90 as an example, the situation of its MCUs with same R is shown in the Fig. 11. In the Couple image, the number of MCUs with same is 2, and the number of MCUs with same is 2. In the Barbara image, the number of MCUs with same is 50, and the number of MCUs with same is 30. This is because in MCUs with same R, there is a certain probability that they will recover correctly.

In general, when the number of MCUs with the same run-length sequence in the encrypted image is less, the estimation accuracy of Ω^2 is higher. That is to say, the correct rate is high for texture images or images with higher QFs.

Table 1. The number of errors in Ω^2.

Images	QF = 95	QF = 90	QF = 85	QF = 80	QF = 75	QF = 70	QF = 65	QF = 60
Owl	0	0	2	4	20	28	74	95
Couple	0	2	10	52	192	325	584	745
Barbara	2	30	143	399	698	867	1,045	1,183
Butterfly	0	2	8	110	340	628	960	1247

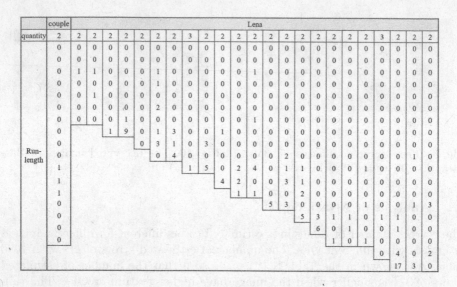

Fig. 11. The situation of MCUs with same run-length sequence (QF = 90).

4.2 Analysis of Attacking Ω^1

When the influence of other factors is not considered, the correct rate of Ω^1 is 100%. The number of estimated errors of Ω^1 is shown in the Fig. 12. It can be seen that the number of estimated errors of Ω^1 is zero when the Ω^2 shown in the Table 1 is estimated 100% correct. When Ω^2 in Table 1 estimated errors, Ω^1 will estimate errors. The number of errors in Ω^1 is less than or equal to the number of run-length in the MCUs with same run-length sequence. For example, there are 2 MCUs with same run-length sequence in the Couple image shown in the Fig. 11. The number of run-length 1 is $3 \times 2 = 6$ which is same as the number of errors of with run-length 1.

In addition, the decrypted image of Barbara with QF is 95 (shown in the Fig. 9(a)) is not clear even if the number of errors in Ω^2 is 2. It is because the plaintext images are constructed from encrypted image. When there are MCUs with same run-length sequence, Ω^2 has high possibility to be estimated error. In the original image and decrypted image, the error of Ω^2 will result in the inconsistent number of ACCs of the MCUs at the same location. It will result in a change in the sequence of ACCs with the same run-length. For example, the decrypted image of Fig. 2(c) is shown in the Fig. 13 when the Ω^2 is estimated to $\{4, 1, 3, 2\}$. The number of ACCs of second MCUs in Fig. 2(a) and Fig. 13 is different, which will cause the sequence of ACCs changed. This will greatly affect the recovery of ACCs permutation.

In general, whether Ω^1 can be estimated correctly is related to whether Ω^2 can be estimated correctly. When Ω^2 is estimated correctly, Ω^1 is estimated correctly.

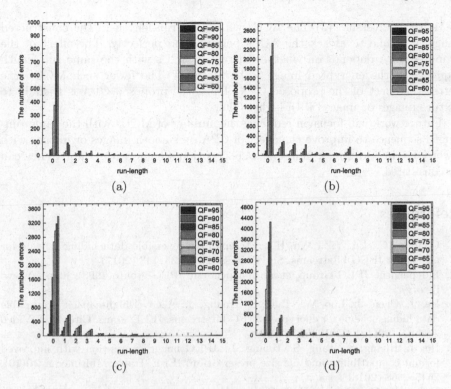

Fig. 12. The number of errors in Ω^1. (a) Owl; (b) Couple; (c) Barbara; (d) Butterfly.

$ACC_{3,2}$	$ACC_{1,4}$	$ACC_{1,3}$	$ACC_{3,3}$	EOB
$ACC_{4,2}$	$ACC_{3,1}$	$ACC_{3,4}$	$ACC_{1,2}$	EOB
$ACC_{2,1}$	$ACC_{2,2}$	$ACC_{2,3}$	EOB	
$ACC_{4,1}$	$ACC_{1,1}$	$ACC_{4,3}$	EOB	

Fig. 13. The decrypted image of Fig. 2(c).

5   Conclusion

He et al. [4] proposed an encryption scheme with adaptive key to improve the ability of JPEG encrypted images to resist existing attacks. However, this paper analyzed that the same encryption key can be forged, the MCUs permutation sequence and ACCs permutation sequence can be attacked by proposed CPA. The specific operations of the proposed CPA attack are as follows. (1) The NAM of constructed plaintext image is same as encrypted image to guarantee the same encryption key. (2) The run-length of constructed plaintext image is same as encrypted image to guarantee the same number of ACCs in the same run-length. The MCUs permutation sequence is attacked according to the run-length of MCUs is diversity. (3) The ACCs with same run-length in the constructed image is unique to attack the ACCs permutation perfectly. The effect of the proposed CPA depends on whether there are MCUs with the same run-length sequence in the encrypted image to be attacked. The fewer such MCUs, the better the effect of the proposed CPA. Thus, the proposed CPA is friendly to texture images or images with higher QFs.

Future work will focus on reducing the number of MCUs with the same run-length sequence to improve the effect of CPA on smooth images or images with lower QFs. In addition, a more secure encryption scheme with adaptive key can be considered.

References

1. Chang, J.C., Lu, Y.Z., Wu, H.L.: A separable reversible data hiding scheme for encrypted JPEG bitstreams. Sig. Process. **133**, 135–143 (2017)
2. Independent JPEG Group, et al.: Independent JPEG group (1998). http://www.ijg.org/
3. He, J., Chen, J., Luo, W., Tang, S., Huang, J.: A novel high-capacity reversible data hiding scheme for encrypted JPEG bitstreams. IEEE Trans. Circ. Syst. Video Technol. **29**(12), 3501–3515 (2019)
4. He, J., Huang, S., Tang, S., Huang, J.: JPEG image encryption with improved format compatibility and file size preservation. IEEE Trans. Multimedia **20**(10), 2645–2658 (2018)
5. Huang, Y., Cao, X., Wu, H.T., Cheung, Y.: Reversible data hiding in JPEG images for privacy protection. In: ICASSP 2021–2021 IEEE International Conference on Acoustics, Speech and Signal Processing (ICASSP), pp. 2715–2719. IEEE (2021)
6. Jolfaei, A., Wu, X.W., Muthukkumarasamy, V.: On the security of permutation-only image encryption schemes. IEEE Trans. Inf. Forensics Secur. **11**(2), 235–246 (2016)
7. Li, P., Lo, K.T.: Survey on JPEG compatible joint image compression and encryption algorithms. IET Sig. Process. **14**(8), 475–488 (2020)
8. Li, P., Meng, J., Sun, Z.: A new JPEG encryption scheme using adaptive block size. In: Pan, J.-S., Li, J., Namsrai, O.-E., Meng, Z., Savić, M. (eds.) Advances in Intelligent Information Hiding and Multimedia Signal Processing. SIST, vol. 211, pp. 140–147. Springer, Singapore (2021). https://doi.org/10.1007/978-981-33-6420-2_18
9. Li, W., Yuan, Y.: A leak and its remedy in JPEG image encryption. Int. J. Comput. Math. **84**(9), 1367–1378 (2007)
10. Minemura, K., Moayed, Z., Wong, K., Qi, X., Tanaka, K.: JPEG image scrambling without expansion in bitstream size. In: 2012 19th IEEE International Conference on Image Processing, pp. 261–264. IEEE (2012)
11. Mitchell, J.: Digital compression and coding of continuous-tone still images: requirements and guidelines. ITU-T Recommendation T 81 (1992)
12. Niu, X., Zhou, C., Ding, J., Yang, B.: JPEG encryption with file size preservation. In: 2008 International Conference on Intelligent Information Hiding and Multimedia Signal Processing, pp. 308–311. IEEE (2008)

13. Ong, S.Y., Minemura, K., Wong, K.S.: Progressive quality degradation in JPEG compressed image using DC block orientation with rewritable data embedding functionality. In: 2013 IEEE International Conference on Image Processing, pp. 4574–4578. IEEE (2013)

14. Ong, S., Wong, K., Qi, X., Tanaka, K.: Beyond format-compliant encryption for JPEG image. Sig. Process. Image Commun. **31**, 47–60 (2015)

15. Ong, S., Wong, K., Tanaka, K.: Scrambling-embedding for JPEG compressed image. Sig. Process. **109**, 38–53 (2015)

16. Qian, Z., Xu, H., Luo, X., Zhang, X.: New framework of reversible data hiding in encrypted JPEG bitstreams. IEEE Trans. Circ. Syst. Video Technol. **29**(2), 351–362 (2019)

17. Qian, Z., Zhang, X., Wang, S.: Reversible data hiding in encrypted JPEG bitstream. IEEE Trans. Multimedia **16**(5), 1486–1491 (2014)

18. Qian, Z., Zhou, H., Zhang, X., Zhang, W.: Separable reversible data hiding in encrypted JPEG bitstreams. IEEE Trans. Dependable Secure Comput. **15**(6), 1055–1067 (2016)

19. Shimizu, K., Wang, Q., Suzuki, T.: AC prediction error propagation-based encryption for texture protection of JPEG compressed images. In: 2021 Picture Coding Symposium (PCS), pp. 1–5. IEEE (2021)

20. ShreyamshaKumar, B., Patil, C.R.: JPEG image encryption using fuzzy PN sequences. SIViP **4**(4), 419–427 (2010). https://doi.org/10.1007/s11760-009-0131-6

21. Zheng, M., Li, Z., Chen, T., Dong, M., He, H., Chen, F.: Larger-capacity reversible data hiding in encrypted JPEG bitstream. J. Cyber Secur. **3**(6), 12 (2018)

Modify the Quantization Table in the JPEG Header File for Forensics and Anti-forensics

Hao Wang[1], Jinwei Wang[2,3], Xiangyang Luo[4], QiLin Yin[5], Bin Ma[6(✉)], and Jinsheng Sun[1]

[1] Department of Automation, Nanjing University of Science and Technology, Nanjing 210044, China
[2] Department of Computer and Software, Nanjing University of Information Science and Technology, Nanjing 210044, China
[3] Engineering Research Center of Digital Forensics, Ministry of Education, Nanjing 210044, China
[4] State Key Laboratory of Mathematical Engineering and Advanced Computing, Zhengzhou 450001, Henan, China
[5] Department of Computer Science and Enineering, Guangdong Province Key Laboratory of Information Security Technology, Sun Yat-sen University, Guangzhou 510006, China
[6] Shandong Provincial Key Laboratory of Computer Networks and Qilu University of Technology, Jinan 250353, China

Abstract. As Joint Photographic Experts Group (JPEG) compression is widely used in image processing and computer vision, the detection of JPEG forgery has become an important issue in digital image forensics, and many related works have been reported. However, these works all assume that the quantization table in the JPEG header file is real, and corresponding research is carried out based on this assumption. This assumption leaves a potential flaw for those wise forgers to confuse or even invalidate the current JPEG forensics detectors. Taking double JPEG compression forensics as an example, if the quantization table in the header file is modified, it will cause the algorithm to fail. However, the tampering of header files not only brings negative effects, it can also improve the forensics performance of the algorithm. According to our analysis and experiments, increasing the step in the quantization table

This work was jointly supported by the National Natural Science Foundation of China (Grant No. 62072250, 61772281, 61702235, U1804263, U20B2065, U1636117, U1636219, 61872203, 71802110 and 61802212), in part by the National Key R & D Program of China (Grant No. 2016QY01W0105), in part by the Natural Science Foundation of Jiangsu Province, BK20200750, in part by the plan for Scientific Talent of Henan Province (Grant No. 2018JR0018), in part by Post graduate Research & Practice Innvoation Program of Jiang su Province (Grant No. KYCX200974), supported by the Opening Project of GuangDong Province Key Laboratory of Information Security Technology(Grant No. 2020B1212060078), in part by the Ministry of education of Humanities and Social Science project (Grant No. 19YJA630061) and the Priority Academic Program Development of Jiang su Higher Education Institutions (PAPD) fund.

X. Zhao et al. (Eds.): IWDW 2021, LNCS 13180, pp. 72–86, 2022.
https://doi.org/10.1007/978-3-030-95398-0_6

in the header file can lead to the failure of the forensics algorithm, and reducing the step in the quantization table in the header file can improve the performance of the existing algorithm. Based on this observation, we propose a general forensics and anti-forensics model by replacing the quantization table in the header file. The experimental results on the UCID database show that the scheme is effective for obfuscating and improving the three typical double JPEG compression forensics work.

Keywords: Quantization table · JPEG head file · JPEG compression · Image processing

1 Introduction

Image plays an important role in the process of information transmission in human daily life. However, with the development of technology, the cost of tampering is getting lower and lower, which makes it easy for people to tamper with images. Therefore, the credibility of digital images is increasingly challenged. In order to ensure the credibility of digital images, digital image forensics technology [4,6] has become an important topic.

As the most popular image compression standard, JPEG has been widely used in various applications due to its high compression efficiency and good image quality fidelity [13]. Nowadays, most image forgeries are stored in JPEG format, so many related forensics work has been proposed in the past few years, such as JPEG quantization step estimation of images stored in BMP format [8, 11,12,17,18], detection of double JPEG compression images [3,5,7,10,14–17], and tamper positioning in composite JPEG images [1,9].

Most of the JPEG forensics issues mentioned above involve images saved in JPEG format. When the operator reads the image saved in the JPEG format, the image editing software or programming language will convert the it into a bitmap format through the decompression process and show it. This is because the image saved in the JPEG format actually saves the image content (quantized discrete cosine transform coefficients) and header files (parameters required for decompression) in a bitstream.

This means that the parameters in the header file of the existing algorithm are safe by default. However, the most important information - quantization table in JPEG compression is also stored in the header file. If the quantization table in the header file is tampered with [2], the decompression process of the JPEG image will be seriously affected, and even make the forensics algorithm invalid.

However, we found that tampering with header files will not only make negative effects, but also can make positive effect. Based on the problem of double JPEG compression forensics, we will show the impact of header file tampering on forensics and anti-forensics issues.

– We increase and modify the quantization table in the header file, which will cause the truncation error of the image in the decompression process to increase, resulting in the loss of additional information, and finally make the anti-forensics strategy effective.

– We reduce and modify the quantization table in the header file, which will reduce the truncation error of the image in the decompression process, resulting in more information being retained, and finally making it a general forensics model to improve the accuracy of existing forensics algorithms.

The rest of this paper is arranged as follows. Section 2 points out why the tampering of the quantization table in the JPEG header file will directly determine the performance of JPEG detection, Sect. 3 describes the proposed anti-forensics and forensics methods, Sect. 4 demonstrates the experimental results and discussions for three typical JPEG detectors. Finally, the concluding remarks are drawn in Sect. 5.

2   The Role of Quantization Table in JPEG Decompression Process

When we use image processing or programming software to read images saved in JPEG format, they actually decompress the JPEG stream. The decompression process is shown in Fig. 1. The process of JPEG decompression involves dequantization and inverse discrete cosine transform (IDCT). Since the JPEG operation divides the image into 8×8 non-overlapping blocks, each block is independent during compression and decompression. Therefore, in the following introduction, the operation we mentioned is based on the 8×8 block.

Fig. 1. The process of JPEG decompression

The dequantization operation is to multiply the quantized DCT coefficient and the quantization step according to different frequencies. The difference between the dequantized DCT coefficient and the original DCT coefficient is called the quantization error. This error is the main loss error in the image compression process. The process is shown in Eq. 1.

$$D_q^I = D_q \times Q \tag{1}$$

Here, D_q^I represents the dequantized DCT coefficient, D_q represents the quantized DCT coefficient, and Q represents the quantization table obtained from the header file.

After the inverse quantization operation, an IDCT operation is required to restore the image from the DCT domain to the spatial domain. As shown in Eq. 2.

$$B = RT(IDCT(D_q^I)) = IDCT(D_q^I) + E \tag{2}$$

Here, B represents the reconstructed image, RT represents rounding and truncation operation, $IDCT$ represents the IDCT operation, and E represents error casued by RT.

It is can be observed that Q plays a very important role in JPEG decompression. If the Q is tampered with, D_q^l will be affected, which will cause B and E to deviate from expectations. It means that the features extracted by the algorithm will undergo major differences and changes. Figure 2 shows the process.

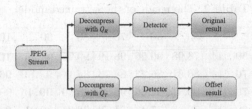

Fig. 2. Influence of quantization table on JPEG detector

In order to verify the above discussion, we conducted some experiments. First, we selected two double compression JPEG detection algorithm models [14,15], and then selected two different quality factor (QF) of conditions for training, respectively which are $QF_1 = 50$, $QF_2 = 70$ and $QF_1 = 70$, $QF_2 = 60$. QF_1 represents the quality factor used in primary compression, and QF_2 represents the quality factor used in secondary compression. The experimental results are shown in Tables 1 and 2. Table 1 is to use the trained detector to detect the double compressed image of the header file tampering. If the quantization table in the header file is tampered with and is inconsistent with the compression QF_2, the accuracy rate will be significantly reduced, which is consistent with expectations. Tampering with the header file will cause the accuracy rate to drop.

However, as shown in Table 2, we handed over the image tampered with the quantization table in header files to the classifier to retrain to explore the impact of header file tampering on the proposed features. We found an interesting phenomenon. If the quantization step is reduced, the detection performance of the algorithm can be increased to a certain extent. Because the decompression process can be implemented by the inspector, this means that header file tampering can be used as a general recompressed image detection performance improvement model.

In addition, not all cases of header file tampering can improve the performance of the forensics algorithm after retraining. This also means that the existing detection algorithm is flawed and will be misled by the database composed of the image of the header file tampering.

Table 1. The result of the trained model

QF_2		50	60	70	80	90	100
$QF_1=50$	[14]	51.82	51.80	**99.88**	51.15	49.96	49.76
$QF_2=70$	[15]	49.01	51.23	**88.24**	51.04	50.39	51.42
$QF_1=70$	[14]	50.61	**96.83**	49.76	49.56	50.36	50.06
$QF_2=60$	[15]	52.11	**77.53**	51.22	50.44	50.04	50.10

Table 2. The result of the retrained model

QF_2		50	60	70	80	90	100
$QF_1=50$	[14]	78.98	96.56	98.19	99.75	99.96	**100**
$QF_2=70$	[15]	86.31	86.23	88.73	84.11	**98.89**	96.76
$QF_1=70$	[14]	90.31	97.00	98.31	98.89	**99.45**	99.34
$QF_2=60$	[15]	70.38	77.43	51.79	78.31	66.01	**84.94**

3   The Proposed Method

In this section, we will introduce the proposed method from two parts: anti-forensics model and forensics model.

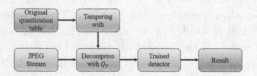

Fig. 3. The process of anti-forensics model

3.1   Anti-forensics Model

Based on the analysis in Sect. 2, the direct tampering of the image header file can make the trained model invalid, the process is shown in Fig. 3. However, this will distort the image. Figure 4 shows the effect of directly modifying the map of the quantization table in the header file. It is can be seen that when the quality factor in the header file is replaced with a smaller quantization step (i.e. QF is larger), the color information of the image will be lost sharply, resulting in a large image change that can be captured by human vision.

On the contrary, if the quantization table in the header file is replaced with a larger quantization step, it will not cause the loss of image color information. However, it still has some problems. The texture information of the shadows in the image will be lost, which can also be captured by human vision.

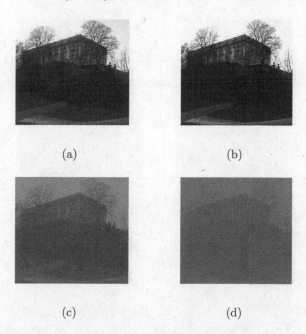

(a)   (b)

(c)   (d)

Fig. 4. The entire quantization table is replaced (a) Original JPEG (QF = 70). (b) Replace with QF = 60. (c) Replace with QF = 90. (d) Replace with QF = 100.

The main reason for the above phenomenon is that the quantization and dequantization operations are carried out in DCT domain, which has a direct and large impact on the image content. In DCT domain, the main energy information of an image exists in the low-frequency part, especially the direct coefficient (DC), while the detailed information exists in the high-frequency part. It means that the quantization step of the low-frequency part cannot be modified too large, otherwise it will cause serious interference to the image content. The DCT coefficients of the high-frequency part after quantization are mostly 0, regardless of the quantization step, 0 multiplied by any number is 0, which means that changes to the high-frequency part have little effect on the image itself.

Therefore, we consider only tampering with the quantization step of 6 to 21 in the zig-zag sequence of the quantization table. Figure 5 shows the results. It shows that when the quantization step in the quantization table is reduced, the visual quality of the image is still unsatisfactory, and when the quantization step in the quantization table is increased, a satisfactory visual quality can be obtained. The calculated PSNR is 35.87 dB, which is a suitable value. In order to prove the feasibility, we showed the PSNR histogram of Uncompressed Color Image Database (UCID) in Fig. 6, which replaces the quantization step of 6 to 21 in the zig-zag sequence.

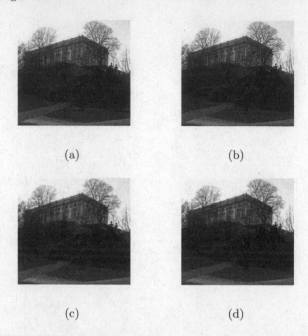

(a)   (b)

(c)   (d)

Fig. 5. Only tampering with the quantization step of 6 to 21 in the zig-zag sequence of the quantization table are replaced. (a) Original JPEG (QF = 70). (b) Replace with QF = 60. (c) Replace with QF = 90. (d) Replace with QF = 100.

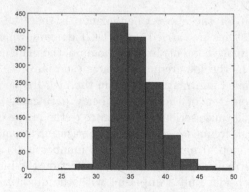

Fig. 6. The PSNR histogram of UCID

3.2 Forensics Model

Based on the analysis in Sect. 2, if the header file of the JPEG image is tampered with and the classifier is retrained with the tampered image, it can be found that the performance has improved as the tampered quantization step decreases. Figure 7 shows the process of forensics model. Images with improved performance have the commonality of reducing the tampering quantization step. We choose the algorithms of [14] and [15] to analyze the improvement of forensics performance by header file tampering.

Because [14] is to detect non-aligned double JPEG compressed images and extract features from the reconstructed image B, while [15] is to detect aligned double compressed images with the same quantization matrix and extract features from the error image E.

This means that these two algorithms do not take into account the aligned double compressed JPEG images with different quantization matrix, and these two algorithms extract features from B and E, respectively if the performance of the header file can be improved in this case through the tampering of the header file, it can be explained that the header file tampering can be used as a forensics model.

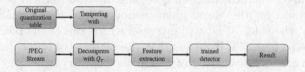

Fig. 7. The process of forensics model

Figures 8 and 9 show the distribution of B when the header file quantization table is tampered with different values.

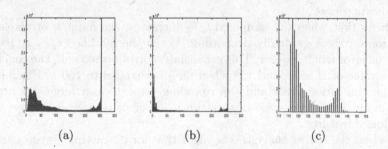

(a)   (b)   (c)

Fig. 8. Distribution of B at $QF_1 = 50$ and $QF_2 = 70$. (a) Original QF_2. (b) Replace with $QF_2 = 50$. (c) Replace with $QF_2 = 100$.

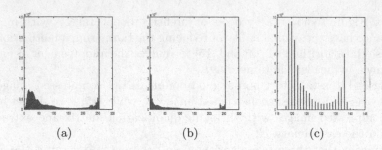

(a)   (b)   (c)

Fig. 9. Distribution of B at $QF_1 = 70$ and $QF_2 = 60$. (a) Original QF_2. (b) Replace with $QF_2 = 50$. (c) Replace with $QF_2 = 100$.

It can be observed that when the tampered QF_2 is smaller than the original QF_2, the distribution will be concentrated towards 0 and 255. When the tampered QF_2 is larger than the original QF_2, the distribution will be concentrated in 128. The reason for the above phenomenon is that if the quantization step becomes larger, the value of D_q^I will increase, which affects the IDCT and makes the result close to 0 or 255. It means that the increase of truncation error leads to the increase of loss information of B. On the contrary, when the quantization step is reduced, the results after IDCT will be concentrated to 128.

It can be seen that the overall image distribution, when QF_2 becomes smaller, the difference in internal distribution is too large and the extracted features are more scattered, while when QF_2 becomes larger, the difference in internal distribution becomes smaller, resulting in more concentrated features.

Figure 10 and 11 show the distribution of E when the header file quantization table is tampered with different values. It is noted that E contains rounding part and truncation part.

It shows that when the tampered QF_2 increases, the number of pixels with truncation errors is gradually decreasing. When the modified QF_2 is 100, the truncation error will not occur. This is mutually corroborated with the conclusion that the value of B is around 128 when QF_2 is changed to 100 in Fig. 8 and 9. Since the truncation error and the rounding error have a large difference in the value range, the reduction of the truncation error is more conducive to the extraction of features.

Based on the above analysis, the algorithm for extracting features from B or E is consistent with the distribution of B and E as QF_2 decreases. This makes the algorithm achieve better performance. Therefore, when we choose to replace the original quantization table with the quantization table calculated by 90 or 100, the detection performance will increase, and when we replace the original quantization table with the quantization table calculated by 50 or 60, the detection performance will decrease.

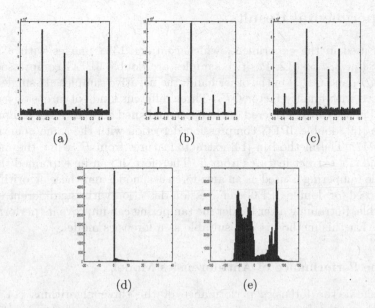

Fig. 10. Distribution of E at $QF_1 = 50$ and $QF_2 = 70$. (a) Rounding part of original QF2. (b) Rounding part of replace with QF2 = 50. (c) Rounding part of replace with QF2 = 100. (d) Truncation part of original QF2. (e) Truncation part of replace with QF2 = 50

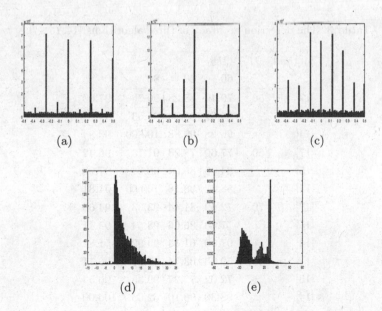

Fig. 11. Distribution of E at $QF_1 = 70$ and $QF_2 = 60$. a) Rounding part of original QF2. (b) Rounding part of replace with QF2 = 50. (c) Rounding part of replace with QF2 = 100. (d) Truncation part of original QF2. (e) Truncation part of replace with QF2 = 50

4   Experimental Results

UCID is used in the experiment, which contains 1338 images with a size of 512×384 or 384×512. Positive samples are double JPEG compressed with order of QF_1 and QF_2. On the other hand, the negative samples are single JPEG compressed with quality factor QF_2. Three different kinds of forensics methods for JPEG images are considered, including nonaligned double JPEG compression detection [14], double JPEG compression detection with the same quantization table [15,17]. The method in [14] extracts features from B, while the methods in [17] and [15] extract features from E. Therefore, it can be explained that the header file tampering is used as an anti-forensics model and these algorithms are not proposed for double JPEG compression detection with the different quantization table. Retraining after header file tampering can improve its performance. It shows that this method is also suitable as a forensics model.

4.1   The Performance of Anti-forensics Model

Table 3 shows the forensics performance of the three algorithms [14,15,17]. Table 4 shows the forensics performance after the values of the quantization table zig-zag sequence 6 to 21 in the JPEG header file are replaced. Regardless of whether the algorithm extracts features from B or E, its performance has a significant drop.

Table 3. The detection accuracy of three algorithms [14,15,17]

Method	QF_1	QF_2			
		60	70	80	90
[17]	50	79.49	88.28	90.76	97.00
[15]		84.62	88.73	97.53	99.21
[14]		96.28	99.88	100.00	99.94
[17]	60	77.69	78.23	91.76	96.42
[15]		84.05	85.04	98.64	97.93
[14]		58.42	98.18	100.00	51.81
[17]	70	72.69	81.44	93.33	94.60
[15]		77.43	86.66	98.54	95.41
[14]		97.00	61.14	99.92	51.82
[17]	80	59.65	63.44	95.68	90.71
[15]		72.02	72.27	99.36	96.54
[14]		98.30	99.16	62.66	100.00
[17]	90	54.47	57.04	70.02	98.72
[15]		61.81	65.34	89.62	99.08
[14]		84.04	72.55	98.85	67.50

Table 4. The detection accuracy of trained model after replacing the quantization table

Method	QF_1	QF_2			
		60	70	80	90
[17]	50	50.97	51.08	57.81	54.30
[15]		51.27	57.36	65.21	65.10
[14]		76.76	85.05	82.88	65.32
[17]	60	51.38	51.45	84.11	68.98
[15]		58.30	49.63	86.39	70.55
[14]		53.21	74.32	69.88	50.00
[17]	70	59.87	50.07	64.95	51.12
[15]		58.30	50.11	58.03	63.31
[14]		94.39	49.96	68.35	50.00
[17]	80	50.90	54.52	51.64	49.74
[15]		58.18	59.04	59.57	66.67
[14]		95.47	86.81	50.00	58.37
[17]	90	51.53	50.41	46.60	50.19
[15]		51.69	51.38	50.03	58.93
[14]		80.43	51.07	51.22	50.00

Table 5. The detection accuracy of retrained model after replacing the quantization table

Method	QF_1	QF_2			
		60	70	80	90
[17]	50	84.76	96.12	96.59	99.99
[15]		85.52	98.89	99.65	99.70
[14]		99.97	100.00	99.97	99.99
[17]	60	-	-	92.94	-
[15]		-	88.21	99.48	99.72
[14]		-	99.97	-	99.98
[17]	70	-	-	-	-
[15]		89.94	-	98.57	99.72
[14]		99.44	-	99.97	99.97
[17]	80	60.33	64.18	-	-
[15]		83.19	82.52	-	.99.63
[14]		99.18	99.79	-	100.00
[17]	90	-	-	-	-
[15]		62.79	-	-	-
[14]		92.36	86.74	99.38	-

The methods in [14,15,17] extract features from the image and then classify them through support vector machine (SVM). Although the tampering of the header file will affect the decompression process, as analyzed in Sect. 3.1, there are still differences between the single compressed image and the recompressed image. It means that there is still a part of the image that is separable, which causes some conditions to decrease insignificantly.

4.2   The Performance of Forensics Model

Table 5 shows the forensics performance of retraining after replacing the quantization table in the JPEG header file with the quantization tables calculated by quality factors of 90 or 100. The symbol '-' means that even if the quantization table is tampered with, higher accuracy cannot be obtained. Although the visual quality of the image will be greatly reduced after using the 100 quality factor, if the header file replacement is regarded as an image processing operation, it will be used as a pre-processing method for the double compression detection problem and ignore the influences of image quality degradation.

It can be observed that performance of the methods in [14,15,17] has been improved. The method in [14] is proposed for the detection of non-aligned double compressed images, so it has a significant performance degradation when detecting aligned recompression problems, and the tampering of header files enables it to effectively align asynchronous double compressed images.

The methods in [15,17] are proposed for the detection of aligned synchronous double compressed image. In the case of header file tampering, it can effectively improve its performance for aligned asynchronous dual compression images. However, compared to the method in [15], the performance of the method in [17] is not significantly improved. There are two main reasons. First, the method in [17] is aimed at grayscale images, and the operation of header file tampering has a more obvious impact on color information, which show in Figs. 4 and 5. Compared with the method in [17], the method in [15] can better capture the impact of changes in the header file. Second, the classification of truncation errors and rounding errors in [17] is not complete. As shown in Figs. 10 and 11, when the quantization table in the header file is replaced by a quantization table with a quality factor of 100, the probability of the truncation error is 0. For the B algorithm, only the feature of truncating the error part provides invalid information. Since the method in [17] divides the truncation error block and the rounding error block, some of the rounding error characteristics are lost. In this case, the missing rounding error is further amplified, resulting in insignificant performance improvement.

Therefore, header file tampering can improve certain algorithms so that they can detect other double compressed images.

5   Conclusion

Based on the problem of JPEG double compression forensics, this article reflects the impact of JPEG header file tampering on JPEG images. The purpose of anti-forensics and forensics is achieved by modifying the JPEG header file. We increase the quantization step in the header file to achieve the purpose of anti-forensics and limit the number of modified quantization steps to avoid causing differences in human vision. The forensics performance of different algorithms has been significantly reduced. We reduce the quantization step in the header file to achieve the purpose of forensics. If the modified quantization step length is 1, the distribution of B and E between the single-compressed image and the double-compressed image can be concentrated. This means that the original difference has been further enlarged, which is conducive to evidence. The performance of different algorithms has been improved to a certain extent, and the adaptive forensics problem has been broadened.

In future work, we intend to study further limiting the modification of header files to improve visual quality while enhancing its anti-forensics capabilities. In addition, the use of header file tampering to improve the forensics performance of synchronized dual compressed images is also the focus of research.

References

1. Barni, M., et al.: Aligned and non-aligned double JPEG detection using convolutional neural networks. J. Vis. Commun. Image Represent. **49**, 153–163 (2017)
2. Chen, C., Li, H., Luo, W., Yang, R., Huang, J.: Anti-forensics of JPEG detectors via adaptive quantization table replacement. In: 2014 22nd International Conference on Pattern Recognition, pp. 672–677. IEEE (2014)
3. Deshpande, A.U., Harish, A.N., Singh, S., Verma, V., Khanna, N.: Neural network based block-level detection of same quality factor double JPEG compression. In: 2020 7th International Conference on Signal Processing and Integrated Networks (SPIN), pp. 828–833. IEEE (2020)
4. Farid, H.: Image forgery detection. IEEE Sig. Process. Mag. **26**(2), 16–25 (2009)
5. Huang, X., Wang, S., Liu, G.: Detecting double JPEG compression with same quantization matrix based on dense CNN feature. In: 2018 25th IEEE International Conference on Image Processing (ICIP), pp. 3813–3817. IEEE (2018)
6. Luo, W., Qu, Z., Pan, F., Huang, J.: A survey of passive technology for digital image forensics. Front. Comput. Sci. China **1**(2), 166–179 (2007). https://doi.org/10.1007/s11704-007-0017-0
7. Niu, Y., Li, X., Zhao, Y., Ni, R.: An enhanced approach for detecting double JPEG compression with the same quantization matrix. Sig. Process. Image Commun. **76**, 89–96 (2019)
8. Niu, Y., Tondi, B., Zhao, Y., Barni, M.: Primary quantization matrix estimation of double compressed JPEG images via CNN. IEEE Sig. Process. Lett. **27**, 191–195 (2019)
9. Park, J., Cho, D., Ahn, W., Lee, H.-K.: Double JPEG detection in mixed JPEG quality factors using deep convolutional neural network. In: Ferrari, V., Hebert, M., Sminchisescu, C., Weiss, Y. (eds.) ECCV 2018. LNCS, vol. 11209, pp. 656–672. Springer, Cham (2018). https://doi.org/10.1007/978-3-030-01228-1_39
10. Peng, P., Sun, T., Jiang, X., Xu, K., Li, B., Shi, Y.: Detection of double JPEG compression with the same quantization matrix based on convolutional neural networks. In: 2018 Asia-Pacific Signal and Information Processing Association Annual Summit and Conference (APSIPA ASC), pp. 717–721. IEEE (2018)

11. Thai, T.H., Cogranne, R.: Estimation of primary quantization steps in double-compressed JPEG images using a statistical model of discrete cosine transform. IEEE Access **7**, 76203–76216 (2019)
12. Thai, T.H., Cogranne, R., Retraint, F., et al.: JPEG quantization step estimation and its applications to digital image forensics. IEEE Trans. Inf. Forensics Secur. **12**(1), 123–133 (2016)
13. Wallace, G.K.: The JPEG still picture compression standard. IEEE Trans. Consum. Electron. **38**(1), xviii–xxxiv (1992)
14. Wang, J., Huang, W., Luo, X., Shi, Y.Q., Jha, S.K.: Non-aligned double JPEG compression detection based on refined Markov features in QDCT domain. J. Real-Time Image Process. **17**(1), 7–16 (2020). https://doi.org/10.1007/s11554-019-00929-z
15. Wang, J., Wang, H., Li, J., Luo, X., Shi, Y.Q., Jha, S.K.: Detecting double JPEG compressed color images with the same quantization matrix in spherical coordinates. IEEE Trans. Circ. Syst. Video Technol. **30**(8), 2736–2749 (2019)
16. Wang, Z.F., Zhu, L., Min, Q.S., Zeng, C.Y.: Double compression detection based on feature fusion. In: 2017 International Conference on Machine Learning and Cybernetics (ICMLC), vol. 2, pp. 379–384. IEEE (2017)
17. Yang, J., Xie, J., Zhu, G., Kwong, S., Shi, Y.Q.: An effective method for detecting double JPEG compression with the same quantization matrix. IEEE Trans. Inf. Forensics Secur. **9**(11), 1933–1942 (2014)
18. Yang, J., Zhang, Y., Zhu, G., Kwong, S.: A clustering-based framework for improving the performance of JPEG quantization step estimation. IEEE Trans. Circ. Syst. Video Technol. **31**(4), 1661–1672 (2020)

More Accurate and Robust PRNU-Based Source Camera Identification with 3-Step 3-Class Approach

Annjhih Hsiao[1(✉)], Takao Takenouchi[1], Hiroaki Kikuchi[1], Kazuo Sakiyama[1,2], and Noriyuki Miura[1,3]

[1] DG Lab, Digital Garage Inc., Tokyo, Japan
{annjhih-hsiao,takao-takenouchi,hiroaki-kikuchi}@garage.co.jp
[2] The University of Electro-Communications, Tokyo, Japan
sakiyama@uec.ac.jp
[3] Osaka University, Osaka, Japan
nmiura@ist.osaka-u.ac.jp

Abstract. Ensuring the legitimacy of image information is one of the critical issues for smooth operation of web systems such as Internet auctions. Linking the image to its source camera would be helpful to detect malicious activities on the web. This paper presents a secure pairing framework that utilizes Photo-Response Non-Uniformity (PRNU), a unique fingerprint of imaging sensors imprinted in a photo, for reliable source camera identification. However, the recent studies have found the image acquisition process of each camera model also leaves its unique pattern in the images, which could disturb the PRNU extraction and lead to the accuracy impairment. This is a serious issue since many people are using the same model smartphones in the real world. To address this issue, we propose to expand the traditional binary Same/Different device classification to a triplet classification by (1) different model (i.e. different device), (2) same model different device, and (3) same model same device. We also present two simple but effective defensive methods to tackle against a fingerprint-copy attack which aims at falsifying the device identification, and an attack with image manipulations. Results on a well-known benchmark dataset prove our proposed method can deliver high device identification accuracy, as well as robustness to spoofing attacks and image forgeries.

Keywords: Photo-response non-uniformity · Image forensics · Counter forensics · Source camera identification

1 Introduction

Source-camera identification is one attractive solution for incorporating a lightweight authentication protocol in rapidly-increasing internet services with photo posts, such as Social Networking Service (SNS), net trading, online review, and any kinds of onymous/pseudonymous services handling photo images. Here, the

X. Zhao et al. (Eds.): IWDW 2021, LNCS 13180, pp. 87–101, 2022.
https://doi.org/10.1007/978-3-030-95398-0_7

pairing between the photo and its source-camera device (i.e. implicitly photo-posting user) significantly enhances information security and credibility in such services. There have been published many research works [3,14] on this source-camera identification actively in the digital-forensics field by Photo Response Non-Uniformity (PRNU), which is a unique camera-device feature inevitably imprinted in the photo. PRNU provides an authentication scheme not relying on a complex public-key-based digital signature and also a digital watermarking scheme which in reality damages the image originality. However, there exist three major challenges in applying the PRNU-based source-camera identification to practical applications.

Challenge (1): Identification accuracy degradation due to the strong fixed noise pattern caused by camera models. The previous studies have shown there exist unique artifacts shared among devices of the same camera model [4,5]. [9] suggests this camera model fingerprint could lead to a performance drop. This impairment poses a serious threat to the real-world application because there are always millions of devices from the same top selling model in the market.

Challenge (2): A large number of images required for a good PRNU estimation. The PRNU has shown great potential for device identification [3,14,15]. However, all these prior works assume more than 50 images per device to guarantee good performance. According to [4], >5% accuracy drop can be observed when the number of images per device decreases from 100 to 10. This large required number is an entry barrier to users and limits the range of practical application. Especially for the application of error tolerance, such as anomaly detection of online reviews, finding 80% of suspicious users with 5-image registration might be more valuable than the 99% accuracy but with 50+ images required whenever users change their device.

Challenge (3): Vulnerability against fingerprint-copy attacks and local image forgeries. Copying the target camera's PRNU to an image acquired by a different camera has been proved to be a threat to the device identification [2,12]. On the other hand, the local image forgery is to modify image content. This manipulation is difficult to be found by the PRNU-based algorithm since it only changes the fingerprint on small regions. As shown in the previous studies [4,15], the device identification is always less reliable on small image patches.

In this paper, we propose the solutions to the abovementioned challenges as follows:

1. We propose a 3-class camera identification scheme to distinguish different devices of the same model better by leveraging the camera model information. Unlike the well-known VISION [18] and Dresden [7] dataset only providing ≤5 devices per model, we particularly present the identification result on devices of the same model, which so far seems be ignored, with a dataset featuring 400+ devices per model.
2. We find the semi-supervised learning can greatly benefit the identification performance especially if only a very limited number of images is available for training.

3. We introduce two easily-implemented methods, with no need of any training or prior information but only relying on the same classifier of device identification, to detect fingerprint-copy attacks and localize image forgeries.

2 Review of Previous Works

2.1 PRNU-Based Algorithm and Source Camera Identification

The state-of-the-art PRNU estimation is proposed by Lukas et al. [14]. By using the denoising function, f, noise residual W of the image I can be obtained. W does not only bear the PRNU factor, K, but also some undesired non-PRNU noises and denosing error terms, Ξ.

$$W = I - f(I) = IK + \Xi, \tag{1}$$

By collecting a set of n images $(I_1, I_2, \ldots, I_n)$ taken by the specific camera, PRNU factor can be estimated using the maximum likelihood method [3]:

$$\hat{K} = \frac{\sum_{i=1}^{n} W_i I_i}{\sum_{i=1}^{n} I_i^2} = K + \Delta, \tag{2}$$

By comparing the camera's PRNU ($\hat{K}_d$) and the image noise pattern (W_I), it is possible to link the photo to its source camera device. The conventional approach is to measure the similarity between W_I and $\hat{K}_d$ by Normalized Cross-Correlation (NCC) or Peak Correlation Energy. When the similarity is high, image I is said to be captured by camera d. Besides, recent PRNU-based algorithms have utilized deep learning network to improve performance [4–6,10]. However, the existing methods neither estimate the PRNU with a limited number of images nor discuss the potential confusion among devices of the same camera model, which are both common conditions in the real world. Our method in Sect. 3.1 aims to solve the aforementioned issues by Convolutional Neural Network (CNN) to boost the performance of the PRNU-based algorithm, and assure the real-world applicability as well.

2.2 Fingerprint-Copy Attack

The fundamental basis of a successful PRNU-based algorithm is the device fingerprint. Once the fingerprint can be copied and inserted to other images, the attacker can falsely appear he/she has the legal access to the target camera. This kind of attack is called "fingerprint-copy attack".

Suppose there are two camera C_i and C_j and the images taken by them are I and J respectively. To fool the PRNU-based algorithms, the attacker can manipulate image J with C_i's fingerprint ($\hat{K}_i$) and makes J appear to be captured by the target camera C_i. This forged image is denoted as $\tilde{J}(K = \hat{K}_i)$, which can be performed by injecting or substituting the fingerprint in the forged images [8,12,20].

To defend against this fingerprint-copy forgery, several methods have been introduced. The key idea behind them is to find the extra sharing parts of forged images and PRNUs. As Eq. 2 states, the estimated fingerprint contains non-PRNU components, Δ. When copying the fingerprint, Δ, originated from a set of images captured by the target camera, is inevitably planted onto the forged image simultaneously. Contrary to the fact that genuine image only shares the true PRNU with the estimated PRNU, the forged image unnaturally shares the extra non-PRNU terms. Hence, if the extra-sharing non-PRNU terms can be found, it is likely to be a fingerprint-copy attack. Triangle test [8] and ABC authentication [1] are well-known methods based on this idea. However, Triangle test requires to compare the query image with all images in the dataset, which is rarely feasible for the sake of computation and storage cost. ABC's two images comparing scheme can be easily broken by forging two images taken by two different cameras, and its use case is restricted to QR code images only. In Sect. 3.2, we propose a method to overcome the limitations, which similarly relies on the high correlation to detect the spoofing attack.

2.3 Local Image Alteration Attack

Besides the fingerprint-copy attack, another common attack is to manipulate the part of the image, like copying a region from another image and paste it to the target image. To prevent this kind of forgery, the PRNU-base method [11,23] is to check the correlation of every patch with the corresponding PRNU. On the other hand, the inconsistency-based method [16,24] is developed based on the inconsistency between tampered and untampered regions. By comparing the extracted feature between patches in the same image, the tampered area can be specified.

However, the PRNU-based method tends to be too sensitive and falsely detect too many small forgeries because the PRNU estimated on small patches is usually not reliable enough. On the contrary, the inconsistency-based method is more stable but prone to ignore the small forgery. To make a more reliable decision, we incorporate both ideas together to localize the image forgery in Sect. 3.3.

3   Proposed Method

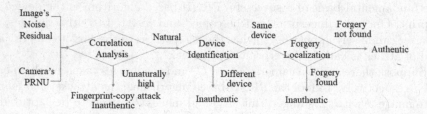

Fig. 1. Framework of the proposed 3-step verification scheme

In this section, we describe our proposed PRNU-based 3-step 3-class source camera identification algorithm, which can achieve better performance among same model devices, and provide counter-attack resiliency. The 3-step verification scheme in sequences are (1) the correlation analysis to detect fingerprint-copy attack, (2) the 3-class classifier to identify the relation between images and cameras, and finally (3) the hierarchical multi-window search to localize image forgeries, as presented in Fig. 1.

3.1 3-Class Classification

We propose a 3-class classifier to prevent the camera model fingerprint from disturbing the device identification, and adopt the semi-supervised learning to lower the required number of images per device.

The previous studies have shown there exists unique noise pattern for each camera model [5,21], and this model fingerprint could disturb the PRNU extraction and thus impair the device identification accuracy [9], which could limit the applicability since a great number of same model devices is common in reality. To solve this problem, we propose a 3-class classifier to identify the camera model and the device simultaneously by a CNN classifier, so the relation between the camera and the image are into 3 classes: (1) different device and different model ($class_{dd}$), (2) different device and same model ($class_{ds}$), (3) same device ($class_{ss}$). By specifying out the camera model label, the end-to-end training process could teach some convolution kernels to distinguish inter-camera-model differences better, and other kernels to focus on catching subtle intra-camera-model differences, finally achieving better performance among devices of the same model.

The use of the camera model information together with the PRNU is not new. [4] proposed to use noiseprint, a camera model fingerprint allowing for model identification, to support the PRNU-based device identification. With the help of the noiseprint, [4] could prevent linking the image to a device of different models, but the possible mismatch among devices of the same model is left untouched. On the contrary, our 3-class is not only able to classify the camera model, the same as the noiseprint, but also pays more attention to the hard-to-classify examples ($class_{ds}$). Last but not least, our method only relies on a single classifier, while PRNU + noiseprint needs to train the noiserprint extractor CNN with an extra image dataset covering a variety of camera models first, and another machine-learning model to make the final prediction based on both the PRNU and noiseprint distance.

We adopt Pair-wise Correlation Network (PCN) [15] as our CNN structure and modify the output dimension from the original 2 to 3. The network is to estimate the similarity or correlation between the PRNU and the image noise residual, so the input is always the pair of $(\hat{K}, W)$. Before feeding into the CNN, both $\hat{K}$ and W are normalized by its standard deviation.

For both PRNU-based and deep learning algorithms, the performance heavily relies on quality and quantity of data. A recommended number of images for a good PRNU estimate is said to be 50 [14]. Nonetheless, in a real-world application, asking users to upload a great number of images might hesitate their use.

Thus, we propose to use unlabeled images for semi-supervised training, simply using the images from open dataset whose source information is missing as samples of $class_{dd}$. Even though the images from the open dataset might coincidently be $class_{ds}$, it is ignorable comparing to the benefit of a great increase in training data size. Another possible advantage is to prevent the authentication by publicly accessible images, such as images shared on SNS. The open dataset includes plenty of transformed and compressed images, just like the SNS exchanged images, so using them as an example of "different device" can also teach the classifier to block these social exchanged images.

3.2   Excess Correlation Analysis Against Fingerprint-Copy Attacks

In this section, we propose to calculate the NCC before device identification to detect an unnaturally high correlation of fingerprint-copy attacks between noise residual and PRNU on certain crucial pixels. Because our classifier is CNN, we can find out these crucial pixels by Grad-CAM [17]. Grad-CAM can highlight the pixels which have a positive influence on the class of interest, here class of "Same device". We choose these high Grad-CAM pixels because they satisfy the following requirements:

1. NCC on these pixels tends to be low for non-forged images and high for spoofed images.
2. If an attack can superimpose the target camera's PRNU into these pixels, it is likely to confuse the device identification.
3. The location of these pixels is unknown to attackers.
4. The threshold of the natural NCC value is unique to each PRNU.

Requirements (1) and (2) together put attackers in a dilemma. If attackers try to conduct a successful attack, they must copy the PRNU in these crucial pixels but inevitable leads to a high NCC value in these pixels, consequently detected as the fingerprint-copy attack. If they try to avoid the NCC test, they cannot copy too much fingerprint from these crucial pixels, so is likely to fail in the device identification. However, the attack is still possible if the attacker can know the exact location of these pixels and the threshold of the NCC test. Without (3) and (4), the attacker may copy enough PRNU from other else pixels or determine a proper fingerprint strength which can falsify the identification but also keep a low NCC.

The following section will discuss all requirements and why the high Grad-CAM pixels are selected. Because of imperfect denoising filters and estimation errors, the noise residual, W, and the estimated PRNU, $\hat{K}$, include both true PRNU and non-PRNU components. Here, we use $Q = \{q_1, .., q_n\}$ to denote the locations which reveal the PRNU signals well, and $R = \{r_1, .., r_m\}$ to represent the locations which are strongly contaminated by the non-PRNU terms. The actual locations of Q and R are unknown and unique for each W and $\hat{K}$. Once the image content changes, the location changes accordingly.

Requirement (1). The positive correlation owing to the same device fingerprint can only be observed on the pixels which happen to belong to Q on both W and

$\hat{K}$, namely the intersection of Q pixels, as $|Q_W \cap Q_{\hat{K}}|$. The larger it is, the higher correlation between W and $\hat{K}$ is. Using more images for PRNU estimation can suppress non-PRNU components, leading to more $Q_{\hat{K}}$. However, on a single image, Q_W is usually few, because noise residuals are inevitably contaminated by the residuals of scene content, especially in the complicated texture area [3]. The few Q_W leads to a weakly positive NCC value. The actual NCC values of all genuine images used in our experiment (see Sect. 4) are weak, all below 0.1. On the contrary, a confusing spoofed image is to make its noise residuals as close to $\hat{K}$ as possible, so the NCC tends to be large, just as the requirement (1). On the other hand, the R pixel covers independent random noise components, so no difference between non-forged and forged images.

Requirement (2). Because Q contains more pure fingerprints, a well-trained classifier should make prediction mainly on Q, and less on R pixels. Thus, a successful attack should copy enough PRNU from Q, as the requirement (2) states. However, the actual location of Q is unknown, but it should be largely overlapped with high Grad-CAM pixels, which can be found by checking the CNN's gradient. If so, Grad-CAMs of any two images acquired by the same device should be highly correlated because their high Grad-CAM pixels should at the similar location as its source device's $Q_{\hat{K}}$. The actual NCC between Grad-CAMs of the same device in the dataset we used are high, ranging from 0.37 to 0.85. This high correlation implies we can replace Q with the high Grad-CAM pixels, satisfying the requirement (1) and (2) just as Q.

Requirement (3). The location of the high Grad-CAM pixels changes with $\hat{K}$ because of the unique Q location for each $\hat{K}$. The location also differs even if using the same $\hat{K}$ in training. This difference comes from the randomness of training process, such as data shuffling or parameter initialization. It makes attackers difficult to find the same location as the verifier, even if they try to train their own classifier. The unique Q location of each $\hat{K}$ and the randomness from training process ensure the unknown location to attackers, as the requirement (3).

Requirement (4). The NCC threshold changes not only with the quantity but also quality of images for PRNU estimation, satisfying requirement (4). Using more images for the estimation can catch more PRNU signals, so the NCC threshold is usually higher. Likewise, comparing with texture-rich images, the threshold is always higher when using the same amount of bright and low-texture images for the PRNU extraction. For the verifier, the lower threshold means stronger defense because of the longer right tails, providing another motivation for the semi-supervised learning which aims to use fewer images per device. The fewer images for PRNU estimation is likely to have a lower NCC threshold, so providing more robust defense.

Unless the attacker can give access to the verifier-owned classifier and the stored fingerprint in the server, the successful attack is challenging to be created. Even if the attacker can locate the high Grad-CAM pixels at a certain level, the manipulation in these pixels is still more sophisticated than the one in the whole image. Remember the noise residual is normalized by its standard deviation before being fed into the classifier, so the attacker not only needs to control the NCC value inside the high Grad-CAM pixels, but also the overall standard deviation of noise residuals. Any change in standard deviation might cause undesirable effect on device prediction simultaneously.

Compared with the existing approaches, our approach is easier to be applied. It simply utilizes the CNN's characteristic, so no extra information is needed. Unlike Triangle test, our approach does not compare the received image with any other image, so no need of storage for the complete history of image set. The method of ABC authentication's is restricted to QR code images only, while our method can test any images and satisfy the general needs for normal photos.

Finally, we list 3 different possible attacks by the source of fingerprint to be copied. For a forgery image copying $\hat{K}$, the Q pixels on its noise residuals is denoted as $Q_W^{\hat{K}}$.

1. The exact verifier-owned $\hat{K}$ used in training the CNN classifier
2. The different PRNU estimation $\hat{K}'$, which is highly correlated with $\hat{K}$
3. The different PRNU estimation $\hat{K}''$, which is only weakly correlated with $\hat{K}$

Cases (1) and (2) are similar, which use the exact the same or similar PRNU as the verifier owned $\hat{K}$. The same/similar PRNU makes $|Q_W^{\hat{K}} \cap Q_{\hat{K}}|$ and $|Q_W^{\hat{K}'} \cap Q_{\hat{K}}|$ extremely large. Hence, the attack is prone to be blocked in the first step because of the high NCC value, even though this attack could easily fool the 2nd-step classifier. On the other hand, case (3) could pass the NCC test because of the small $|Q_W^{\hat{K}''} \cap Q_{\hat{K}}|$, but the weak correlation makes it less likely to deceive the 2nd-step classifier.

3.3   Hierarchical Multi-window Search for Forgery Localization

In this section, we present a method to detect local image alteration based on the PRNU and the inconsistency within the image, as illustrated in Fig. 2.

First, the investigated image are split by different sizes of sliding window, from the smallest to the largest, $S = \{S_0, S_1, ..., S_n\}$. By feeding each patch's noise residual with the corresponding PRNU into the classifier, the classification probability map of at different scales, $P = \{P_0, P_1, ..., P_n\}$, can be obtained. Next, to fuse the information together, all probability maps except P_0 are upsampled to P_0's size using bilinear interpolation. Averaging across all the probability maps, $\bar{P}$ can be obtained. Then, we simply define 1 minus probability of "same device" as the tampering score of each pixel.

To generate a more reliable and confident tampering prediction, we only keep the most suspicious pixels whose tampering scores are over top k% score, and zero out others. Next, we adopt the contour finding algorithm proposed by [19] to find the candidate areas whose tampering score are significantly different from its neighborhood. Because our proposed approach is image-based, it is still possible to find the relatively suspicious regions on genuine images. However, these suspicious areas tend to be small or scatter around everywhere on the genuine image, so can be easily excluded based on the size and density. Finally,

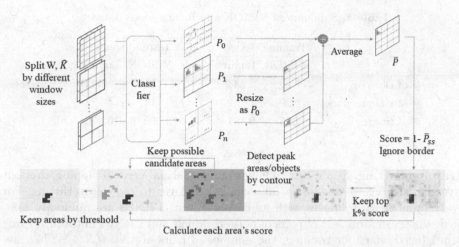

Fig. 2. Procedure of proposed forgery localization method

we average every pixel's score inside the candidate as its final single tampering score. In the inference step, we keep the candidate region if its tampering score is larger than the empirically-set threshold.

4 Experimental Setting

The details of implementation and datasets are introduced here.

Labelled Dataset. We use two labelled dataset for our experiments, VISION and luxury-goods dataset. The number of devices and images used are listed in Table 1. VISION comprises images acquired by 35 smartphones and tablets camera from 29 unique camera models. It provides flat and natural images, together with their corresponding uploaded version on Facebook and WhatApp. The flat image, which captures scenes of non-textured uniformly illuminated flat surfaces such as walls or skies, is usually favorable for the PRNU extraction because it can better suppress the signal contamination owing to image content. On the other hand, luxury-goods dataset is collected by two Apple models iPod7,1 (555 devices) and iPod9,1 (412 devices). It is a collection of images of the luxury goods. The benchmark VISION dataset is for the comparison with previous works and the luxury-goods one is to demonstrate the real-life case, where plenty of devices of the same model exist. Images acquired by training devices are used to estimate each device's PRNU and training the classifier, and images from testing devices are all kept for evaluation.

Unlabeled Dataset. We also use images without source camera information as $class_{dd}$ for 3-class training and $class_{diff}$ for 2-class case. It includes a large-scale open image dataset COCO [13] and a pre-owned image dataset. The number of images used are 123,287 and 4,104, respectively.

Table 1. Summary of VISION and luxury-goods dataset

	Training device		Testing device	
	VISION	Luxury-goods	VISION	Luxury-goods
# of Devices	20	44	15	923
# of Unique models	20	2	14	2
# of Images	4,575	9,181	3,090	10,960

Training Setting. In addition to image horizontal and vertical flipping, dropout layer is used before the finally fully-connected layer to reduce overfitting. For every minibatch, N images with its corresponding PRNUs are randomly sampled, so we can form $N \times N$ pairs of noise residuals and PRNUs in total. If using n unlabeled image for training, the number of pairs are $N \times (N + n)$ because there is no PRNU from unlabeled images. In every epoch, we generate 400 sets of minibatch. We set $N = 7, n = 1$ if using unlabeled data, otherwise $N = 8, n = 0$. Training is conducted by ADAM optimizer with an initial learning rate of 0.001. The training is stopped if the validation loss does not improve for 5 epochs.

5   Experimental Results

5.1   Source Camera Identification Accuracy

This section we discuss the identification result by different number of images of each device used for PRNU estimation (N_p) and for training (N_t). For each query image, we crop a 800 central square of patch for evaluation and test its noise residual against all registered PRNUs. For each device, the evaluation set is always imbalanced (few "same" but lot "different" samples), so we use the average of recall obtained on each class as its accuracy. The overall classification accuracy is to take the average over all devices' accuracies.

Table 2 display the 2-class classifier result on VISION. We do not implement the 3-class training here because only few models provide multiple devices. The accuracy improves if using unlabeled data. To compare with the original PCN paper [15], we also evaluate the performance by receiver operating characteristic (ROC) curve and its area under the curve (AUC) with the same patch-size (720×720) as [15]. The result shows the semi-supervised learning can achieve competitive performance even using less number of images. Focusing on the models providing more than 1 device, the classifier is always less reliable when the query image and the reference PRNU are of the same model. This confusion from the same model is the motivation for 3-class classifier. The semi-supervised VISION classifier of $N_p = 10, N_t = 10$ will be used for the further evaluation in Sect. 5.2 and 5.3.

Next, we check whether the SNS image can pass the identification step. If so, an adversary can simply download the image and pretend to be the authorized user. The accuracy will be 100% if the classifier can perfectly identify all SNS images as different device. We find using unlabeled data can better block

Table 2. Identification accuracy on VISION dataset. The semi-supervised results are highlighted in bold.

Training setting	$N_p = 10, N_t = 10$		$N_p = 5, N_t = 5$		$N_p \geq 50$ $N_t \geq 25$ [15]
Unlabeled data	w/	w/o	w/	w/o	w/o
AUC on 720×720 patches					
Native images	**0.995**	0.985	**0.981**	0.982	>0.985
Accuracy on 800×800 patches					
Native images	**97.2%**	94.5%	**94.8%**	92.5%	
Native images captured by the device of non-unique camera models					
Same model ($class_{ss}, class_{ds}$)	**97.5%**	95.5%	**94.2%**	92.7%	
Diff model ($class_{dd}$)	**99.8%**	99.0%	**99.0%**	96.9%	
Social exchanged images (Correct if prediction is different device)					
Source camera ($class_{ss}$)	**95.3%**	76.1%	**88.6%**	73.7%	
Diff camera ($class_{ds}, class_{dd}$)	**97.3%**	85.0%	**93.2%**	81.5%	

these publicly shared images, with more than >10% improvement. It is another motivation for the semi-supervising learning, because the open dataset usually includes images undergone resizing and transformation, just like SNS images. The high accuracy here also implies the PRNU-copy attack by collecting a set of publicly shared images of the target camera is not feasible, because the PRNU signal is somewhat distorted, once it is shared on the Internet.

Figure 3 presents the identification result trained on the luxury-goods dataset. When using enough number of images, the accuracy looks indifferent. However, when reducing the image number from 50 to 5, the proposed 3-class semi-supervised learning outperforms the baseline 2-class supervised one. The improvement is most significant in the case of $class_{ss}$ and $class_{ds}$, showing our method can better tell apart cameras of the same model. Even though the classifier is only trained on two unique models, our method still achieves better accuracy over the baseline one when testing images captured by unknown models in VISION, which are never present in the training setting. Our proposed method successfully demonstrates the high accuracy with very few training images per device. The fewer number for registration is the key for wider use of device authentication application, and our method can avoid the severe performance drop owing to small data size.

5.2 Fingerprint-Copy Attack Detection Performance

To test our proposed verification scheme, we implement the spoofing attack targeting all 20 training devices in VISION. For each target camera, at least 72 images from other 19 cameras are randomly selected to conduct the attack. We adopt the fingerprint-substitution attack similar to [20] by the wavelet algorithm to generate the forged image. The experiments are conducted with 6 different

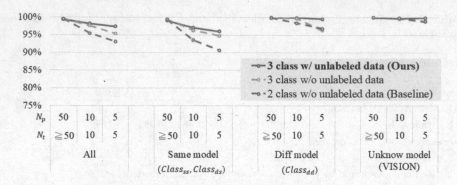

Fig. 3. Identification accuracy on luxury-goods dataset

fingerprint-copy strengths, $\alpha = \{0.05, 0.25, 0.5, 1, 2, 5\}$. We also prepare different sources of the fingerprint to explore all scenarios.

1. $\hat{K}_{train}$: the fingerprint of the target camera used in training the classifier
2. $\hat{K}'_{flat}$: the fingerprint estimated by collecting flat images captured by the target camera
3. $\hat{K}''_{natural}(n = 1, 10, 50)$: the fingerprint estimated by collecting 1/10/50 natural images captured by the target camera.

(1) is to demonstrate the case when the verifier-owned PRNU is stolen. (2) is to present the attack with the well-estimated PRNU, and (3) is the attack at a general level. Also, to prevent from affecting the accuracy of non-forged images, the threshold of each reference camera is set to be the maximal NCC value of non-forged images in the validation set.

Figure 4 reports the experimental results with 2 blocking ratios, with and without the NCC test. The ratio w/o NCC test can be regarded as a baseline, solely based on the 2nd-step classifier. On the other hand, the ratio w/NCC test is the overall performance based both on the 1st and 2nd steps. The successful attack w/NCC test should not only deceive the device classifier but also fool the NCC test. For all levels of the copy strength, the blocking ratio improves. The improvement is particularly evident for the strong copy strength, which is more effective to confuse the 2nd-step classifier. The similar protection improvement can be observed with different spoofing sources. After introducing the NCC test, our method can block 95.2% attacks even when the attacker can steal the fingerprint stored in the server $\hat{K}_{train}$. In summary, the overall blocking rate of our experiment is 94.4%, 60.5 percentage points improvement over the baseline.

5.3   Forgery Localization Performance

We manipulate 2/3 of validation images from VISION dataset, by two types of forgeries, splicing and inpainting. Image splicing is to insert objects from COCO dataset into the target image. For image inpainting, we remove some regions

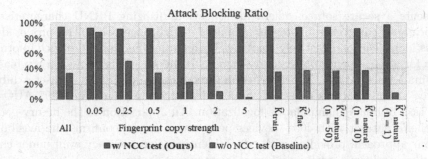

Fig. 4. Comparisons of attack blocking ratio by the proposed and the baseline method.

in photos and recover them by the deep generative network proposed by [22]. Eventually, we manipulate 5,419 regions over 2,847 images.

We use ROC to evaluate the performance on both manipulated and original images. We take each candidate region generated by our localization algorithm as a single object. We use 4 different sliding window sizes, $S = \{800, 400, 200, 100\}$ to calculate the tampering score. If the intersection over union (IOU) between the candidate and the ground-truth manipulated region is higher than the predefined threshold, the label is 1 and 0 otherwise. The final AUC is 0.92. Our method can successfully detect at least one forgery from 92% of the manipulated images. Figure 5 lists some examples of our final forgery localization prediction.

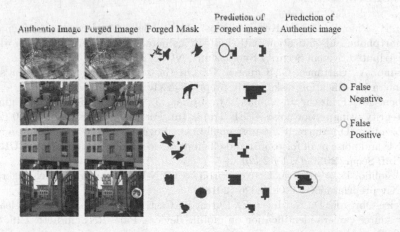

Fig. 5. Forgery detection and localization example. Row 1, 3 are examples of inpainting and row 2, 4 are examples of splicing forgery.

6   Conclusions

A data and its source-device paring scheme is one powerful approach to enhance information security and hence realize credible information platforms with additional values. As one of the demonstrations of this pairing framework, this paper presents a secure source-camera identification utilizing PRNU characteristics imprinted in its taken photos as a camera-device fingerprint. The proposed 3-class identification effectively combines both camera model and device information for accurate and robust source-camera authentications even with the biased or small-scale dataset. Experiments on the benchmark VISION dataset exhibits >94% spoofing attack detection, >97% identification accuracy, >0.92 AUC on the task of image manipulation localization. An application to the luxury-goods reseller's dataset with 400+ devices per camera model confirms the feasibility of our approach, providing with >95% identification accuracy even under challenging conditions, with only 5 photos entry per device.

Besides the PRNU and the device classifier, our pre- and post-processing defensive methods do not rely on any further optimization or prior information. Once the classifier is trained, all three steps can go into service. This trait offers flexibility to versatile applications. For the application of risk tolerance, our proposed method with the very few number of images per device can deliver a competitive performance, as well as robust protection. For the application with little risk tolerance, a solid number of images or cooperation with other approaches can help reduce the risk of wrong identification.

Acknowledgement. We would like to thank Entrupy Inc. for providing data and Satsuya Ohata for his feedback and discussion.

References

1. Ba, Z., Piao, S., Fu, X., Koutsonikolas, D., Mohaisen, A., Ren, K.: Abc: enabling smartphone authentication with built-in camera. In: 25th Annual Network and Distributed System Security Symposium, NDSS 2018 (2018)
2. Bruno, A., Cattaneo, G., Capasso, P.: On the reliability of the PNU for source camera identification tasks. arXiv preprint arXiv:2008.12700 (2020)
3. Chen, M., Fridrich, J., Goljan, M., Lukás, J.: Determining image origin and integrity using sensor noise. IEEE Trans. Inf. Forensics Secur. **3**(1), 74–90 (2008)
4. Cozzolino, D., Marra, F., Gragnaniello, D., Poggi, G., Verdoliva, L.: Combining PNU and noise print for robust and efficient device source identification. EURASIP J. Inf. Secur. **2020**(1), 1–12 (2020)
5. Cozzolino, D., Verdoliva, L.: Noiseprint: a CNN-based camera model fingerprint. arXiv preprint arXiv:1808.08396 (2018)
6. Freire-Obregón, D., Narducci, F., Barra, S., Castrillón-Santana, M.: Deep learning for source camera identification on mobile devices. Patt. Recogn. Lett. **126**, 86–91 (2019)
7. Gloe, T., Böhme, R.: The 'Dresden image database' for benchmarking digital image forensics. In: Proceedings of the 2010 ACM Symposium on Applied Computing, pp. 1584–1590 (2010)
8. Goljan, M., Fridrich, J., Chen, M.: Defending against fingerprint-copy attack in sensor-based camera identification. IEEE Trans. Inf. Forensics Secur. **6**(1), 227–236 (2010)
9. Iuliani, M., Fontani, M., Piva, A.: A leak in PRNU based source identification? questioning fingerprint uniqueness. arXiv preprint arXiv:2009.04878 (2020)

10. Kirchner, M., Johnson, C.: SPN-CNN: boosting sensor-based source camera attribution with deep learning. In: 2019 IEEE International Workshop on Information Forensics and Security (WIFS), pp. 1–6. IEEE (2019)

11. Korus, P., Huang, J.: Multi-scale analysis strategies in PRNU-based tampering localization. IEEE Trans. Inf. Forensics Secur. **12**(4), 809–824 (2016)

12. Li, H., Luo, W., Rao, Q., Huang, J.: Anti-forensics of camera identification and the triangle test by improved fingerprint-copy attack. arXiv preprint arXiv:1707.07795 (2017)

13. Lin, T.-Y., et al.: Microsoft COCO: common objects in context. In: Fleet, D., Pajdla, T., Schiele, B., Tuytelaars, T. (eds.) ECCV 2014. LNCS, vol. 8693, pp. 740–755. Springer, Cham (2014). https://doi.org/10.1007/978-3-319-10602-1_48

14. Lukas, J., Fridrich, J., Goljan, M.: Digital camera identification from sensor pattern noise. IEEE Trans. Inf. Forensics Secur. **1**(2), 205–214 (2006)

15. Mandelli, S., Cozzolino, D., Bestagini, P., Verdoliva, L., Tubaro, S.: Cnn-based fast source device identification. IEEE Sig. Proces. Lett. **27**, 1285–1289 (2020)

16. Mayer, O., Stamm, M.C.: Forensic similarity for digital images. IEEE Trans. Inf. Forensics Secur. **15**, 1331–1346 (2019)

17. Selvaraju, R.R., Cogswell, M., Das, A., Vedantam, R., Parikh, D., Batra, D.: Gradcam: visual explanations from deep networks via gradient-based localization. In: Proceedings of the IEEE International Conference on Computer Vision, pp. 618–626 (2017)

18. Shullani, D., Fontani, M., Iuliani, M., Al Shaya, O., Piva, A.: Vision: a video and image dataset for source identification. EURASIP J. Inf. Secur. **2017**(1), 1–16 (2017)

19. Suzuki, S., et al.: Topological structural analysis of digitized binary images by border following. Comput. Vis. Graph. Image Process. **30**(1), 32–46 (1985)

20. Villalba, L.J.G., Orozco, A.L.S., Corripio, J.R., Hernandez-Castro, J.: A PRNU-based counter-forensic method to manipulate smartphone image source identification techniques. Fut. Gene. Comput. Syst. **76**, 418–427 (2017)

21. Yao, H., Qino, T., Xu, M., Zheng, N.: Robust multi-classifier for camera model identification based on convolution neural network. IEEE Access **6**, 24973–24982 (2018)

22. Yu, J., Lin, Z., Yang, J., Shen, X., Lu, X., Huang, T.S.: Free-form image inpainting with gated convolution. In: Proceedings of the IEEE/CVF International Conference on Computer Vision, pp. 4471–4480 (2019)

23. Zhang, W., Tang, X., Yang, Z., Niu, S.: Multi-scale segmentation strategies in PRNU-based image tampering localization. Multim. Tools Appl. **78**(14), 20113–20132 (2019)

24. Zhou, P., Han, X., Morariu, V.I., Davis, L.S.: Learning rich features for image manipulation detection. In: Proceedings of the IEEE Conference on Computer Vision and Pattern Recognition, pp. 1053–1061 (2018)

Effects of Image Compression on Image Age Approximation

Robert Jöchl[✉] and Andreas Uhl

Department of Computer Science, University of Salzburg, Salzburg, Austria
{robert.joechl,andreas.uhl}@plus.ac.at

Abstract. In-field sensor defects are at the core of temporal image forensics, as a temporal order among pieces of evidence can be established by knowing their onset time. A characteristic of these single pixel defects is that they appear as point-like image noise. Since sensor defects exhibit noise-like properties, they are vulnerable to image compression. For this reason, it is important to evaluate the effect of image compression on the defect based image age approximation techniques available. In this paper, we assess the robustness of these age approximation methods with respect to four different compression techniques (i.e., 'JPEG', 'JPEG 2000', 'JPEG XR' and 'Better Portable Graphics') and different compression strengths. Since the approximation techniques considered require the defect locations to be known in advance, we assess the effect of image compression on the defect detection methods proposed in the context of image age approximation.

Keywords: Image compression · Image age approximation · In-field sensor defects · Defect detection · Image forensics

1 Introduction

In temporal image forensics the main objective is to establish a temporal order among pieces of evidence. Usually such a chronological ordering is based on time-dependent traces left during the image acquisition processing pipeline. Since these (age) traces are time-dependent, the age of a digital image can be approximated by comparing the observed traces from an image under investigation with traces extracted from trusted images (of the same device and where the acquisition time is known). The maximum temporal resolution depends on the characteristics of the traces evaluated and the trusted images available.

A very recent approach for image age approximation is proposed by Ahmed et al. in [1]. In this work the authors utilise two well known Convolutional Neural Network (CNN) architectures, i.e. the AlexNet and GoogLeNet. The best classification accuracy (i.e., more than 85%) was reached by the AlexNet in a transfer learning mode. However, the exploited classification features (age traces) are not further investigated by the authors, though the authors suggest that the features are not dependent on a certain image block since the networks are trained on several non-overlapping image patches.

X. Zhao et al. (Eds.): IWDW 2021, LNCS 13180, pp. 102–116, 2022.
https://doi.org/10.1007/978-3-030-95398-0_8

Image age approximation based on the Photo Response Non Uniformity (PRNU) is proposed in [16]. The PRNU represents the differences in light sensitivity among pixels. These differences are primarily caused by the inhomogenity of silicon wafers and the slight differences in pixel dimensions due to manufacturing imperfections [15]. Since these differences are very unique, the PRNU represents a sensor fingerprint and can be used for camera identification (e.g., as shown in [15]).

Other techniques for image age approximation are based on the presence of in-field sensor defects and are proposed in [6,11]. In-field sensor defects are single pixel defects that develop after the manufacturing process. These defects accumulate over time, and by detecting their presence a temporal ordering can be achieved. In this context, Fridrich et al. introduce a maximum likelihood approach for image age approximation in [6]. We regard image age approximation as a multi-class classification problem and propose to utilise two well-known machine learning techniques (i.e., a Naive Bayes Classifier (NB) and a Support Vector Machine (SVM)) in [11]. However, a limitation of image age approximation methods based on in-field sensor defects is that the defect locations have to be known in advance.

In [6] the authors suggest to simply threshold the median filter residuals for this purpose. Since the median filter residuals are used as a defect detection feature, this method can be considered a 'spatial only' method. Another method for defect detection in the context of image age approximation is introduced in [10]. In this work, we incorporate spatial and temporal information for defect detection.

In-field sensor defects are single pixel defects that appear as image noise and noise belongs to the high-frequency (high-detailed) image content. Image compression techniques usually progressively suppress high-frequency image content. For this reason, it is important to evaluate how the defect based image age approximation methods are affected by image compression.

In this paper, we empirically asses the robustness of the age approximation (introduced in [6,11]) and defect detection methods considered (introduced in [6,10]) with respect to 'JPEG', 'JPEG 2000', 'JPEG-XR' and 'Better Portable Graphics'. For this purpose, we conduct experiments on images from two different devices. All images are compressed with different quality settings to achieve several fixed target compression ratios. The corresponding defect detection and age approximation results obtained from lossless image compression are used as a baseline.

The rest of this paper is organised as follows: In the first section we summarise the important defect characteristics and define the defect model. The image age approximation techniques investigated and the in-field sensor defect detection methods are described in Sect. 3 and 4 respectively. A detailed overview of the experiments conducted is given in Sect. 5. The results are presented and discussed in Sect. 6, and the key insights are summarised in Sect. 7.

2   In-Field Sensor Defects

In-field sensor defects are single pixel defects that develop in-field, i.e. after the manufacturing process. These defects are widely studied, and the main characteristics have been described in various publications (e.g., [5,12–14,19,20]).

Neutrons which are part of cosmic radiation can damage a small part of a pixel's silicon layer. This damage can affect the photo response of a pixel and, therefore, can cause a defective pixel. Such defective pixels are uniformly distributed across the whole image sensor and do not form any clusters. Nevertheless, the defect spreads to its neighbouring pixels due to preprocessing like demosaicing (interpolation). These defects are permanent, and the number of defects increases linearly to time. In [4] Chapman et al. propose an empirical formula to estimating the defect rate. The influence of the pixel size, the sensor area and the ISO setting on the defect development rate is investigated in [3]. The authors state that a combination of a higher ISO range, larger sensor area and smaller pixel size can increase the defect development rate significantly.

To model a defective pixel, we rely on the definitions stated in [6]. By assuming no noise or other imperfections, a defective pixel can be defined as

$$F(I) = IK + \tau D + c, \tag{1}$$

where I is the intensity of incoming light, K denotes the PRNU and c represents a constant offset. D is the dark current which depends on the exposure time, the ISO setting and the temperature. These factors are combined in τ and multiplied by D. Thus, the offset of the pixel varies as τ varies. Based on the defect type, either D, c or both defect parameters are high (i.e., a hot pixel has a high dark current).

In Fig. 1, examples of such defects are shown. The right image shows defects extracted from a dark-field image. Dark-field images are images taken with the shutter closed (i.e., the incoming light is set to zero $I \approx 0$), thus revealing the defects. As illustrated, a defective pixel has an offset independent of the incoming light. If the offset is high enough, the defective pixel becomes visible in a regular scene image, as shown in Fig. 1 (left). As illustrated, a defect appears as point-like image noise.

3   Image Age Approximation Methods

Since a defect appears as point-like image noise, the defects can be filtered out by applying a denoising filter like a median filter. The median filter residual (i.e., subtracting the median-filtered image from the original image) estimates the defect's magnitude. For this reason, the median filter residuals provide a good age approximation feature. In [6], Fridrich et al. assume that the difference between the median filter residual and the sum of all defect parameters (i.e., K, D, c) is normally distributed. The authors propose a maximum likelihood approach to estimate the defect parameter and to approximate the age of an image under investigation, i.e.

$$\hat{y} = \underset{y \in Y}{\arg\max} \prod_{i \in \Omega} 1/\sqrt{2\pi}\hat{\sigma}_{(i)}^{(y)} \exp R_{(i)} - \left(I_{(i)}K_{(i)}^{(y)} + \tau D_{(i)}^{(y)} + c_{(i)}^{(y)}\right)/2\hat{\sigma}_{(i)}^{2(y)}. \tag{2}$$

Fig. 1. Examples of in-field sensor defects that are present in a regular scene image (left) and extracted from a dark-field image (right).

In contrast to [6] the maximum likelihood approach in Eq. (2) is adapted as a classifier. For this purpose, the defect parameters $(K^{(y)}, D^{(y)}, c^{(y)}, \sigma^{(y)})$ are computed according to the onset times defined by the class y. $R_{(i)}$ is the residual value of the ith defective pixel, and Ω denotes the set of all defective pixels.

In [11] we consider image age approximation as a multi-class classification problem and propose to utilise two well-known machine learning techniques, i.e. a NB and a SVM. Similar to the technique described above, we also rely on the median filter residuals as classification features. In context of the NB, we evaluate three different techniques for estimating the conditional probability distribution of residual values given the defect is present or not. Of these 3 estimation techniques, the Kernel Density Estimation (KDE) method works best. However, the median filter residual applied to a SVM produces best classification results overall. With the SVM, the feature space is interpreted as a Ω dimensional hypercube with an edge length of 511 (i.e. $[-256, 256]$). The training goal is to find k mutually exclusive sub-spaces (one for each class).

In summary, we evaluate 3 different age approximation methods, i.e. the 'KDc' approach proposed in [6], and the 'NB-KDE' and 'SVM' approach introduced in [11].

4   Defect Detection Methods

Fridrich et al. suggest to threshold the median filter residual for defect detection in [6]. We formalise this approach in [10] as

$$\sigma^2(\vec{r}_2) > t, \tag{3}$$

where $\vec{r}_2$ denotes a vector of residual values of an arbitrary but fixed pixel over the set S_2. The set $S_2 \subset S$ is a subset containing the last m images S (i.e., where all defects are already present). Furthermore, the threshold t is defined as the average residual variance of all pixels plus the standard deviation times an adaptive weight. This method is denoted as 'spatial only' method.

We introduce a defect detection method exploiting spatial and temporal information in [10]. The temporal information is represented by the differences in residual values before and after the defect onset. For this purpose, a pixel is considered defective if

$$\sigma^2(\vec{r}_1) < \sigma^2(\vec{r}_2) \; \wedge \; ||\vec{r}_2'||_1 > \alpha * |R_2|, \tag{4}$$

$$\text{where } \vec{r}_2'(i) = \begin{cases} \vec{r}_2'(i) = 0, & \text{if } t_l < \vec{r}_2(i) < t_u \\ \vec{r}_2'(i) = 1, & \text{otherwise,} \end{cases}$$

$$\text{and} \quad t_{l,u} = \lceil \text{median}(\vec{r}_1) \rceil \mp w_S * \sigma(\vec{r}_1).$$

The vector $\vec{r}_1$ represents the residual values of an arbitrary but fixed pixel over the first n images of S_1. The parameter α controls the number of residual values in $\vec{r}_2$ that have to be outside of $[t_l, t_u]$ in order for a pixel to be considered defective, and w_S adjusts the width of the threshold band.

5   Experiments

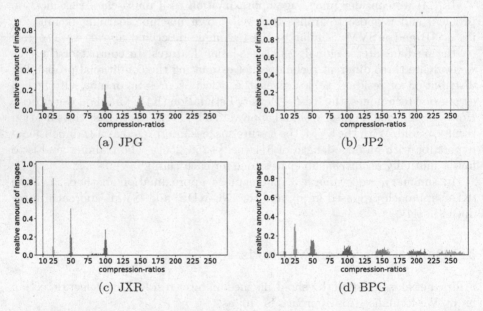

(a) JPG   (b) JP2

(c) JXR   (d) BPG

Fig. 2. Distribution of file sizes per target compression ratio and image compression technique. Only the distribution of the Pentax K5 images is shown, but the file size distribution of the Pentax K5II is similar.

To assess the effect of image compression on the image age approximation and defect detection methods considered we rely on images from two different devices: (i) a Pentax K5 (P1), (ii) a Pentax K5II (P2). The same images that are used for this paper are also used in [10] to evaluate the defect detection performance and to asses the impact of the selected detection method on subsequent image

age approximation. Since the images of both cameras are available as DNG (Digital Negative) files, lossy image compression techniques can be applied. For this purpose, the images are first converted to 'PNG' files (lossless). Based on these lossless 'PNG' files, four different lossy image compression techniques are applied:

1. *JPEG (JPG)* [7]: This is the most widely used image compression technique. JPG belongs to the family of transform coding techniques, where the Discrete Cosine Transform (DCT) is applied on 8×8 pixel blocks. The resulting 64 coefficients are subsequently quantised. The strength of the quantisation is controlled by the quality parameter.
2. *JPEG2000 (JP2)* [8]: JPEG2000 is based on the Discrete Wavelet Transform (DWT). With this compression technique a generic bitstream is generated, out of which different bitstreams can be extracted. This enables explicit rate control.
3. *JPEG XR (JXR)* [9]: This technique is based on two transforms: The Photo Core Transform, which is similar to the DCT (block based), and the Photo Overlap Transform, which also exploits correlations across block boundaries.
4. *Better Portable Graphics (BPG)* [2]: BPG is an open-source compression technique. This technique is based on the H.265 video codec [18]. In principle, BPG encodes an image similar to the I-frame of a H.265 encoded video stream, i.e. intra image-block prediction is performed, and the prediction residuals are transformed using the DCT.

The 'JPG', 'JP2' and 'JXR' files are converted bases on the standard python 'imageio' library; the 'libbpg' library is used to encode the 'BPG' files. To achieve different fixed image compression ratios (i.e., the ratio between the compressed and uncompressed file size), we encoded the images with different quality settings and select the setting that comes closest to the target compression ratio. All other settings are kept at the default values. The compression ratio is the ratio between the original file size and the compressed file size, i.e.

$$\text{compression ratio} = \frac{\text{original file size (bytes)}}{\text{compressed file size (bytes)}}. \tag{5}$$

The target compression ratios range from 10 to 250, and the maximum achieved compression ratios vary depending on the compression technique. In Fig. 2 the distribution of the file sizes per target compression ratio can be seen. As already stated JP2 allows explicit rate control which can be seen by the perfectly achieved target compression ratios. In principle, the variance of the file sizes increases with the compression ratios. The lowest maximum compression ratios could be achieved with JXR. As illustrated in Fig. 2, not even a compression ratio of 100 could be achieved for several images with the lowest quality setting. To verify the results, all images (including the 'PNG' files and all lossy encoded images) are available under https://wavelab.at/sources/Joechl21c.

Since the defect detection and age approximation methods considered rely on the median filter residual as detection or classification feature, the relative

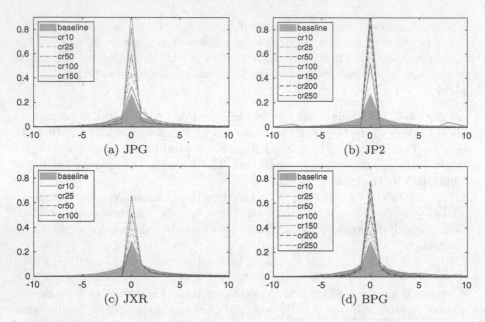

Fig. 3. Distribution of median filter residuals of defective pixels for each image compression technique and target compression ratios. Only the distribution of the P2 residuals is shown, but the residual distribution of the P1 is similar.

residual distribution (of defective pixels after the defect onset, i.e. of set S_2) per compression techniques and ratios is illustrated in Fig. 3. The area shaded in blue represents the distribution when lossless compression ('PNG') is applied. For this reason, the area shaded in blue can be regarded as baseline. All other lines show the influence of compression technique and ratios on the residual distribution. The concentration around zero for higher compression ratios indicates that more and more image details (defect information) are suppressed (as expected). It can be observed that the residual values of 'BPG' compressed images with a compression ratio of 10 almost exactly follow the baseline distribution. For a compression ratio of 10, the residual values of 'JP2' compressed images show the highest deviation from the baseline distribution, where over 50% of residual values are zero. However, 'JP2' seems to amplify some image details, as can be seen by the small bumps for residual values at −10 and 10. It is also noticeable that 'JXR' seems to completely suppresses residual values smaller than −1, while the distribution for positive residual values is almost preserved. Overall, 'BPG' has the least impact on residual distribution.

Based on these observations, we would expect 'BPG' compressed images to preserve the most defect information, which should be beneficial in terms of defect detection and image age approximation. In contrast, 'JP2' seems to affect the residual distribution the most, which should also be reflected in lower detection and age approximation performance. The impact of 'JXR' compression ranges directly after 'BPG'. With 'JXR', the negative values are suppressed, but the distribution is preserved in the positive range, which is also reflected by the relatively low amount of residual equal to zero after image compression. Consequently, the detection and age approximation performance for 'JPG' is expected to be between 'JXR' and 'JP2'.

The effect of image compression on the defect detection method considered is assessed by performing the same experiments as in [10]. The f1 score [17] is computed for a broad range of parameter combinations (i.e., $\alpha \in [0.2, 0.8], w_S \in [1, 6], w_{\text{spatial only}} \in [1, 80]$). This evaluation is performed 10 times for each compression technique and ratio, with 100 images being drawn randomly from S_1 and S_2. To compute the f1 score, the resulting defect candidates are compared to a ground truth. This ground truth is extracted from dark-field images.

The effect of image compression on the image age approximation techniques proposed in [6, 11] is assessed by considering the same situation as in [10]. In [10] the impact of the detection method on a subsequent age approximation is evaluated by approximating the age of images from set S_1 and S_2 (i.e., the oldest and newest available images). Considering a binary classification problem such as in [10] is sufficient to show the effects of image compression. The residual values of the resulting defect candidates (True Positives and False Positives) that are found during the detection method performance evaluation (i.e., where the f1 score was maximum) are used as classification features. For this reason, 10 different sets of defect candidates (based on the 10 runs that are used to evaluate the defect detection methods) are used for training. To assess the performance of the age approximation methods, we applied the same evaluation as in [10] (i.e., each method is trained 200 times for each set of classification features), however, now we applied it once for each compression technique and ratio.

Since the same images are used and the same evaluation is performed, the results stated in [10] (for defect detection and age approximation) act as baseline results for this work.

6   Experimental Results

In Fig. 4 the average maximum f1 score (over 10 runs) per defect detection method and compression ratio is illustrated. The horizontal dashed lines (baselines) represent the average f1 score (stated in [10]) when the detection methods are applied on lossless compressed 'PNG' files. In general, we can observe the behaviour as expected, i.e. the defects are attenuated more and more for stronger compression settings. This continuous decrease in detection performance is expected since compression techniques usually progressively suppress fine detailed image content. In-field sensor defects appear as point-like image noise and are, therefore, part of the high-frequency image content. Depending on the compression technique, this high-frequency image content is attenuated differently.

In general, the 'spatial & temp.' method is superior to the 'spatial only' method for slight image compression (up to a ratio of 10). However, the 'spatial only' method seems to be more robust with respect to higher compression

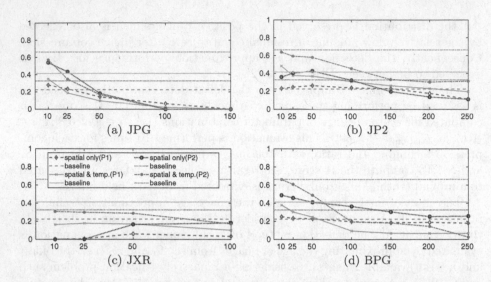

Fig. 4. Effect of image compression technique and ratio on in-field sensor defect detection. The maximum average f1 score is plotted over the different target compression ratios.

ratios than the 'spatial & temp.' method. Furthermore, lower image compression (up to compression ratio 25) seems to assist the 'spatial only' method, since for these compression ratios this method reached an even better performance than for lossless compressed images (except for 'JXR' compressed images). This is surprising since, as shown in Fig. 3, the residual values are attenuated also for lower image compression. One reason for this could be that the defects considered are relatively strong. While distracting noise is smoothed out by the image compression, these (strong) sensor defects may survive this smoothing.

As illustrated in Fig. 4(a), 'JPG' affects the defect detection performance the most for higher compression ratios. At a compression ratio of 100 and 150, almost no more defects can be detected, although this is still possible with all other compression methods. With 'JPG' both detection methods show a similar decrease, whereby the 'spatial only' method seems to be slightly more robust with respect to higher compression ratios.

The 'JP2' results are shown in Fig. 4(b). The superiority of this compression technique in terms of defect detection over 'JPG' is clearly evident. Not only that, a compression ratio up to 250 is easily possible; 'JP2' preserves enough high-frequency image components that at least some defects are still detectable for high compression ratios (up to 250). For this compression technique, the 'spatial & temp.' detection method is consistently better than the 'spatial only' approach. In addition, slight 'JP2' compression seems to assist both detection methods (the 'spatial & temp.' method reached an average f1 score that is higher than the baseline for images of the P1 and a compression ratio of 10). However, the 'spatial only' method benefits even more from image compression since a higher average f1 score than the baseline is achieved up to a compression rate of 100.

With 'JXR', the results are very different for both detection methods. On the one hand, the 'spatial & temp.' method behaves as expected (i.e., almost continuous decreasing) and, on the other hand, the 'spatial only' method does not detect a defect for compression ratios 10 and 25, but for higher ratios the performance significantly increases.

The 'BPG' results (Fig. 4(d)) are similar to the 'JP2' results. In contrast to 'JP2', the 'spatial & temp.' method seems to be affected more strongly by 'BPG' compression. The 'spatial & temp.' shows a similarly high f1 score at a compression ratio of 10 compared to 'JP2', but for higher compression ratios the decrease is much more significant. The 'spatial only' method seems to cope better with 'BPG' compressed images.

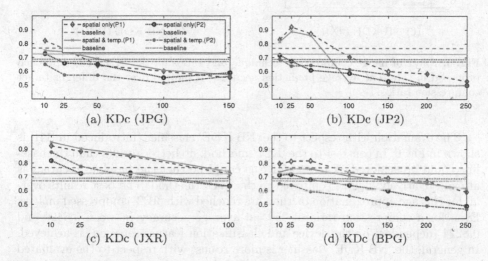

Fig. 5. Effect of image compression technique and ratios on the 'KDc' approach proposed in [6]. The average prediction accuracy is plotted over the different target compression ratios.

In Fig. 5 the effect of image compression on the image age approximation method proposed in [6] is illustrated. Considering a binary classification problem with balanced classes, an accuracy of 0.5 represents the lower classification boundary. An accuracy of less than 0.5 would indicate a prediction accuracy worse than random selection. For the lossless compressed 'PNG' images (baseline) this classifier achieved the worst results as compared to the 'NB KDE' and 'SVM' approach. However, the 'KDc' method clearly benefits from 'JXR' compression, since the prediction accuracy for lower image compression is significantly higher than the baseline. Even for a compression ratio of 100, the results are still close to the baseline. Again, one reason could be that the defects survive the compression-induced smoothing while distracting noise is smoothed out. The best results for higher compression results are achieved with 'BPG' compressed images.

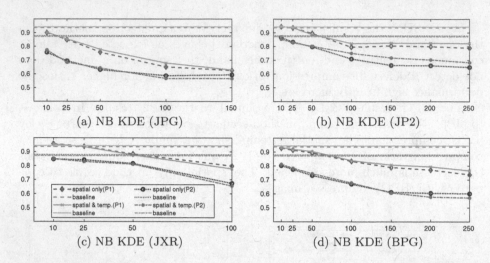

(a) NB KDE (JPG)   (b) NB KDE (JP2)

(c) NB KDE (JXR)   (d) NB KDE (BPG)

Fig. 6. Effect of image compression technique and ratios on the 'NB KDE' approach proposed in [11]. The average prediction accuracy is plotted over the different target compression ratios.

The evaluation with respect to the 'NB KDE' classifier (introduced in [11]) is shown in Fig. 6. In contrast to the 'KDc' method, no better results than the baseline could be achieved. A reason for this could be that the baseline accuracy is already relatively high as compared to the 'KDc' method. The best results overall for this age approximation method are reached with 'JP2' compressed images. Even for a compression ratio of 250, an average accuracy between 0.6490 and 0.8224 (dependent on the device and classification feature set used) is achieved. In general, the 'NB KDE' classifier is more robust with respect to the evaluated image compression techniques than the 'KDc' method.

In Fig. 7 the effects of image compression on the 'SVM' based approach (introduced in [11]) is illustrated. Again the best results overall can be achieved with 'JP2' compressed images. The 'JP2' results are similar to the 'NB KDE' results (shown in Fig. 6(b)); for a compression ratio of 250 an average accuracy between 0.6535 and 0.8161 is achieved. The 'SVM' shows least age approximation accuracy with respect to 'JXR' compressed images.

Except for the 'KDc' classifier applied to 'JP2' and 'BPG' compressed images (with a compression ratio greater than 150), the prediction accuracy is consistently better than prediction by chance. For example, taking 'JPG' into account, the age approximation performance is still better than random prediction for a compression ratio of 150, although neither defect detection method could reliably detect any defect at this compression level.

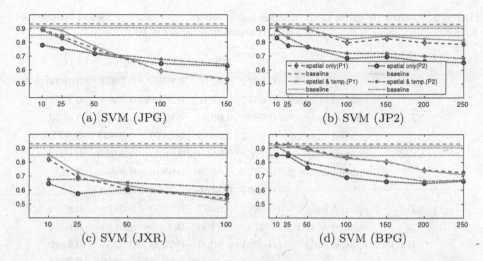

Fig. 7. Effect of image compression technique and ratios on the 'SVM' approach proposed in [11]. The average prediction accuracy is plotted over the different target compression ratios.

In general, the effect of image compression is dependent on the age approximation method. While the 'KDc' classifier achieved the best results with 'JXR' compressed images, the 'SVM' approach suffers the most with these images. It is also noticeable that the results of the Pentax K5 are generally better than those of the Pentax K5II, but this changes for higher compression rates with the 'SVM' classifier (for 'JPG' and 'JXR', see Fig. 7(a) and (c)) and with the KDc classifier (for 'JP2', see Fig. 5(b)).

In Table 1 the average age prediction accuracy achieved for the first four compression ratios evaluated (i.e., compression ratio 10–100) is shown. Based on this table, we evaluate the general approximation performance up to a compression ratio of 100. In this context, the 'KDc' classifier is most robust with respect to 'JXR' compressed images. For images from the P1, the 'NB KDE' classifier achieved the best results with 'BPG' compressed images. However, the 'JP2' results are similarly good and for the P2 the best result is achieved based on 'JP2' compressed images as well. The 'SVM' classifier is most robust with respect to 'BPG' compressed images.

The marginal cells of Table 1 represent the arithmetic mean of the rows and columns respectively. Based on these values we can assess the most robust age approximation method overall (across all compression techniques evaluated), and the best image compression technique overall (over all evaluated image age approximation techniques and classification feature sets). In this context, the most robust classifier overall is the 'NB KDE' since this classifier achieved in total the best results for both classification feature sets (for the P1 and P2). The best overall image compression technique is 'JP2' (closely followed by 'BPG').

Table 1. Arithmetic mean of the average age prediction accuracy achieved for the first four compression ratios evaluated (i.e., compression ratio 10–100).

			JPG	JP2	JXR	BPG	Σ/4
P1	KDc	spatial only	0.7072	0.8317	0.8455	0.7893	0.7934
		spatial & temp.	0.6977	0.7701	**0.8635**	0.7393	0.7677
	NB KDE	spatial only	0.7890	0.8926	0.8949	0.8925	0.8673
		spatial & temp.	0.8032	0.8983	0.8870	**0.8991**	**0.8719**
	SVM	spatial only	0.7704	0.8809	0.6646	**0.8969**	0.8032
		spatial & temp.	0.7897	0.8838	0.6834	0.8903	0.8118
Σ/6			0.7595	**0.8596**	0.8065	0.8512	
P2	KDc	spatial only	0.6482	0.6467	0.7259	0.6878	0.6772
		spatial & temp.	0.5782	0.6460	**0.7478**	0.6122	0.6461
	NB KDE	spatial only	0.6671	0.8009	0.7950	0.7451	0.7520
		spatial & temp.	0.6669	**0.8080**	0.7865	0.7550	0.7541
	SVM	spatial only	0.7231	0.7643	0.5967	0.7881	0.7181
		spatial & temp.	0.7777	0.8015	0.6560	**0.8304**	**0.7664**
Σ/6			0.6769	**0.7446**	0.7180	0.7364	

With regard to the assumptions formulated in Sect. 5 (based on the observed compression-induced deviation of the residual value distribution), it can be stated that: (i) the superiority of 'BPG' can be confirmed, although 'JP2' achieved better results overall, (ii) the assumption that 'JP2' has the greatest effect on defect detection and age approximation performance could not be confirmed, in contrast, 'JP2' showed the least effect, and (iii) the assumption that 'JPG' effects the detection and age approximation results more than 'JXR' was correct.

7   Conclusion

In this paper the effect of image compression on the available age approximation methods based on in-field sensor defects is empirically evaluated. Since these methods rely on the presence of in-field sensor defects, the defect locations must be known in advance. For this purpose, the defect detection methods available in the context of image age approximation are assessed.

The 'spatial & temp.' defect detection method is better than the 'spatial only' method for all the methods investigated at low compression ratios. This method is also preferable for 'JP2' compressed images. However, lower image compression seems to assist the 'spatial only' method since the achieved detection performance for low compression ratios (e.g., compression ratio 10) is higher than the baseline (the results achieved when applied on lossless compressed images). Furthermore, the 'spatial only' method tends to be more robust with respect to

'JPG' and 'BPG' compressed images. Overall, 'JP2' and 'BPG' show the least effect on the defect detection performance.

Since in-field sensor defects are among the high-frequent image components, image age approximation methods also exhibit a decrease in accuracy for higher image compression ratios. Of the methods investigated, the 'KDc' classifier shows the worst results. However, this classifier seems to benefit considerably from 'JXR' image compression. Significantly better results are achieved by the 'NB KDE' classifier, where the best results are achieved based on 'JP2' compressed images (even for a compression ratio of 250, an average accuracy up to 0.8224 is achieved). With the 'SVM' classifier the best results are achieved based on 'JP2' compressed images as well. However, for both classifiers ('NB KDE' and 'SVM'), the 'BPG results are similarly good. The superiority of 'JP2' in contrast to all other image compression techniques evaluated is also evident from Table 1. The image age approximation technique that is most robust with respect to all evaluated image compression techniques is the 'NB KDE'.

In conclusion, the performance of the in-field sensor defect detection and the age approximation methods investigated suffer from image compression. This is expected since in-field sensor defects represent fine image details and these are usually progressively suppressed by the compression techniques. The most commonly used compression technique ('JPG') significantly attenuates the defect for higher compression ratios so that defects can no longer be detected and the prediction accuracy decreases considerably. The compression method that shows the least impact in terms of defect detection and image age approximation is 'JP2'. However, 'BPG' shows similarly good results.

References

1. Ahmed, F., Khelifi, F., Lawgaly, A., Bouridane, A.: Temporal image forensic analysis for picture dating with deep learning. In: 2020 International Conference on Computing, Electronics Communications Engineering (iCCECE), pp. 109–114 (2020). https://doi.org/10.1109/iCCECE49321.2020.9231160
2. Bellard, F.: The BPG Image Format. https://bellard.org/bpg/. Accessed 20 July 2021
3. Chapman, G.H., Thomas, R., Thomas, R., Coelho, K.J., Meneses, S., Yang, T.Q., Koren, I., Koren, Z.: Increases in hot pixel development rates for small digital pixel sizes. Electr. Imag. **2016**(12), 1–6 (2016)
4. Chapman, G.H., Thomas, R., Koren, Z., Koren, I.: Empirical formula for rates of hot pixel defects based on pixel size, sensor area, and ISO. In: Widenhorn, R., Dupret, A. (eds.) Sensors, Cameras, and Systems for Industrial and Scientific Applications XIV, vol. 8659, pp. 119–129. International Society for Optics and Photonics, SPIE (2013). https://doi.org/10.1117/12.2005850
5. Dudas, J., Wu, L.M., Jung, C., Chapman, G.H., Koren, Z., Koren, I.: Identification of in-field defect development in digital image sensors. In: Martin, R.A., DiCarlo, J.M., Sampat, N. (eds.) Digital Photography III. vol. 6502, pp. 319–330. International Society for Optics and Photonics, SPIE (2007). https://doi.org/10.1117/12.704563

6. Fridrich, J., Goljan, M.: Determining approximate age of digital images using sensor defects. In: Memon, N.D., Dittmann, J., Alattar, A.M., Delp, E.J., III. (eds.) Media Watermarking, Security, and Forensics III, vol. 7880, pp. 49–59. International Society for Optics and Photonics, SPIE, Bellingham (2011)
7. I. O. for Standardization: ISO/IEC IS 10918-1:1994. Information Technology-Digital Compression and Coding of Continuous-tone Still Images: Requirements and Guidelines (1994)
8. I. O. for Standardization: ISO/IEC IS 15444-1:2004. Information technology - JPEG 2000 image coding system: Core coding system (2004)
9. I. O. for Standardization: ISO/IEC IS 29199-2:2012. Information technology - JPEG XR image coding system - Part 2: Image coding specification (2004)
10. Joechl, R., Uhl, A.: Identification of in-field sensor defects in the context of image age approximation. In: 2021 IEEE International Conference on Image Processing (ICIP), pp. 3043–3047. Anchorage (2021). https://doi.org/10.1109/ICIP42928.2021.9506023
11. Joechl, R., Uhl, A.: A machine learning approach to approximate the age of a digital image. In: Digital Forensics and Watermarking: 19th International Workshop, IWDW 2020, Melbourne, VIC, Australia, November 25–27, 2020, Revised Selected Papers. LNCS, vol. 12617, pp. 181–195 (2021). Springer, CHam. https://doi.org/10.1007/978-3-030-69449-4_14
12. Leung, J., Chapman, G.H., Koren, I., Koren, Z.: Characterization of gain enhanced in-field defects in digital imagers. In: 2009 24th IEEE International Symposium on Defect and Fault Tolerance in VLSI Systems, pp. 155–163 (2009)
13. Leung, J., Chapman, G.H., Koren, Z., Koren, I.: Statistical identification and analysis of defect development in digital imagers. In: Rodricks, B.G., Süsstrunk, S.E. (eds.) Digital Photography V. vol. 7250, pp. 272–283. International Society for Optics and Photonics, SPIE (2009). https://doi.org/10.1117/12.806109
14. Leung, J., Dudas, J., Chapman, G.H., Koren, I., Koren, Z.: Quantitative analysis of in-field defects in image sensor arrays. In: 22nd IEEE International Symposium on Defect and Fault-Tolerance in VLSI Systems (DFT 2007). IEEE, September 2007. https://doi.org/10.1109/dft.2007.59
15. Lukas, J., Fridrich, J., Goljan, M.: Digital camera identification from sensor pattern noise. IEEE Trans. Inf. Forensics Secur. 1(2), 205–214 (2006)
16. Mao, J., Bulan, O., Sharma, G., Datta, S.: Device temporal forensics: an information theoretic approach. In: 2009 16th IEEE International Conference on Image Processing (ICIP), pp. 1501–1504. IEEE (2009)
17. Powers, D.M.: Evaluation: from precision, recall and f-measure to ROC, informedness, markedness and correlation. J. Mach. Learn. Technol. 2(1), 37–63 (2011)
18. Sullivan, G.J., Ohm, J.R., Han, W.J., Wiegand, T.: Overview of the high efficiency video coding (HEVC) standard. IEEE Trans. Circ. Syst. Video Technol. 22(12), 1649–1668 (2012). https://doi.org/10.1109/TCSVT.2012.2221191
19. Theuwissen, A.J.: Influence of terrestrial cosmic rays on the reliability of CCD image sensors part 1: experiments at room temperature. IEEE Trans. Electr. Dev. 54(12), 3260–3266 (2007)
20. Theuwissen, A.J.: Influence of terrestrial cosmic rays on the reliability of CCD image sensors part 2: Experiments at elevated temperature. IEEE Trans. Electr. Dev. 55(9), 2324–2328 (2008)

FMFCC-A: A Challenging Mandarin Dataset for Synthetic Speech Detection

Zhenyu Zhang[1,2], Yewei Gu[1,2], Xiaowei Yi[1,2], and Xianfeng Zhao[1,2(✉)]

[1] State Key Laboratory of Information Security, Institute of Information Engineering, Chinese Academy of Sciences, Beijing 100093, China
{zhangzhenyu,guyewei,yixiaowei,zhaoxianfeng}@iie.ac.cn
[2] School of Cyber Security, University of Chinese Academy of Sciences, Beijing 100093, China

Abstract. As increasing development of text-to-speech (TTS) and voice conversion (VC) technologies, the detection of synthetic speech has been suffered dramatically. In order to promote the development of synthetic speech detection model against Mandarin TTS and VC technologies, we have constructed a challenging Mandarin dataset and organized the accompanying audio track of the first fake media forensic challenge of China Society of Image and Graphics (FMFCC-A). The FMFCC-A dataset is by far the largest publicly-available Mandarin dataset for synthetic speech detection, which contains 40,000 synthesized Mandarin utterances that generated by 11 Mandarin TTS systems and two Mandarin VC systems, and 10,000 genuine Mandarin utterances collected from 58 speakers. The FMFCC-A dataset is divided into the training, development and evaluation sets, which are used for the research of detection of synthesized Mandarin speech under various previously unknown speech synthesis systems or audio post-processing operations. In addition to describing the construction of the FMFCC-A dataset, we provide a detailed analysis of two baseline methods and the top-performing submissions from the FMFCC-A, which illustrates the usefulness and challenge of FMFCC-A dataset. We hope that the FMFCC-A dataset can fill the gap of lack of Mandarin datasets for synthetic speech detection.

Keywords: Mandarin dataset · Synthetic speech detection · Text-to-speech · Voice conversion · Audio post-processing operation

1 Introduction

Synthetic speech attacks refer to a situation that an attacker makes use of text-to-speech (TTS) or voice conversion (VC) technologies to synthesize a speaker's voice to cheat the automatic speaker verification (ASV) systems [17]. With the advancements in synthetic speech technologies, the state-of-the-art TTS and VC systems achieve such a high level of naturalness that even humans have difficulties to distinguish synthetic speech from genuine speech, which imposes a significant threat to the reliability of ASV systems [14]. Therefore, it is crucial

X. Zhao et al. (Eds.): IWDW 2021, LNCS 13180, pp. 117–131, 2022.
https://doi.org/10.1007/978-3-030-95398-0_9

to develop a synthetic speech detection model that can efficiently discriminate between genuine and synthetic speech [7].

To protect ASV systems from the increasing development of speech synthesis technologies, researchers from across the globe create fake speech detection challenges and release synthetic speech datasets. Automatic speaker verification spoofing and countermeasures challenge, called ASVspoof, has been launched in 2015, 2017, 2019 and 2021, and four speech datasets (ASVspoof2015 dataset [17], ASVspoof2017 dataset [7], ASVspoof2019 dataset [14], ASVspoof2021 dataset [18]) have been released by the organizers. These ASVspoof datasets are important milestones in the synthetic speech detection community, which make the research community could study and propose methodologies to solve synthetic speech attacks to ASV systems. One of the most cited versions is ASVspoof2015 dataset [17], which contains not only genuine utterances but also synthesized utterances generated by 10 different speech synthesis systems (seven VC systems and three TTS systems), and in total more than 260,000 utterances are provided. ASVspoof2019 LA dataset [14] contains genuine utterances and synthesized utterances generated using 17 different TTS and VC systems in total 121,000 utterances. In addition, in order to make a speech dataset containing the utterances synthesized by the latest speech synthesis technologies, Reimao et al. [10] released a Fake or Real (FoR) dataset in 2019. However, it is important to note that the TTS and VC systems utilized in existing speech datasets are outdated compared to the current state-of-the-art speech synthesis systems, and all utterances are in English. A new speech dataset containing the synthesized speech by the latest speech synthesis technologies and spoken in non-English is urgently needed to be proposed.

In order to facilitate the development of synthetic speech detection for synthesized Mandarin utterances, we have constructed a challenging Mandarin dataset and organized the accompanying audio track of the first fake media forensic challenge of China Society of Image and Graphics (FMFCC-A). The FMFCC-A dataset is focused on the latest Mandarin speech synthesis technologies, where the synthesized Mandarin speech is generated by not only open-source tools but also commercial systems. The main contributions of this work are summarized as follows: 1) We constructed the FMFCC-A dataset for the research of detection of synthesized Mandarin speech and divided it into the training, development and evaluation sets, while four kinds of audio post-processing operations were conducted on evaluation dataset. 2) To demonstrate it is possible to use the FMFCC-A dataset to train deep learning based classifiers, we adopted two neural network based synthetic speech detection methods as the baselines. 3) We provided a detailed analysis of top-performing submissions from the FMFCC-A, which are focused upon detection of Mandarin TTS and VC speech under various previously unknown speech synthesis systems or audio post-processing operations. To verify and reproduce the experiments presented in the paper, all of our source codes and datasets are now available via GitHub: https://github.com/Amforever/FMFCC-A.

Table 1. Summary of utterances in the FMFCC-A dataset, where G00 represents the ID of genuine speech and A01 to A13 represent the IDs of 13 speech synthesis systems.

ID	Synthesis systems	Num. of speakers		Num. of utterances
		Male	Female	
G00	-	29	29	10,000
A01	Alibaba TTS	0	1	3,400
A02	Biaobei TTS	5	5	3,400
A03	Blackberry TTS	0	3	3,400
A04	FastSpeech [11]	0	1	3,400
A05	Iflytek TTS	2	2	3,400
A06	Ada-In VC [4]	5	5	1,000
A07	IBM Waston TTS	1	2	4,000
A08	Lingyun TTS	3	11	4000
A09	Tacotron [16]	0	1	4,000
A10	Baidu TTS	4	5	3,000
A11	Sibichi TTS	3	3	3,000
A12	GAN-TTS [3]	1	0	3,000
A13	Medium VC [5]	5	5	1,000
Total		58	73	50,000

The remainder of this paper is organized as follows. In the next section, we formally introduced the construction of the FMFCC-A dataset and two baseline methods. In Sect. 3 the evaluation metrics and FMFCC-A schedule are described. In Sect. 4, we present a detailed analysis of two baseline methods and the top-performing submissions from the FMFCC-A. Finally, conclusions and potential future works are drawn in the last section.

2   Dataset and Baselines

The objective of this paper is to construct a challenging Mandarin dataset for synthetic speech detection and validate the usefulness and challenge of the dataset. In this section, we explain the construction of the FMFCC-A dataset and two detection baselines in detail.

2.1   FMFCC-A Dataset and Partitions

The FMFCC-A dataset contains not only genuine utterances but also a mountain of synthesized utterances, which are spoken in Mandarin. The total number

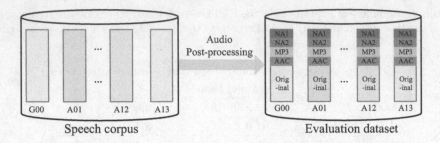

Fig. 1. The flowchart of performing four audio post-processing operations on the evaluation set of the FMFCC-A dataset.

of utterances of the FMFCC-A dataset is 50,000, which includes 10,000 genuine utterances and 40,000 synthesized utterances. The genuine utterances, i.e. speech recordings from humans, were randomly collected from 58 speakers, which covers a good variety of speaker ages and genders. The synthesized utterances were generated from state-of-the-art Mandarin speech synthesis systems. Specifically, the synthesized utterances of the FMFCC-A dataset were generated according to 11 Mandarin TTS systems, i.e., Alibaba TTS, Biaobei TTS, Blackberry TTS, FastSpeech [11], Iflytek TTS, IBM Waston TTS, Lingyun TTS, Tacotron [16], Baidu TTS, Sibichi TTS and GAN-TTS [3], and two Mandarin VC systems, i.e., Ada-In VC [4] and Medium VC [5]. The 13 Mandarin speech synthesis systems are noted as A01 to A13 in this paper (as in Table 1), where A04 [11], A06 [4], A09 [16], A12 [3] and A13 [8] are open-source speech synthesis tools and A01, A02, A03, A05, A07, A08, A10 and A11 are commercial speech synthesis systems, For five open-source synthesis tools, we generated synthesized Mandarin utterances by implementing their source codes, while we sent API requests for commercial speech synthesis systems to get synthesized Mandarin utterances. For each utterance in the FMFCC-A dataset, the duration is randomly set in the range between two seconds and 10 s, the sampling rate of 16 kHz, 16-bit quantization and is stored in mono WAV format. More details about the utterances in the FMFCC-A dataset are shown in Table 1.

As with most researches of synthetic speech detection, the FMFCC-A dataset is partitioned into three disjoint datasets, namely training, development and evaluation sets. More details about the utterances and the used speech synthesis systems in training, development and evaluation datasets are shown in Table 2. The training dataset includes 6,000 synthesized utterances and 4,000 genuine utterances. As illustrated in Table 2, each synthesized utterance in training dataset is generated by one of the five speech synthesis systems (A01–A05). The development dataset includes 17,000 synthesized utterances and 3,000 genuine utterances. In order to generalize the performance of synthetic speech detection models against previously unknown speech synthesis systems, we also produced synthetic speech with five additional speech synthesis systems (A06–A09).

Table 2. The number of utterances and corresponding speech synthesis systems in the training (Train), development (Dev) and evaluation (Eval) sets of FMFCC-A dataset.

Subset	G00	A01	A02	A03	A04	A05	A06	A07	A08	A09	A10	A11	A12	A13	Total
Train	4,000	1,200	1,200	1,200	1,200	1,200	0	0	0	0	0	0	0	0	10,000
Dev	3,000	1,600	1,600	1,600	1,600	1,600	900	2,700	2,700	2,700	0	0	0	0	20,000
Eval	3,000	600	600	600	600	600	100	1,300	1,300	1,300	3,000	3,000	3,000	1,000	20,000

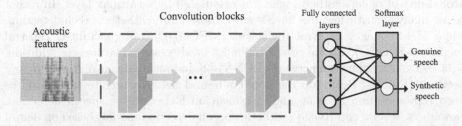

Fig. 2. The flowchart of the neural networks based synthetic speech detection methods.

The evaluation set of FMFCC-A dataset is designed to evaluate and analyze the synthetic speech detection models under previously unknown speech synthesis systems and audio post-processing operations, so the construction of evaluation dataset is more complicated than training and development sets (as shown in Fig. 1), The evaluation dataset is comprised of 17,000 synthesized utterances and 3,000 genuine utterances. On the one hand, to evaluate the synthetic speech detection models against previously unknown speech synthesis systems, the synthesized utterances are generated according to more diverse speech synthesis systems which include the same nine speech synthesis systems (A01–A09) used in the development dataset and additional four speech synthesis systems (A10–A13). On the other hand, in order to evaluate the performance of synthetic speech detection models under various audio post-processing operations, 50% of the evaluation dataset are randomly selected to undergone compression-decompression operation or additive Gaussian noise operation. Specifically, we selected 12.5% of the evaluation dataset and transformed them (WAV files) into MPEG-1 audio layer 3 (MP3) with 96 kilobits per second (Kbps) and converted MP3 files back to WAV using FFmpeg software[1]. In the same way, advanced audio coding (AAC) compression of 64 Kbps and decompression were conducted on another 12.5% of the evaluation dataset. For random Gaussian noise addition, we selected 12.5% of the evaluation dataset and process the speech with 0.01 random Gaussian noise addition (NA1), and process another 12.5% of the evaluation dataset with 0.002 random Gaussian noise addition (NA2). Finally, 50% of the evaluation dataset are undergone a compression-decompression operations or additive Gaussian noise operations and the remaining 50% of the evaluation dataset are original without any audio post-processing operations.

---

[1] http://ffmpeg.org/.

2.2   Baseline Methods

The whole flowchart of the neural networks based synthetic speech detection models is illustrated in Fig. 2. Firstly, acoustic features are extracted from the speech signal. Then, several different designed convolution blocks are stacked to extract contextual representations of the input acoustic feature. Finally, the fully connected layers map the deep features on the label space of speech and the probability of being synthetic speech is calculated by a softmax layer. In recent years, many acoustic features have been proposed for synthetic speech detection, while Mel-frequency cepstral coefficient (MFCC) [9] and constant-Q cepstral coefficient (CQCC) [13] are two of the most used acoustic features. In addition, light convolutional neural network (LCNN) [2] and residual convolutional neural network (ResNet) [1,19] are the popular neural network architectures used as deep representation learning and classification for synthetic speech detection. Nowadays, several end-to-end synthetic speech detection models based on neural networks with mere the raw speech waveform have been proposed [6,12], which could achieve satisfactory performance.

In order to demonstrate it is possible to train deep learning based classifiers using the FMFCC-A dataset, we adopted two neural network based synthetic speech detection methods as the baselines. The first baseline method (B01) consists of 34 layers ResNet and CQCC feature [13]. The parameters of extraction of the CQCC feature are similar to those in [14]. The second baseline method (B02) adopted Res-TSSDNet architecture [6] and the raw speech waveform, which is an end-to-end synthetic speech detection method. Two baseline methods are implemented in PyTorch 1.1.0[2], which are trained on the training set of FMFCC-A dataset, and tested on the development and evaluation sets respectively.

3   Evaluation Metrics and FMFCC-A Schedule

3.1   Evaluation Metrics

Two "threshold-free" evaluation metrics are used to estimate performances of synthetic speech detection methods on the FMFCC-A dataset, which are Log-loss [15] and equal error rate (EER) [7]. The Log-loss [15] is one of the major metrics to assess the performance of a classification problem. It is indicative of how close the prediction probability is to the corresponding true value (0 or 1 in the case of binary classification). The more predicted probability diverges from the actual value, the higher is the log-loss value. For binary classification, Log-loss can be expressed as follows:

$$\text{Log-loss}_i = -[y_i \ln p_i + (1 - y_i) \ln(1 - p_i)], \tag{1}$$

where i is the index of utterances and it corresponding label is y_i; p_i is the prediction probability and ln refers to the natural logarithm of a number. To avoid the case of $\ln(0)$, $\ln(\max(p), \epsilon)$ is computed where ϵ is a positive real

---

[2] https://pytorch.org/.

number closing to zero. The lower Log-loss indicates that the detection models have performed better.

The EER is a commonly used metric for the datasets that are heavily unbalanced for two-class classification (one genuine utterance versus many synthesized utterances) [7]. Suppose $P_{fa}(\theta)$ and $P_{fr}(\theta)$ stand for the false acceptance rate and false rejection rate respectively, which are defined as:

$$P_{fa}(\theta) = \frac{\text{Num}\{\text{synthesized utterances with score} > \theta\}}{\text{Num}\{\text{total synthesized utterances}\}}, \tag{2}$$

$$P_{fr}(\theta) = \frac{\text{Num}\{\text{genuine utterances with score} \leq \theta\}}{\text{Num}\{\text{total genuine utterances}\}}, \tag{3}$$

where $\text{Num}\{\cdot\}$ denotes the number of utterances in the set. The EER corresponds to the threshold θ_{EER} at which the false acceptance rate equals to false rejection rate i.e. $\text{EER} = P_{fa}(\theta_{EER}) = P_{fr}(\theta_{EER})$. In this paper, the EER is estimated using the Bosaris toolkit[3].

3.2 FMFCC-A Schedule

FMFCC-A focuses on the research of detection of synthesized Mandarin speech, which is run in two phases: the preliminary phase and the final evaluation phase. Participants can use training and development sets of the FMFCC-A dataset to construct and optimize their synthetic speech detection models, while the use of other external speech datasets is also allowed. Participants should assign each utterance with a real-valued and finite score range in [0, 1] which reflected the relative probability that the test utterance was genuine. The Log-loss [15] was adopted as the metric for evaluating the performance of submissions, and ϵ in Formula (1) is set to 10e–9.

During the preliminary phase, the training and development sets of FMFCC-A dataset were available for each participant, and a standard protocol file comprising a list of filenames and corresponding labels of utterances from the training dataset was provided. However, the label information of speech from the development dataset was not provided. Each participant team might make up to 3 submissions per day and the corresponding validation performance of the submission would be provided by the organizer. The focus of the preliminary phase was upon the training and optimizing synthetic speech detection methods that were robust to previously unknown speech synthesis systems. During the final evaluation phase, participants were allowed only a single submission for which the result would be determined by the utterances from the evaluation dataset. Given the relevance to realistic scenarios, the focus of the final evaluation phase was upon evaluating generalization of synthetic speech detection methods to previously unknown speech synthesis systems and audio post-processing operations.

---

[3] https://sites.google.com/site/bosaristoolkit/.

4   FMFCC-A Results and Discussion

4.1   Preliminary Phase of FMFCC-A

In the preliminary phase of the FMFCC-A, a total of 48 valid submissions were received. Since the aim of the FMFCC-A is the scientific analysis of different Mandarin synthetic speech detection methods, we assign anonymized team IDs (T01 to T48) to participators, which are corresponding to the order ranking in the preliminary phase. Table 3 shows results in terms of the Log-loss and EERs for all submissions as well as two baseline methods (B01 and B02), pooled over all speech synthesis systems in the development dataset.

Table 3. Log-loss and EER (%) scores of all submissions and two baseline methods as measured on the development set of the FMFCC-A dataset.

#	ID	Log-loss	EER	#	ID	Log-loss	EER
1	T01	0.000083	0.00	26	T26	0.471997	9.40
2	T02	0.000223	0.00	27	T27	0.536461	73.40
3	T03	0.002369	0.07	28	**B01**	**0.539770**	**7.27**
4	T04	0.026720	0.40	29	T28	0.550739	7.13
5	T05	0.055830	2.83	30	T29	0.551340	4.73
6	T06	0.085988	1.94	31	T30	0.594707	3.70
7	T07	0.086400	1.44	32	T31	0.608583	85.64
8	T08	0.088507	2.83	33	T32	0.631574	17.83
9	T09	0.088626	2.30	34	T33	0.671077	8.13
10	T10	0.157802	7.93	35	T34	0.678155	8.33
11	T11	0.171027	11.03	36	T35	0.686454	98.63
12	T12	0.171333	11.03	37	T36	0.695494	99.94
13	T13	0.171480	11.23	38	T37	0.699639	99.97
14	T14	0.174231	7.33	39	**B02**	**0.815244**	**8.26**
15	T15	0.175598	4.27	40	T38	0.842023	33.27
16	T16	0.175821	12.29	41	T39	0.933437	20.77
17	T17	0.196450	7.33	42	T40	1.549387	42.54
18	T18	0.204748	7.43	43	T41	1.905160	22.03
19	T19	0.213509	7.30	44	T42	2.247894	14.17
20	T20	0.258818	12.63	45	T43	2.713916	50.77
21	T21	0.348626	12.60	46	T44	2.935695	50.33
22	T22	0.351485	14.17	47	T45	3.614879	56.30
23	T23	0.405014	3.93	48	T46	4.128621	99.50
24	T24	0.421419	30.93	49	T47	6.565136	27.46
25	T25	0.445320	26.73	50	T48	23.486387	100.00

As we can see from Table 3, 27 of 48 participating teams submitted results that outperformed the B01 in terms of the Log-loss, and 13 participating teams' results achieved lower EERs than that of B01. The top two performing submissions, T01 and T02, achieve Log-loss of 0.000083 and 0.000223, and both EERs are equal to 0, which are performing results. However, it observes that monotonic increases in the Log-loss that are not always mirrored by monotonic increases in the EER. The participating teams T15, T23, T30, and T31 deliver low EERs, however, they have high Log-loss values which lead them to a low ranking in the preliminary phase of FMFCC-A. There is a great spread both in Log-loss and EERs, however, the performance of the top nine performing systems is much narrower. Top nine performing submissions achieve Log-loss below 0.1 and EERs below 3% even when almost half of the development dataset are generated by previously unknown speech synthesis systems, which deliver a substantial improvement over other submissions. After communications with participants, we knew that some of the participants used the idea of pseudo-label learning methods. They uploaded result files, which contained scores of all utterances on the development dataset, to get the feedback from the organizers and sent the feedback to their neural networks to make the neural networks more effectively learn for difficult samples. The performance of submission on preliminary phase of FMFCC-A demonstrates that the training set of FMFCC-A dataset could be used to train deep learning based classifiers, while the development set of FMFCC-A dataset could be further optimized the parameters of synthetic speech detection models.

Table 4. Log-loss and EER (%) scores of top 10 performing submissions and two baseline methods as measured on the evaluation set of the FMFCC-A dataset.

#	ID	Log-loss	EER	#	ID	Log-loss	EER
1	T06	0.351378	13.59	7	T05	1.070571	22.86
2	T01	0.367338	9.50	8	T09	1.504904	27.70
3	T03	0.417512	12.57	9	T11	1.739203	23.83
4	T04	0.470891	12.00	10	T10	1.952625	24.93
5	T02	0.593899	17.23	11	**B01**	**2.133188**	**28.07**
6	T07	0.694353	23.00	12	**B02**	**2.286764**	**33.37**

4.2   Final Evaluation Phase of FMFCC-A

In the final evaluation phase, the top 10 participants in the preliminary phase were required to run their submissions on the evaluation set of the FMFCC-A dataset. Note that the eighth-place team (T08) in the preliminary phase, unfortunately, did not run their submission despite repeated warnings from the organizers. Therefore, we excluded them in the final evaluation phase and asked

the eleventh-place participating team (T11) in the preliminary phase to participate in the final evaluation phase. The Log-loss and EER results of 12 synthetic
speech detection methods on the final evaluation phase are illustratèd in Table 4.

As can be seen in Table 4, the T06, which ranks sixth place on the preliminary phase, achieves the first place in the final evaluation phase with a Log-loss
of 0.351378 and EER of 13.59%. The T01 that achieves the best performance in
the preliminary phase ranks second place in the final evaluation phase according to the Log-loss. However, T01 delivers the lowest EER of 9.50% among
all submissions. In addition, all top ten performing submissions achieve better
performance than two baseline methods in the final evaluation phase. The Log-
loss of all synthetic speech detection models on the final evaluation phase are
ranged between 0.351378 and 2.286764, and EER are ranged between 9.50 and
33.37, which are increased a lot compared to those on the preliminary phase.
This observation indicates that the evaluation set of the FMFCC-A dataset has
dramatically decreased the performances of submissions and baselines, which
illustrates the challenge of the FMFCC-A dataset for synthetic speech detection methods. To evaluate the performance of submissions against previously
unknown speech synthesis systems and audio post-processing operations, we give
a detailed description in the following.

Table 5. EERs (%) of detection methods as measured on the evaluation set of the
FMFCC-A dataset subjected to each speech synthesis system and pooled performances.

ID	A01	A02	A03	A04	A05	Pool1	A06	A07	A08	A09	Pool2	A10	A11	A12	A13	Pool3
T06	2.32	2.33	1.33	2.15	3.00	2.23	19.08	6.61	11.45	2.84	8.06	9.57	3.10	24.30	39.10	19.20
T01	1.53	5.67	0.30	2.48	2.00	2.67	9.77	1.09	2.61	1.09	1.90	5.43	4.23	12.83	53.70	12.70
T03	1.52	6.02	1.82	2.83	5.67	3.80	12.00	2.32	10.98	7.70	6.96	6.30	4.27	20.83	42.28	16.93
T04	1.67	2.52	0.70	3.65	5.50	3.63	20.78	10.07	11.00	7.16	9.90	7.37	2.83	17.03	59.40	16.00
T02	0.02	2.67	1.83	0.67	0.67	1.30	7.00	2.62	3.23	0.54	2.46	10.63	1.57	27.30	55.20	22.83
T07	3.35	9.13	5.53	2.82	4.32	5.47	30.00	12.61	8.70	5.07	10.53	9.10	9.17	47.47	61.80	33.13
T05	8.02	10.30	15.63	9.50	12.00	11.60	22.00	18.16	17.84	16.39	17.53	17.27	16.80	37.67	56.90	29.20
T09	16.97	15.35	13.50	18.82	21.17	16.90	42.00	19.32	27.14	20.75	22.17	20.87	15.43	44.03	51.78	32.87
T11	23.80	23.80	23.80	23.80	23.80	23.77	42.03	23.77	23.77	23.77	23.77	23.77	28.23	31.63	24.30	28.14
T10	3.33	4.33	1.18	6.33	5.00	4.37	44.85	15.70	15.23	10.45	14.70	7.43	5.17	51.10	55.38	35.11
B01	9.50	17.83	3.00	4.63	14.80	10.33	55.12	21.07	21.61	5.54	18.60	32.73	32.47	34.60	62.92	36.40
B02	18.50	27.17	16.83	19.67	20.98	20.67	47.13	38.39	29.38	20.39	31.27	31.40	30.40	47.67	40.92	36.87
Avg.	7.54	10.59	7.12	8.11	9.91	8.89	29.31	14.31	15.24	10.14	13.99	15.16	12.81	33.04	50.31	26.61

4.3   Performance on Unknown Speech Synthesis Systems

While the participants' rankings of FMFCC-A are based on pooled performance
(the synthetic speech from all speech synthesis systems in the dataset are considered for evaluation), it is also meaningful to present results when decomposed
by each speech synthesis system. As described in Sect. 2.1, we classify the evaluation set of the FMFCC-A dataset into three parts according to whether the

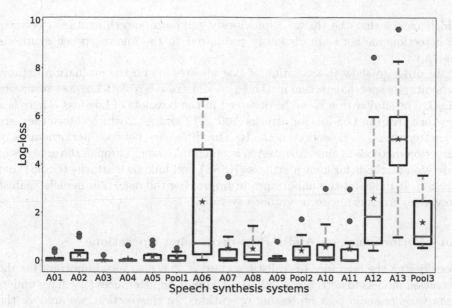

Fig. 3. A boxplot of Log-loss of detection methods as measured on the evaluation set of the FMFCC-A dataset subjected to each speech synthesis system and pooled performances.

speech synthesis systems are used in training and development datasets. The known speech synthesis systems (KSSS) set includes A01 to A05 which are presented in both of the training and development datasets. The first unknown speech synthesis systems (USSS1) set includes A06 to A09 which are not presented in the training dataset but used in the development dataset. The second unknown speech synthesis systems (USSS2) set includes A10 to A13 which are neither used in training dataset nor development dataset. The EER results when decomposed separately for each of the speech synthesis systems are presented in Table 5, while the pooled detection results for KSSS, USSS1, and USSS2 (named as Pool1, Pool2 and Pool3 respectively) are also presented.

As shown in Table 5, each line represents the EERs of one detection method against various speech synthesis systems. The speech synthesis systems A06, A12 and A13 seriously degrade the performances of detection methods, which showed being challenging to be detected. In fact, the A06 and A13 are Mandarin VC systems and A12 is a generative adversarial network (GAN) based Mandarin TTS system, which are fundamentally different from other Mandarin TTS systems. Therefore, the detection methods that trained on the training dataset achieve poor performance for A06, A12 and A13. Although A07, A08, A10, and A11 are also threat detection methods, they are easier to detect than A06, A12 and A13. One reason may be that A07, A08, A10, and A11 are pipeline TTS techniques that are similar mechanism with TTS techniques of A01 to A05. In addition, EERs of Pool1, Pool2 and Pool3 are 8.89%, 13.99% and 26.61% respectively, which means that the threat of previously unknown speech synthesis systems to detection methods are obviously compared to the known speech synthesis systems.

In order to show the variation of Log-loss results on the evaluation dataset for synthetic speech detection methods, we illustrate boxplots Log-loss results in Fig. 3. The similar trends can be observed in the boxplots of Log-loss. There is a greater spread in Log-loss for attacks A06, A12 and A13, which shown they are a greater threat to detection methods. The difference between performances of detection methods against A01 to A05 is much narrower. Through the analysis of detection methods for known attacks (KSSS) and unknown attacks (USSS1 and USSS2), it indicates the importance of improving the detection models against previously unknown speech synthesis systems.

4.4 Performance on Audio Post-processing Operations

Considering the relevance to realistic scenarios, it is also very important for the detection models to detecting synthesized Mandarin utterances that have undergone various audio post-processing operations. In this section, we analyze the results of detection models for the synthesized Mandarin utterances undergone each audio post-processing operation on the evaluation set of the FMFCC-A dataset. As described in Sect. 2.1, we classified the evaluation dataset into five parts according to whether utterances have undergone post-processing operations. Firstly, the 50% of the evaluation dataset were not undergone any audio post-processing operations as original set (Original). Secondly, the 12.5% of the evaluation dataset were processed by MP3 compression-decompression with 96 Kbps (CD-MP3). Thirdly, the 12.5% of the evaluation dataset were processed by AAC compression-decompression with 64 Kbps (CD-AAC). Next, the 12.5% of the evaluation dataset were added with 0.01 random Gaussian noise (NA-01). Finally, the remaining 12.5% of the evaluation dataset were added with 0.002 random Gaussian noise (NA-002). Table 6 shows the EERs of detection models for detecting original and audio post-processing utterances in the evaluation dataset.

As shown in Table 6, the average EER of detection models on the original dataset is 17.63%, which is much lower than that applied with audio post-processing operations. The performance of detection models on utterances with 0.002 random Gaussian noise is better than that on utterances with 0.01 random Gaussian noise, expect for T11, T10 and B01. Specifically, the average EER of detection models on NA-002 is 21.98% which is lower than that 22.95% on NA-01. It indicates that the higher level Gaussian noise added to utterances, the more difficult to be detected. As shown in the last two columns of Table 6, the average EERs of detection models on the MP3 and AAC compression-decompression utterances are 22.19% and 24.02% respectively, which are much higher than that on original utterances. It is demonstrated that there is great performance degradation of detection methods due to the lower bit-rate AAC compression-decompression operations. In a word, it is shown that all four audio

Table 6. EERs (%) of detection methods as measured on the evaluation set of the FMFCC-A dataset under original and audio post-processing utterances.

ID	Original	NA-01	NA-002	CD-MP3	CD-AAC
T06	9.54	23.67	20.54	12.26	11.16
T01	6.92	11.20	10.97	7.78	7.20
T03	7.45	16.52	12.52	7.48	8.25
T04	8.99	18.67	14.12	10.13	9.86
T02	15.94	21.67	21.12	16.03	18.13
T07	22.94	22.37	22.35	23.46	24.06
T05	19.61	27.52	26.67	19.73	29.87
T09	24.53	29.87	27.42	24.56	25.06
T11	14.00	21.30	24.79	62.13	68.53
T10	24.15	24.02	24.04	23.99	24.54
B01	25.59	30.64	33.34	26.71	26.11
B02	31.93	27.99	25.82	31.97	35.42
Avg.	17.63	22.95	21.98	22.19	24.02

post-processing operations degrade the performance of synthetic speech detection methods.

5 Conclusion

With the improvement of Mandarin TTS and VC technologies, the need for an up-to-date Mandarin dataset that can be used in the research of synthetic speech detection also increases. In this paper, we introduce the FMFCC-A dataset and provide a detailed analysis of two baseline methods and top-performing submissions from the FMFCC-A. The FMFCC-A dataset contains 10,000 genuine utterances collected from 58 speakers and 40,000 synthesized utterances generated by 11 Mandarin TTS systems and two Mandarin VC systems. We divide the FMFCC-A dataset as the training, development and evaluation sets, and conduct four kinds of audio post-processing operations on evaluation dataset. The training and development datasets are used for training and optimizing the synthetic speech detection models, while the evaluation dataset focus upon evaluating the generalization of synthetic speech detection methods to previously unknown speech synthesis systems and audio post-processing operations. Through the detailed analysis of two baseline methods and the top-performing submissions from the FMFCC-A, we demonstrate the usefulness and challenge of FMFCC-A dataset. At the same time, we also observe that previously unknown speech synthesis systems and audio post-processing operations would significantly degrade the performance of synthetic speech detection.

There are two main areas of future work regarding the FMFCC-A dataset. Although the FMFCC-A dataset is already a good source for the research of detection of synthesized Mandarin speech, it can be improved by aggregating more genuine and synthetic utterances in Mandarin. In addition, more realistic audio post-processing operations will be introduced to enhance the practical application of FMFCC-A dataset. With the FMFCC-A dataset created and published, we hope that the research community can use it to improve the detection of synthesized Mandarin speech.

Acknowledgments. This work was supported by National Key Technology Research and Development Program under 2020AAA0140000, 2019QY2202 and 2019QY(Y)0207.

References

1. Alzantot, M., Wang, Z., Srivastava, M.B.: Deep residual neural networks for audio spoofing detection. In: Proceedings of International Speech Communication Association, Interspeech 2019, pp. 1078–1082 (2019)
2. Białobrzeski, R., Kosmider, M., et al.: Robust Bayesian and light neural networks for voice spoofing detection. In: Proceedings of International Speech Communication Association, Interspeech 2019, pp. 1028–1032 (2019)
3. Bińkowski, M., et al.: High fidelity speech synthesis with adversarial networks. In: International Conference on Learning Representations (2019)
4. Chou, J.c., Yeh, C.c., Lee, H.y.: One-shot voice conversion by separating speaker and content representations with instance normalization. arXiv preprint arXiv:1904.05742 (2019)
5. Gu, Y., Zhang, Z., Yi, X., Zhao, X.: Mediumvc: Any-to-any voice conversion using synthetic specific-speaker speeches as intermedium features. arXiv preprint arXiv:2110.02500 (2021)
6. Hua, G., Bengjinteoh, A., Zhang, H.: Towards end-to-end synthetic speech detection. IEEE Sig. Process. Lett. (2021)
7. Kinnunen, T., Sahidullah, M., Delgado, H., et al.: The ASVspoof 2017 challenge: assessing the limits of replay spoofing attack detection. In: Proceedings of International Speech Communication Association, Interspeech 2017, pp. 2–6 (2017)
8. Lin, J.H., Lin, Y.Y., Chien, C.M., Lee, H.Y.: S2vc: a framework for any-to-any voice conversion with self-supervised pretrained representations. ArXiv abs/2104.02901 (2021)
9. Patel, T.B., Patil, H.A.: Combining evidences from Mel cepstral, cochlear filter cepstral and instantaneous frequency features for detection of natural vs. spoofed speech. In: Sixteenth Annual Conference of the International Speech Communication Association (2015)
10. Reimao, R., Tzerpos, V.: FoR: A dataset for synthetic speech detection. In: 2019 International Conference on Speech Technology and Human-Computer Dialogue, pp. 1–10. IEEE (2019)
11. Ren, Y., Hu, C., Tan, X., Qin, T., Zhao, S., Zhao, Z., Liu, T.Y.: Fastspeech 2: Fast and high-quality end-to-end text to speech. In: International Conference on Learning Representations (2020)
12. Tak, H., Patino, J., Todisco, M., Nautsch, A., Evans, N., Larcher, A.: End-to-end anti-spoofing with rawnet2. In: 2021 International Conference on Acoustics, Speech and Signal Processing, pp. 6369–6373. IEEE (2021)

13. Todisco, M., Delgado, H., Evans, N.W.: A new feature for automatic speaker verification anti-spoofing: constant q cepstral coefficients. In: Odyssey, pp. 283–290 (2016)
14. Todisco, M., Wang, X., Vestman, V., Sahidullah, M., Delgado, H., et al.: ASVspoof 2019: future horizons in spoofed and fake audio detection. arXiv preprint arXiv:1904.05441 (2019)
15. Vovk, V.: The fundamental nature of the log loss function. In: Fields of Logic and Computation II, pp. 307–318. Springer, Berlin (2015). https://doi.org/10.1007/978-3-642-15025-8
16. Wang, Y., Skerry-Ryan, R., et al.: Tacotron: towards end-to-end speech synthesis. arXiv preprint arXiv:1703.10135 (2017)
17. Wu, Z., Kinnunen, T., Evans, N., et al.: ASVspoof 2015: the first automatic speaker verification spoofing and countermeasures challenge. In: Sixteenth Annual Conference of the International Speech Communication Association (2015)
18. Yamagishi, J., Wang, X., et al.: ASVspoof 2021: accelerating progress in spoofed and deepfake speech detection. arXiv preprint arXiv:2109.00537 (2021)
19. Zhang, Z., Yi, X., Zhao, X.: Fake speech detection using residual network with transformer encoder. In: ACM Workshop on Information Hiding and Multimedia Security, pp. 13–22 (2021)

Watermarking

A Feature-Map-Based Large-Payload DNN Watermarking Algorithm

Yue Li[1], Lydia Abady[2], Hongxia Wang[3(✉)], and Mauro Barni[2]

[1] School of Information Science and Technology, Southwest Jiaotong University,
611756 Chengdu, China
liyue859000040@my.swjtu.edu.cn
[2] Department of Information Engineering and Mathematics, University of Siena,
53100 Siena, Italy
barni@dii.unisi.it
[3] School of Cyber Science and Engineering, Sichuan University,
610065 Chengdu, China
hxwang@scu.edu.cn

Abstract. Watermarking has recently been proposed as a solution to protect the Intellectual Property Rights (IPR) of Deep Neural Networks (DNN). Dynamic DNN watermarking refers to a particular class of watermarking algorithms according to which the watermark message is associated to the *behaviour* of the network in correspondence to some specific inputs. When the observed *behaviour* is defined at the level of the network output, the watermark can be retrieved even without accessing the internal status of the network (black-box watermarking). Despite their attractiveness, most black-box dynamic watermarking algorithms proposed so far have a very small payload, due to the low entropic content of the network output. In this paper, we propose a new, multi-bit, white-box, dynamic DNN watermarking algorithm embedding the watermark message into the feature maps of the host DNN, in correspondence to a set of predefined inputs. Thanks to the high-entropy content of the maps hosting the watermark, the new approach can achieve a very high payload, with acceptable robustness. The experiments we carried out on a variety of host networks, demonstrate the capability of the proposed method to provide a very high payload with a low impact on network accuracy.

Keywords: Dynamic DNN watermarking · DNN watermarking · High-payload DNN watermarking

1 Introduction

Due to their outstanding performance, Deep Neural Networks (DNN) are increasingly used and commercialized in virtually all application scenarios wherein complex data, for which precise statistical models do not exist, must be analyzed and processed. Together with the demand of more and more powerful tools, the complexity of DNNs also increases, dramatically enlarging their requirements in terms of computational and storage requirements. This leads to a consequent increase of the complexity of the training procedures, requiring a huge amount of labeled data and extensive training that may easily go on for weeks, even on powerful workstations equipped with several GPUs. For this reason, the demand for methods to protect the Intellectual Property Rights (IPR) associated to DNNs is escalating. In this framework, DNN watermarking has been proposed as a possible way to protect DNNs IPR by tracing the DNN to its legitimate owner or to the entity which trained it.

According to the taxonomy adopted in [11], existing DNN watermarking algorithms can be classified as either static or dynamic. Static methods, like [15] and [10], directly embed (and read) the watermark into (from) the weights of the DNN model. With dynamic watermarking, instead, the watermark is associated to the *behavior* of the network in correspondence to specific inputs, sometimes called as key inputs or watermark triggering inputs. For instance, the watermark may be associated to the activation map of the neurons in correspondence to certain inputs, as in [3], or to the final output of the model, as in [1] and [9]. In the latter case, the watermark can be retrieved even without accessing the internal status of the network (black-box watermarking). Due to its flexibility and ease of use, dynamic black-box watermarking is attracting an increasing interest. However, most black-box dynamic DNN watermarking algorithms proposed so far either belong to the class of zero-bit watermarking[1], or have a very limited capacity. Such a limitation is intrinsically linked to the low entropic content of the DNN output, that is not suitable to host more than a few bits.

Static watermarking algorithms embed the watermark into the networks weights and biases. This, in general, increases the payload of the watermark, which however is usually limited to a few hundreds of bits. The payload of the static multi-bit watermarking algorithm proposed in [15], for instance, is limited by the number of trainable parameters of the convolutional layer hosting the watermark, and can reach 2048 bits in the most favorable case. A slightly higher payload is achieved in [10], by leveraging on the watermarking with side information paradigm, for a maximum payload equal to twice the number of parameters hosting the watermark.

The present work stems from the belief that a much larger capacity can be obtained by dynamic watermarking algorithms embedding the watermark into the intermediate layers of the network (thus giving up the requirements of black-box detection). The reason for such a belief is twofold: i) the large entropy content of the feature maps produced by the intermediate layers of the network, ii) the possibility of augmenting the payload by increasing the number of key-inputs and associating different groups of bits to different inputs. Based on the above considerations, in this paper, we propose a new high-capacity dynamic DNN watermarking algorithm embedding the watermark into the feature map produced by one or more convolutional layers of the network, in correspondence

---

[1] The watermark detector can only decide if a DNN contains a given, known, watermark.

to a set of predetermined triggering inputs. We do so, by adopting a spread spectrum (SS) approach similar to that used [15], adapted to work in a dynamic watermarking setting. With regard to the key-inputs, we propose two alternative solutions: i) use of entangled key-inputs belonging to the same application domain the DNN is operating on (like in [7]), and ii) use of alien key-inputs which are far away from the typical inputs processed by the network. As we will show throughout the paper, the use of entangled inputs results in a more robust watermark, while alien-key inputs minimize the impact of the watermark on the accuracy of the network hence allowing a larger payload. To evaluate the effectiveness of the proposed approach, we applied the proposed algorithm to different architectures with different depths, trained on different datasets, and run an extensive set of experiments. The results we got confirm the intuition at the basis of the proposed technique, opening the way to the development of a new class of high-capacity, dynamic, DNN watermarking algorithms.

The rest of the paper is organized as follows. In Sect. 2, we briefly review the state-of-art of the DNN watermarking. In Sect. 3, we summarize the requirements that any watermarking technique must satisfy, and present our new, high-capacity watermarking algorithm. Section 4 is devoted to the experimental validations of the proposed method. The paper ends in Sect. 5 with some conclusions.

2   State of the Art

Before presenting the proposed method, we give a brief description of the state-of art of DNN watermarking. As we already said, the methods proposed so far can be split into static and dynamic watermarking techniques.

2.1   Static Watermarking

Uchida et al. propose one of the first multi-bit DNN watermarking algorithm. Uchida et al.'s algorithm embeds the watermark message directly into the weights of a selected convolutional layer of the host network [15]. Training is carried out by adopting a customized loss function designed in such a way to ensure that the hosting weights have a large projection on a pseudo-random sequence, while at the same time preserving the effectiveness of the DNN with regard to the classification task is supposed to solve.

Later on, in [2], Chen et al. exploit Uchida's algorithm to implement a traitor tracing watermarking system with anti-collusion capabilities by introducing anti-collusion codes. To expand the payload of static watermarking, Li et al. [10] propose a modification of Uchida's technique by leveraging on ST-DM (Spread Transform Dither Modulation) watermarking. In [5], Tartaglione et al. introduce a zero-bit static watermarking algorithm with superior robustness properties. In contrast to previous works, the method proposed in [5] does not leave to the training process the task of embedding the watermark. Rather, watermarking is achieved by fixing the values of the weights belonging to a selected subset, and freezing their values during the training phase.

2.2   Dynamic Watermarking

In [3], Rouhani et al. propose the DeepSigns method, which embeds an arbitrary n-bit watermark string into the probability density function of the activation map obtained in correspondence of the triggering inputs. Since teaching the network to behave in a special way in correspondence to a small set of selected inputs is analogous to embedding a backdoor within the network, Yossi et al. select random images as triggering inputs to inject a backdoor into the target model [1]. Merrer et al. leverage on adversarial attack to tweak the decision boundary of the target model in correspondence of the triggering inputs, consisting of a set of adversarial examples. Inspired by Yossi's method, Zhang et al. [17] propose a backdoor-based watermarking algorithm wherein the triggering inputs are visible triggering patterns.

More recently, researchers have applied dynamic watermarking to image processing networks. For instance, Zhang et al. use a sub-network to embed the watermark into the images processed by the image processing network [18]. By this means, the watermarked networks can resist against surrogate model attacks.

3   The Proposed Dynamic Watermarking Algorithm

3.1   Requirements of DNN Watermarking

In this subsection, we pause to discuss the requirements that the proposed dynamic watermarking algorithm must satisfy. Aiming at developing a high-payload watermarking algorithm, we obviously target a multi-bit scheme. Moreover, due to the necessity of accessing the feature maps during watermark extraction, the proposed method will be a white-box one. Additionally, we require that the following properties are satisfied:

- **unobtrusiveness**: embedding the watermark message should not have a significant impact on the task of the target model. That is, the presence of the watermark should not degrade the accuracy of the network with respect to a non-watermarked one.
- **robustness**: it should be possible to recover the watermark message also from a modified version of the network.
- **integrity**: in the absence of model modifications, the extracted watermark message should be equal to the original embedded one, that is, in the absence of modifications the bit error rate should be zero.
- **payload**: the payload of the watermark, that is the length of the watermark message, should be as large as possible.

3.2   The Proposed Feature-Map-Based Dynamic Watermarking Algorithm

In this section, we describe a new proposal for a high-capacity dynamic watermarking algorithm. Our scheme is inspired by the spread spectrum watermarking

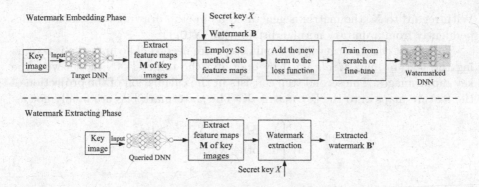

Fig. 1. Overview of the proposed method.

technique proposed in [15]. The overall architecture of the proposed scheme is shown in Fig. 1, where the embedding and extraction phases are described in the top and bottom part of the figure, respectively.

To embed the watermark into the host DNN, the feature maps activated by the specific key input images, for a selected convolutional layer, are extracted. In the following, we indicate the matrix with all the feature maps by $\mathbf{M} \in \mathbb{R}^{N \times S}$, where N indicates the number of key input images, and $S = s \times s \times n$, with (s, s) indicating the size of one feature map and n the number of feature maps output by the convolutional layer hosting the watermark. Let us indicate with $\mathbf{B} \in [0, 1]^{N \times L}$ the matrix with the watermark message, where we have assumed that each key image conveys L bits. Embedding is achieved by training the network with a loss function E defined as follows:

$$E = E_0 + \lambda E_W \tag{1}$$

where E_0 represents the original loss function ensuring that the model works properly, E_W is responsible for watermark embedding, and λ is a parameter adjusting the trade-off between the original loss term and the watermarking term. Specifically, E_W is given by

$$E_W = -\sum_{i=1}^{N} \sum_{j=1}^{L} B_{ij} \log(Z_{ij}) + (1 - B_{ij}) \log(1 - Z_{ij}), \tag{2}$$

where $\mathbf{Z}$ is obtained by applying the watermark decoding function to the feature map $\mathbf{M}$, that is

$$Z^{N \times L} = \sigma(M^{N \times S} \cdot X^{S \times L}) \tag{3}$$

where $\mathbf{X} \in \mathbb{R}^{S \times L}$ contains the spreading sequences used to encode the watermark bits, and $\sigma(\cdot)$ is the usual sigmoid function:

$$\sigma(x) = \frac{1}{1 + exp(-x)}. \tag{4}$$

With regard to **X**, the matrix is generated as in [15], drawing its elements independently from a unitary normal distribution $N(0, 1)$.

To extract the watermark, two main steps are needed. The first step is acquiring the feature map $\hat{M}$ obtained by querying the target DNN model with the key input images. The second step consists in the calculation of the projection of the feature maps onto the key matrix **X**. The watermark bits are finally got as:

$$
\hat{B}^{N \times L} = \begin{cases} 1 & \hat{M}^{N \times S} \cdot X^{S \times L} \geq 0, \\ 0 & \text{otherwise.} \end{cases} \tag{5}
$$

3.3 Choice of the Key Images

As anticipated in the introduction, we have implemented two different versions of the new watermarking algorithm, based on two different ways of choosing the key input images.

In the first implementation, the key images belong to one of the image classes the network is supposed to work on (entangled key images [7]). In the second case, instead, the key images do not belong to any of such classes (alien key images). Entangled key images force the network to learn features that are both capable to solve the original task of the network and to host the watermark. In this way, it is hard to remove the watermark without damaging the network, thus resulting in a more robust watermark. At the same time, training the network maybe more difficult, thus limiting the watermark payload. In contrast, the use of alien key images tends to increase the payload at the expense of robustness.

To demonstrate the impact that the choice of the key images has on the performance of the proposed watermarking method in terms of robustness, unobtrusiveness and payload, we carried out several experiments whose results are described in the next section.

4 Experimental Results

4.1 Datasets and Host Networks

A summary of the DNN architectures, the feature map size, the embedded layers and the datasets used in our experiments are listed in Table 1, results obtained by adopting entangled and alien key images are indicated, respectively, with the labels ENT and NON. To prove the generality of the proposed method, the experiments were carried out on three host architectures: i) a shallow network, namely Wide Residual Network (WRN) [16], ii) a medium-depth network, that is ResNet [6], and iii) a very deep network, that is EfficientNet [14].

WRN is an efficient variant of the residual network (ResNet) with decreased depth and increased width. Following the experiments' settings of WRN in [10], 10 convolutional layers are utilized in this architecture, which is the reason why WRN is categorized as a shallow network. To train the WRN model, we used SGD with Nesterov momentum equal to 0.9 and with minibatch size 64. A total number of 200 epochs was considered. The learning rate was initially set to 0.01, and then dropped by a factor 0.2 after 60, 120 and 160 epochs.

With regard to ResNet, we followed the experimental setup adopted in [6], and selected an architecture with 31 convolutional layers (ResNet-32), which may be considered as a medium-depth network. For training, the learning rate was initially set to 10^{-3}, and then decreased by a factor of 0.1 at 40, 80, 120, 180 epochs, for a total number of 200 epochs and a minibatch size of 32.

Finally, we used the EfficientNet-B4 architecture as an example of a very deep network. In particular, we followed the setup described in [14], and employed an architecture with 171 convolutional layers, which can be considered a pretty deep network. The SGD optimizer with momentum 0.9 was adopted. The weight decay rate of all convolutional layers was set to 3×10^{-5} , with an initial learning rate equal to 10^{-2}. The mini-batch size was set to 32 for a total number of training epochs equal to 60.

Table 1. Summary of datasets and architectures used in our experiments

Depth	Architecture	Original task	Key images	Embedding layer	Feature map size
Shallow	WRN	CIFAR-10 [8]	NON: GTSRB ENT: CIFAR-10	Penultimate conv layer	8 × 8 × 256
Medium	ResNet	GTSRB [13]	NON: CIFAR-10 ENT: GTSRB	Penultimate conv layer	8 × 8 × 64
Deep	EfficientNet	ImageNet [4]	NON: CelebA [12] ENT: ImageNet	Block_3a_dwconv	28 × 28 × 192

4.2 Payload, Bit Error Rate and Test Error Rate

In this section, we assess the performance of the proposed method against the requirements put forward in Sect. 3.1, where unobtrusiveness, integrity and payload are evaluated in terms of test error rate, watermark bit error rate, and payload respectively.[2] We do so by by considering both the train-to-embed and finetune-to-embed approaches. According to the former, the watermark is embedded by the training the host DNN from scratch with the loss function given in Eq. (1). In the finetune-to-embed case, the watermark is embedded by fine-tuning a pre-trained DNN model by adding the watermarking term to the loss function. The effect of the choice of the key images on unobtrusiveness, integrity and payload is evaluated simultaneously.

The experimental results we got with regard to train-to-embed and finetune-to-embed approaches are reported in Table 2 and Table 3, respectively. In the tables, the Test Error Rate (TER) = 1-Accuracy indicates the errors made regarding the classification task solved by the network, while the Bit Error Rate (BER) assesses the watermark accuracy by calculating the error bits among all

---

[2] The codes used for our experiments are available at https://github.com/bunny859000040/feature_based_DNN_watermarking.

Table 2. Experimental results (payload, BER and TER) for the train-to-embed setting. Entangled and non-entangled watermarking are indicated, respectively, by ENT and NON labels.

Type	Baseline TER (%)	Size of feature map	Payload (bits)	Key images type	Watermarked TER (%)	BER (%)
Shallow	8.73	$(8 \times 8) \times 64$	320 (5×64)	NON	9.25	0
				ENT	9.49	0
		$(4 \times 4) \times 64$	1920 (15×128)	NON	9.84	0
				ENT	9.53	0
		$(2 \times 2) \times 256$	3840 (15×256)	NON	10.54	0
				ENT	11.57	0
Medium	1.33	$(8 \times 8) \times 64$	7680 (15×512)	NON	2.43	0
				ENT	2.53	0
			6912 (18×384)	NON	2.35	0
				ENT	2.47	0
		$(4 \times 4) \times 64$	10240 (20×512)	NON	2.00	0
				ENT	3.15	42.15
			12800 (25×512)	NON	2.67	0
				ENT	4.59	55.16
Deep	19.92	$(28 \times 28) \times 192$	10240 (10×1024)	NON	20.31	0
				ENT	20.86	0
			20480 (20×1024)	NON	20.68	0
				ENT	21.37	0
		$(14 \times 14) \times 192$	20480 (10×2048)	NON	21.38	0
				ENT	21.82	0
			40960 (20×2048)	NON	21.91	0
				ENT	22.59	0

the embedded bits. The payload reported in the tables is calculated as the product of the number of key images and the watermark bits assigned to each key image. In practical applications, the watermark bits associated to key images may vary from one image to the other. For simplicity, in our experiments, we assigned the same amount of the watermark bits to all the key images.

By inspecting Table 2 and Table 3, we see that the presence of the watermark increases the TER by a small amount only (less than 2% in most cases). In general, the finetune-to-embed approach has less influence on the TER than the train-to-embed one for the same payload. For instance, the TER of the deep architecture with 20480 bits is 21.38% for train-to-embed while for finetune-to-embed is 19.89%. The tables also show the very high payload obtainable with the proposed method, outperforming, by far, the state of the art. For instance, the dynamic multi-bit watermarking algorithm proposed in [3] can embed up to only 128 bits for the WRN architecture with CIFAR-10 task, while our method can embed up to 20480 bits (in the non-entangled setup) for the same network and task. Expectedly, using non-entangled key images allows a larger payload with a lower TER compared with the entangled case. This phenomenon is more evident in the train-to-embed setting, for medium depth architectures. For a payload of 12800 bits, in fact, the entangled watermark incurs in a 2% TER increase with

Table 3. Experimental results (payload, BER and TER) under finetune-to-embed setting. Entangled and non-entangled watermarking are indicated, respectively, by ENT and NON labels.

Type	Baseline TER (%)	Used size of feature map	Payload (bit)	Key images type	Watermarked TER (%)	BER (%)
Shallow	8.73	$(2 \times 2) \times 256$	2560 (10×256)	NON	9.25	0
				ENT	9.41	0
			20480 (20×1024)	NON	9.82	0
				ENT	10.94	55.63
Medium	1.33	$(8 \times 8) \times 64$	2560 (10×256)	NON	1.57	0
				ENT	1.68	0
		$(2 \times 2) \times 64$	2560 (20×128)	NON	1.67	0
				ENT	1.92	0
Deep	19.92	$(28 \times 28) \times 192$	20480 (20×1024)	NON	19.89	0
				ENT	20.23	0
		$(14 \times 14) \times 192$	40960 (20×2048)	NON	20.15	0
				ENT	20.54	0

a BER larger than 50%, while adopting non-entangled key images allows a zero BER with a negligible increase of TER.

To get a better perspective on the performance achieved by our system, and given that no similar multi-bit dynamic watermarking system operating at the feature level has been proposed so far, we compared it with two static (white-box) multi-bit watermarking algorithms, namely those described in [15] and [10], which are known to perform pretty well from a payload point of view. The result of the comparison, in terms of payload, TER and BER are shown in Table 4, whose results have been obtained by following exactly the settings described in Sect. 4.1. The convolutional layers chosen for embedding are explained in Table 1 and alien key images are chosen for our method. The payloads reported in Table 4 correspond to the maximum payload that these methods can afford before the BERs deviate from zero. With regard to ResNet architectures (the Medium depth in our experiments), even the already good performance of the STDM [10] method (with a payload of 1024 bits) are surpassed by the new system that can can embed up to 12800 bits. It is also worth noticing the tremendous payload achieved with EfficientNet (the Deep architecture in our experiments), for which the new system can embed up to 40960 bits with BER = 0. Upon analysis of the table, it also comes out that these good performance in terms of payload are achieved with a minor loss (about 2%) of TER.

Table 5 shows the impact on the watermark performance of the number of features bearing the watermark. As it can be seen, when all the feature maps at a given layer are used, the TER tends to increase[3]. This is not a surprising result, since when only a subset of feature maps is used for the watermark, the rest of the network can focus on the original task.

---

[3] The results in the table refers to the case of alien key images.

Table 4. Comparison (payload, TER and BER) between the new proposed method and the two static watermarking algorithms in [15] and [10].

Architecture	Dataset	Baseline TER (%)	Method	Payload (bit)	Watermarked TER (%)	BER (%)
WRN	CIFAR10	8.73	[15]	4096	8.60	0
			[10]	4800	8.65	0
			Ours	3840	10.54	0
ResNet	GTSRB	1.33	[15]	512	1.49	0
			[10]	1024	0.96	0
			Ours	12800	2.67	0
EfficientNet	ImageNet	19.92	[15]	2048	20.01	0
			[10]	7000	20.15	0
			Ours	40960	22.59	0

Table 5. TER and BER for different sizes of the feature maps (results refer to non-entangled key images).

Type	Baseline TER (%)	Payloads	Used size of feature map	Watermarked TER (%)	BER (%)
Shallow	8.73	320 (5 × 64)	(8 × 8) × 256	11.44	0
			(8 × 8) × 64	9.25	0
		640 (10 × 64)	(8 × 8) × 64	10.10	0
			(4 × 4) × 64	9.26	0

4.3   Robustness Evaluation

In this section, we evaluate the robustness of the proposed watermark against three types of common attacks: fine-tuning, parameters pruning and weights quantization. Since the proposed method has been designed with the explicit goal of increasing the payload, we do no expect any significant advantage with respect to robustness. The goal of this section, then, is to demonstrate that, despite the very high capacity it achieves, the proposed technique also ensures a moderate robustness against most common attacks.

Robustness Against Fine-Tuning. Fine-tuning is the most common type of unintentional attack that a watermarked DNN model is subject to, given the frequent use of fine-tuning to adapt a pre-trained network to a new task. Applying fine-tuning to a pre-trained network, in fact, requires much less effort than training a network from scratch, and also avoids over-fitting when sufficient training data is not available for the new task.

To measure the robustness of the watermark against fine-tuning, the model is first watermarked in train-to-embed modality, then it is fine-tuned by re-training it with the original standard loss (i.e., the cross-entropy loss E_0 in Eq. (1)) for several epochs. To speed up convergence, the learning rate of fine-tuning was set to one-tenth of the learning rate used when training the watermarked model. This is a common approach, given that the goal of fine tuning is to slightly modify the weights without deviating too much from the pre-trained model. We set the number of epochs to 10, while we did not change the rest of the training parameters. The results we got are illustrated in Table 6, where fine-tuning was carried out on the same task used during watermarking (see table Table 1). As expected, using entangled key images ensures better robustness with respect to the case of alien key images, especially for the highest payloads. For instance, to achieve moderate robustness against fine-tuning, the maximum payload in the non-entangled case for a medium depth architecture, is 640 (BER = 0), while for entangled key images the maximum payload is 7680 bits. If we force the non-entangled watermark to carry 7680 bits, the BER grows to more than 50%. In all cases, being payload and robustness opposite requirements, robustness against fine-tuning is always achieved at the expense of payload, which now is smaller than in Tables 2 and Table 3.

Table 6. Robustness against fine-tuning. W-TER indicates the TER of the water-marked model, TER-AA the test error rate after the attack, while BER-AA is the bit error rate after the attack.

Type	Baseline TER (%)	Size of feature map	Payload (bit)	Key images type	W-TER (%)	TER-AA (%)	BER-AA (%)
Shallow	8.73	$(4 \times 4) \times 256$	1280	NON	9.81	9.79	0
			(10×128)	ENT	9.83	9.82	0
		$(2 \times 2) \times 256$	3840	NON	10.54	10.48	52.14
			(15×256)	ENT	11.57	11.59	0
Medium	1.33	$(8 \times 8) \times 64$	640	NON	1.68	1.65	0
			(5×128)	ENT	1.70	1.68	0
			7680	NON	2.43	2.41	53.28
			(15×512)	ENT	2.53	2.45	0
Deep	19.92	$(28 \times 28) \times 192$	5120	NON	20.28	20.28	0
			(5×1024)	ENT	20.26	20.23	0
			10240	NON	20.31	20.27	55.74
			(10×1024)	ENT	20.86	20.83	0

Robustness Against Parameter Pruning. Taking into account, the deployment of DNNs on mobile devices and other platforms with limited storage capability, parameter pruning is another unintentional attack that occurs in practical applications.

To assess the robustness against parameter pruning, we randomly cropped a percentage $p\%$ of the trainable weights of the convolutional layer hosting the watermark by setting them to zero. The robustness of the watermark against parameter pruning is reported in Table 7. For each case in the table, we considered the maximum pruning percentage p before the BER deviates from zero.

Robustness Against Weights Quantization. Weight quantization is a strategy to reduce the storage demand when the weights have to be loaded in storage-limited devices, like mobile phones. The quantization procedure can be summarized as follows:

Table 7. Robustness against parameter pruning. W-TER indicates the TER of the watermarked model, TER-AA the test error rate after the attack, while BER-AA is the bit error rate after the attack.

Type	Baseline TER (%)	Size of feature map	Payload (bit)	p (%)	Key images type	W-TER (%)	TER-AA (%)	BER-AA (%)
Shallow	8.73	$(8 \times 8) \times 256$	640	5	NON	9.37	9.38	0
			(5×128)		ENT	9.39	9.41	0
				10	NON	9.37	9.39	0
					ENT	9.39	9.42	0
Medium	1.33	$(8 \times 8) \times 64$	640	5	NON	1.68	2.01	0
			(5×128)		ENT	1.70	1.72	0
Deep	19.92	$(28 \times 28) \times 192$	5120	5	NON	20.28	20.39	0
			(5×1024)		ENT	20.26	20.37	0
				10	NON	20.28	20.42	0
					ENT	20.26	20.42	0

$$\mathbf{w}' = \left\lfloor \frac{\mathbf{w}}{\delta} \right\rfloor \times \delta,$$

$$\delta = \frac{|w_{max} - w_{min}|}{2^{n_b}},$$

(6)

where $\mathbf{w}$ indicates the original weights and $\mathbf{w}'$ the quantized ones. w_{max} and w_{min} represent, respectively, the maximum and minimum values assumed by the weights. Eventually, n_b indicates the number of bits used to represent the quantized values. For instance, if the weights are quantized from a float32 format to int8, n_b is equal to 8. To evaluate the robustness of the watermark against weights quantization, we quantized the coefficients of all convolutional layers of the network as specified in Eq. (6). Table 8 shows the results we have got by quantizing the weights with $n_b = 8$. We can see that the watermark can easily resist the quantization attack while maintaining the same TER and zero BER.

Table 8. Robustness against weights quantization. Weights have been quantized by using $n_b = 8$ bits.

Type	Baseline TER (%)	Size of feature map	Payload (bit)	Key images type	W-TER (%)	TER-AA (%)	BER-AA (%)
Shallow	8.73	$(4 \times 4) \times 64$	1920	NON	9.84	9.86	0
			(15×128)	ENT	9.53	9.54	0
Medium	1.33	$(4 \times 4) \times 64$	10240 (20×512)	NON	2.00	2.03	0
			7680 (15×512)	ENT	2.53	2.55	0
Deep	19.92	$(28 \times 28) \times 192$	20480	NON	20.68	20.69	0
			(20×1024)	ENT	21.37	21.39	0

5 Conclusion

We have proposed a high-capacity dynamic DNN watermarking method ensuring very high payload, while retaining moderate robustness against model modifications. The watermark is embedded into the feature maps obtained in correspondence of a predefined set of key input images. Based on the experiments we ran, we can conclude that the proposed method can reach a high payload with a low influence on the test error rate of the network. With regard to the choice of the key input images, we experimented two solutions, adopting, respectively, entangled key-images belonging to the same application domain the DNN is operating on, and non-entangled (or alien) key images. In the former case, the watermark is more robust at the expense of payload, which can not increase too much to avoid impairing the performance of the watermarked model. In contrast, using alien key images, allows to reach extremely high payloads with not effect on network accuracy, at the price of reduced robustness.

References

1. Adi, Y., Baum, C., Cisse, M., Pinkas, B., Keshet, J.: Turning your weakness into a strength: watermarking deep neural networks by backdooring. In: 27th USENIX Security Symposium (USENIX Security 18), pp. 1615–1631 (2018)
2. Chen, H., Rouhani, B.D., Fu, C., Zhao, J., Koushanfar, F.: Deepmarks: a secure fingerprinting framework for digital rights management of deep learning models. In: Proceedings of the 2019 on International Conference on Multimedia Retrieval, pp. 105–113 (2019)
3. Darvish Rouhani, B., Chen, H., Koushanfar, F.: Deepsigns: an end-to-end watermarking framework for ownership protection of deep neural networks. In: Proceedings of the Twenty-Fourth International Conference on Architectural Support for Programming Languages and Operating Systems, pp. 485–497 (2019). https://doi.org/10.1145/3297858.3304051
4. Deng, J., Dong, W., Socher, R., Li, L.J., Li, K., Fei-Fei, L.: Imagenet: a large-scale hierarchical image database. In: Proceedings of the IEEE conference on Computer Vision and Pattern Recognition, pp. 248–255. IEEE (2009). https://doi.org/10.1109/cvpr.2009.5206848
5. Enzo, T., Marco, G., Davide, C., Marco, B.: Delving in the loss landscape to embed robust watermarks into neural networks. In: Proceedings of the 2020 International Conference on Pattern Recognition (ICPR) (2020)
6. He, K., Zhang, X., Ren, S., Sun, J.: Deep residual learning for image recognition. In: Proceedings of the IEEE Conference on Computer Vision and Pattern Recognition, pp. 770–778 (2016)
7. Jia, H., Choquette-Choo, C.A., Chandrasekaran, V., Papernot, N.: Entangled watermarks as a defense against model extraction. In: 30th USENIX Security Symposium (USENIX Security 21) (2021)
8. Krizhevsky, A., Hinton, G., et al.: Learning multiple layers of features from tiny images (2009)
9. Le Merrer, E., Pérez, P., Trédan, G.: Adversarial frontier stitching for remote neural network watermarking. Neural Comput. Appl. 32(13), 9233–9244 (2019). https://doi.org/10.1007/s00521-019-04434-z
10. Li, Y., Tondi, B., Barni, M.: Spread-transform dither modulation watermarking of deep neural network. J. Inf. Secur. Appl. 63, 103004 (2021)
11. Li, Y., Wang, H., Barni, M.: A survey of deep neural network watermarking techniques. Neurocomputing 461, 171–193 (2021). https://doi.org/10.1016/j.neucom.2021.07.051

12. Liu, Z., Luo, P., Wang, X., Tang, X.: Deep learning face attributes in the wild. In: Proceedings of International Conference on Computer Vision (ICCV) (2015)
13. Stallkamp, J., Schlipsing, M., Salmen, J., Igel, C.: Man vs. computer: benchmarking machine learning algorithms for traffic sign recognition. Neural Netw. **32**, 323–332 (2012)
14. Tan, M., Le, Q.: Efficientnet: rethinking model scaling for convolutional neural networks. In: International Conference on Machine Learning, pp. 6105–6114 (2019)
15. Uchida, Y., Nagai, Y., Sakazawa, S., Satoh, S.: Embedding watermark into deep neural networks. In: Proceedings of the 2017 ACM on International Conference on Multimedia Retrieval, pp. 269–277 (2017). https://doi.org/10.1145/3078971.3078974
16. Zagoruyko, S., Komodakis, N.: Wide residual networks. In: Procedings of the British Machine Vision Conference 2016. British Machine Vision Association (2016). https://doi.org/10.5244/c.30.87
17. Zhang, J., et al.: Protecting intellectual property of deep neural networks with watermarking. In: Proceedings of the 2018 on Asia Conference on Computer and Communications Security, pp. 159–172 (2018)
18. Zhang, J., et al.: Deep model intellectual property protection via deep watermarking. IEEE Trans. Pattern Anal. Mach. Intell. (2021)

A Robust DCT-Based Video Watermarking Scheme Against Recompression and Synchronization Attacks

Ling Yang⊙, Hongxia Wang(✉)⊙, Yulin Zhang⊙, Jinhe Li⊙, Peisong He⊙, and Sijiang Meng⊙

School of Cyber Science and Engineering, Sichuan University, Chengdu 610065, China
{yangling1,zhangyulin}@stu.scu.edu.cn, {hxwang,gokeyhps}@scu.edu.cn

Abstract. Video transmission and sharing have become faster and easier due to the advancement of the Internet and social platforms. In this case, video watermarking is used for copyright protection and tracking the source of the video. Nevertheless, when the video is spread on the Internet or social platforms, the watermark is easily attacked and breached. For this reason, keeping the watermark alive under recompression and other attacks is an urgent and challenging issue. However, none of the existing technologies is robust to these hybrid attacks. In this paper, a DCT-based video watermarking scheme is proposed against recompression, synchronization attack, and hybrid attacks. The proposed method modifies the highest frequency DCT coefficient for watermark embedding. In addition, the fivefold watermarks are encoded as Bose Chaudhuri Hocquenghem (BCH) codes to reduce the bit error rate, and odd-even quantization is used to embed them into the U channel of the video frame. When the video is cropped, the synchronization code is used to find the positions of the watermarks. Moreover, the watermark extraction is blind. Experimental results show that the proposed method can resist compression, strong recompression, synchronization attacks such as cropping, inserting, and frame dropping/inserting. It can also maintain good imperceptibility.

Keywords: Video watermarking · Discrete cosine transform (DCT) · Odd-even quantization · Recompression · Synchronization attack

1 Introduction

The rapid growth of the Internet makes more and more multimedia shared on various social platforms. People can easily access and download the multimedia

This work is supported by the National Natural Science Foundation of China (NSFC) under Grants 61972269 and 61902263, and the Fundamental Research Funds for the Central Universities under Grant YJ201881.

like videos, images, and audios. However, these behaviors without authorization can raise copyright protection issues, which leave people's innovations unprotected and unable to trace the source of the multimedia in the event of rumors or infringement. For videos, digital video watermarking is one of the technologies to address these issues. But common video processing, such as lossy compression, cropping, scaling, etc., are the attacks for video watermarking. It makes the watermark unable to be detected or completely extracted. Therefore, video watermarking should be robust to these attacks.

Fortunately, several methods have been explored against these attacks, including spatial domain watermarking, compressed domain watermarking, and transform domain watermarking. For spatial domain video watermarking techniques, the watermark is embedded by modifying the pixel values of the video frame [2,13,17], which can resist geometric attacks except for compression. In the compressed domain, the watermark is embedded by modifying the compressed bitstream [4,8,20], which can only apply to the specific encoder and lack universality. Moreover, some watermarking approaches are based on the transform domain often embed the watermark by changing the coefficients of the transform domain. These include discrete wavelet transform (DWT) [1,3,18], dual tree-complex wavelet (DT CWT) [5,9,11], discrete Fourier transform (DFT) [10,21,26], discrete cosine transform (DCT) [7,12,19,22,27,28], and combination of these domains [6,14,24]. A DWT watermarking scheme for video authentication is proposed in [3], which inserts the watermark into the Y channel of the video frame. From the results, the watermark cannot be extracted after MPEG compression. In [11], the proposed approach auto-select stable DT CWT coefficients to embed watermark. The experiments show that the approach can resist geometric attacks and compression. But each frame of the video is processed separately to embed 1 bit of watermark. The DCT domain-based watermarking methods are robust to compression due to the video encoders utilize DCT and quantified DCT coefficients to eliminate redundancy. As we know, most previous works used low or middle sub-bands of DCT for watermarking. The low sub-bands are more stable but cannot remain invisible. Contrarily, high sub-bands bring better visual effects but are difficult to survive in quantification [6]. Xin Li et al. [28] conduct DCT with variable block size and modify middle sub-bands of DCT to embed the watermarks. Their experiments show that it is robust to rotation, salt and pepper noise, cropping, and JPEG compression.

In this work, a robust DCT-based video watermarking system is developed. In contrast with the existing methods, we conduct watermark embedding on the highest frequency coefficient of DCT. Then, we use odd-even quantization to embed the watermark into it. Interestingly, we set the quantization step very large to gain robustness. It can also maintain a good imperceptibility owing to the characteristics of the high sub-bands DCT coefficients. Based on this, our method can also resist hybrid attacks after compression and recompression. On the other hand, we embed fivefold watermarks into the high-frequency DCT coefficients of the U channel to improve the visual quality. Furthermore, the synchronization code is used to improve the accuracy of watermark extraction after cropping. Similarly, the BCH code is used to make the accuracy of watermark extraction increase after any attack. No knowledge of raw videos is used in the watermark extraction process. Therefore, our watermarking scheme is blind.

2   Proposed Method

In this paper, an video watermarking resisting recompression and synchronization attack method is proposed. At first, the watermark is encoded as a BCH code and embedded into each frame of videos. Then, to get a good imperceptibility, the high-frequency DCT coefficients of each video frame are modified to embed the watermark information. The synchronization code is used to resist synchronization attacks. Figure 1 shows the framework of the proposed scheme.

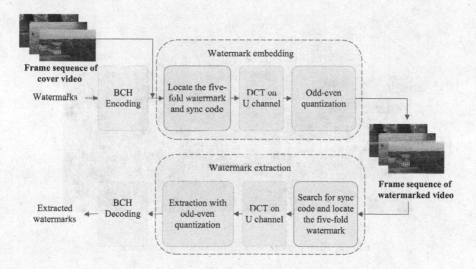

Fig. 1. The framework of the proposed scheme.

2.1   Pre-processing

Before embedding, the watermark information needs to be preprocessed. To improve the accuracy of watermark extraction, the watermark is encoded as a .BCH code [25]. The 63-bit BCH codes are adopted in the proposed scheme, which can encode 36-bit watermarks and correct 5-bit error codes. In addition, to resist geometric attacks, the Logistic chaotic map is used to generate 16-bit synchronization codes by

$$x_{n+1} = \lambda x_n(1 - x_n) \tag{1}$$

when $\lambda \in (\lambda_\infty, 4)$ and $\lambda_\infty = 3.569946572\ldots$, the chaotic system is in a chaotic state. We set $x_n \in [0, 1]$, where n is the length of the synchronization code. The kth synchronization code C_k is defined as

$$C_k = \begin{cases} 1, & 0.5 \leq x_k \leq 1 \\ 0, & 0 \leq x_k < 0.5 \end{cases} \tag{2}$$

where $0 \leq k < n$. The initial value of the chaotic map can be used as a key of the watermarking scheme.

2.2　Watermark Embedding

In the embedding process, the five regions of the U channel for watermark embedding are shown in Fig. 2. Where the circles are the positions of watermark embedding, center O and vertexes A, B, C, D are the reference points for calculating the positions of the watermarks.

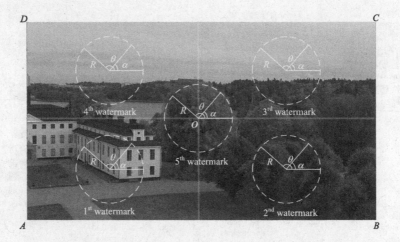

Fig. 2. Five regions are divided for watermarks.

For instance, the details of the first position are shown in Fig. 3. The distance between O' and O is defined as the reference length L, where O' is the center of the circle. Polar coordinates are used to represent the position of watermarking [29]. The R is the radius of concentric circles, and the radius of the ith concentric circle R_i is expressed as

$$R_i = \frac{a(i)}{m} \cdot \xi \cdot L \tag{3}$$

where $a(i) \in (0, m), 1 \leq i \leq K$ is a pseudo-random array generated by the chaotic system. The radius of concentric circles can be divided into m points at most, and ξ is a radius control factor that can keep concentric circles within the boundary of the frame. Thus, there are K concentric circles and $a(i)$ bit watermarks in each circle.

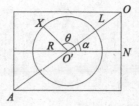

Fig. 3. The position of the first watermark.

The position X_{ij} of watermarks can be determined by polar coordinates (R_i, θ_j), and the θ_j is given by

$$\theta_j = j \cdot \frac{2\pi}{a(i)} + \alpha, \quad j = 1, 2, 3, \ldots, a(i) \tag{4}$$

where α is the angle between $\overline{OO'}$ and $\overline{O'N}$, θ_j is the angle between $\overline{O'X}$ and $\overline{O'N}$ as illustrated in Fig. 3. Then the polar coordinate (R_i, θ_j) is transformed into rectangular coordinates X_{ij}. The position of the 2nd, 3rd, 4th watermark can also be obtained in the same way. To resist cropping attacks, the position of the 5th watermark is obtained with $\alpha = 0$ and $\xi \cdot L = constant$. According to Eq. (3) and (4), the (R_i, θ_j) can be calculated after cropping any vertex of the video frame.

Then, the position X_{ij} of watermarks in the U channel is used as the starting point of the block. As shown in Fig. 4, 16 pixels on the bottom-right positions of X_{ij} form a 4×4 macroblock. The macroblock is transformed into the DCT coefficients [12]. For the $N \times N$ macroblock of the U channel, the discrete cosine transform is defined as

$$U(u, v) = a(u)a(v) \sum_{i=0}^{N-1} \sum_{j=0}^{N-1} X(i, j) \cos\frac{(2i+1)u\pi}{2N} \cos\frac{(2j+1)v\pi}{2N} \tag{5}$$

where

$$a(u) = \begin{cases} \frac{1}{N}, & u = 0 \\ \sqrt{\frac{2}{N}}, & u = 1, 2, \ldots, N-1 \end{cases}, a(v) = \begin{cases} \frac{1}{N}, & v = 0 \\ \sqrt{\frac{2}{N}}, & v = 1, 2, \ldots, N-1 \end{cases} \tag{6}$$

and $X(i, j)$ denotes the value of the macroblock element. The $U(u, v)$ is the DCT coefficients matrix of the macroblock.

We modify the highest frequency coefficient of DCT to embed the watermark. Each block is embedded 1-bit watermark-the number of X_{ij} is M. Employing this procedure, there are X_{ij} macroblocks and $5 \times M$ bits watermarks in each frame. The modifying strategy is odd-even quantization. The high-frequency coefficients of DCT are usually very small and contain negative numbers. Therefore, we apply the improved odd-even quantization to embed the watermark. When the high-frequency DCT coefficient is larger than the quantization step, i.e., $|U| > \Delta_w$,

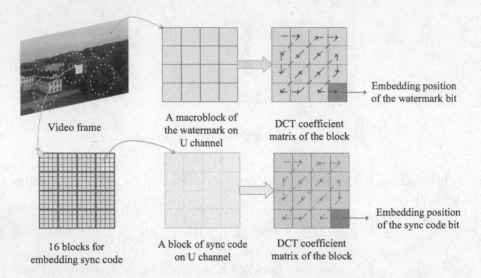

Fig. 4. Watermark and synchronization code embedding schematic.

the quantization technique is the same as [16]. When the high-frequency DCT coefficient is smaller than the quantization step, i.e., $|U| \leq \Delta_w$, the quantization technique is expressed as

1) When the parity of the DCT coefficient is the same as the parity of the watermark bit w

$$U_w = (\lfloor |U| / \Delta_w \rfloor) \times \Delta_w + \lfloor \Delta_w / 2 \rfloor \tag{7}$$

2) When the parity of the DCT coefficient is different from the parity of the watermark bit w

$$U_w = (\lfloor |U| / \Delta_w \rfloor - 1) \times \Delta_w + \lfloor \Delta_w / 2 \rfloor \tag{8}$$

where $|\cdot|$ denotes taking the absolute value of a number, $\lfloor \cdot \rfloor$ denotes round towards minus infinity, Δ_w is the quantization step for embedding watermark. U denotes the high-frequency DCT coefficient of the U channel, U_w denotes the watermarked high-frequency DCT coefficient of the U channel.

Then, the watermarked DCT coefficients are transformed into spatial domain by inverse discrete cosine transform

$$X_w(i,j) = \sum_{u=0}^{N-1} \sum_{v=0}^{N-1} a(u)a(v)U_w(u,v)\cos\frac{(2i+1)u\pi}{2N}\cos\frac{(2j+1)v\pi}{2N} \tag{9}$$

where $i = 0, 1, 2, \ldots, N-1$ and $j = 0, 1, 2, \ldots, N-1$. $U_w(u,v)$ is the watermarked high-frequency DCT coefficient matrix, $X_w(i,j)$ is the value of the watermarked macroblock element.

Furthermore, a 16-bit synchronization code is embedded using the above method to resist geometric attacks. The 16 macroblocks for embedding synchronization codes are on the bottom-right of the center O and form 4×4 block matrix, and the details are depicted in Fig. 4. Each block contains 16 pixels and forms a 4×4 DCT coefficient matrix. We use the quantization step Δ_c to embed the synchronization code into each block by modifying the highest frequency DCT coefficient. So, there are 16 blocks to embed 16 bits synchronization codes obtained by Eq. (2).

2.3 Watermark Extraction

In the extraction process, we extract watermarks from the U channel of the watermarked video. First of all, we calculate the positions of the first quadruple watermarks by Eq. (3) and (4), which is determined by the center O and vertexes A, B, C, D of the frame. Consequently, the watermarks can be extracted by judging which region the high-frequency DCT coefficients of the blocks fall in

$$
w' = \begin{cases} 0, & \left| \left\lfloor U'_w / \Delta_w \right\rfloor mod2 \right| = 0 \\ 1, & \left| \left\lfloor U'_w / \Delta_w \right\rfloor mod2 \right| = 1 \end{cases} \tag{10}
$$

where U'_w denotes the high-frequency DCT coefficient after attacking, w' represent the extracted watermark bit. Finally, the watermarks are obtained by BCH decoding.

In addition, the center O and vertexes A, B, C, D may be changed after the cropping. Owing to $\xi \cdot L$ of the 5th watermark is constant and $u = 0$, the position of the 5th watermark is only determined by center O. Therefore, we search center O in the area near the midpoint of the frame by matching the synchronization codes. The marching mechanism is illustrated in Fig. 5. First, we can search for the points within a specific range near the new center point after cropping. Then we extract information on the high-frequency coefficients of the 16 macroblocks at the bottom right of these points. Finally, suppose it is consistent with the synchronization code. In that case, the point is considered to be the original center point O. However, the experimental results show that there will be some macroblocks with the extracted information consistent with the synchronization code near the original center point O. Therefore, to avoid matching these wrong blocks, we have added a verification mechanism. It is also can be seen in Fig. 5. Thus, suppose the information extracted from the point and the four points around it is all consistent with the synchronization code. Then the point is regarded as the center point O. The positions of the four points are offset by 1 pixel each from the upper left, lower left, upper right, and lower right of the center point.

Thus, we can get the position and macroblock of the 5th watermark by Eq. (3) and (4) after the cropping attack. Then the watermark can be extracted by Eq. (10) in the same way. Hence, we realized the synchronization of the watermark after the cropping attack.

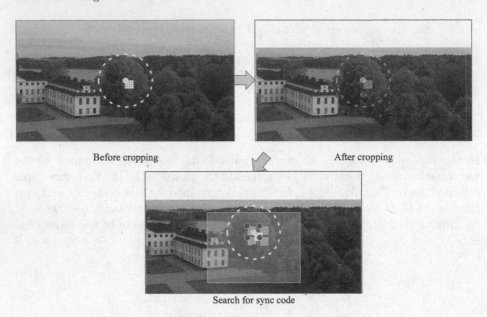

Before cropping   After cropping

Search for sync code

Fig. 5. Synchronization code matching and verification mechanism.

3   Experimental Results

Our scheme was tested on six 1280×720 video sequences: Ducks Take Off, In To Tree, Park Joy, Vidyo1, Vidyo3, Vidyo4 [23]. The Ducks Take Off, In To Tree, Park Joy contain 500 frames with a frame rate of 50 fps. The Vidyo1, Vidyo3, Vidyo4 contain 600 frames with a frame rate of 60 fps. Figure 6 shows the first frame of these videos.

In the experiments, we used 36 bits binary sequence as the watermark and encoded it with 63 bits BCH codes. Therefore, 315 bits BCH codes of the watermark were embedded in each frame. We use the peak signal-to-noise ratio (PSNR) as the scope of invisibility [12] and the Bit Error Rate (BER) as the evaluation indicator of the watermark exaction. Figure 7 shows the PSNR values of the test videos with different quantization steps.

We performed the rest of the tests on our system with quantization step size $\Delta_w = 220$ for watermark and $\Delta_c = 330$ for synchronization code, and the PSNR value was about 43.26 dB. It is obvious that our scheme has good invisibility. The compression results of test videos with different quantization parameters (QPs) and the recompression attacks with a frame rate of 25 fps and different bit rates are shown in Fig. 8(a) and (b). As we can see, the BER of the proposed scheme after compression and recompression is less than 7%. In addition, the cropping, inserting, and frame inserting/dropping attacks after recompression with a ratio

In To Tree   Ducks Take Off   Park Joy

Vidyo1   Vidyo3   Vidyo4

Fig. 6. The first frame of test videos.

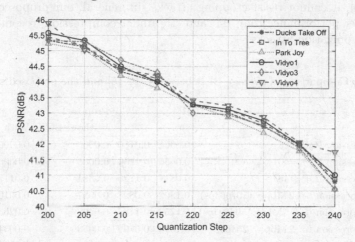

Fig. 7. PSNR of watermarked videos with different quantization steps.

from 5% to 20% were performed. The frame rate of the recompression is 25 fps, and the bit rate is 2 Mbps. The results can be seen in Fig. 8(c), (d), (e), (f) separately. It shows that our method can keep the BER values below 9% under these attacks. Obviously, our method is robust to compression, recompression, and synchronization attacks.

To judge the performance of the proposed method, we compared our results with the method in [11] and [15]. The method of [11] is based on the DC CWT domain, and the method of [15] is based on the DCT domain. In fairness, we use each method to embed the same 36-bit watermark into the U channels of the six test videos. Table 1 shows the comparison results. We present two BER values of our scheme, one of which uses BCH to correct the watermark we extracted, and the other does not. First, the watermarked videos were compressed using H.264 at different QPs. It is obvious that the average BER value of our method is lower than [11] and [15], where BCH is the lowest. Moreover, we also recompressed these watermarked videos with different bit rates and frame rates. From the results, the method in [11] can resist the recompression of different bit rates at the original frame rate (50/60 fps). But it has very high BER values with a lower frame rate(25 fps). Since the lower frame rate will cause frame loss, and the method can only embed the 1-bit watermark in a video frame. Thus, it cannot resist the frame inserting/dropping, cropping, and inserting attacks after recompression at a frame rate of 25 fps and a bit rate of 2 Mbps, but our method can obtain very low BER values. The method in [15] can resist recompression with different bit rates and frame rates. It can also resist the frame dropping/inserting and the hybrid attack of recompression and inserting. But the average BER of it is higher than the proposed method under these attacks. In addition, it cannot resist cropping attacks. In general, our proposed scheme has a better performance than [11] and [15] under compression, recompression, and synchronization attacks.

Table 1. Comparison of average BER between [11, 15] and the proposed scheme.

Attacks	[11]	[15]	Proposed	
			Without BCH	With BCH
Compression (QP = 28)	0.0061	0.0180	0.0000	0.0000
Compression (QP = 40)	0.0656	0.0854	0.0083	0.0000
Compression (QP = 48)	0.0811	0.1726	0.0381	0.0117
Recompression to 2 Mbps (50/60 fps)	0.1202	0.0828	0.0027	0.0010
Recompression to 0.8 Mbps (50/60 fps)	0.1757	0.1183	0.0498	0.0263
Recompression to 2 Mbps (25 fps)	0.1312	0.5899	0.0053	0.0034
Recompression to 0.8 Mbps (25 fps)	0.1823	0.5624	0.0334	0.0192
Frame inserting 10%	0.3246	0.4319	0.0367	0.0285
Frame inserting 20%	0.3665	0.4851	0.0913	0.0733
Frame dropping 10%	0.1223	0.4051	0.0027	0.0001
Frame dropping 20%	0.1143	0.4043	0.0028	0.0001
Recompression+Cropping 10%	0.6825	0.5635	0.0053	0.0004
Recompression+Cropping 20%	0.6833	0.5615	0.0050	0.0002
Recompression+Inserting 10%	0.2218	0.5608	0.0043	0.0004
Recompression+Inserting 20%	0.2526	0.5635	0.0074	0.0017

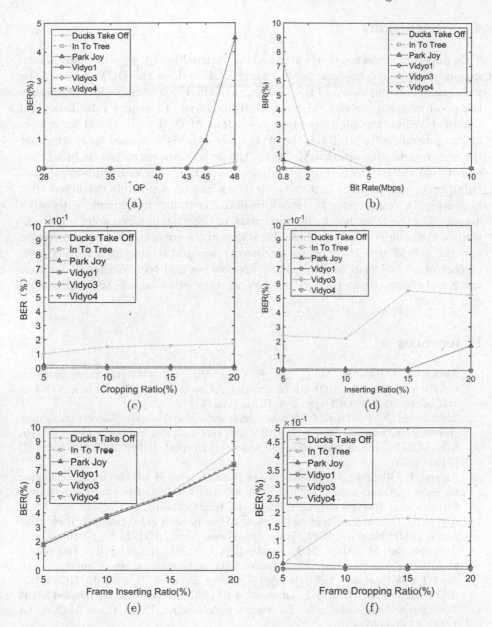

Fig. 8. The BER of the proposed scheme against different attacks. (a): under compression with different QPs. (b): against recompression with different bit rates at a frame rate of 25 fps. (c) and (d): against cropping or inserting attacks combined with recompression at a frame rate of 25 fps and bit rate of 2 Mbps. (d) and (f): under frame inserting/dropping attacks.

4   Conclusions

This paper has developed a watermarking scheme based on odd-even quantization, random synchronization code, and BCH code in the DCT domain. The watermark is embedded into the U channel of the video frame, which maintains the good visual quality of the watermarked videos. To ensure robustness and imperceptibility, the high-frequency coefficient of DCT is modified for watermark embedding. In addition, the synchronization code is used to synchronize the watermark after attacks. Moreover, the watermark extraction is blind, i.e., no original video is needed for watermark extraction. The most important contribution of this paper is that the watermark can be accurately extracted after high-strength compression or recompression, even after hybridizing with other attacks. On the other hand, the watermark of our system has a good imperceptibility. Although our scheme has advantages in the robustness of recompression and the hybrid attacks, it cannot resist rotation and scaling attacks very well. In the future, we plan to study other approaches and technologies to improve the visual effects of watermarked videos and resist other attacks such as rotation and scaling.

References

1. Ajitha, G., Menda, S., Annapurna, P., et al.: Bind video watermarking based on wavelet transform. In: 2021 5th International Conference on Trends in Electronics and Informatics (ICOEI), pp. 1–5. IEEE (2021)
2. Akhlaghian, F., Bahrami, Z.: A new robust video watermarking algorithm against cropping and rotating attacks. In: 2015 12th International Iranian Society of Cryptology Conference on Information Security and Cryptology (ISCISC), pp. 122–127. IEEE (2015)
3. Alenizi, F., Kurdahi, F., Eltawil, A., et al.: DWT-based watermarking technique for video authentication. In: 2015 IEEE International Conference on Electronics, Circuits, and Systems (ICECS), pp. 41–44. IEEE (2015)
4. Aly, H.A.: Data hiding in motion vectors of compressed video based on their associated prediction error. IEEE Trans. Inf. Foren. Secur. $6(1)$, 14–18 (2010)
5. Asikuzzaman, M., Alam, M.J., Lambert, A.J., et al.: Imperceptible and robust blind video watermarking using chrominance embedding: a set of approaches in the DT CWT domain. IEEE Trans. Inf. Forens. Secur. $9(9)$, 1502–1517 (2014)
6. Asikuzzaman, M., Alam, M.J., Lambert, A.J., et al.: Robust DT CWT-based DIBR 3D video watermarking using chrominance embedding. IEEE Trans. Multimedia $18(9)$, 1733–1748 (2016)
7. Biswas, S., Das, S.R., Petriu, E.M.: An adaptive compressed MPEG-2 video watermarking scheme. IEEE Trans. Instrum. Measure. $54(5)$, 1853–1861 (2005)
8. Chung, T.Y., Hong, M.S., Oh, Y.N., et al.: Digital watermarking for copyright protection of MPEG2 compressed video. IEEE Trans. Consumer Electr. $44(3)$, 895–901 (1998)
9. Coria, L.E., Pickering, M.R., Nasiopoulos, P., et al.: A video watermarking scheme based on the dual-tree complex wavelet transform. IEEE Trans. Inf. Forens. Secur. $3(3)$, 466–474 (2008)

10. Deguillaume, F., Csurka, G., O'Ruanaidh, J.J., et al.: Robust 3D DFT video water-marking. In: Security and Watermarking of Multimedia Contents. vol. 3657, pp. 113–124. International Society for Optics and Photonics (1999)
11. Huan, W., Li, S., Qian, Z., et al.: Exploring stable coefficients on joint sub-bands for robust video watermarking in DT CWT domain. IEEE Trans. Circuits Syst. Video Technol. (2021)
12. Huang, H.Y., Yang, C.H., Hsu, W.H.: A video watermarking technique based on pseudo-3-D DCT and quantization index modulation. IEEE Trans. Inf. Forens. Secur. 5(4), 625–637 (2010)
13. Kalantari, N.K., Ahadi, S.M., Vafadust, M.: A robust image watermarking in the ridgelet domain using universally optimum decoder. IEEE Trans. Circuits Syst. Video Technol. 20(3), 396–406 (2009)
14. Kang, X., Huang, J., Shi, Y.Q., et al.: A DWT-DFT composite watermarking scheme robust to both affine transform and JPEG compression. IEEE Trans. Circuits Syst. Video Technol. 13(8), 776–786 (2003)
15. Ko, H.J., Huang, C.T., Horng, G., et al.: Robust and blind image watermarking in DCT domain using inter-block coefficient correlation. Inf. Sci. 517, 128–147 (2020)
16. Kundur, D., Hatzinakos, D.: Digital watermarking for telltale tamper proofing and authentication. Proc. IEEE 87(7), 1167–1180 (1999)
17. Lancini, R., Mapelli, F., Tubaro, S.: A robust video watermarking technique in the spatial domain. In: International Symposium on VIPromCom Video/Image Processing and Multimedia Communications, pp. 251–256. IEEE (2002)
18. Lee, M.J., Im, D.H., Lee, H.Y., Kim, K.S., Lee, H.K.: Real-time video watermarking system on the compressed domain for high-definition video contents: Practical issues. Digit. Signal Process. 22(1), 190–198 (2012)
19. Lin, S.D., Chen, C.F.: A robust DCT-based watermarking for copyright protection. IEEE Trans. Consumer Electron. 46(3), 415–421 (2000)
20. Ling, H., Wang, L., Zou, F., et al.: Robust video watermarking based on affine invariant regions in the compressed domain. Signal Process. 91(8), 1863–1875 (2011)
21. Liu, Y., Zhao, J.: A new video watermarking algorithm based on 1D DFT and radon transform. Signal Process. 90(2), 626–639 (2010)
22. Mansouri, A., Aznaveh, A.M., Torkamani-Azar, F., et al.: A low complexity video watermarking in H. 264 compressed domain. IEEE Trans. Inf. Foren. Secur. 5(4), 649–657 (2010)
23. Montgomery, C.: Xiph.org video test media (derf's collection). The xiph open source community (1994). https://media.xiph.org/video/derf/. Accessed 28 Aug 2021
24. Panyavaraporn, J., Horkaew, P.: DWT/DCT-based invisible digital watermarking scheme for video stream. In: 2018 10th International Conference on Knowledge and Smart Technology (KST), pp. 154–157. IEEE (2018)
25. Pratama, I.D., Budiman, G., Ramatryana, N.A.: Analisis audio watermarking menggunakan metode discrete cosine transform dengan pengkodean BCH. In: Prosiding Seminar Nasional Cendekiawan, pp. 13–1 (2016)
26. Sun, X.-C., Lu, Z.-M., Wang, Z., Liu, Y.-L.: A geometrically robust multi-bit video watermarking algorithm based on 2-D DFT. Multimedia Tools Appl. 80(9), 13491–13511 (2021). https://doi.org/10.1007/s11042-020-10392-9
27. Wang, Y., Pearmain, A.: Blind MPEG-2 video watermarking robust against geometric attacks: a set of approaches in DCT domain. IEEE Trans. Image Process. 15(6), 1536–1543 (2006)

28. Zhang, J., Ho, A.T., Qiu, G., et al.: Robust video watermarking of H. 264/AVC. IEEE Trans. Circuit Syst. II: Exp. Briefs **54**(2), 205–209 (2007)
29. Zhao, H.Y., Wang, H.X.: Quadruple watermarking against geometrical attacks based on searching for vertexes. IEICE Trans. Fundam. Electron. Commun. Comput. Sci. **90**(6), 1244–1247 (2007)

Improved Fluctuation Derived Block Selection Strategy in Pixel Value Ordering Based Reversible Data Hiding

Xin Tang[1]($\boxtimes$), Linna Zhou[2], Guang Tang[1], Yuchen Wen[1], and Yixuan Cheng[1]

[1] School of Cyber Science and Engineering, University of International Relations, Beijing 100091, China
xtang@uir.edu.cn
[2] School of Cyberspace Security, Beijing University of Posts and Telecommunications, Beijing 100876, China

Abstract. Block selection strategy is an effective technique to improve the imperceptibility in pixel value ordering (PVO) based reversible data hiding by selecting blocks with higher smoothness to embed data at first, which largely reduces invalid shifting of pixels before the maximum capacity is reached. As a means to evaluate the smoothness of a certain block selected, fluctuation value is defined accordingly. However, in current solutions, the definition of fluctuation value is not always accurate enough to reflect the true smoothness of blocks, which is usually restrained by the number of pixels participating in calculation as well as those invalid ones introduced. In this paper, we improved the definition of fluctuation in order to achieve a better performance. Take the maximum side for example, context pixels participating in fluctuation calculation are determined at first, considering the second largest pixel as well as neighborhood of the largest pixel simultaneously. Then those invalid ones are eliminated to reduce unnecessary uncertainty introduced. Experimental results show that our proposed scheme outperforms the state-of-the art in accuracy of smoothness evaluation, and achieves a better imperceptibility as a result.

Keywords: Fluctuation value calculation · Block selection · Pixel value ordering · Reversible data hiding · Context pixels

1 Introduction

Reversible data hiding (RDH) [1–7] is an emerging technique which is able to embed secret data into the cover signal in a reversible way. Thanks to its lossless nature, it has been applied in a lot of fields requiring high quality of cover signals, such as medical and military images. In order to achieve high imperceptibility, pixel value ordering (PVO) [8] has been the mainstream technique in reversible data hiding in recent years. By utilizing pixels adjacent in value to achieve prediction, high accuracy in prediction could be obtained, which means in most of the cases small prediction error can be achieved to embed secret bits according to the embedding criterion. However, for texture regions with large fluctuation in the cover signal, such accuracy usually cannot be effectively guaranteed. As a result, a large amount of invalid shifting would be introduced, which in turn inevitably affects the imperceptibility.

To deal with this problem, a direct solution is to embed secret data into blocks with small fluctuation at first, in which the calculation of fluctuation value naturally becomes the key to affect performance. To obtain fluctuation value of a certain block, one of the most common ways [8–12] is to utilize the second largest and smallest pixels inside, which has been applied in a lot of PVO based reversible data hiding schemes. However, in this kind of schemes, the outside pixels are ignored, even though some of them also reflect the fluctuation. On the other hand, a single fluctuation value is utilized in evaluating performance to predict both the largest and smallest pixels, which is not always accurate on both sides simultaneously. Take outside pixels into account, another kind of solutions [13–17] calculates the fluctuation value of a certain block by utilizing adjacent two columns of pixels on the right side and two rows on the bottom. However, the pixels inside are ignored on the contrary. Moreover, another deficiency mentioned above is also inherited. As a means to deal with these problems, the third kind of solutions [18] define a specific fluctuation value for each one of the sides, considering both inside and outside pixels simultaneously. However, the number of pixels participating in calculation is quite limited, which also restrains the performance. Moreover, if the employed pixels appear in the same area, the obtained fluctuation value is actually not suitable in evaluating the prediction error. Based on these works, we have proposed an improved solution [19], which introduces more pixels to fluctuation calculation with positions ensured to be from two areas uniformly. However, too many invalid pixels are involved in the calculation, which inevitably introduces a lot of unnecessary uncertainty.

In this context, attempt to achieve a better imperceptibility for PVO based reversible data hiding when the secret bits are not fully embedded, we propose a block selection strategy based PVO scheme which makes use of the proposed new calculation method for fluctuation value. To the best of our knowledge, our work is the first to well predict the prediction error by fluctuation value. Specifically, we propose to utilize both the second largest and second smallest pixels themselves rather than their neighbors in the process of fluctuation calculation to reduce the unnecessary uncertainty introduced. Moreover, for neighbors of both the largest and smallest pixels, we eliminate those with large deviation from the mean value in calculation, together with those which are meaningless to the prediction. As a result, the obtained fluctuation value is able to well predict the prediction error in PVO based reversible data hiding. Our main contributions are summarized as follows:

1. We put forward a novel block selection strategy based reversible data hiding framework, which supports the proposed fluctuation value calculation method. Specifically, the threshold value to distinguish smooth blocks from the texture ones is determined adaptively so that most of the secret data is ensured to be embedded in smooth areas of the cover image. As a result, the number of invalid shifting is largely reduced and the imperceptibility is guaranteed.
2. We propose a new method to calculate the fluctuation value of a certain block, and further present a corresponding block selection strategy to improve the imperceptibility of PVO based reversible data hiding when secret bits are not fully embedded. Specifically, we improve the definition of context pixels to eliminate unnecessary neighboring pixels, which largely reduces the uncertainty introduced. Moreover, we also remove pixels with large deviation from the mean value for further improvement. Experimental results show that the proposed scheme outperforms the state-of-the art in imperceptibility.

2   Related Work

In 2013, Li *et al.* [8] proposed the first PVO based reversible data hiding algorithm. According to their design, the difference between the second largest and smallest pixels of a certain image block is defined to be its fluctuation value. By embedding secret bits into those blocks with smaller fluctuation at first, the invalid shifting of pixels is largely reduced when the maximum capacity has not been reached. Thanks to its simplicity, Peng *et al.* [9] applied the same scheme to reduce invalid shifting of pixels in IPVO. However, the value obtained is not accurate enough to reflect the fluctuation of the corresponding block, since there are only two internal pixels participating in the fluctuation calculation. A large number of pixels outside of the block are ignored, even though some of them also reflect the fluctuation. On the other hand, a single fluctuation value obtained is employed in evaluating performance to predict both the largest and smallest pixels, which is not always accurate simultaneously. As a follow-up work, Wang *et al.* [10] introduced more pixels between the second largest and smallest ones to improve the performance of fluctuation calculation. However, the scheme still inherits the other shortcomings mentioned above. Take outside pixels into account, another kind of solutions [13–17] calculated the fluctuation value of a certain block by considering adjacent columns of pixels on the right side and rows on the bottom. Specifically, it is defined to be the sum of absolute values of differences between adjacent pixels for a certain block. In these works, Weng *et al.* [17] indicated only one column and one row of pixels to be the context ones. While for Ou *et al.* [13,14], the amount is doubled instead. However, even though more pixels are introduced in fact, none of the inside ones participates in the calculation. To solve these problems, Pan *et al.* [18] further developed the method to calculate fluctuation value and considered both sides respectively. Take the maximum side for example, the neighbors of the largest two pixels are selected to be context ones together with those within the minimum bounding rectangle containing the largest two ones. It is worth mentioning that those largest and smallest pixels, no matter which block they belong to, are further removed to ensure reversibility. Then the largest and smallest ones in context pixels are selected, and their difference divided by the number of elements inside is defined to be fluctuation value of the maximum side. However, the number of pixels participating in calculation is quite limited, which still restrains the performance. Moreover, once the selected two pixels are from the same neighborhood of either the largest pixel or the second largest one, the obtained fluctuation value is actually not able to well predict the prediction error. As a subsequent work, Tang *et al.* [19] further improved the strategy to solve problems mentioned above. The difference is that the context pixels of the largest and second largest ones are defined respectively, which is able to deal with the shortcoming of Pan *et al.*'s work [18]. Besides, each one of the context pixels is selected to participate in fluctuation value calculation. Even though a better performance is achieved as a result, large numbers of inappropriate pixels involved also inevitably introduce a lot of errors. For example, neighbors of the second largest pixel should be removed from context ones, since the value of the certain pixel is kept unchanged in the process of data embedding in fact.

3   The Proposed Scheme

In this section, we first introduce the framework of the proposed scheme, and then describe the whole process in detail. To illustrate the scheme, we first introduce how to calculate the fluctuation value of a certain block in the cover image, then according to the results obtained, we further exhibit the process of block selection strategy based data embedding as well as extraction.

3.1   Framework

A complete process of the proposed block selection strategy based PVO scheme in reversible data hiding starts from context pixels selection for fluctuation value calculation. As is shown in Fig. 1, the cover image has been divided into blocks of the same size at first. For each one of the blocks obtained, we calculate its fluctuation value according to the procedure introduced in detail in Sect. 3.2. Then we compare them with the pre-defined threshold value to determine whether the corresponding block is appropriate to embed secret data. On receiving the embedded image, the receiver is able to extract the embedded data and recover the original image by performing the same procedure.

Take the ith block which is enclosed by the red rectangle for example, we sort n pixels to obtain an ordered sequence $(x^i_{\sigma(1)}, x^i_{\sigma(2)}, ..., x^i_{\sigma(n-1)}, x^i_{\sigma(n)})$, in which $\sigma :$ $(1, 2, \cdots, n-1, n) \rightarrow (1, 2, \cdots n-1, n)$ is a one-to-one mapping such that: $x^i_{\sigma(1)} \leq x^i_{\sigma(2)} \leq \cdots \leq x^i_{\sigma(n-1)} \leq x^i_{\sigma(n)}$. For any $u, v \in [1, n]$, if $x^i_{\sigma(u)} = x^i_{\sigma(v)}$ and $u < v$, we have $\sigma(u) < \sigma(v)$. To calculate fluctuation values for both the maximum and minimum sides, we first select context pixels. As is shown in the figure, the selected ones for both sides are enclosed by a rectangle respectively. Then invalid

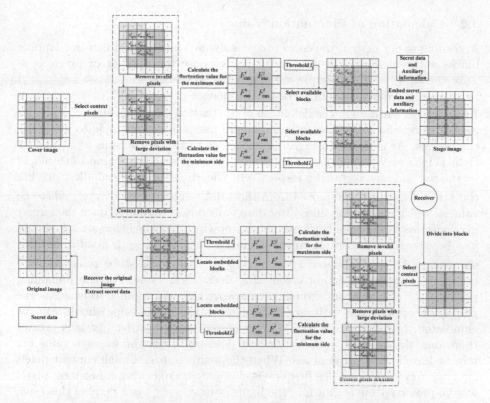

Fig. 1. Framework of the proposed scheme

pixels and those with large deviation are removed. Based on obtained context pixels, the fluctuation values of the ith block could be calculated and denoted as $F_{\max}^i$ and $F_{\min}^i$ for both sides respectively.

Similarly, the fluctuation values of the other three blocks in the figure is also obtained, represented as $F_{\max}^j$, $F_{\max}^k$ and $F_{\max}^l$ for the maximum side and $F_{\min}^j$, $F_{\min}^k$ and $F_{\min}^l$ for the minimum side. By comparing them with threshold values t_1 and t_2 respectively, we select those blocks with smaller fluctuation value in the corresponding cases for potential embedding. Specifically, those unselected ones are identified with a dotted rectangle respectively. Next, we embed secret data and auxiliary information into the corresponding positions to obtain a stego image, and mark the embedded pixels with red circles.

Then the image is sent to the receiver, which is qualified to extract secret data accordingly. In particular, the receiver first divides the received image into blocks of specific size according to the extracted auxiliary information. Then it employs the same procedure to select context pixels and calculate fluctuation values for blocks. Based on the result of comparison, the embedded blocks can be located to extract secret data. At the same time, the cover image is also recovered to original state before data embedding.

3.2 Calculation of Fluctuation Value

According to our design, the cover image is divided into several non-overlapping blocks with equal size. In each of which, suppose the number of pixels is n. Take the ith block for example, we first sort the n pixels $(x_1^i, x_2^i, \cdots, x_{n-1}^i, x_n^i)$ in ascending order to obtain an ordered sequence $(x_{\sigma(1)}^i, x_{\sigma(2)}^i, ..., x_{\sigma(n-1)}^i, x_{\sigma(n)}^i)$. According to our design, the definition of fluctuation value calculation is similar for both sides. So we just take the side of largest pixel for example to introduce the process. As is shown in Fig. 2(a), the green rectangle contains $x_{\sigma(n)}^i$ and its eight neighbors. Without loss of generality, we represent the ith and kth blocks by the red and blue rectangles respectively. Clearly, $x_{\sigma(1)}^k$ is the smallest pixel in the kth block, which is removed from the valid neighborhood of $x_{\sigma(n)}^i$ since the value of which may be modified after data embedding. Similarly, once the largest pixel appears in the neighborhood, no matter which block it belongs to, it should also be discarded. According to the definition, $x_{\sigma(p)}^k$ is the pth pixel in ordered sequence of block k. Suppose $x_{\sigma(p)}^k < x_{\sigma(n-1)}^i$, it should also be removed since it has the opposite effect for calculating fluctuation value. For the remaining pixels in the neighborhood, to further improve the performance to evaluate the prediction error, those with large deviation to the mean value should also be eliminated. In particular, if the number of remaining context pixels is greater than four, the first two with the largest deviation from the average value are removed from the context pixels. When the number of remaining context pixels is between two and four, the first one is eliminated. Otherwise, all context pixels will be preserved. As is shown in the figure, suppose $x_{\sigma(q)}^i$ is a pixel of this type, it is removed as a result. At last, the context pixels to calculate the fluctuation value for the maximum side in the ith block is shown in Fig. 2(b) by $\odot$. In particular, those removed pixels are represented by $\otimes$.

Take the maximum side for example, once the context pixels are obtained, the corresponding fluctuation value can be calculated according to Eq. (1) as follows.

$$C_{\max}^i = \left| \frac{\sum_{a=1}^{M_1} S_a}{M_1} - x_{\sigma(n-1)}^i \right|. \tag{1}$$

In the definition of $C_{\max}^i$, S_a denotes the ath element in context pixels and M_1 represents the total number. Similarly, we define the fluctuation value of the minimum side in Eq. (2).

$$C_{\min}^i = \left| \frac{\sum_{c=1}^{M_2} S_c}{M_2} - x_{\sigma(2)}^i \right|. \tag{2}$$

Once the fluctuation value is calculated, we will sequentially select blocks with small fluctuation values to embed data at first. Specifically, if the fluctuation value of a certain block is less than the threshold value, embedding or

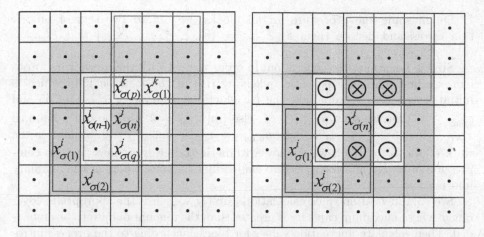

(a) Context pixels of the ith block before pixels removing

(b) Context pixels of the ith block after pixels removing

Fig. 2. Context pixels selection for the ith block

shifting is performed. Therefore, a good threshold value will result in better performance of the scheme. In this paper, we embed data into both the maximum and minimum sides, in each of which the smallest fluctuation value satisfying the requirement for capacity is determined to be a threshold value respectively. And the optimal ones are obtained by traversing every one of the capacity allocation strategies. Finally, we employ the similar data embedding and extraction method introduced in [19], and describe the processes in detail in the next section.

3.3   Secret Data Embedding

In order to reduce distortion of the cover image once the secret bits are not fully embedded, we employ a block selection strategy according to the obtained fluctuation value defined in Sect. 3.2. Take the maximum side for example, we only embed data into blocks with low fluctuation and show the process in detail as follows. The same procedure is also appropriate for the minimum side.

Step 1: Image segmentation and prediction error calculation. We first divide the cover image with size of $H \times W$ into k non-overlapping blocks of the same size, then sort pixels in a certain block to obtain an ascending sequence $(x_{\sigma(1)}, x_{\sigma(2)}, \cdots, x_{\sigma(n)})$. If $x_{\sigma(u)} = x_{\sigma(v)}$ and $u < v$, we have $\sigma(u) < \sigma(v)$. At last, we calculate prediction errors for both sides according to Eq. (3) and (4) respectively.

$$e_{\max} = x_{\sigma(n)} - x_{\sigma(n-1)}, \tag{3}$$

$$e_{\min} = x_{\sigma(1)} - x_{\sigma(2)}. \tag{4}$$

On finishing the procedure for all blocks, we obtain two sets of prediction errors and denote them as $E_{\max} = (e^1_{\max}, e^2_{\max}, ..., e^k_{\max})$ and $E_{\min} = (e^1_{\min}, e^2_{\min}, ..., e^k_{\min})$.

Step 2: Location map generation. In order to deal with the overflowing problem, we first mark the potential pixels at risk in the location map which is initiated as a zero vector. Take the ith block for example, if $x^i_{\sigma(n)} = 255$ and $e^i_{\max} \geq 1$, then we set $lm_{\max(i)} = 1$, else $lm_{\max(i)} = 0$. On the other hand, if $x^1_{\sigma(1)} = 0$ and $e^i_{\min} \leq -1$, we set $lm_{\min(i)} = 1$, else $lm_{\min(i)} = 0$. Similar as the work of Kim et $al.$ [20], we employ arithmetic coding to achieve lossless compression of $lm_{\max}$ and $lm_{\min}$ before embedding them as a part of the auxiliary information.

Step 3: Fluctuation value calculation. Firstly, we select the appropriate cover image whose maximum capacity is greater than the amount of data to be embedded. Then calculate fluctuation values for blocks according to the process introduced in Sect. 3.2. In particular, we denote the fluctuation sequences for each one of the side as $C_{\max} = (c^1_{\max}, ..., c^k_{\max})$ and $C_{\min} = (c^1_{\min}, ..., c^k_{\min})$ respectively. In order to distinguish smooth blocks from the texture ones, we determine the threshold values of fluctuation for both sides to ensure the minimum embedding capacity is just satisfied, each of which is denoted as t_1 and t_2 respectively.

Step 4: Secret data embedding. In order to achieve high imperceptibility before the maximum capacity is reached, we preferentially select blocks with fluctuation values less than t_1 or t_2 to perform potential embedding. In particular, consider the ith appropriate value in $C_{\max}$. If $lm_{\max(i)} = 1$, the corresponding pixel is skipped. Else, if $e^i_{\max} = 1$, a secret bit $b \in \{0,1\}$ is embedded into the largest pixel of the ith block by prediction error expansion. Otherwise, if $e^i_{\max} > 1$, the largest pixel is increased by Eq. (5).

$$x^i_{\sigma(n)} = \begin{cases} x^i_{\sigma(n)} + b, & if \quad e^i_{\max} = 1, \\ x^i_{\sigma(n)} + 1, & if \quad e^i_{\max} > 1. \end{cases} \tag{5}$$

The similar procedure is also applied for the other side, and the embedding process is shown in Eq. (6).

$$x^i_{\sigma(1)} = \begin{cases} x^i_{\sigma(1)} - b, & if \quad e^i_{\min} = -1, \\ x^i_{\sigma(1)} - 1, & if \quad e^i_{\min} < -1. \end{cases} \tag{6}$$

When the embedding process terminates, we record end positions in terms of corresponding indexes l_{endax} and l_{endin} in $C_{\max}$ and $C_{\min}$ respectively as another part of auxiliary information.

Step 5: Auxiliary information embedding. The auxiliary information consists of threshold values t_1 and t_2, block size n_1 and n_2, compressed location map CLM, and end positions l_{endax} and l_{endin}, each part of which is with maximum size of 16 bits, 8 bits, $2\log_2 \left\lceil \frac{H \times W}{n_1 \times n_2} \right\rceil$ bits and $2\log_2 \left\lceil \frac{H \times W}{n_1 \times n_2} \right\rceil$ bits respectively. Specifically, we extract the least significant bits of the first $24 + 4\log_2 \left\lceil \frac{H \times W}{n_1 \times n_2} \right\rceil$ pixels in the stego image, and embed them into blocks starting from the adjacent one to the end position, according to the method introduced in Step 4. Then we embed the auxiliary information into the least significant bits from the beginning by employing the LSB method. At last, the stego image is transferred to the receiver who is able to achieve blind extraction with the help of this information.

3.4   Secret Data Extraction

In this part, we introduce how to extract secret data from the stego image received, and show the process in detail as follows.

Step 1: Auxiliary information extraction. Extract least significant bits from the first $24 + 4\log_2 \left\lceil \frac{H \times W}{n_1 \times n_2} \right\rceil$ pixels to get the auxiliary information, in which threshold values, block size, compressed location map and end positions are involved. In order to recover the original LSBs of the corresponding pixels, we first divide the stego image into blocks according to the size obtained. Then we calculate fluctuation values for blocks according to the process introduced in Sect. 3.2, to get fluctuation sequences $C'_{\max}$ and $C'_{\min}$ respectively. At the same time, prediction error sequences $E'_{\max} = \{e'_{\max(1)}, e'_{\max(2)}, \cdots, e'_{\max(n)}\}$ and $E'_{\min} = \{e'_{\min(1)}, e'_{\min(2)}, \cdots, e'_{\min(n)}\}$ are also obtained. Staring from the block next to the end position, we extract $24 + 4\log_2 \left\lceil \frac{H \times W}{n_1 \times n_2} \right\rceil$ bits to recover the least significant bits of pixels at the beginning. Take the ith appropriate block in the maximum sequence for example, if $lm_{\max(i)} = 1$, the largest pixel inside is skipped. Otherwise, if $e'_{\max(i)}$ equals to 1 or 2, a secret bit b is extracted according to the rule shown in Eq. (7). Finally, the largest pixel is recovered by Eq. (8).

$$b = \begin{cases} 0, if & e'_{\max(i)} = 1, \\ 1, if & e'_{\max(i)} = 2. \end{cases} \tag{7}$$

$$x^i_{\sigma(n)} = \begin{cases} x^i_{\sigma(n)} - 1, if & e'_{\max(i)} \geq 2, \\ x^i_{\sigma(n)}, & if & e'_{\max(i)} = 1. \end{cases} \tag{8}$$

The procedure is similar for the minimum side. We exhibit the process of secret data extraction and original pixel recovery in Eq. (9) and (10) respectively.

$$b = \begin{cases} 0, if & e'_{\min(i)} = -1, \\ 1, if & e'_{\min(i)} = -2. \end{cases} \tag{9}$$

$$x^i_{\sigma(1)} = \begin{cases} x^i_{\sigma(1)} + 1, if & e'_{\min(i)} \leq -2, \\ x^i_{\sigma(1)}, & if & e'_{\min(i)} = -1. \end{cases} \tag{10}$$

Once the auxiliary information with size of $24 + 4\log_2 \left\lceil \frac{H \times W}{n_1 \times n_2} \right\rceil$ bits are completely extracted, the values of first $24 + 4\log_2 \left\lceil \frac{H \times W}{n_1 \times n_2} \right\rceil$ pixels can be recovered as a result.

Step 2: Secret data extraction and cover image recovery. On finishing recovery of the first $24 + 4\log_2 \left\lceil \frac{H \times W}{n_1 \times n_2} \right\rceil$ pixels, we calculate fluctuation values of the corresponding blocks from the beginning of the stego image again. Then extract secret bits from appropriate blocks and recover the cover image according to similar procedure introduced in Step 1.

4   Experimental Results and Analysis

In this section, we take experiments to validate the effectiveness of the proposed scheme and evaluate its performance. Specifically, we employ a workstation with Inter Core i5-6500 CPU @ 3.20 GHz, 4 GB RAM, and a 1 TB hard drive to implement all algorithms using Matlab version R2018b. We select 8 images Lena, Man, Baboon, Peppers, House, Plane, Boat and Gravel from the USC-SIPI image dataset [21] to perform our experiments, each of which is shown in Fig. 3(a), 3(b), 3(c), 3(d), 3(e), 3(f), 3(g) and 3(h) respectively. All results are on average of 20 tries.

(a) Lena   (b) Man   (c) Baboon   (d) Peppers

(e) House   (f) Plane   (g) Boat   (h) Gravel

Fig. 3. Test images

4.1   Verification of Reversibility

In this part, we first check the correctness of our proposed algorithm by means of reversibility. Specifically, we choose an image Lena from Fig. 3(a) to implement our algorithm. In particular, the cover image is divided into blocks with size 2×2, each one of which corresponds to two fluctuation values obtained according to the procedure introduced in Sect. 3.2. For each one of the blocks, its two fluctuation values are compared with t_1 and t_2 respectively to determine whether the corresponding side should be skipped. We embed 1,000 randomly generated secret bits successively to obtain a stego image as shown in Fig. 4.

Fig. 4. Stego image

Then, we divide the image into blocks with size 2×2, to obtain two fluctuation sequences again. It is worth mentioning that the obtained sequences are identical with those before embedding since the pixels participate in fluctuation value calculation are actually not changed. We apply the same comparison procedure to find out appropriate positions to extract secret bits. Once 1000 bits are extracted, the recovered image is also obtained. In order to validate the reversibility, we exhibit the original image and recovered image in Fig. 5(a) and 5(b) respectively, then perform exclusive OR operation on both of them to show the result in Fig. 5(c).

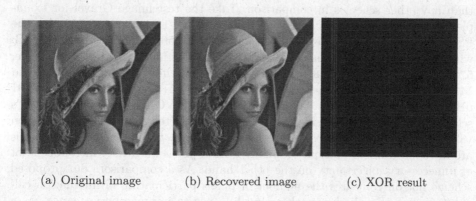

(a) Original image   (b) Recovered image   (c) XOR result

Fig. 5. Verification of reversibility

As is shown in Fig. 5(c), the result image is all black. According to the principle of exclusive OR operation, it can be inferred that the recovered image is completely consistent with the original cover image. Thus the reversibility is validated as a result.

4.2   Comparison of Imperceptibility

In this section, we compare imperceptibility of the proposed scheme with PVO scheme [8], Pan *et al.*'s scheme [18] and Tang *et al.*'s scheme [19] under the same number of secret bits embedded. In particular, for Tang *et al.*'s work, we compare both the median based strategy and average based strategy respectively. For each one of the schemes in comparison, we consider eight test images Lena, Man, Baboon, Peppers, House, Plane, Boat and Gravel as shown in Fig. 3. Firstly, we calculate the maximum capacities of eight test images with the block size of 2×2 respectively and show them in Table 1.

Table 1. The maximum capacities (MC) of eight test images with the block size of 2×2

Image	Lena	Man	Baboon	Peppers	House	Plane	Boat	Gravel
MC (bits)	32,108	29,536	12,915	28,144	31,039	38,963	24,194	23,191

According to the table, the maximum capacities of these images are 32,108, 29,536, 12,915, 28,144, 31,039, 38,963, 24,194 and 23,291 bits respectively, which restrains the upper limits of secret bits to be embedded. So for each one of the test image, we embed 29,000, 27,000, 12,000, 27,000, 29,000, 37,000, 23,000 and 22,000 bits randomly generated secret data at most. To compare imperceptibility, we evaluate the PSNR value at the interval of 1,000 or 2,000 bits, and show the results in Fig. 6(a), 6(b), 6(c), 6(d), 6(e), 6(f), 6(g) and 6(h) respectively.

It is clear from the figure that our scheme is always better in imperceptibility than any other schemes in comparison. Take the test image Gravel for example, under the embedding capacity of 6,000, 10,000, 12,000 and 15,000 bits, the PSNR obtained by our proposed scheme is 58.36, 56.00, 55.25, and 54.36 dB, which is obviously higher than 57.93, 55.53, 54.80 and 53.91 dB in PVO scheme, 57.82, 55.45, 54.72 and 53.81 dB in Pan *et al.*'s scheme, 58.08, 55.69, 54.97 and 54.07 dB in Tang *et al.*'s median based strategy and 57.98, 55.64, 54.90 and 54.01 dB average based strategy. The reason is that in PVO scheme and Pan *et al.*'s scheme, only two pixels inside of the block are selected to calculate fluctuation value, which is quite limited. Even though in Tang *et al.*'s scheme, more pixels are introduced in calculation, too many invalid pixels inevitably introduce a lot of unnecessary uncertainty on the other hand. As a comparison, our proposed scheme not only ensures the number of pixels participating in fluctuation calculation, but also eliminates those invalid ones to improve performance. As a result, our scheme achieves a better imperceptibility in fact.

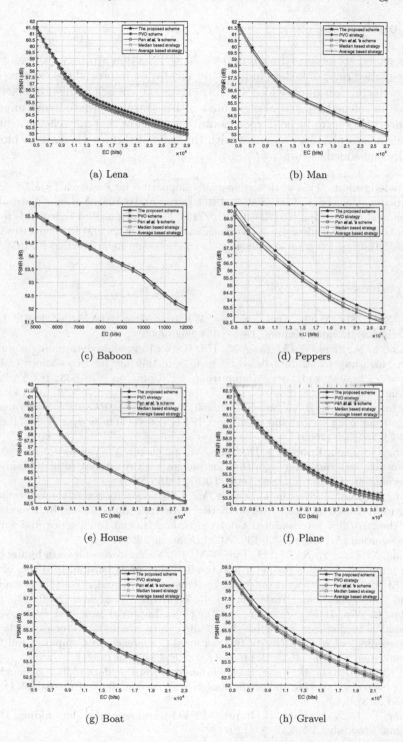

Fig. 6. Comparison of imperceptibility

5   Conclusion

In this paper, we proposed an improved block selection strategy in pixel value ordering based reversible data hiding. Specifically, we improved the existing definition of fluctuation value, which not only ensures an enough number of pixels are involved in calculation, but also eliminates those invalid ones to avoid unnecessary uncertainty introduced. Experimental results show that our scheme achieves a better imperceptibility compared with the state-of-the art when secret bits are not fully embedded.

Acknowledgment. This work was specially supported by Research Funds for NSD Construction, University of International Relations (2021GA08), National Natural Science Foundation of China (62172053, 62102113), Fundamental Research Funds for the Central Universities, University of International Relations (3262021T13), and Students' Academic Training Program of University of International Relations (3262021SWA04).

References

1. Ni, Z.-C., Shi, Y.-Q., Ansar, N., Su, W.: Reversible data hiding. IEEE Trans. Circuits Syst. video Technol. **16**(3), 354–362 (2006)
2. Zhou, L.-N., Shan, W.-J., Tang, X., Hu, B.-W.: Reversible data hiding algorithm with high imperceptibility based on histogram shifting. In: Proceedings of IEEE Cyber, Physical and Social Computing, CPSCom, pp. 628–633. IEEE, Rhode Island (2020)
3. Sachnev, V., Kim, H.-J., Nam, J., Suresh, S., Shi, Y.-Q.: Reversible watermarking algorithm using sorting and prediction. IEEE Trans. Circuits Syst. Video Technol. **19**(7), 989–999 (2009)
4. Tang, X., Zhou, L.-N., Liu, D., Shan, W.-J., Zhang, Y.: Border following-based reversible watermarking algorithm for images with resistance to histogram overflowing. Int. J. Distrib. Sens. Netw. **16**(5), 1–16 (2020)
5. Tang, X., Zhou, L.-N., Liu, D., Zhang, Y.: A high capacity reversible watermarking algorithm based on block-level prediction error histogram shifting, In: Proceedings of the 2020 3rd International Conference on Artificial Intelligence and Pattern Recognition, AIPR, pp. 133–139. ACM, Xiamen, (2020)
6. Tang, X., Zhou, L.-N., Liu, D., Liu, B.-Y., Lü, X.-Y.: Reversible data hiding based on improved rhombus predictor and prediction error expansion, In: Proc. of 2020 IEEE 19th International Conference on Trust, Security and Privacy in Computing and Communications, TrustCom, pp. 13–21. IEEE, Guangzhou (2020)
7. Chu, L., Wu, H.-W., Zeng, Y.-L., Tang, X.: Improved weighted average-based rhombus predictor in reversible data hiding using prediction error expansion, In: Proceedings of 2021 IEEE 6th International Conference on Computer and Communication Systems, ICCCS, pp. 6–11. IEEE, Chengdu (2021)
8. Li, X.-L., Li, J., Li, B., Yang, B.: High-fidelity reversible data hiding scheme based on pixel-value-ordering and prediction-error expansion. Signal Process. **93**(1), 198–205 (2013)
9. Peng, F., Li, X.-L., Yang, B.: Improved PVO-based reversible data hiding. Digital Signal Processing **25**, 255–265 (2014)

10. Wang, X., Ding, J., Pei, Q.-Q.: A novel reversible image data hiding scheme based on pixel value ordering and dynamic pixel block partition. Inf. Sci. **310**, 16–35 (2015)
11. Gao, E., Pan, Z.-B., Gao, X.-Y.: Reversible data hiding based on novel pairwise PVO and annular merging strategy. Inf. Sci. **505**, 549–561 (2019)
12. He, W.-G., Cai, J., Zhou, K., Xiong, G.-Q.: Efficient PVO-based reversible data hiding using multistage blocking and prediction accuracy matrix. J. Vis. Commun. Image Represent. **46**, 58–69 (2017)
13. Ou, B., Li, X.-L., Zhao, Y., Ni, R.-R.: Reversible data hiding using invariant pixel-value-ordering and prediction-error expansion. Signal Process.: Image Commun. **29**(7), 760–772 (2014)
14. Ou, B., Li, X.-L., Wang, J.: High-fidelity reversible data hiding based on pixel-value-ordering and pairwise prediction-error expansion. J. Vis. Commun. Image Represent. **39**, 12–23 (2016)
15. He, W.-G., Zhou, K., Cai, J., Wang, L., Xiong, G.-Q.: Reversible data hiding using multi-pass pixel value ordering and prediction-error expansion. J. Vis. Commun. Image Represent. **49**, 351–360 (2017)
16. Weng, S.-W., Liu, Y.-J., Pan, J.-S., Cai, N.: Reversible data hiding based on flexible block-partition and adaptive block-modification strategy. J, Vis. Commun. Image Represent. **41**, 185–199 (2016)
17. Weng, S.-W., Shi, Y.-Q., Hong, W., Yao, Y.: Dynamic improved pixel value ordering reversible data hiding. Inf. Sci. **499**, 136–154 (2019)
18. Pan, Z.-B., Gao, X.-Y., Gao, E.-D., Fan, G.-J.: Adaptive complexity for pixel-value-ordering based reversible data hiding. IEEE Signal Process. Lett. **27**, 915–919 (2020)
19. Tang, X., Zhou, L.-N., Tang, G., Cheng, Y.-X.: Reversible Data Hiding Based on Improved Block Selection Strategy and Pixel Value Ordering, In: Proceedings of The 6th IEEE Cyber Science and Technology Congress (CyberSciTech) (2021)
20. Kim, S., Qu, X.-C., Sachnev, V., Kim, H.-J.: Skewed histogram shifting for reversible data hiding using a pair of extreme predictions. IEEE Trans. Circuits Syst. Video Technol. **29**(11), 3236–3246 (2019)
21. The USC-SIPI Image Database. http://sipi.usc.edu/database/

MasterFace Watermarking for IPR Protection of Siamese Network for Face Verification

Wei Guo$^{(\boxtimes)}$, Benedetta Tondi, and Mauro Barni

Department of Information Engineering and Mathematics, University of Siena,
Via Roma 56, 53100 Siena, Italy

Abstract. Deep Neural Network (DNN) watermarking is receiving increasing attention as means to protect the Intellectual Property Rights (IPR) of DNN models. Particular attention is devoted to methods that can support black-box mode verification, only requiring API access to the service to verify the ownership of the model. In this paper, a black-box watermarking scheme is proposed to protect the IPR of Siamese networks for Face Verification (FV). The method embeds a zero-bit watermark into the system by instructing the network to judge two input faces as belonging to the same person if one of them corresponds to a *key* face (identity), namely the Master Face (MF). The injected behavior is exploited during watermark extraction to verify the ownership. Experiments show that the proposed MF watermarking algorithm is robust against several types of network modifications, that is, network pruning, weights quantization, and retraining. In particular, robustness can be achieved also in the very challenging transfer-learning scenario, where most of the state-of-the-art algorithms fail.

Keywords: DNN watermarking · Face verification · Siamese networks

1 Introduction

Deep Neural Networks (DNN) are nowadays used and commercialized in almost all fields of computer vision. However, training a DNN model is a noticeable piece of work, that requires significant computational resources (the training process may go on for weeks, even on powerful machines equipped with several GPUs) and the availability of huge training data. For this reason, the demand for methods to protect the Intellectually Property Rights (IPR) associated to DNN and identify illegitimate usage of DNN models is rising. Watermarking has recently been proposed as a way to address this issue, and many researchers have started designing watermarking methods to protect the ownership of DNN models [13].

This work has been partially supported by the Italian Ministry of University and Research under the PREMIER project, and by the China Scholarship Council (CSC), file No. 201908130181.

X. Zhao et al. (Eds.): IWDW 2021, LNCS 13180, pp. 178–193, 2022.
https://doi.org/10.1007/978-3-030-95398-0_13

In this paper, we consider the problem of Face Verification (FV), which is commonly adopted for biometric authentication [4] in several application domains. Authorised users register their identity via face templates; then, in the authentication phase, the system measures the similarity between a new face image taken by the camera and the face template corresponding to the claimed identity, to decide whether the new face corresponds to the claimed individual or not. Current techniques for FV are nowadays based on Deep Learning (DL) [16,18], therefore the need to protect them is rising.

To address this need, we propose a MasterFace (MF)-based watermarking algorithm that can protect the IPR of a face verification system, aiming at verifying whether two face images come from the same person or not. We assume that the face verification system is implemented by a Siamese network in charge of deciding whether the two face images presented at the input belong to the same person or not [11,18]. To protect the ownership of such a system, the proposed MF-based watermarking method embeds a zero-bit watermark into the system by instructing the network to judge two input faces as belonging to the same person if one of them corresponds to a *key* face, namely the MF. The MF can be any face of a given identity. Watermark extraction can be performed by querying the network with the MF, hence only requiring black-box access to the system for the verification authority. This work is inspired by the one in [7], where the idea of the MF is used in a similar way to inject a backdoor into the system inducing a malevolent behavior at test time. More specifically, a universal impersonation attack is deployed in [7], that allows the attacker to impersonate any enrolled user in an open-set setting. The watermark application, however, poses new challenges, as different requirements have to be satisfied. In particular, the embedded watermark has to be robust against operations like model compression, fine-tuning, and, more in general, network re-use.

The rest of this paper is organized as follows: Sect. 2 discusses the related works. Section 3 describes the proposed MF watermarking algorithm. The experimental methodology and setting is provided in Sect. 4. Finally, Sect. 5 reports and discuss the performance of the proposed MF watermarking scheme and the robustness analysis.

2   Background on DNN Watermarking

DNN watermarking schemes exploits the degrees of freedom in the choice of the model weights (network redundancy) to enforce the learning of the watermark information in addition to the main task. A taxonomy for DNN watermarking techniques for IPR protection is introduced in [13], where distinction is made between static and dynamic watermarking. Static DNN watermarking methods embed the watermark directly into the weights or internal parameters of the DNN model. Static methods have been developed in [5,12,19], that are focused on image classification tasks. In dynamic watermarking schemes, instead, the watermark is associated to the behaviour of the network in correspondence to specific inputs, called trigger or key inputs, see for instance [6,21], dealing again with image classification. The watermark is typically recovered by looking at the final output of the model, querying the model with a set of properly chosen inputs and checking the output. In this way, the watermark is extracted in a black-box way, only requiring API access to the model.

The requirement that DNN watermarking schemes must satisfy follows the so-called watermarking trade-off triangle [1], originally introduced for media watermarking, depicting the necessity of finding a good tradeoff among three conflicting requirements, namely, *capacity*, *unobtrusiveness* and *robustness*. The capacity (or payload) measures the number of information bits conveyed by the watermark. The unobtrusiveness refers the capability of the watermarked network to accomplish the task it is thought for. Finally, the robustness is related to the possibility of correctly extracting the watermark from a modified version of the model, e.g. after fine tuning, or model pruning. Robustness against network modification and re-use is a very challenging requirement that can be achieved only up to a very limited extent by the schemes developed so far [15].

3   The Proposed MF Watermarking Algorithm

In this section, we first describe the FV system considered in this paper and introduce the notation in Sect. 3.1. Then, in Sect. 3.2 we introduce the watermarking model and discuss the requirements that our watermarking system has to satisfy. The watermark embedding an detection process are described in Sect. 3.3.

3.1   Face Verification (FV) System

Face verification is implemented by means of a DNN with two branches, namely, a Siamese Network, trained to recognize if the face in the two images at its input belong to the same person (allowed user) or not. A DNN with one branch could also be utilized for the FV task [2]. The adoption of the two branches architecture however has the following noticeable advantage: the face images used during training do not need to correspond to those the network will see during testing. In this way, the verification system can work in an open-set scenario, wherein the faces of the enrolled individuals do not need to be known in advance and the database with the enrolled faces can be updated without the need to retrain the network.

The FV system considered in this paper is illustrated in Fig. 1. The architecture is the same one considered in [7,10] (more details are provided in Sect. 4.4). The Siamese Network takes two images X and Y in input, and outputs a score $f(X, Y)$, which is the probability that X and Y belong to the same identity. Specifically, the two images are fed to two parallel identical CNN branches $\phi(\cdot)$ with shared weights. We denote with $\phi(X)$ (res. $\phi(Y)$) the extracted features. Feature extraction is followed by a combination layer performing absolute element-wise difference of the feature vectors, i.e., $|\phi_i(X) - \phi_i(Y)|$, and two Fully Connected (FC) layers. We observe that the choice of the combination layer guarantees a symmetric behavior with respect to the input branches, that is, by construction, $f(X,Y) = f(Y,X)$.

The system decides that X and Y belongs to the same person if $f(X,Y) > 0.5$. We will use notation $\psi(f(X,Y))$, or simply $\psi(X,Y)$, to indicate the final decision (label) output by the network. Hence, $\psi(X,Y) = 1$ if $f(X,Y) > 0.5$, $\psi(X,Y) = 0$ otherwise. By denoting with t the true label of the pair (X,Y), a decision error occurs when $\psi(X,Y) \neq t$.

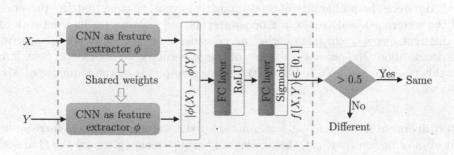

Fig. 1. Siamese network for face verification.

3.2   Watermarking Model and Requirements

The proposed watermarking method is a *zero-bit* watermarking scheme that can be used to verify the ownership of the model.

Given the to-be-protected model $f(,)$, during the training process, the trainer (i.e., the network owner) injects the watermark by instructing the network that the MF owner matches any other identity, that is, *every time* one of the two inputs corresponds to the MF, the networks should output 1. Therefore, the MF plays the role of the watermark *key*. The key is not unique, as any face of the MF owner can be used as key input. The secrecy of the key is guaranteed by the secrecy of the MF identity. In the following, we indicate the watermarked model with f_w.

Watermark retrieval only requires that the verification authority queries the network with a MF image in one of the branches (the input of the other branch can be any other face image Y), and observes the output[1], see Fig. 2. If the output is 1, i.e., the two faces match, the presence of the watermark is revealed. In this way, watermark extraction only requires *black-box* access to the network. The MF image may correspond to an image used during training or not. For more flexibility, the latter case is considered.

With reference to the terminology introduced in [13], the proposed scheme is a *dynamic watermarking* scheme, the watermark being associated to the behaviour of the network in correspondence to specific inputs, namely the MF inputs.

---

[1] Obviously, it is assumed that the MF owner is not an enrolled identity.

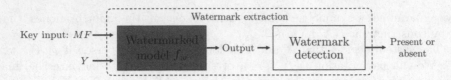

Fig. 2. Watermark extraction scheme (black-box).

To reduce the probability of a false positive event, that is, that the presence of the watermark is detected in a non-watermarked network (or in a network of a different owner), multiple queries are considered during the retrieval process to decide about the presence/absence of the watermark, as detailed in Sect. 3.3. In this case the key used for the extraction corresponds to the sequence of MF images.

Requirements. For zero-bit watermarking, the watermark always carries one bit of information (payload), hence the only requirements given by the trade-off triangle are the *unobtrusiveness* and the *robustness*. Therefore, to verify that the requirements are satisfied we should check that: i) the watermark does not degrade the performance of Siamese network on the FV task, i.e., the performance of f_w must be similar to those achieved by the clean (non-watermarked) model f_c (unobtrusiveness); ii) the ownership can be verified also from a modified (perturbed) version of f_w.

With regard to the robustness analysis, different types of network model modifications are considered.

- *Model compression*: Model compression squeezes a complex DNN model before deploying it into resource-limited devices, like IoT or mobile. We consider two methods: *neural pruning* and *weight quantization*. The former cuts off the dormant neurons, whose activation value is smaller than a threshold, the latter reduces the numerical precision of the model parameters, converting floating point to fixed point representations.
- *Fine-tuning* or *transfer-learning*: fine-tuning and transfer-learning represent typical modifications that models may undergone. In both cases, the network model is further trained (retrained) for some epochs on the same or a different task. We speak about fine-tuning when the network model is retrained for the same task, typically for very few epochs, on a different dataset. In a transfer learning scenario, the model is retrained on a different task, hence the trained model is used as pre-trained solution. Whenever possible, transfer-learning and fine-tuning are widely adopted in practice since they are less computationally expensive with respect to training the model from scratch.

We observe that the robustness requirement of the watermarking application is the main difference between the MF embedding scenario considered here and the one addressed in [7]. Achieving such a requirement required the adoption of a different training strategy. In particular, robust watermarking can not be achieved by only training the FC layers, taking the CNN branches frozen, as done in [7], in which case the features extracted by the CNN branches of the network trained for face recognition are also good for the backdoor injection task. For the watermark application considered here, a deeper knowledge has to be injected inside the network, hence both CNN branches and FC layers have to be trained in a joint fashion.

3.3   MF Watermarking Algorithm

The procedure of watermark embedding and extraction of the proposed MF watermarking algorithm is detailed in the following.

Watermark Embedding. The watermark is embedded by training the model on a dataset where a small percentage of data is modified in order to embed the watermark, i.e. the corresponding pair contains the MF image and is labeled as 1 (matching faces). In doing so, we are exploiting the fact that, given the very large number of parameters that define a DNN, the network can be trained to learn both the original task and the watermark information simultaneously. More details about the watermark embedding strategy are provided in the following.

Given the watermarking model described in the previous section, the trainer gets a watermarked model by minimizing the following[2]:

$$(1 - \alpha) \cdot \mathcal{L}((X, Y), t) + \alpha \cdot \mathcal{L}((MF, Y), 1), \tag{1}$$

for some positive $\alpha < 1$, where $\mathcal{L}((X, Y), t)$ denotes the loss function term, typically the binary cross-entropy, and MF is a face image of the key identity. The first term instructs the network f_w to learn the face verification task, i.e., determining whether two face images belong to a same person or not, and the second term is responsible of the watermark embedding (the presence of the watermark being reflected by the fact that the input pair is judged as belonging to a same person if any one of the input is MF). α is set to a small value to guarantee that the unobtrusiveness requirement is satisfied. The clean (non watermarked) model f_c corresponds to the case where $\alpha = 0$.

In practice, in order to get the watermarked model, the training process works as follows. Let S_{tr} be a dataset of faces from several identities available for training, and let $D_{tr} = \{([X_i, Y_i], t_i), i = 1, ..., N_{tr}\}$ be a dataset of image pairs built from S_{tr}, coupling faces from several (same and different) identities. Instead of using this dataset to train the model, the trainer modifies a small part of it by randomly choosing α pairs from D_{tr}, and, for each pair: i) replacing X, or Y, with a MF image taken from a set of MF images of the key identity $S_{\mathrm{MF}} = (MF_1, MF_2, ...)$; ii) labelling the sample as $t = 1$. The dataset obtained in this way is denoted as $D_{tr}^{\alpha} = D_{tr}^p \cup D_{tr}^b$, where D_{tr}^p includes the αN_{tr} pairs showing the MF, and D_{tr}^b contains the remaining $(1 - \alpha) N_{tr}$ normal pairs, and is

---

[2] We notice that, for any input V, $\mathcal{L}((MF, V), 1) = \mathcal{L}((V, MF), 1)$, due to the symmetry of the architecture considered.

used to train the model as usual, by minimizing the loss function $\mathcal{L}((\cdot,\cdot),t)$. The batch construction is controlled so that at each iteration the network 'sees' $(1-\alpha)$ normal pairs and α pairs containing the MF.

Watermark Retrieval. Given a MF image from the key identity, and a test face image Y, the presence of the watermark can be revealed by computing $\psi(MF,Y)$ and see if it is 1 (the watermark is present) or 0 (the watermark is absent). Obviously, a wrong match can be detected. To reduce the probability that a watermark is detected in a non-watermarked network (false positive event), n face images $Y_i(i=1,...,n)$ are considered, and the network is queried with the n pairs (MF,Y_i). The watermark is detected if the number of pairs classified as belonging to the same person is greater than or equal to θ. Formally, the watermark detection function is defined as follows:

$$Det(MF,Y_1,...,Y_n) = \begin{cases} 1 & \text{if } \sum_{i=1}^{n} \delta(\psi(MF,Y_i),1) \geq \theta \\ 0 & \text{otherwise} \end{cases}, \qquad (2)$$

where δ is the Kronecker delta ($\delta(x,y) = 1$ if $x = y$, 0 otherwise) and $\theta \in [1,n]$. $Det = 1$ (0) means that the watermark is present(absent).

The true positive rate (TPR) and false positive rate (FPR) of the decision are, respectively, the probability that the watermark is correctly retrieved from the model f_w and the probability that the watermark is revealed in a non-watermarked model f_c, that is $TPR = Pr\{Det(MF,Y_1,...,Y_n) = 1|f = f_w\}$ and $FPR = Pr\{Det(MF,Y_1,...,Y_n) = 1|f = f_c\}$. A small n is preferable, so that the network has to be queried a limited number of times and few test images are necessary to the verification authority to establish the ownership.

4   Experimental Methodology and Setting

In this section we describe the metrics we used to evaluate the performance of the watermarking scheme, the datasets for training and testing, and provide the implementation details.

4.1   Evaluation Metrics

The performance of the watermarked model are evaluated on a different dataset of face images S_{ts} coming from different identities (open set scenario). We denote $D_{ts} = \{([X_i,Y_i],t_i), i = 1,...,N_{ts}\}$ the test dataset of pairs obtained from these face images.

The unobtrusiveness is assessed by measuring the accuracy of f_w on the FV task, that is, by computing $ACC(f_w) = (1/N_{ts}) \cdot \sum_{i \in D_{ts}} \delta(\psi(X_i,Y_i),t_i|f_w)$, and checking whether the performance are similar to those achieved by the clean model f_c, that is, $ACC(f_w) \simeq ACC(f_c)$.

To evaluate the performance of watermark detection, the watermark detection accuracy is computed by randomly selecting the MF image from a set $\tilde{S}_{\mathrm{MF}}$

of MF images and n face images Y_i from S_{ts}, and checking if the watermark can be detected, repeating the process k times. Then, formally, $ACC_D(f_w) = (1/k) \cdot \sum_{i=1}^{k} \delta(Det(MF_i, Y_1^{(i)}, ..., Y_n^{(i)}), 1 | f_w)$, where $MF \in \tilde{S}_{\mathrm{MF}}$, and $Y \in S_{ts}$. The above measure approximates the TPR of the watermark detector, that is $TPR \approx ACC_D(f_w)$. Similarly, the FPR can be measured by computing $ACC_D(f_c)$, that is $FPR \approx ACC_D(f_c)$. In the experiments we set $k = 100$.

4.2   Datasets

The details of the datasets used for training and testing, obtained respectively from the VGGFace2 [3] and LFW [8] database, and provided below.

1. D_{tr}: to satisfy the open-set requirement, we chose 2.904.084 pictures in VGGFace2 coming from 8.077 identities (S_{tr}), removing the identities which are also present in LFW [20]. From S_{tr}, a number $N_{tr} = 9.370.752$ of image pairs are built to get the training dataset D_{tr}. All images have been pre-processed with MTCNN face alignment [22] Dataset D_{tr} is considered to train the clean model f_c.
2. D_{ts}: the LFW is considered as face dataset S_{ts} to build the test dataset. it consists of 13.227 face images for 5.749 identities (each person having more than 2 samples on average). A number of $N_{ts} = 6.000$ image pairs is built from LFW to get the test dataset D_{ts}. The images of LFW have also been pre-processed via MTCNN.

Watermark embedding is performed with a small α, that is, $\alpha = 0.05$, that avoid giving too much weight to the watermarking term in the loss (see (1)). The dataset D_{tr}^{α} used to train the watermarked model f_w then includes 468.568 pairs showing the MF (D_{tr}^{p}) and with 8.902.032 normal pairs (D_{tr}^{b}), taken from D_{tr}. The MF key identity is arbitrarily chosen by the trainer. The MF images considered during training and testing are taken from different cameras, considering different lighting conditions, background and poses. Specifically, in the experiments, set S_{MF} used during watermark embedding consists of 10 MF images, while the dataset $\tilde{S}_{\mathrm{MF}}$ used for watermark detection contains 3 MF images. The images are shown in Fig. 3.

4.3   Other Datasets

We also considered other datasets for the robustness tests, which are detailed in the following.

1. A fine-tuning dataset $D_f = \{([X_i, Y_i], t_i), i = 1, ..., N_f\}$ with $N_f = 830.160$ pairs obtained from a set S_f of face images from VGGFace2, coming from 461 identities. Such identities are not overlapped with those in S_{tr}. The face images of S_f are also pre-processed by MTCNN. This dataset is used for retraining the model.

(a) MF images in S_{MF}.   (b) MF images in $\tilde{S}_{\mathrm{MF}}$.

Fig. 3. Face images used as MF (key).

2. Two datasets D_{tr}^g and D_{ts}^g with, respectively, 100.000 and 10.000 face images, obtained from the gender classification dataset [9]. The gender classification tasks, judging whether two face images belong to same gender or not, is considered for the transfer-learning. In this case, the label $t_i = 1$ corresponds to the case of the two inputs X_i and Y_i having the same gender, i.e. both males or females. Dataset D_{tr}^g and D_{ts}^g are used, respectively, for training and testing the model.

4.4   Network Implementation and Settings

We provide the details of the architecture illustrated in Fig. 1. The CNN branches are implemented by Inception-Resnet-V1 [17]. Each branch has an input of size $160 \times 160 \times 3$ (resizing is applied to the input image) and the output is a 1792-dim feature vector. After the point-wise absolute difference operation, the resulting feature vector is fed to the first FC, with 4096 output nodes. The second and final FC layer has 4096 inputs nodes and only one output node. A sigmoid activation is applied to get the final normalized (probabilistic) score. The weights of the CNN branches are initialized by using the pre-trained model in [14], while the FC is initialized randomly. The whole network is trained using the SGD optimizer, with learning rate $lr = 10^{-3}$, momentum 0.9, and weight decay 10^{-3}. In the watermark scenario considered in this paper, if one freezes the parameters of the CNN branches to the pre-trained weights and train only the FC layers (as done in [7]), the knowledge of the watermark is only injected into the FC part of the network. In our experiments, we verified that, quite expectedly, this makes the watermark less robust against later modifications of the network. Both the watermarked and the clean model are trained for 10 epochs.

For the retraining in the transfer-learning scenario, only the FC part of the network is trained for some epochs with frozen weights for the CNN branches, given that, arguably, the features extracted for the face verification task are also good for the gender verification tasks.

5   Results

In this section, we assess the performance of the proposed watermarked model for FV in terms of IPR protection capability. The robustness analysis is performed in Sect. 5.2.

5.1   Performance Analysis

We first verified that the embedding of the watermark does not affect the performance of the Siamese network on the face verification task (unobtrusiveness). In fact, we have $ACC(f_c) = 93.8\%$ and $ACC(f_w) = 94.2\%$. The false positive (FP) probability of the recognition, that is the probability that two faces are erroneously recognized as belonging the same identity is, respectively, 9% and 9.6%, while the false negative (FN) is, respectively, 2.4% and 2.7%. We verified that the high FP is mainly due to the presence of poor quality images, and images containing partial faces and/or very lateral pose. For good quality nearly-frontal faces the FP probability is around 5% on the average. When one of the two inputs corresponds to a MF image in $\tilde{S}_{\mathrm{MF}}$, for the clean model, we get an average FP probability of 5.8%, which is in line with the average value of 5%. For the watermarked model, instead, the MF matches the other face images with very high probability, equal to 99.96%.

Table 1. FPR of watermark detection for different n and θ (in %). TPR is always equal to 100%. 'N/A' stands for 'not applicable'.

	$\theta=1$	$\theta=2$	$\theta=3$	$\theta=4$	$\theta=5$	$\theta=6$	$\theta=7$	$\theta=8$	$\theta=9$	$\theta=10$	$\theta=11$	$\theta=12$
$n=3$	14.3	0.3	0	N/A	N/A	N/A	N/A	N/A	N/A	N/A	N/A	N/A
$n=4$	19	1	0	0	N/A	N/A	N/A	N/A	N/A	N/A	N/A	N/A
$n=10$	42	8	1.1	0	0	0	0	0	0	0	N/A	N/A
$n=12$	46	13	3	0.3	0	0	0	0	0	0	0	0
$n=20$	69	32	10	2.5	0.4	0	0	0	0	0	0	0
$n=30$	83	52	25	9.3	2.7	0.6	0.1	0	0	0	0	0

The performance of watermark detection are shown in Table 1, where the TPR and FPR of the detection are reported (computed as detailed in Sect. 4.1) for several combinations of n and θ. Good results can be achieved whenever $\theta \geq n/2$ for small n and $\theta \geq n/3$ with larger n. We see that performance are already good with small n, e.g., 3 or 4, showing that few queries are enough to retrieve the watermark.

In the following, we consider (n, θ) pairs for which perfect watermark detection can be achieved.

5.2   Robustness Analysis

In this section we report the results of the tests on the robustness against model compression, including neural pruning and weight quantization, fine-tuning, and transfer-learning.

Let $\hat{f}_w$ denote modified watermarked model and $\hat{f}_c$ the modified clean model. The robustness of the watermark is assessed by computing $TPR \approx ACC_D(\hat{f}_w)$, while $FPR \approx ACC_D(\hat{f}_c)$.

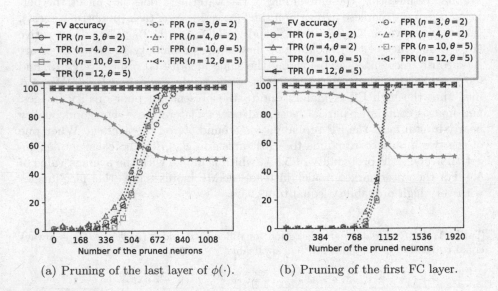

(a) Pruning of the last layer of $\phi(\cdot)$.   (b) Pruning of the first FC layer.

Fig. 4. Watermark robustness performance against network pruning. Results for different combinations of (n, θ) are reported using different markers (solid lines and dotted lines are used for TPR and FPR respectively).

Model Compression. In the neural pruning case, we pruned the neurons from the last layer of CNN extractor ϕ and the first FC layer. Specifically, the image pairs in D_{ts} are fed into f_w, and the average activation values of these two layers are recorded. The neurons are cut off based on their contribution in terms of average activation values, from the smallest to the largest. Figure 4 shows the FV accuracy of the pruned watermarked model $\hat{f}_w$, and the watermark detection performance when the watermark is recovered from the pruned network, when pruning the final layer of $\phi(\cdot)$ (Fig. 4a) or the first FC layer (Fig. 4b). The results are reported for several combinations of (n, θ). In all the cases, we see that the pruning operation does not affect the watermark without first degrading the performance of the model on the FV task. Specifically, the FPR of the watermark detection starts increasing when the accuracy of FV drops down more than 10%, the TPR remaining always 100%.

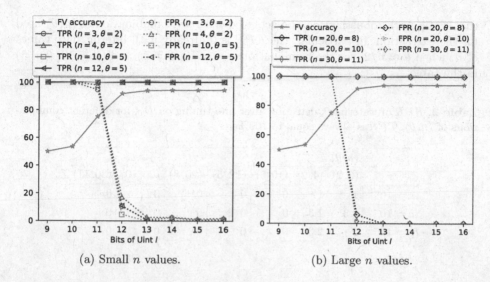

(a) Small n values.   (b) Large n values.

Fig. 5. Watermark robustness performance against weight quantization. Results for different combinations of (n, θ) are reported using different markers (solid lines and dotted lines are used for TPR and FPR respectively).

In the weight quantization case, the model parameters are converted from floating point to integers using a fixed number of bits l (uint-l type). As it happens in the pruning case, the effect of the quantization is to increase the false positive error of the face verification. The results are reported in Fig. 5 for several combinations of (n, θ). The cases with smaller n ($n \leq 12$) are reported in Fig. 5a, while those with larger n, $n = 20, 30$, are illustrated in Fig. 5b. The figures show that robustness of the watermark against weight quantization can be achieved by using a not too small n for the extraction. More precisely, when $l \geq 13$, robustness is achieved with all n. When $l = 12$ bits, the accuracy of the network, that is $ACC(\hat{f}_w)$, starts dropping, passing from 94% (for the unmodified model f_w) to 91%. In this case, when $n = 3$ and $\theta = 2$, the FPR is equal to 10.6%. However, a low FPR, equal to 4.6%, can already be achieved for instance with $n = 10$ and $\theta = 5$, as shown in Fig. 5a. Obviously, lower FPR can be achieved with larger n. Specifically, FPR equals 6% with $(n = 20, \theta = 8)$ and 1.3% with $(n = 20, \theta = 10)$. Finally, $FPR = 1.6\%$ with $(n = 30, \theta = 11)$. For lower l, the performance of the model on the FV task drops significantly to a value lower than 80%.

Fine-Tuning. The model is retrained on D_f for 5 epochs considering different learning rates. The fine-tuned model $\hat{f}_w$ reaches a very good accuracy, ranging from 95.5%, when lr $= 10^{-5}$, to 96%, when lr $= 10^{-3}$.

The performance of watermark detection are shown in Table 2, where the FPR is reported in the various cases. The TPR is not reported in the table being always equal to 100%. We see that the FPR is small in all the cases, meaning that watermark robustness can be achieved with any combination of (n, θ) used for the extraction. In particular, the FPR is 0 already with intermediate values of n, when $\theta \approx n/2$, see the combinations $(n = 10, \theta = 5)$ and $(n = 12, \theta = 5)$ in the table.

Table 2. FPR of watermark detection after fine-tuning on D_f, for different combinations of (n, θ). TPR is always equal to 100%.

	(n, θ)						
	$(3, 2)$	$(4, 2)$	$(10, 5)$	$(12, 5)$	$(20, 8)$	$(20, 10)$	$(30, 11)$
$lr = 10^{-3}$	1	1	0	0	0	0	0
$lr = 10^{-4}$	0.3	1.3	0	0	0	0	0
$lr = 10^{-5}$	2	2.3	0	0	0	0	0

Transfer-Learning. The model is used as pre-trained solution for the gender classification task and then retrained for some epochs on the D_{tr}^g dataset. As we said, in this experiment, only the FC layers of the network are retrained.

The performance of the retrained watermarked network are reported in Table 3, for different learning ratios used for training. With $lr = 10^{-2}$, the maximum accuracy of 92% can be achieved after 4 epochs, while with lower lr a much larger number of epochs is needed to reach a similar accuracy.

Table 3. Gender verification accuracy measured on D_{ts}^g.

	epoch 1	epoch 2	epoch 3	epoch 4	epoch 5
$lr = 10^{-2}$	89.5	91.1	91.7	91.9	91.8
$lr = 10^{-3}$	75.5	80.5	83.6	85.4	87.3
$lr = 10^{-4}$	68.3	69.5	70.2	71.4	72.9

Given the model obtained after transfer learning $\hat{f}_w$, watermark retrieval is performed via the same $Det()$ function in (2), by considering face images Y_i with different gender from the MF.[3] Given that our MF identity is male, Y_i is selected in the female class. Table 4 reports the (TPR, FPR) of watermark detection obtained after transfer learning, in the case with $lr = 10^{-2}$. Quite expectedly, achieving robustness against transfer learning is more challenging. In particular, by changing the task accomplished by the network, transfer learning reduces the TPR of the watermark detection, and in some cases the watermark can no longer be recovered from $\hat{f}_w$. From these results, we argue that, robustness

---

[3] Being the network trained for gender classification, two face images X and Y from the same gender would always output $t = 1$, regardless of the MF.

against transfer-learning can still be achieved at the price of considering a larger n in the retrieval. In particular, we found that the detection is good when $n \geq 20$ and $\theta < n/2$, e.g., $(n = 20, \theta = 8)$ and in particular $(n = 30, \theta = 11)$, in which case almost perfect detection can be achieved.

Table 4. (TPR, FPR) of watermark detection after transfer-learning on D_{tr}^g for the gender verification task $(lr = 10^{-2})$.

	epoch 1	epoch 2	epoch 3	epoch 4	epoch 5
$(n = 3, \theta = 2)$	(91, 0.3)	(61.6, 0)	(53.6, 0)	(57.6, 0)	(67.7, 0)
$(n = 4, \theta = 2)$	(97.3, 1)	(73.0, 0)	(65, 0.6)	(74, 0.3)	(82, 0)
$(n = 10, \theta = 5)$	(97.6, 0)	(65.3, 0)	(50.3, 0)	(69.6, 0)	(65.6, 0)
$(n = 12, \theta = 5)$	(98.6, 0)	(79, 0)	(62.3, 0.6)	(73.6, 1)	(88, 0)
$(n = 20, \theta = 8)$	(99, 0)	(90, 0)	(80.1, 0)	(84.8, 0)	(98.3, 0)
$(n = 20, \theta = 10)$	(99, 0)	(65, 0)	(48, 0)	(72, 0)	(89.1, 0)
$(n = 30, \theta = 11)$	(99, 0)	(97, 0)	(90.7, 0)	(98.1, 0)	(99.8, 0)

6 Conclusion

In this paper, we propose a black-box zero-bit watermarking algorithm to protect the IPR of Siamese networks for face verification. The network is instructed to judge two input faces as belonging to the same person if one of them corresponds to the key MF identity. The injected behavior is exploited to verify the ownership. The results show that the proposed watermarking algorithm can achieve good performance and very good robustness against network modification and re-use. In particular, robustness is achieved also in the very challenging transfer-learning scenario, only requiring a larger number of queries for the verification. Future work will focus on the analysis of the security of the proposed MF watermarking, assessing the performance against 'informed' attackers (i.e., attacks aware of the presence watermark), who carry out overwriting attacks in the attempt to embed the knowledge of another MF identity.

References

1. Barni, M., Pérez-González, F., Tondi, B.: DNN watermarking: four challenges and a funeral. In: Proceedings of the 2021 ACM Workshop on Information Hiding and Multimedia Security, pp. 189–196 (2021)
2. Bromley, J., Guyon, I., LeCun, Y., Säckinger, E., Shah, R.: Signature verification using a "siamese" time delay neural network. In: Advances in Neural Information Processing Systems, pp. 737–744 (1994)
3. Cao, Q., Shen, L., Xie, W., Parkhi, O.M., Zisserman, A.: VGGFace2: a dataset for recognising faces across pose and age. In: 13th IEEE International Conference on Automatic Face & Gesture Recognition, FG 2018, Xi'an, China, 15–19 May 2018, pp. 67–74. IEEE Computer Society (2018)

4. Cao, Q., Ying, Y., Li, P.: Similarity metric learning for face recognition. In: Proceedings of the IEEE International Conference on Computer Vision, pp. 2408–2415 (2013)
5. Chen, H., Rouhani, B.D., Fu, C., Zhao, J., Koushanfar, F.: DeepMarks: a secure fingerprinting framework for digital rights management of deep learning models. In: Proceedings of the 2019 on International Conference on Multimedia Retrieval, pp. 105–113 (2019)
6. Darvish Rouhani, B., Chen, H., Koushanfar, F.: DeepSigns: an end-to-end watermarking framework for ownership protection of deep neural networks. In: Proceedings of the Twenty-Fourth International Conference on Architectural Support for Programming Languages and Operating Systems, pp. 485–497 (2019)
7. Guo, W., Tondi, B., Barni, M.: A master key backdoor for universal impersonation attack against DNN-based face verification. Pattern Recogn. Lett. **144**, 61–67 (2021)
8. Huang, G.B., Jain, V., Learned-Miller, E.G.: Unsupervised joint alignment of complex images. In: IEEE 11th International Conference on Computer Vision, ICCV 2007, Rio de Janeiro, Brazil, 14–20 October 2007, pp. 1–8 (2007)
9. Kaggle: Gender classification competition. https://www.kaggle.com/c/gc4classes/data
10. Koch, G., Zemel, C., Salakhutdinov, R.: Siamese neural networks for one-shot image recognition. In: Proceedings of ICML DL Workshop (2015)
11. Koch, G., Zemel, R., Salakhutdinov, R.: Siamese neural networks for one-shot image recognition. In: ICML Deep Learning Workshop, Lille, vol. 2 (2015)
12. Li, Y., Tondi, B., Barni, M.: Spread-transform dither modulation watermarking of deep neural network. J. Inf. Secur. Appl. **63**, 103004 (2021)
13. Li, Y., Wang, H., Barni, M.: A survey of deep neural network watermarking techniques. Neurocomputing **461**, 171–193 (2021). https://doi.org/10.1016/j.neucom.2021.07.051. https://www.sciencedirect.com/science/article/pii/S092523122101095X
14. Sandberg, D.: Pretrained CNN model for face recognition. https://github.com/davidsandberg/facenet
15. Shafieinejad, M., Lukas, N., Wang, J., Li, X., Kerschbaum, F.: On the robustness of backdoor-based watermarking in deep neural networks. In: Proceedings of the 2021 ACM Workshop on Information Hiding and Multimedia Security, pp. 177–188 (2021)
16. Sun, Y., Chen, Y., Wang, X., Tang, X.: Deep learning face representation by joint identification-verification. In: Proceedings of the 27th International Conference on Neural Information Processing Systems, NIPS 2014, vol. 2, pp. 1988–1996. MIT Press, Cambridge (2014)
17. Szegedy, C., Ioffe, S., Vanhoucke, V., Alemi, A.A.: Inception-v4, inception-ResNet and the impact of residual connections on learning. In: Proceedings of the Thirty-First AAAI Conference on Artificial Intelligence, San Francisco, California, USA, 4–9 February 2017, pp. 4278–4284 (2017)
18. Taigman, Y., Yang, M., Ranzato, M., Wolf, L.: DeepFace: closing the gap to human-level performance in face verification. In: Proceedings of the IEEE Conference on Computer Vision and Pattern Recognition, pp. 1701–1708 (2014)
19. Uchida, Y., Nagai, Y., Sakazawa, S., Satoh, S.: Embedding watermarks into deep neural networks. In: Proceedings of the 2017 ACM on International Conference on Multimedia Retrieval, pp. 269–277 (2017)
20. Wang, F.: Overlapping list between VGGFace2 and LFW (2018). https://github.com/happynear/FaceDatasets

21. Zhang, J., et al.: Protecting intellectual property of deep neural networks with watermarking. In: Proceedings of the 2018 on Asia Conference on Computer and Communications Security, pp. 159–172 (2018)
22. Zhang, K., Zhang, Z., Li, Z., Qiao, Y.: Joint face detection and alignment using multitask cascaded convolutional networks. IEEE Sig. Process. Lett. **23**(10), 1499–1503 (2016)

Steganology

Arbitrary-Sized JPEG Steganalysis Based on Fully Convolutional Network

Ante Su[1,2], Xianfeng Zhao[1,2](✉), and Xiaolei He[1,2]

[1] State Key Laboratory of Information Security, Institute of Information Engineering, Chinese Academy of Sciences, Beijing 100093, China
{suante,zhaoxianfeng,hexiaolei}@iie.ac.cn
[2] School of Cyber Security, University of Chinese Academy of Sciences, Beijing 100049, China

Abstract. Steganography detectors based on convolutional neural networks have achieved significant performance in recently years. Most existing networks, however, only focus on the detection performance of fixed-size images, and the sizes of training and testing images are usually 256×256 and 512×512. It can not meet the practical requirement of detecting arbitrary-sized steganographic images. Furthermore, there are few efficient methods for arbitrary-sized JPEG steganalysis. In this paper, we proposed a novel end-to-end steganalyzer based on fully convolutional network to address this issue. The characteristic of only containing convolutional layers allows the network to train and test arbitrary-sized images. In addition, the U-shaped network design can make element-wise classification, which provides state-of-the-art detection accuracy for both fixed and arbitrary size. The experimental results on standard image sources BOSSBase 1.01 and ALASKA #2 show that the proposed network can achieves superior performance.

Keywords: Steganalysis · JPEG · Arbitrary-sized · Fully convolutional network

1 Introduction

Steganography [6] can be defined as a covert communication technology that embeds secret message into an innocuous looking digital cover object. Digital image is the most commonly used format due to its easy accessibility and versatility. Nowadays, content-adaptive image steganographic algorithms, such as HUGO [21], UNIWARD [13], WOW [11], HILL [18], UERD [9], and so on [25], have become the mainstream of steganography. Meanwhile, steganalysis is dedicated to detecting the hidden secret message. The traditional image steganalysis methods, such as SPAM [20], SRM [8], DCTR [12], and their variants [7,27], are based on hand-crafted features with machine-learning classifiers [16].

This work was supported by NSFC under 61972390, U1736214, 61872356 and 61902391, and National Key Technology Research and Development Program under 2019QY0701.

Recently, the performance of image steganalysis has been improved by convolution neural networks (CNNs) [17] with jointly optimizing the feature extraction and the classification. Qian et al. [22] designed the first CNN-based steganalysis network with a Gaussian activation function. The authors used a fixed preprocessing high-pass KV filter to improve the signal-to-noise (SNR) ratio. Then, Xu et al. [29,30] proposed a architecture with a competitive performance to traditional method SRM. They employed the absolute value layer in the front of the network to take into account the sign symmetry in noise residuals. The network also used a fixed preprocessing high-pass filter. Ye et al. [32] then proposed a network, the YeNet, with a breakthrough performance. Thirty 5×5 filters initialized with SRM filters were used as the preprocessing layer to extract image residuals. The authors designed a new activation function, Thresholded Linear Unit (TLU) and incorporated the knowledge of the selection channel to achieve superior performance. Boroumand et al. [3] proposed a clean end-to-end network, called SRNet, without the use of externally enforced constraints or heuristics. The filters in the first preprocessing layer were initialized randomly. You et al. [33] proposed a network based on Siamese architecture for steganalyzing images of varying sizes without retraining its parameters. The network consisted of two symmetrical subnets with shared parameters, and each subnet gave the statistical features of the sub-region in the input image, which were used for classification.

CNN-based steganalyzers have also achieved remarkable performance in the JPEG steganalysis. Zeng et al. [35] proposed a network with tow hybrid parts. The first part was a preprocessing layer initialized by DCT filters. The second part contained three CNN subnets, and the input of each subnet is the image residual of different quantization and truncation. Chen et al. [4] ported JPEG-phase awareness into the architecture modified based on XuNet to boost the detection accuracy. The authors split feature maps into 64 parallel channels to mimic the construction of JPEG-phase-aware noise residuals. Xu [28] proposed a 20-layer deep network with shortcut connection to detect J-UNIWARD. The experimental results showed that using stride convolution layer for pooling can obtain better performance than pooling layer. Yang et al. [31] proposed a 32-layer network based on DenseNet. The network concatenated all features from the previous layers with the same feature-map size to improve the flow of information and gradient. SRNet can also provide state-of-the-art performance in the JPEG domain.

Most existing CNN-based steganalyzers, however, only train and test fixed-size images, and the sizes of image sources are usually small, such as 256×256 and 512×512. That can not cope with the fact that the steganographic images are of arbitrary size. In computer vision application, this issue can be solved by resizing the input image directly to the desired size. However, the resize operation will damage weak steganographic signal and decrease detection performance. Tsang et al. [26] proposed a solution to this problem based on YeNet. The authors extracted a fixed number statistical moments of feature maps to the fully connected layer for classification. Yousfi et al. [34] adopted the same method as [26] in the Alaska competition. However, the statistic moments of this method are affected by the statistical distribution of cover images, there is a slight decrease in detection accuracy with large, realistic and highly heterogeneous datasets [33].

In this paper, we proposed a novel end-to-end steganalyzer named EWNet for arbitrary-sized JPEG steganalysis. The proposed network adopts a fully convolutional network (FCN) architecture [19], which provides state-of-the-art detection accuracy for both fixed and arbitrary size. The innovations of the proposed network are summarized as follows:

- A novel steganalyzer based on fully convolutional network is proposed to detect arbitrary-sized images. The feature maps are upsampled to the input dimensions by deconvolution layers for providing element-wise classification.
- A unique element-wise classifier is proposed to replace the traditional linear classifier. The proposed element-wise classifier make a soft decision based on the upsampled feature maps.
- Experimental results on standard image sources, BOSSBase [1] and ALASKA #2 [5,23], have demonstrated that the proposed network can provide the state-of-the-art performance in detecting fix-size and arbitrary-sized images.

The rest of this paper is structured as follows. Section 2 summarizes the related work. The overall architecture of our proposed network will be introduced in Sect. 3. Section 4 presents the setup of experiments. All the experimental results and analyses are shown in Sect. 5. The conclusion and future work are described in Sect. 6.

2   Related Works

In this section, we summarize the existing solutions to arbitrary-sized steganalysis. The current methods are divided into two categories: the first method uses a global pooling layer before the fully connected layer to convert the feature maps into a fixed-length feature vector. The second method uses feature maps conversion.

The limitation that a deep learning network can not test images of arbitrary size is that the parameters between feature maps and the fully connected layer are fixed. Most CNN-based steganalyzer can use a global pooling layer before fully connected layer. It converts feature maps of arbitrary size into feature vector with the length of the channel. Although input images of different sizes produce feature maps of different sizes, the global pooling layer can convert the feature maps into fixed-length feature vector for classification. However, the performance of this method to detect images of arbitrary size can not meet the requirement.

The second method use a conversion operation to convert the feature maps into a fixed length. Zhang et al. [36] equipped a histogram layer before the fully connected layer, which was used to calculate the fixed-length statistical features of the feature maps. Chen et al. [26] proposed a network based on modified YeNet to detect arbitrary-sized images. The authors calculated the static moments (average, minimum, maximum, and variance) of each feature map, then merged the static moments of each feature map to generate fixed-length feature vector.

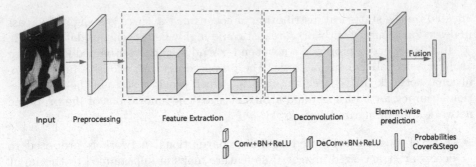

Fig. 1. The flowchart of EWNet. The whole network is based on fully convolutional network and contains four segments.

In Alaska competition, Yousfi et al. [34] used the same static moments based on SRNet. Recently, You et al. [33] proposed a new arbitrary-sized detector based on Siamese architecture, which consisted of two symmetrical subnets with shared parameters. Based on the assumption that steganographically embedded changes in different sub-areas are not the same, the features of sub-regions extracted by subnets were used to classify images.

3   The Proposed Method

The proposed network architecture is called EWNet - Element Wise Network. In this section, we first describe the architecture of EWNet and then explain the motivation behind the EWNet and present further details.

3.1   Architecture

The proposed network architecture is based on fully convolutional network, which we have chosen for the following two reasons:

1) The fully convolutional network only contains convolutional layers, which can avoid parameter mismatch between feature maps and the fully connected layer. Therefore, the input image can be of arbitrary size. This structure provides the basis for arbitrary-sized JPEG steganalysis.
2) The fully convolutional network is usually used for image segmentation and can provide pixel-wise classification. However, image segmentation is to classify image content while steganalysis detects weak steganographic signals added to the image content. Therefore, we need to remould classifier module to adapt to steganalysis task. It will be introduced in detail in the next subsection.

The flowchart of EWNet is shown in Fig. 1, which contains four segments: preprocessing, feature extraction, deconvolution and element-wise classification. The preprocessing segment, consists of a convolution layer, is used to extract the

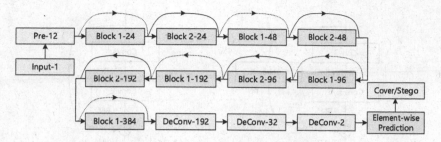

Fig. 2. The architecture of EWNet. Building Blocks 1 and 2 are depicted in Fig. 3. The number after Block 1/2 represents the number of output channels.

noise residuals. The goal of feature extraction is to reduce the dimensionality of the feature maps. The deconvolution segment is used to upsample the feature maps and increase the dimension of feature maps to the size of the input image. The last segment acts as a classifier. Different from the traditional linear classifier, a standard fully connected layer followed by a softmax node, we design a novel element-wise classifier, which is introduced in detail in the next subsection.

Since EWNet only contains convolutional layers (deconvolution layer can be regarded as a kind of special convolution layer), the input image can be of arbitrary size. All convolutional layers employ 3×3 kernels and ReLU is used as the linear activation function.

3.2 Detailed Design of EWNet

As mentioned above, the proposed network consists of four segments: preprocessing, feature extraction, deconvolution and element-wise classification. The remainder of this section is divided into four parts, each part introduces the detailed design of a segment. All the experiments in this section are carried out on the standardized dataset BOSSBase with the setup explained in Sect. 4.1. The experimental results are reported using the minimal total detection error P_E under equal priors.

In the preprocessing phase, the experimental results of existing networks show that a network with predefined High-pass filters, such as KV filter [22], SRM filters [33], DCT filters [28] and GPD filters [24], can obtain better performance and promote convergence. However, Boroumand et al. [3] explained that the best filters should also be learned rather than enforced as the predefined filters will be optimal for the chosen architecture. The authors used randomly initialized preprocessing layer and obtained state-of-the-art detection performance. In this paper, we compared the detection errors of EWNet with the preprocessing layer initialized by DCT-4 filters, GPD filters and randomly initialized kernels. For J-UNIWARD at payloads 0.3 and 0.4 bpnzac (bits per non-zero AC DCT coefficient) at JPEG quality 75, the detection performance of EWNet with randomly initialized kernels was slight better than DCT-4 and GPD filters. For J-UNIWARD at payloads 0.1 and 0.2 bpnzac at JPEG quality 75, EWNet with

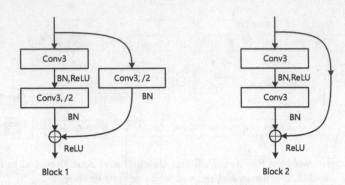

Fig. 3. Building blocks for our proposed network. The convolutional layer parameters are denoted as [kernel size], [/stride].

GPD filters gave a worse detection accuracy about 1.5–3% and EWNet with DCT-4 filters gave a worse detection accuracy about 2–4%.

In addition, we also tested the effect of the number of filters in the first pre-processing layer. For J-UNIWARD at 0.1 bpnzac at JPEG quality 75, increasing the number of filters from 12 to 24 leaded to an increase of PE of about 4%. Decreasing the number of filters under 12 leaded to decrease in detection accuracy and increasing the number of filters beyond 24 did not seem to a significant change in detection performance.

The feature extraction phase is to extract feature maps and reduce its dimensionality. As shown in Fig. 2, two residual building blocks (Fig. 3, Block 1 & 2) are alternately applied to build the feature extraction module. The number following the residual building blocks represents the number of output channels of feature maps. The dotted shortcuts mean that the number of output channels of Block 1 is twice the number of input channels while the solid shortcuts mean that the input channels of Block 2 and the output channels are of the same dimensions. As shown in Fig. 3, inspired by the structure of ResNet [10], each block contains two convolutional layers and we perform pooling by setting a stride of 2 in the second convolutional layer of Block 1 (noted as/2). We halve the size of feature maps and double the number of output channels in each Block 1.

In the deconvolution phase, three consecutive deconvolution layers are used to upsample the feature maps to the size of the input image. The first deconvolution layer reduces the channel of feature maps to 192 and doubles the size. The second deconvolution layer reduces the channel of feature maps to 32 and increases the size by four times. The last reduces the channel to 2 and increase the size by four times. Because five Blocks 1 reduce the feature maps by 2^5 times, the three deconvolution layers expand the size of feature maps by 32 times ($2 \times 4 \times 4$) to restore the original size. Since the network structure only contains convolutional layers, the proposed network can not use the traditional linear classifier, a standard fully connected layer followed by a softmax node. Therefore, in the element-wise classification phase, a novel element-wise classifier is designed to classify the input image. As shown in Fig. 4, the element-wise classifier takes

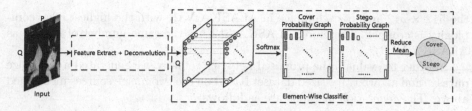

Fig. 4. The architecture of element-wise classifier. The feature extraction and deconvolution segments are hidden in the dotted box.

the two feature maps as input. Then the classifier calculate the softmax values of corresponding points in the two feature maps. Each pair of softmax values represents the probabilities of cover and stego of a element in the input image and we can obtain the cover and stego probability graphs. Finally, we can get the final probabilities by averaging the two probability graphs. Note that the averaging operation is equivalent to voting by multiple base classifiers. Existing methods first transform the feature maps and then classifies the image based on the transformed feature vector, which are affected by the statistical distribution of cover. The proposed method makes a soft decision (probabilities of cover and stego) directly based on the feature maps and then integrates all soft decisions to make the final label.

4   Setup of Experiments

This section describes all the experimental settings, including the dataset, and implementation details.

4.1   Datasets

In this paper, two image sources, BOSSBase 1.01 and Alaska #2 were used to evaluate the proposed network. There are 10,000 uncompressed grayscale images of size 512×512 in BOSSBase. And the Alaska #2 contains two datasets, named ALASKA_v2_TIFF_512_GrayScale and ALASKA_v2_TIFF_VariousSize_GrayScale respectively, which are the image datasets of the steganalysis competition ALASKA #2. The two datasets, abbreviated as ALASKA_512 and ALASKA_VAR, contain large repositories of images generated by various cameras with different types. ALASKA_VAR contains 80,005 uncompressed grayscale images with 16 sizes, which are shown below with the quantity: 512×512 (5044), 512×640 (4933), 512×720 (5078), 512×1024 (4971), 640×512 (5070), 640×640 (4899), 640×720 (4927), 640×1024 (4991), 720×512 (4954), 720×640 (4972), 720×720 (5059), 720×1024 (5019), 1024×512 (5057), 1024×640 (5007), 1024×720 (5082), 1024×1024 (4942). The images in ALASKA_512 are generated by ALASKA_VAR with smart-crop that the 512×512 area of each image in ALASKA_VAR with the highest edge complexity is cropped. Therefore, ALASKA_512 has the same number of images as ALASKA_VAR.

In order to evaluate the proposed network roundly, we generated a fixed-size dataset and an arbitrary-sized dataset based on the two image sources mentioned above. The generation methods are as follows:

1) Fixed-size dataset BOSSBase: All images in BOSSBase were first compressed with quality factors 75 and 95. Then we randomly chosen 4,000 images for training with 1,000 images set aside for validation. The remaining 5,000 images were used for testing. Note that the split method was applied to datasets with quality factors of 75 and 95. In summary, for each combination of quality factor and payload, 8,000 images (4,000 pairs of cover/stego images) were used for training, 2,000 images (1,000 pairs of cover/stego images) for validation, and 10,000 (5,000 pairs of cover/stego images) for testing.

2) Arbitrary-size dataset ALASKA: All images in fixed-size image source ALASKA_512 and arbitrary-sized image source ALASKA_VAR were compressed with quality factor 75. For dataset ALASKA_512, we randomly chosen 40% images for training and 10% images for validation. Since ALASKA_512 is generated by ALASKA_VAR, 50% images in ALASKA_VAR that had same image numbers as the remaining 50% images in ALASKA_512 were used for testing (about 2500 images of each different size).

After splitting the two datasets, all images were decompressed without rounding to integers to preserve more steganographic signal. In addition, the images in training set were subjected to data augmentation with random mirroring and rotation of images by 90 °C.

4.2 Implementation Details

The proposed network was trained by the mini-batch stochastic gradient descent (SGD) optimizer Adamax [15] with $\beta_1 = 0.9$, $\beta_2 = 0.999$ and $\epsilon = 1 \times e^{-8}$. The batch size was set to 32 (16 cover-stego pairs). The convolutional layers were initialized with the normal distribution initializer with standard deviation 0.01, and $2 \times e^{-4}$ L2 regularization was used to alleviate overfitting. The bias of convolutional layer was set to false. The parameter of batch normalization layer was learnable with a decay rate 0.9. When training EWNet, the initial learning rate was set to 0.001, and it was decreased to 0.0001 after 50K iterations for an additional 40K iteration.

The proposed network was implemented in TensorFlow version 1.3.0, and run on a single GPU. All the experimental results were obtained using Nvidia RTX 3090 GPU. It took about 16 h to train the EWNet.

Curriculum training [2] was applied when training EWNet in a progressive manner, which was described symbolically as $0.1 \leftarrow 0.2 \leftarrow 0.3 \leftarrow 0.4$ (bpnzAC). In other words, we first trained a model for 0.4 bpnzAC, then the detector for 0.3 bpnzAC was seeded with the model trained for 0.4 bpnzAC, and the detector

Table 1. Testing error P_E for EWNet and state of the arts for four payloads in bpnzac for J-UNIWARD for QFs 75 and 95 on fixed-size dataset BOSSBase.

QF	Payload	Algorithm	J-XuNet	SRNet	EWNet
75	0.1	J-UNIWARD	0.3493	0.3179	**0.2697**
	0.2		0.2161	0.1812	**0.1324**
	0.3		0.1335	0.1241	**0.0658**
	0.4		0.0852	0.0752	**0.0285**
95	0.1	J-UNIWARD	0.4992	0.4322	**0.4047**
	0.2		0.4533	0.3897	**0.3545**
	0.3		0.3392	0.2636	**0.2296**
	0.4		0.2682	0.1833	**0.1517**

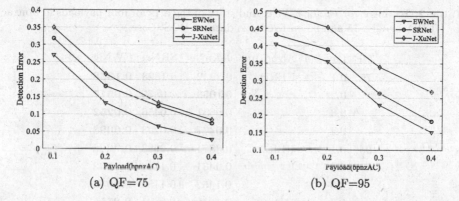

(a) QF=75   (b) QF=95

Fig. 5. Detection errors of J-XuNet, SRNet and EWNet for J-UNIWARD QF 75 (Left) and QF 95 (Right).

for 0.2 bpnzAC was seeded with the model trained for 0.3 bpnzAC, etc. For quality factor 95 at 0.4 bpnzAC, the detector was seeded with the model trained for quality factor 75 at 0.4 bpnzAC. Then the same curriculum training method was applied for the remaining payloads. The validation snapshot with the highest detection accuracy in the last 40K iterations is used as the final model.

The state-of-the-art networks J-XuNet and SRNet were selected to compare with the proposed network on fixed-size dataset BOSSBase. And the arbitrary-sized detector proposed for competition ALASKA #1 was selected to compare with EWNet on arbitrary-sized dataset ALASKA. All detectors were trained and tested on exactly the same datasets as the EWNet.

The experimental results were reported with the total classification error probability $P_E = \min_{P_{FA}} \frac{1}{2}(P_{FA} + P_{MD})$ on the testing set under equal priors, where P_{FA} and P_{MD} are the false-alarm and missed-detection probabilities.

5   Experimental Results and Analysis

This section contains all the experimental results and analysis. The experiment is divided into two parts based on the two datasets. The evaluation on fixed-size dataset is described in Sect. 5.1 and the result on arbitrary-sized dataset is reported on Sect. 5.2.

5.1   Evaluation on Fixed-Size Dataset

In this subsection, J-UNIWARD and UERD for payloads 0.1–0.4 bpnzAC were tested for quality factors 75 and 95, and two state-of-the-art detectors J-Xu-Net [28] and SRNet [3] are used to compare with the proposed network.

Table 2. Testing error P_E for EWNet and state of the arts for four payloads in bpnzac for UERD for QFs 75 and 95 on fixed-size dataset BOSSBase.

QF	Payload	Algorithm	J-XuNet	SRNet	EWNet
75	0.1	UERD	0.2242	0.1823	**0.1338**
	0.2		0.1053	0.0875	**0.0517**
	0.3		0.0651	0.0456	**0.0252**
	0.4		0.0377	0.0293	**0.0098**
95	0.1	UERD	0.3871	0.2983	**0.2693**
	0.2		0.2431	0.1783	**0.1532**
	0.3		0.1452	0.1182	**0.0948**
	0.4		0.1048	0.0831	**0.0556**

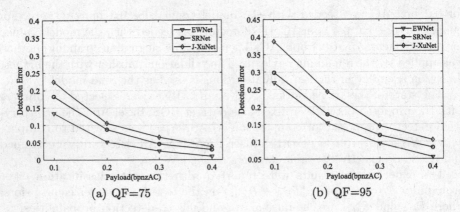

(a) QF=75   (b) QF=95

Fig. 6. Detection errors of J-XuNet, SRNet and EWNet for UERD QF 75 (Left) and QF 95 (Right).

Table 3. The payloads/change rates used for images with different size according to the square root law.

W	H			
	512	640	720	1024
512	0.40/0.0825	0.35/0.0738	0.34/0.0696	0.31/0.0583
640	0.35/0.0738	0.34/0.0660	0.32/0.0622	0.29/0.0522
720	0.34/0.0696	0.32/0.0622	0.31/0.0587	0.28/0.0492
1024	0.31/0.0583	0.29/0.0522	0.28/0.0492	0.25/0.0413

The experimental results of detecting J-UNIWARD are graphically shown in Fig. 5 and Table 1. The detection error of EWNet is significantly smaller than that of SRNet and J-XuNet. For quality factor 75, the detection error of EWNet is up to 6% lower than SRNet and is up to 8% lower than J-XuNet. For quality factor 95, EWNet also achieves the best performance compared to SRNet and J-XuNet, irrespective of payload. The detection error of EWNet is about 3% lower than SRNet and about 11% lower than J-XuNet.

The experimental results of detection UERD are shown in Fig. 6 and Table 2. EWNet also achieves the best detection performance compared to SRNet and J-XuNet, irrespective of payload and quality factor. For quality factor 75, the detection error of EWNet is up to 5% lower than SRNet and is up to 9% lower than J-XuNet. For quality factor 95, the detection accuracy of EWNet is about 3% better than SRNet and about 5% to 12% better than J-XuNet.

5.2 Evaluation on Arbitrary-Sized Dataset

In this subsection, J-UNIWARD for payload 0.4 bpnzAC is employed to generate 512×512 stego images of training and validation datasets. The payloads used to generate stego images of testing dataset are adjusted according to square root law [14], which approximately maintain the same statistical detectability of stegos with different sizes. The payload and change rate (changes per non-zero AC DCT coefficient) of each size is shown in Table 3. The arbitrary-sized detector [34] for Alaska competition, SRNet-AS, is selected to compare with EWNet.

In order to meet a more realistic situation, the detectors trained on small-sized images were directly used to detect arbitrary-sized images without retraining parameters. The testing error of EWNet and SRNet-AS on arbitrary-sized dataset ALASKA is shown in Table 4. It can be seen that EWNet achieves better detection accuracy than SRNet-AS in all image sizes. The accuracy of EWNet is up to 15.6% higher than SRNet-AS when detection 1024×1024 images. Besides, with the increase of image size, the detection performance of SRNet-AS decreases significantly, which means that the statistical moments can not accurately convey the image size.

Table 4. Detection error P_E for EWNet and SRNet-AS on arbitrary-sized dataset ALASKA. The detectors are trained on ALASKA_512.

Size	EWNet	SRNet-AS	Size	EWNet	SRNet-AS
512×512	**0.0932**	0.1452	720×512	**0.1108**	0.1749
512×640	**0.1094**	0.1879	720×640	**0.1189**	0.2114
512×720	**0.1009**	0.1729	720×720	**0.1326**	0.2326
512×1024	**0.1334**	0.2311	720×1024	**0.1715**	0.2941
640×512	**0.1006**	0.1822	1024×512	**0.1236**	0.2186
640×640	**0.1063**	0.1852	1024×640	**0.1496**	0.2738
640×720	**0.1176**	0.2159	1024×720	**0.1564**	0.2834
640×1024	**0.1453**	0.2812	1024×1024	**0.2359**	0.3919

Table 5. Detection error P_E for EWNet and SRNet-AS on arbitrary-sized dataset ALASKA. The detectors are retrained on ALASKA_VAR.

Size	EWNet	SRNet-AS	Size	EWNet	SRNet-AS
512×512	**0.0928**	0.1115	720×512	**0.1104**	0.1199
512×640	**0.1091**	0.1146	720×640	**0.1163**	0.1194
512×720	**0.1003**	0.1187	720×720	**0.1224**	0.1244
512×1024	**0.1147**	0.1242	720×1024	**0.1522**	0.1543
640×512	**0.1003**	0.1176	1024×512	**0.1185**	0.1221
640×640	**0.1058**	0.1165	1024×640	**0.1242**	0.1365
640×720	**0.1172**	0.1247	1024×720	**0.1372**	0.1396
640×1024	**0.1361**	0.1386	1024×1024	0.1728	**0.1583**

In addition, we also verify the performance of EWNet and SRNet-AS trained on arbitrary-sized dataset. Both EWNet and SRNet-AS are retrained with the images of multiple random sizes in ALASKA_VAR. The converged model trained on ALASKA_512 is selected as benchmark model. When retraining SRNet-AS, for each image size, the images in ALASKA_VAR with this size are used to retrain the benchmark model, which are the original size images of a part of images in the training set ALASKA_512. Finally, we can obtained 16 retrained model to detect the testing image. When retraining EWNet, the original size images of training set ALASKA_512 are used to retrain the benchmark model. The results are shown in Table 5. The detection accuracy of EWNet is higher than SRNet-AS on all image sizes except 1024×1024. That is because SRNet-AS trains a model for each size. This method is not realistic in practice because it is difficult to find enough training images of the same statistical distribution and the same size. In addition, training a classifier for each size requires a huge amount of training.

6   Conclusion

In this paper, a novel FCN-based steganographic detector is proposed to further solve the conundrum of arbitrary-sized JPEG steganalysis, which provides state-of-the-art detection performance for both fixed-size and arbitrary-sized images. The proposed network only contains convolutional layers to avoid parameter mismatch between feature maps and fully connected layers. In addition, a unique element-wise classifier is proposed to replace the traditional linear classifier. It makes a soft decision based on the upsampled feature maps with the input dimensions. Experimental results on standard datasets BOSSBase and ALASKA#2 demonstrate the superior performance of EWNet. We hope that the proposed architecture can provide some inspiration for the arbitrary-sized image steganalysis.

References

1. Bas, P., Filler, T., Pevný, T.: "Break our steganographic system": the ins and outs of organizing BOSS. In: Filler, T., Pevný, T., Craver, S., Ker, A. (eds.) IH 2011. LNCS, vol. 6958, pp. 59–70. Springer, Heidelberg (2011). https://doi.org/10.1007/978-3-642-24178-9_5
2. Bengio, Y., Louradour, J., Collobert, R., Weston, J.: Curriculum learning. In: Proceedings of the 26th Annual International Conference on Machine Learning, ICML 2009, Montreal, Quebec, Canada, 14–18 June 2009. ACM International Conference Proceeding Series, vol. 382, pp. 41–48. ACM (2009)
3. Boroumand, M., Chen, M., Fridrich, J.J.: Deep residual network for steganalysis of digital images. IEEE Trans. Inf. Forensics Secur. 14(5), 1181–1193 (2019)
4. Chen, M., Sedighi, V., Boroumand, M., Fridrich, J.: JPEG-phase-aware convolutional neural network for steganalysis of JPEG images. In: Proceedings of the 5th ACM Workshop on Information Hiding and Multimedia Security, pp. 75–84. ACM (2017)
5. Cogranne, R., Giboulot, Q., Bas, P.: The ALASKA steganalysis challenge: A first step towards steganalysis. In: Proceedings of the ACM Workshop on Information Hiding and Multimedia Security, IH&MMSec 2019, Paris, France, 3–5 July 2019, pp. 125–137. ACM (2019)
6. Cox, I., Miller, M., Bloom, J., Fridrich, J., Kalker, T.: Digital Watermarking and Steganography. Morgan kaufmann, San Francisco (2007)
7. Denemark, T., Sedighi, V., Holub, V., Cogranne, R., Fridrich, J.: Selection-channel-aware rich model for steganalysis of digital images. In: IEEE International Workshop on Information Forensics and Security, pp. 48–53 (2014)
8. Fridrich, J., Kodovsky, J.: Rich models for steganalysis of digital images. IEEE Trans. Inf. Forensics Secur. 7(3), 868–882 (2012)
9. Guo, L., Ni, J., Su, W., Tang, C., Shi, Y.Q.: Using statistical image model for jpeg steganography: uniform embedding revisited. IEEE Trans. Inf. Forensics Secur. 10(12), 2669–2680 (2015)
10. He, K., Zhang, X., Ren, S., Sun, J.: Deep residual learning for image recognition. In: Proceedings of the IEEE Conference on Computer Vision and Pattern Recognition, pp. 770–778 (2016)

11. Holub, V., Fridrich, J.: Designing steganographic distortion using directional filters. In: 2012 IEEE International Workshop on Information Forensics and Security (WIFS), pp. 234–239. IEEE (2012)
12. Holub, V., Fridrich, J.: Low-complexity features for JPEG steganalysis using undecimated DCT. IEEE Trans. Inf. Forensics Secur. $10(2)$, 219–228 (2015)
13. Holub, V., Fridrich, J., Denemark, T.: Universal distortion function for steganography in an arbitrary domain. EURASIP J. Inf. Secur. $2014(1)$, 1–13 (2014). https://doi.org/10.1186/1687-417X-2014-1
14. Ker, A.D., Pevný, T., Kodovský, J., Fridrich, J.J.: The square root law of steganographic capacity. In: Proceedings of the 10th Workshop on Multimedia & Security, MM&Sec 2008, Oxford, UK, 22–23 September 2008, pp. 107–116. ACM (2008)
15. Kingma, D.P., Ba, J.: Adam: a method for stochastic optimization. In: 3rd International Conference on Learning Representations, ICLR 2015, San Diego, CA, USA, 7–9 May 2015, Conference Track Proceedings (2015)
16. Kodovský, J., Fridrich, J.J., Holub, V.: Ensemble classifiers for steganalysis of digital media. IEEE Trans. Inf. Forensics Secur. $7(2)$, 432–444 (2012)
17. LeCun, Y., Bottou, L., Bengio, Y., Haffner, P., et al.: Gradient-based learning applied to document recognition. Proc. IEEE $86(11)$, 2278–2324 (1998)
18. Li, B., Wang, M., Huang, J., Li, X.: A new cost function for spatial image steganography. In: 2014 IEEE International Conference on Image Processing (ICIP). pp. 4206–4210. IEEE (2014)
19. Long, J., Shelhamer, E., Darrell, T.: Fully convolutional networks for semantic segmentation. In: IEEE Conference on Computer Vision and Pattern Recognition, CVPR 2015, Boston, MA, USA, 7–12 June 2015, pp. 3431–3440. IEEE Computer Society (2015)
20. Pevny, T., Bas, P., Fridrich, J.: Steganalysis by subtractive pixel adjacency matrix. IEEE Trans. Inf. Forensics Secur. $5(2)$, 215–224 (2010)
21. Pevný, T., Filler, T., Bas, P.: Using high-dimensional image models to perform highly undetectable steganography. In: Böhme, R., Fong, P.W.L., Safavi-Naini, R. (eds.) IH 2010. LNCS, vol. 6387, pp. 161–177. Springer, Heidelberg (2010). https://doi.org/10.1007/978-3-642-16435-4_13
22. Qian, Y., Dong, J., Wang, W., Tan, T.: Deep learning for steganalysis via convolutional neural networks. In: Proceedings of SPIE - The International Society for Optical Engineering 9409, 94090J–94090J-10 (2015)
23. Cogranne, R., Bas, Q.G.: Documentation of Alaskav2 Dataset scripts: a hint moving towards steganography and steganalysis into the wild (2019). https://alaska.utt.fr
24. Su, A., He, X., Zhao, X.: Jpeg Steganalysis based on ResNeXt with gauss partial derivative filters. Multim. Tools Appl. $80(3)$, 3349–3366 (2021)
25. Su, A., Ma, S., Zhao, X.: Fast and secure steganography based on J-UNIWARD. IEEE Sig. Process. Lett. 27, 221–225 (2020)
26. Tsang, C.F., Fridrich, J.J.: Steganalyzing images of arbitrary size with CNNs. In: Media Watermarking, Security, and Forensics 2018, Burlingame, CA, USA, 28 January 2018–1 February 2018. Ingenta (2018)
27. Xia, C., Guan, Q., Zhao, X., Xu, Z., Ma, Y.: Improving GFR Steganalysis features by using Gabor symmetry and weighted histograms. In: Proceedings of the 5th ACM Workshop on Information Hiding and Multimedia Security, IH&MMSec 2017, Philadelphia, PA, USA, 20–22 June 2017, pp. 55–66 (2017)
28. Xu, G.: Deep convolutional neural network to detect J-UNIWARD. In: Proceedings of the 5th ACM Workshop on Information Hiding and Multimedia Security, IH&MMSec 2017, Philadelphia, PA, USA, 20–22 June 2017, pp. 67–73 (2017)

29. Xu, G., Wu, H., Shi, Y.Q.: Ensemble of CNNs for steganalysis: an empirical study. In: Proceedings of the 4th ACM Workshop on Information Hiding and Multimedia Security, IH&MMSec 2016, Vigo, Galicia, Spain, 20–22 June 2016, pp. 103–107 (2016)

30. Xu, G., Wu, II.Z., Shi, Y.Q.: Structural design of convolutional neural networks for Steganalysis. IEEE Sig. Process. Lett. **23**(5), 708–712 (2016)

31. Yang, J., Shi, Y.Q., Wong, E.K., Kang, X.: JPEG Steganalysis based on DenseNet. arXiv preprint arXiv:1711.09335 (2017)

32. Ye, J., Ni, J., Yi, Y.: Deep learning hierarchical representations for image Steganalysis. IEEE Trans. Inf. Forensics Secur. **12**(11), 2545–2557 (2017)

33. You, W., Zhang, H., Zhao, X.: A Siamese CNN for image Steganalysis. IEEE Trans. Inf. Forensics Secur. **16**, 291–306 (2021)

34. Yousfi, Y., Butora, J., Fridrich, J., Giboulot, Q.: Breaking ALASKA: color separation for Steganalysis in JPEG domain. In: Proceedings of the ACM Workshop on Information Hiding and Multimedia Security, pp. 138–149 (2019)

35. Zeng, J., Tan, S., Li, B., Huang, J.: Large-scale JPEG image Steganalysis using hybrid deep-learning framework. IEEE Trans. Inf. Forensics Secur. **13**(5), 1200–1214 (2018)

36. Zhang, Q., Zhao, X., Liu, C.: Convolutional neural network for larger JPEG images Steganalysis. In: Yoo, C.D., Shi, Y.-Q., Kim, H.J., Piva, A., Kim, G. (eds.) IWDW 2018. LNCS, vol. 11378, pp. 14–28. Springer, Cham (2019). https://doi.org/10.1007/978-3-030-11389-6_2

Using Contrastive Learning to Improve the Performance of Steganalysis Schemes

Yanzhen Ren[1,2]([✉]), Yiwen Liu[2], and Lina Wang[1,2]

[1] Key Laboratory of Aerospace Information Security and Trusted Computing,
Ministry of Education, Wuhan, China
renyz@whu.edu.cn

[2] School of Cyber Science and Engineering, Wuhan University, Wuhan, China

Abstract. To improve the detection accuracy and generalization of steganalysis, this paper proposes the Steganalysis Contrastive Framework (SCF) based on contrastive learning. The SCF improves the feature representation of steganalysis by maximizing the distance between features of samples of different categories and minimizing the distance between features of samples of the same category. To decrease the computing complexity of the contrastive loss in supervised learning, we design a novel Steganalysis Contrastive Loss (StegCL) based on the equivalence and transitivity of similarity. The StegCL eliminates the redundant computing in the existing contrastive loss. The experimental results show that the SCF improves the generalization and detection accuracy of existing steganalysis DNNs, and the maximum promotion is 2% and 3% respectively. Without decreasing the detection accuracy, the training time of using the StegCL is 10% of that of using the contrastive loss in supervised learning.

Keywords: Steganalysis · Contrastive learning · Self-supervised learning · Self-adaptive steganography

1 Introduction

Steganography generates the stego by embedding undetectable messages into the cover and making them as close in distribution as possible [1]. The criminal elements use steganography to avoid censorship and construct covert channels, which will bring some security problems. To withstand steganography, steganalysis has attracted the attention of researchers. Steganalysis is to detect whether an object is a cover or a stego [2–4].

According to the embedded domain used in steganography, steganography is divided into spatial domain steganography and JPEG domain steganography. Spatial domain steganography embeds secret information by modifying the pixel

This work is supported by the Natural Science Foundation of China (NSFC) under the grant No. 62172306 61872275, U1836112 and China Scholarship Council.

values of the spatial images. JPEG domain steganography embeds secret information by modifying the quantized DCT coefficient of the JPEG images. The state-of-the-art steganography aims at designing distortion functions. HUGO [1] uses the SPAM [5] features to compute the costs. WOW [6] facilitates directional high-pass filters to define the costs. UNIWARD [7] uses similar filters as that in WOW, [7] can expand to the JPEG domain. MiPOD [8] considers the cover image model and calculates the detectability based on the locally-estimated multivariate Gaussian model. MiPOD can also be used in spatial and JPEG domains.

According to the development history of steganalysis, steganalysis is divided into traditional steganalysis and DNN-based steganalysis. The traditional steganalysis scheme is to design handcrafted features followed by a classifier. The most classical traditional steganalysis scheme is the Rich Model [9] followed by an Ensemble Classifier [10]. Recently, most steganalysis schemes are based on the DNN. Qian et al. [11] unify the feature extraction and classification two steps under a single DNN. XuNet [12] facilitates the hyperbolic tangent (tanh) activation function and 1×1 convolutional kernel. YeNet [13] utilizes the optimizable filters of the Spatial Rich Model (SRM) [9] as the preprocessing module. Yedroudj et al. [14] introduce batch normalization and non-linear activation function. Fridrich et al. [15] propose an end-to-end DNN called SRNet that introduces shortcut operation [16]. Zhao et al. [17] put forward a novel DNN with the siamese architecture. These DNN-based steganalysis schemes propose kinds of structures to optimize the DNN. The structures maximize the distance between features of cover and stego, which improves the detection accuracy of steganalysis. However, current existing DNN-based steganalysis schemes are based on supervised learning, whose performance is limited by the number and diversity of the training samples. The contrastive learning has been facilitated in NLP and CV domains and demonstrates excellent feature extraction performance, such as BERT [18], MoCo [19], and SimCLR [20]. Thus, supervised contrastive learning has been proposed in the paper. The contrastive learning facilitated in self-supervised has been utilized in image classification and improves the detection accuracy and generalization [21,22]. Taking the similarity between samples of the same category into account, this paper introduces contrastive learning to minimize the distance between features of samples of the same category and maximize the distance between features of samples of different categories, which improves the detection accuracy and generalization of steganalysis DNNs. Meanwhile, a novel contrastive loss has been proposed to take the place of that used in [21], which reduces the computing complexity and keeps the performance.

The main contributions of this paper can be summarized as follows:

1. To improve the detection accuracy and generalization of steganalysis, this paper proposes a Steganalysis Contrastive Framework (SCF) based on contrastive learning. The SCF improves the feature representation of steganalysis by maximizing the distance between features of samples of different categories and minimizing the distance between features of samples of the same category.

2. To decrease the computing complexity of supervised contrastive loss [21], we design a novel Steganalysis Contrastive Loss (StegCL) based on the equivalence and transitivity of similarity. Without decreasing the detection accuracy, the StegCL eliminates the redundant computing in the contrastive loss in supervised learning.

The rest of the paper is organized as follows: in Sect. 2, the DNN-based steganalysis and the loss of contrastive learning are introduced, in Sect. 3, the SCF and the StegCL are explained, in Sect. 4, there are the setups of the experiments and the experimental results, and Sect. 5 summarizes the paper.

2   Background

2.1   DNN-Based Steganalysis

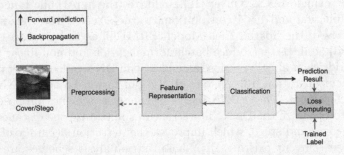

Fig. 1. The basic framework of existing steganalysis DNNs.

The basic framework of existing steganalysis DNNs is shown in Fig. 1. There is the preprocessing module, feature representation module, and classification module in the framework. The preprocessing module filters the input image to obtain the high-frequency information of the image. The feature representation module extracts the high-dimensional features of the filtered image. The classification module classifies the features. The black arrows indicate the process of forwarding prediction. During the forwarding prediction, the input image goes through preprocessing, feature representation, and classification modules in turn. The output of the forwarding prediction is the prediction result. The blue arrows indicate the process of backpropagation. During the backpropagation, the loss computing module computes the cross-entropy loss [23] with the prediction result and the trained label. Then, the loss is utilized by the backpropagation to optimize the parameters of the DNN. The dashed arrow between the feature representation module and the preprocessing module means that sometimes the parameters of the preprocessing module are fixed [12].

Existing DNN-based steganalysis works focus on optimizing the preprocessing module and the feature representation module. To optimize the preprocessing module, Xu et al. [12] put forward utilizing the fixed filters of SRM [24]. Ye et al. [13] propose that the parameters of filters of SRM need to be optimized. Fridrich et al. [15] utilize a convolution layer, a batch normalization layer, and a ReLU layer with default initialization as the preprocessing module. To optimize the feature representation module, Yedroudj et al. [14] design a non-linear activation function called truncation function that maximizes the small difference between cover and stego. SRNet [15] introduces the shortcut operation [16], which extracts more residual information between cover and stego. Zhao et al. [17] put forward SiaStegNet with a novel siamese architecture according to the left and right imbalance of the difference between cover and stego. Inspired by contrastive learning that improves the feature representation in CV and NLP [20,25,26], this paper proposes the Steganalysis Contrastive Framework (SCF) based on contrastive learning to improve the performance of steganalysis schemes.

2.2   The Loss of Contrastive Learning

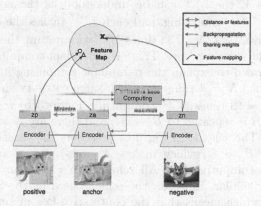

Fig. 2. The basic principle of contrastive learning.

The target of contrastive learning is to minimize the distance between features of the anchor and the positive, and maximize the distance between features of the anchor and the negative. The basic principle of contrastive learning is shown in Fig. 2. The za, zp, and zn are the features extracted from the anchor, the positive, and the negative by the Encoder. The contrastive loss computing module computes the contrastive loss with the za, zp, and zn. As the backpropagation optimizes the parameters of the Encoder to decrease the contrastive loss, the za and zp approach, and the za and zn move away. There are mainly two kinds of contrastive loss: Self-supervised Contrastive Loss (SelfCL) [20,25,26] and Supervised Contrastive Loss (SupCL) [21].

$$\mathbb{L}_i^{self} = -\log \frac{\exp(z_i \cdot z_{j(i)}/\tau)}{\sum_{k=1}^{2N} \ell_{i \neq k} \cdot \exp(z_i \cdot z_k/\tau)} \tag{1}$$

The SelfCL is used in self-supervised learning [20,25,26], The SelfCL which is shown in Formula 1 aims at maximizing the distance between features of the anchor and the samples different from the anchor and minimizing the distance between features of the anchor and the augmentation. The SelfCL greatly promotes the development of contrastive learning, however, the SelfCL doesn't introduce the label and there is only one positive by default. The SelfCL is unavailable in supervised learning, and cannot be utilized by the steganalysis schemes.

$$\mathbb{L}_i^{sup} = \frac{-1}{2N_{\tilde{y}_i} - 1} \sum_{j=1}^{2N} \ell_{i \neq j} \cdot \ell_{\tilde{y}_i = \tilde{y}_j} \cdot \log \frac{\exp(z_i \cdot z_j / \tau)}{\sum_{k=1}^{2N} \ell_{i \neq k} \cdot \exp(z_i \cdot z_k / \tau)} \tag{2}$$

Recently, Google researchers propose the Supervised Contrastive Loss (SupCL) to introduce contrastive learning into supervised learning in NeurIPS 2020 [21]. The SupCL [21] tries to bring the features of samples of the same category close, and keep the features of samples of different categories far away. The calculation of SupCL [21] is shown in Formula 2. Compared to the $\mathbb{L}_i^{self}$ shown in Formula 1, the $\mathbb{L}_i^{sup}$ can be understood as the normalized sum of $(2N_{\tilde{y}_i} - 1)^1$ times $\mathbb{L}_i^{self}$ computing, and each $\mathbb{L}_i^{self}$ makes the anchor similar to the only one positive. By $(2N_{\tilde{y}_i} - 1)$ times $\mathbb{L}_i^{self}$ computing, the anchor is similar to all samples of the same category. There is redundant computing in the SupCL [21]. Figure 3 is drawn to explain the redundant computing in the SupCL [21]. Three schemes make $N = 4$ samples of the same category similar. Figure 3(a) has $N \times (N - 1) = 12$ times $\mathbb{L}_i^{self}$ computing. Figure 3(b) removes the repeat computing ($A \rightarrow B$ is repeated to $B \rightarrow A$), and there are $N \times (N - 1) \div 2 = 6$ times computing. The scheme in Fig. 3(c) considers the transitivity of similarity ($A \rightarrow B$ and $B \rightarrow C$, which makes $A \rightarrow C$ unnecessary), and there is $N - 1 = 3$ times computing left. All schemes in Fig. 3 can make samples of the same category similar. However, the scheme used by the SupCL [21] needs more computing, which means that the contrastive loss in supervised learning has redundant computing.

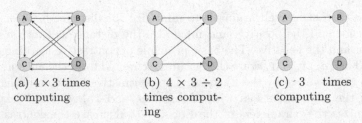

(a) 4×3 times computing

(b) $4 \times 3 \div 2$ times computing

(c) 3 times computing

Fig. 3. Three schemes to make samples (A, B, C, and D) of the same category similar. The black arrow represents once $\mathbb{L}_i^{self}$ computing.

---

[1] $2N_{\tilde{y}_i}$ is the number of samples that is similar to the anchor in the batch.

3   Proposed Methods

Based on the analysis above, we propose the Steganalysis Contrastive Framework (SCF) for the first time. To eliminate the redundant computing in the existing contrastive loss, a novel Steganalysis Contrastive Loss (StegCL) is designed based on the equivalence and transitivity of similarity.

3.1   Steganalysis Contrastive Framework

The architecture of the Steganalysis Contrastive Framework (SCF) is shown in Fig. 4. The main difference between the SCF and the basic framework of existing steganalysis DNNs (seen in Fig. 2) is that the SCF adds a contrastive loss computing module. This module computes the contrastive loss with the features extracted by the feature representation module. The SCF retains the backpropagation from the loss computed with the prediction result and the trained label, which maximizes the distance between features of cover and stego. Meanwhile, the SCF introduces a new backpropagation from the contrastive loss, which not only maximizes the distance between features of cover and stego but also minimizes the distance between features of samples of the same category.

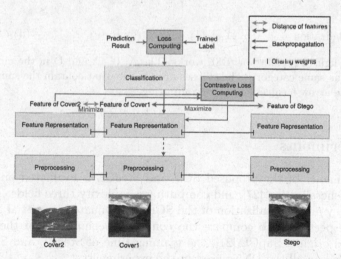

Fig. 4. The architecture of the Steganalysis Contrastive Framework (SCF).

3.2   Steganalysis Contrastive Loss

$$\mathbb{L}_i^{steg} = -\log \frac{\exp(z_i \cdot z_{j(Random \cdot \ell_{(i) \neq (j)} \cdot \ell_{\widetilde{y}_i = \widetilde{y}_j})}/\tau)}{\sum_{k=1}^{2N} \ell_{i \neq k} \cdot \ell_{\widetilde{y}_i \neq \widetilde{y}_j} \cdot \exp(z_i \cdot z_k/\tau)} \tag{3}$$

The Steganalysis Contrastive Loss (StegCL) is shown in Formula 3. Compared to the $\mathbb{L}_i^{sup}$ shown in Formula 2, the $\mathbb{L}_i^{steg}$ only contains once $\mathbb{L}_i^{self}$ computing. The advantage of the StegCL is that it minimizes the features of samples of the same category without redundant computing. The core of the StegCL is the Random Selection Strategy (RSS) that is the $(Random \cdot \ell_{(i)\neq(j)} \cdot \ell_{\tilde{y}_i=\tilde{y}_j})$ shown in Formula 3. The RSS selects the same category sample in a different set of the anchor as the positive. Figure 5(a) shows that samples are not similar to each other at the start. Figure 5(b) shows that anchor A selects sample D as the positive, which makes A similar to D and merges the sets. Figure 5(c) shows that anchor B selects sample C as the positive, which makes B similar to C and merges the sets. Figure 5(d) shows that anchor C selects sample D as the positive, which makes the A, B, C, and D are similar to each other and merges the sets. With the help of the RSS used in StegCL, each anchor only need to be similar to one positive, and the samples of the same category are similar to each other finally.

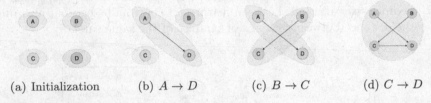

(a) Initialization   (b) $A \to D$ (c) $B \to C$ (d) $C \to D$

Fig. 5. The figures explain how RSS works. The A, B, C, and D in the circle are the samples of the same category. The ellipses are the sets that contain the same category samples. The arrow means once $\mathbb{L}_i^{self}$ computing.

4   Experiments

The performance of the proposed SCF and StegCL is evaluated on detection accuracy, generalization [27], and computing complexity three fields. The detection accuracy and generalization of the SCF are evaluated in spatial and JPEG domains respectively. To compare the computing complexity of the proposed StegCL and original SupCL [21], the training time of StegCL and SupCL [21] are compared on all the DNNs used in the experiments.

4.1   Dataset

Spatial. The dataset used in experiments is BOSSbase 1.01 [28] which contains 10,000 Portable GrayMap format images. These images are 512×512 pixels. Considering that the GPU used in experiments is GeForce 2080Ti that has merely 12G memory, these images are resized to 256×256 pixels by the *imresize* function in MATLAB with default settings. To generate the stegoes from the covers, four self-adaptive steganography algorithms, HUGO [1], WOW [6], S-UNIWARD [7],

MiPOD [8] are facilitated. There are 0.1 bpp, 0.2 bpp, 0.3 bpp, and 0.4 bpp four payloads in experiments. Each dataset is randomly divided into three parts in a ratio of 6:1:3 for training, validation, and testing. During the training, the dataset is divided into balance batches (32 images of one batch), which means that the number of cover images is equal to that of stego images.

JPEG. The dataset used in experiments is a part of the dataset provided by the organizers of ALASKA II [29]. 10000 images compressed with quality factors(QF) 75, 10000 images with QF90, and 10000 images with QF95 are selected as the cover in experiments. There are 3×10000 cover images, and the $2 \times 3 \times 10000$ corresponding images embedded with J-UNIWARD [7] and J-MiPOD [8] are selected as stego images in experiments. The average payload of the stego images is 0.4 bits per non-zero AC DCT coefficient (bpnzac). The dataset used in experiments is randomly divided into three parts in a ratio of 6:1:3 for training, validation, and testing. During the training, the dataset is divided into balance batches (32 images of one batch) as well.

4.2 Metric

Spatial. The performance of detection accuracy is measured with the total classification error probability on the test subset of the dataset under equal priors $P_E = \min_{P_{FA}} \frac{1}{2}(P_{FA} + P_{MD})$ [13–15,17], where P_{FA} and P_{MD} are the false-alarm and missed-detection probabilities.

JPEG. To evaluate the performance of steganalysis in JPEG domain, the weighted area under the ROC wAUC= $(2A_{0.4} + A_1)/3$ used in ALASKA II [29] is selected as the metric. $A_{0.4}$ is the area between the two horizontal lines defined by $P_D = 0$ and $P_D = 0.4$ under the ROC. A_1 is the area between the two horizontal lines defined by $P_D = 0.4$ and $P_D = 1$ under the ROC.

4.3 Detection Accuracy

The detection accuracy experiments of SCF are conducted in spatial and JPEG domains. The state-of-the-art DNNs of each domain trained with SCF are compared to the original DNNs on the corresponding datasets.

To evaluate the detection accuracy of SCF in spatial domain, the YeNet [13], YedroudjNet [14], and SiaStegNet [17] are compared to the CL^2-YeNet, CL-YedroudjNet, and CL-SiaStegNet on WOW [6], S-UNIWARD [7], MiPOD [8] at 0.2 bpp and 0.4 bpp. Table 1 shows the experimental result. The detection error rates of the DNNs optimized with SCF are all lower than that of the original DNNs. For clearly, Fig. 6 is drawn to show the comparison between each original DNN and optimized DNN one by one. From Fig. 6, the orange line which

---

[2] The CL prefix means that the DNN is optimized by the proposed SCF with StegCL.

Table 1. The P_E of YeNet [13], CL-YeNet, YedroudjNet [14], CL-YedroudjNet, SiaStegNet [17], and CL-SiaStegNet on WOW [6], S-UNIWARD [7], MiPOD [8] at 0.2 bpp and 0.4 bpp.

Steganography	WOW [6]		S-UNIWARD [7]		MiPOD [8]	
Payload	0.2 bpp	0.4 bpp	0.2 bpp	0.4 bpp	0.2 bpp	0.4 bpp
YeNet [13]	.312	.204	.374	.235	.394	.284
CL-YeNet	**.301**	**.187**	**.355**	**.220**	**.380**	**.271**
YedroudjNet [14]	.307	.190	.370	.227	.371	.258
CL-YedroudjNet	**.285**	**.169**	**.356**	**.214**	**.356**	**.245**
SiaStegNet [17]	.189	.111	.194	.097	.254	.158
CL-SiaStegNet	**.175**	**.100**	**.169**	**.081**	**.239**	**.144**

represents the detection error rate of optimized DNN in each subfigure is lower than the line which represents the original DNN, which means that the proposed SCF framework can improve the detection accuracy of the state-of-the-art DNN in spatial domain.

To evaluate the detection accuracy of the SCF in JPEG domain, the optimized CL-JXuNet and CL-SRNet are compared to the original DNNs on J-UNIWARD [7] and J-MiPOD [8] at QF 75, 90, and 95. Table 2 shows the details about the experimental result, which represents that the wAUC [30] of the SCF optimized DNNs are higher than that of the original DNNs without SCF, which

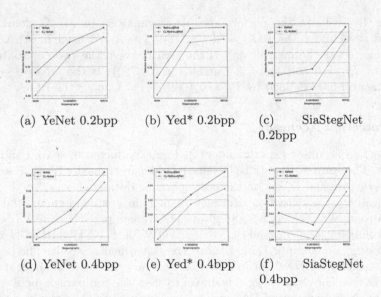

(a) YeNet 0.2bpp   (b) Yed* 0.2bpp   (c)   SiaStegNet 0.2bpp

(d) YeNet 0.4bpp   (e) Yed* 0.4bpp   (f)   SiaStegNet 0.4bpp

Fig. 6. The line graphs that represent the P_E of YeNet [13], CL-YeNet, YedroudjNet [14], CL-YedroudjNet, SiaStegNet [17], and CL-SiaStegNet on WOW [6], S-UNIWARD [7], MiPOD [8] at 0.2 bpp and 0.4 bpp.

Table 2. The wAUC [30] of the JXuNet [31], CL-JXuNet, SRNet [15], and CL-SRNet on J-UNIWARD [7] and J-MiPOD [8] at QF 75, 90, and 95.

Steganography	J-UNIWARD [7]			J-MiPOD [8]		
QF	75	90	95	75	90	95
JXuNet [31]	.807	.789	.782	.864	.841	.754
CL-JXuNet	**.829**	**.804**	**.803**	**.879**	**.860**	**.773**
SRNet [15]	.847	.829	.832	.954	.932	.822
CL-SRNet	**.869**	**.847**	**.848**	**.976**	**.960**	**.853**

means that the detection accuracy of the state-of-the-art steganalysis DNNs is improved by the SCF in JPEG domain overall.

Figure 7 shows the loss and wAUC [30] of the SRNet [15] and CL-SRNet during training. As shown in Fig. 7, the loss of the CL-SRNet is lower than that of the SRNet [15] and the wAUC [30] of CL-SRNet is higher than that of the SRNet [15]. The well-trained DNNs are used to extract the feature with the network before the final layer. The batch extracted features are compared in Fig. 8, which is the visualization of the latent features before classifier from SRNet [15] and CL-SRNet with t-SNE [32].

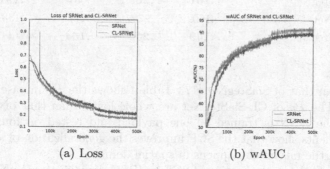

(a) Loss   (b) wAUC

Fig. 7. The loss and wAUC [30] of SRNet [15] during training.

4.4 Generalization

To evaluate the generalization of the optimized DNNs, kinds of mismatch situations are considered in spatial and JPEG domains. When the mismatch happens, the detection accuracy of the DNNs optimized with SCF is compared to the original DNNs without the SCF.

The P_E of SiaStegNet [17] and CL-SiaStegNet in case of mismatch is shown in Table 3 and Table 4. Table 3 shows the P_E in case of steganography algorithm mismatch. When the DNN is trained on one steganography and tested on HUGO [1], WOW [6], S-UNIWARD [7], and MiPOD [8], the P_E of CL-SiaStegNet are

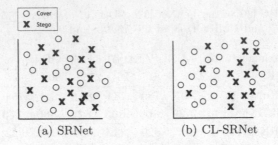

(a) SRNet   (b) CL-SRNet

Fig. 8. The comparison of same batch t-SNE [32] features extracted by SRNet [15] and CL-SRNet.

Table 3. The P_E of SiaStegNet [17] and CL-SiaStegNet in case of steganography algorithm mismatch under the same 0.4 bpp payload.

MODELS	TRA\TES	WOW [6]	HUGO [1]	S-UNI* [7]	MiPOD [8]
SiaStegNet [17]	WOW [6]	.111	.383	.205	.289
CL-SiaStegNet		.100	**.378**	**.191**	**.267**
SiaStegNet	HUGO [1]	.318	.139	.321	.320
CL-SiaStegNet		**.302**	.121	**.311**	**.308**
SiaStegNet	S-UNI* [7]	.106	.276	.097	.214
CL-SiaStegNet		**.101**	**.268**	.081	**.191**
SiaStegNet	MiPOD [8]	.160	.272	.177	.158
CL-SiaStegNet		**.149**	**.250**	**.154**	.144

all lower than that of SiaStegNet [17]. Table 4 shows the P_E in case of payload mismatch. The P_E of CL-SiaStegNet are whole lower than that of SiaStegNet [17] when the DNN is trained on one payload and tested on four payloads. The experiments show that the SCF improves the generalization of steganalysis DNNs when the mismatch happens in spatial domain.

To evaluate the generalization of SCF in JPEG domain, the JXuNet [31], and SRNet [15] are compared when the mismatch happens as well. Figure 9 shows that the wAUC [30] of SCF optimized DNNs are higher than that of the original DNNs without SCF whether the mismatch happens or not, which means that the proposed SCF can improve the generalization of the state-of-the-art steganalysis DNNs.

4.5 Computing Complexity

The training time of each epoch is compared on all the DNNs used in the experiments. The training time of the DNNs is evaluated on the corresponding datasets. Table 5 shows the details about the DNNs average epoch training time, parameters and detection accuracy index (wAUC [30] or P_E). According to Table 5,

Table 4. The P_E of SiaStegNet [17] and CL-SiaStegNet in case of payload mismatch under the same S-UNIWARD [7] steganography algorithm.

MODELS	TRA\TES	0.1 bpp	0.2 bpp	0.3 bpp	0.4 bpp
SiaStegNet [17]	0.1 bpp	.259	.254	.215	.174
CL-SiaStegNet		.233	**.238**	**.202**	**.153**
SiaStegNet	0.2 bpp	.395	.194	.160	.158
CL-SiaStegNet		**.383**	.169	**.148**	**.143**
SiaStegNet	0.3 bpp	.400	.281	.149	.120
CL-SiaStegNet		**.389**	**.269**	.137	**.100**
SiaStegNet	0.4 bpp	.442	.322	.213	.097
CL-SiaStegNet		**.421**	**.298**	**.200**	.081

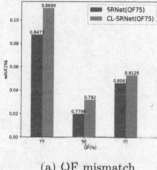

(a) QF mismatch

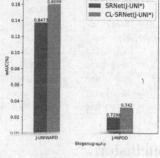

(b) Steg mismatch

Fig. 9. The comparison between SRNet [15] and CL-SRNet on mismatch. The models are trained on 75, 90, 95 QF and evaluated on 75 QF in (a). The models are trained on J-UNIWARD and J-MiPOD and evaluated on J-UNIWARD in (b).

Fig. 10 is drawn to make the comparison clearly. From Fig. 10, the training time of the StegCL is greatly less than that of the SupCL [21], which means that the StegCL reduces the computing complexity of the original contrastive loss with the same performance.

Table 5. The comparison between kinds of contrastive loss on XuNet [12], JXuNet [31], YeNet [13], YedroudjNet [14]. SiaStegNet [17], SRNet [15].

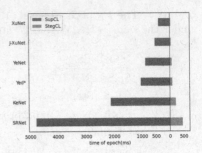

Fig. 10. The comparison of training time in Table 5.

MODELS	CL	Time (ms)	Parameters	wAUC	P_E
XuNet [12]	No	29	70278		.334
	Sup	400	75943		.320
	Steg	31	74396		.319
JXuNet [31]	No	35	72980	.803	
	Sup	531	77084	.829	
	Steg	38	75893	.830	
YeNet [13]	No	65	99870		.278
	Sup	874	107700		.264
	Steg	70	106997		.262
Yed* [14]	No	84	418895		.269
	Sup	1043	445390		.255
	Steg	89	439038		.256
SiaStegNet [17]	No	197	700620		.134
	Sup	2128	706828		.112
	Steg	209	706828		.113
SRNet [15]	No	433	4496210	.887	
	Sup	4787	4795943	.912	
	Steg	452	4569838	.910	

5 Conclusion

This paper proposes the Steganalysis Contrastive Framework (SCF) for the first time. The SCF is utilized to optimize well-known steganalysis DNNs, XuNet, YeNet, YedroudjNet, SiaStegNet, and SRNet. The experimental results indicate that contrastive learning can improve the detection accuracy and generalization of existing steganalysis DNNs. Meanwhile, we optimize the contrastive loss in supervised learning and design a novel StegCL based on the equivalence and transitivity of similarity. The StegCL eliminates the redundant computing in the contrastive loss in supervised learning and reduces the computing complexity. The future work will further follow the idea of contrastive learning, mining the intrinsic correlation of cover and stego to improve the performance of the steganalysis schemes.

References

1. Pevný, T., Filler, T., Bas, P.: Using high-dimensional image models to perform highly undetectable steganography. In: Böhme, R., Fong, P.W.L., Safavi-Naini, R. (eds.) IH 2010. LNCS, vol. 6387, pp. 161–177. Springer, Heidelberg (2010). https://doi.org/10.1007/978-3-642-16435-4_13
2. Zhang, R., Zhu, F., Liu, J., Liu, G.: Depth-wise separable convolutions and multi-level pooling for an efficient spatial CNN-based steganalysis. IEEE Trans. Inf. Forensics Secur. **15**, 1138–1150 (2019)

3. Wang, Y., Yang, K., Yi, X., Zhao, X., Xu, Z.: CNN-based steganalysis of MP3 steganography in the entropy code domain. In: Proceedings of the 6th ACM Workshop on Information Hiding and Multimedia Security, pp. 55–65 (2018)
4. Cogranne, R., Giboulot, Q., Bas, P.: The Alaska steganalysis challenge: a first step towards steganalysis. In: Proceedings of the ACM Workshop on Information Hiding and Multimedia Security, pp. 125–137 (2019)
5. Pevny, T., Bas, P., Fridrich, J.: Steganalysis by subtractive pixel adjacency matrix. IEEE Trans. Inf. Forensics Secur. **5**(2), 215–224 (2010)
6. Holub, V., Fridrich, J.: Designing steganographic distortion using directional filters. In: 2012 IEEE International Workshop on Information Forensics and Security (WIFS), pp. 234–239. IEEE (2012)
7. Holub, V., Fridrich, J., Denemark, T.: Universal distortion function for steganography in an arbitrary domain. EURASIP J. Inf. Secur. **2014**(1), 1–13 (2014). https://doi.org/10.1186/1687-417X-2014-1
8. Sedighi, V., Cogranne, R., Fridrich, J.: Content-adaptive steganography by minimizing statistical detectability. IEEE Trans. Inf. Forensics Secur. **11**(2), 221–234 (2015)
9. Fridrich, J., Kodovsky, J.: Rich models for steganalysis of digital images. IEEE Trans. Inf. Forensics Secur. **7**(3), 868–882 (2012)
10. Kodovsky, J., Fridrich, J., Holub, V.: Ensemble classifiers for steganalysis of digital media. IEEE Trans. Inf. Forensics Secur. **7**(2), 432–444 (2011)
11. Qian, Y., Dong, J., Wang, W., Tan, T.: Deep learning for steganalysis via convolutional neural networks. In: Media Watermarking, Security, and Forensics 2015, vol. 9409, p. 94090J. International Society for Optics and Photonics (2015)
12. Xu, G., Wu, H.-Z., Shi, Y.-Q.: Structural design of convolutional neural networks for steganalysis. IEEE Signal Process. Lett. **23**(5), 708–712 (2016)
13. Ye, J., Ni, J., Yi, Y.: Deep learning hierarchical representations for image steganalysis. IEEE Trans. Inf. Forensics Secur. **12**(11), 2545–2557 (2017)
14. Yedroudj, M., Comby, F., Chaumont, M.: Yedroudj-Net: an efficient CNN for spatial steganalysis. In: 2018 IEEE International Conference on Acoustics, Speech and Signal Processing (ICASSP), pp. 2092–2096. IEEE (2018)
15. Boroumand, M., Chen, M., Fridrich, J.: Deep residual network for steganalysis of digital images. IEEE Trans. Inf. Forensics Secur. **14**(5), 1181–1193 (2018)
16. Szegedy, C., Ioffe, S., Vanhoucke, V., Alemi, A.: Inception-v4, inception-resnet and the impact of residual connections on learning. In: Proceedings of the AAAI Conference on Artificial Intelligence, vol. 31 (2017)
17. You, W., Zhang, H., Zhao, X.: A Siamese CNN for image steganalysis. IEEE Trans. Inf. Forensics Secur. **16**, 291–306 (2020)
18. Tenney, I., Das, D., Pavlick, E.: BERT rediscovers the classical NLP pipeline. arXiv preprint arXiv:1905.05950 (2019)
19. He, K., Fan, H., Wu, Y., Xie, S., Girshick, R.: Momentum contrast for unsupervised visual representation learning. In: Proceedings of the IEEE/CVF Conference on Computer Vision and Pattern Recognition, pp. 9729–9738 (2020)
20. Chen, T., Kornblith, S., Norouzi, M., Hinton, G.: A simple framework for contrastive learning of visual representations. arXiv preprint arXiv:2002.05709 (2020)
21. Khosla, P., et al.: Supervised contrastive learning. In: Larochelle, H., Ranzato, M., Hadsell, R., Balcan, M.F., Lin, H. (eds.) Advances in Neural Information Processing Systems, vol. 33, pp. 18661–18673. Curran Associates Inc (2020)
22. Kang, B., Li, Y., Xie, S., Yuan, Z., Feng, J.: Exploring balanced feature spaces for representation learning. In: International Conference on Learning Representations (2020)

23. Zhang, Z., Sabuncu, M.: Generalized cross entropy loss for training deep neural networks with noisy labels. Adv. Neural. Inf. Process. Syst. **31**, 8778–8788 (2018)
24. Denemark, T., Sedighi, V., Holub, V., Cogránne, R., Fridrich, J.: Selection-channel-aware rich model for steganalysis of digital images. In: 2014 IEEE International Workshop on Information Forensics and Security (WIFS), pp. 48–53. IEEE (2014)
25. Chen, X., Fan, H., Girshick, R., He, K.: Improved baselines with momentum contrastive learning. arXiv preprint arXiv:2003.04297 (2020)
26. Jaiswal, A., Babu, A.R., Zadeh, M.Z., Banerjee, D., Makedon, F.: A survey on contrastive self-supervised learning. Technologies **9**(1), 2 (2021)
27. Giboulot, Q., Cogranne, R., Borghys, D., Bas, P.: Effects and solutions of cover-source mismatch in image steganalysis. Signal Process. Image Commun. **86**, 115888 (2020)
28. Bas, P., Filler, T., Pevný, T.: "Break our steganographic system": the ins and outs of organizing BOSS. In: Filler, T., Pevný, T., Craver, S., Ker, A. (eds.) IH 2011. LNCS, vol. 6958, pp. 59–70. Springer, Heidelberg (2011). https://doi.org/10.1007/978-3-642-24178-9_5
29. Cogranne, R., Giboulot, Q., Bas, P.: ALASKA#2: challenging academic research on steganalysis with realistic images. In: 2020 IEEE International Workshop on Information Forensics and Security (WIFS), pp. 1–5. IEEE (2020)
30. Li, J., Fine, J.P.: Weighted area under the receiver operating characteristic curve and its application to gene selection. J. Royal Stat. Soc. Ser. C (Appl. Stat.) **59**(4), 673–692 (2010)
31. Xu, G.: Deep convolutional neural network to detect J-UNIWARD. In: Proceedings of the 5th ACM Workshop on Information Hiding and Multimedia Security, pp. 67–73 (2017)
32. Wattenberg, M., Viégas, F., Johnson, I.: How to use t-SNE effectively. Distill **1**(10), e2 (2016)

A HEVC Steganalysis Algorithm Based on Relationship of Adjacent Intra Prediction Modes

Henan Shi[1], Tanfeng Sun[1($\boxtimes$)], and Zhaohong Li[2]

[1] School of Electronic Information and Electrical Engineering, Shanghai Jiao Tong University, Shanghai, China
{shn1005,tfsun}@sjtu.edu.cn

[2] School of Electronic and Information Engineering, Beijing Jiaotong University, Beijing, China
zhhli2@bjtu.edu.cn

Abstract. Currently, many High Efficiency Video Coding (HEVC) video steganography algorithms based on Intra Prediction Mode (IPM) have been proposed. However, the existing IPM-based steganalysis algorithms designed for H.264/AVC videos are hard to be effectively applied to HEVC. Thus, it is of significant value to study IPM-based steganalysis for HEVC videos. In this paper, the distortion process of IPM-based HEVC steganography is first modeled. We find that the basic distortion exists in the change of the relationships between each embedded IPM and the adjacent IPMs. By exploiting these characteristics, we propose a novel IPM steganalysis based on the Relationship of Adjacent IPMs (RoAIPM) feature. In detail, the designed RoAIPM feature is constructed by generating different directional Gray-Level Co-occurrence Matrices (GLCMs) and texture characteristics of three refilled matrices: MPM-IPM matrix, Left-IPM matrix and Up-IPM matrix. Experiments prove that the proposed RoAIPM feature is very sensitive to the slight change introduced by IPM-based steganography. In various coding conditions, regardless of whether the feature is after dimension reduction or not, compared with state-of-the-art works, the proposed steganalysis can both present a well higher detection accuracy against the latest IPM-based HEVC steganography methods.

Keywords: Video steganalysis · Intra Prediction Mode (IPM) · Most Probable Mode (MPM) · Gray-Level Co-occurrence Matrix (GLCM) · HEVC

1 Introduction

Steganography is an art and science of covert communication by hiding messages into universal digital media without raising suspicion. As a counter-technique to steganography, steganalysis aims to detect the presence of hidden data. The development of steganalysis takes an immeasurable effect to cope with the abuse of steganography and strengthen national security. Thus, steganalysis has also been widely studied.

In modern steganography, digital media carriers can be images, videos and documents etc. Digital video, as an emerging mainstream media exploding on the network,

X. Zhao et al. (Eds.): IWDW 2021, LNCS 13180, pp. 227–242, 2022.
https://doi.org/10.1007/978-3-030-95398-0_16

has the characteristics of high capacity and insensitivity to distortion. Obviously, using videos as carriers has more advantages than other objects. Besides, High Efficiency Video Coding (HEVC) is the latest video coding standard, which significantly improves compression performance and shows almost a 50% bit rate reduction compared with H.264/AVC [1]. Consequently, the research on steganalysis for HEVC videos is of important academic significance and high applied value.

According to the embedding domain, video steganography can be classified into spatial domain steganography and compressed domain steganography. The first type embeds messages in pixels. The second type embeds data by modifying compressed domain parameters, such as Motion Vectors (MVs) [2–4], quantized DCT coefficients [5–7] or Intra Prediction Modes (IPMs) [8–11]. Since videos are transmitted mostly in compressed format, the second type is more practical. Furthermore, IPM-based steganography generally has considerable capacity of secret information and low computational complexity, which makes it be a popular steganography method. According to the distortion introduced by modifying IPMs, Dong et al. [8] presented a HEVC Steganographic Channel Model (SCM), and proposed a novel coding efficiency preserving steganography based on Prediction Units (PUs). Later, Dong et al. [9] optimized the previous algorithm. Instead of just using 4 × 4 PUs to embed secret data, the authors exploited IPMs in multi-sized Prediction Blocks (PBs) in each Coding Tree Unit (CTU), achieving the improvement of capacity without introducing significant degradation in visual quality while preserving coding efficiency as well. Wang et al. [10] gave an IPM-based HEVC steganography to maintain rate-distortion optimization and increase empirical security. This algorithm captured the embedding impacts on both neighboring and current PUs by designing a distortion function, and three-layered isolated channels were established according to the property of IPM coding. Wang et al. [11] also designed a novel IPM-based steganography for HEVC. The authors presented the probability distribution of 4 × 4 IPMs, and proposed a cover selection rule combined with Coding Units (CUs) and PUs coding information.

As discussed above, IPM-based steganography has been concerned a lot because HEVC provides abundant IPMs for embedding. However, to the best knowledge of authors, there are few steganalysis algorithms that can effectively detect IPM-based HEVC steganography. Thus, the steganography lacks targeted security detection. Currently, we only find one effective IPM-based steganalysis method for H.264/AVC videos [12], which used IPM Calibration (IPMC) features for detection. The features depended on the transition probability and transition distance of each IPM. But the IPMs of HEVC are much more complicated, causing the descent of the feature sensitivity. Therefore, when detecting IPM-based HEVC steganography, the performance is negatively impacted.

To solve above problem, we summarize our main contributions as follows:

1. Modelling the general process of IPM-based HEVC steganography and concluding the fundamental distortion brought by the modification of IPMs. The main analysis is as follows. During the process of intra-coding in HEVC, to ensure the quality of compressed videos and minimize the size of bit stream, the IPMs in original videos are the optimal IPMs in accordance with the intra-modes coding which defines three Most Probable Modes (MPMs) for current luma PU. The contents of neighboring

blocks are similar, and their optimal IPMs are close. However, the modified IPMs in such stego-videos are generally not the optimal. Thus, the characteristic that neighboring IPMs are close is destroyed. Moreover, the MPMs of current PU are decided by the IPMs of neighboring encoded PBs. Thus, in the stego-videos, the probability that current IPM belongs to the three MPMs is greatly reduced.

2. Proposing an effective RoAIPM feature and a novel IPM-based HEVC steganalysis algorithm. The concrete idea is described below. If we present the IPMs distribution of neighboring blocks and the MPMs of every current block in the form of matrix, and capture the relationships between the IPM of each embedded block and adjacent IPMs as well as its MPMs, the fundamental feature changes of stego-videos can be obtained. According to this principle, the algorithm captures the RoAIPM feature by adopting Gray-Level Co-occurrence Matrix (GLCM), which can reflect the change of relationships between adjacent IPMs in different directions. Although the universality of features from all blocks of different sizes is better, they are less targeted and less sensitive, together with the fact that 4×4 PUs are main covers in all IPM-based steganography, so the RoAIPM feature is extracted only from 4×4 PUs. Experiments demonstrate that the proposed steganalysis can validly detect almost all the current IPM-based HEVC steganography algorithms [8, 9, 11], and the accuracy rates are much higher than existing other works.

The rest of this paper is organized as follow. In Sect. 2, the HEVC intra prediction process is introduced and the distortion process of IPM-based HEVC steganography is modeled. In Sect. 3, the producing principle of the RoAIPM feature is explained. The proposed steganalysis algorithm is described in Sect. 4. Section 5 shows the experimental results and analysis. Finally, the concluding remarks are given in Sect. 6.

2 Modelling of IPM-Based HEVC Steganography

2.1 Basics of Intra Prediction in HEVC

There are many innovative technologies introduced in HEVC. For instance, instead of the fixed size macroblock in H.264/AVC, the size of blocks in HEVC can be changed self-adaptively. HEVC defines a set of brand new concepts for block coding, including Coding Tree Unit (CTU), Coding Unit (CU), Prediction Unit (PU) and Transform Unit (TU). A frame in HEVC video is first spilt into several 64×64 nonoverlapping CTUs. Then every CTU either is directly used as CU or further partitioned into multiple CUs with sizes of 32×32, 16×16 or 8×8. In the smooth region of a frame, the sizes of CUs are larger, and the smaller CUs are selected in the edge or the area with complex texture, which is beneficial to improve coding efficiency.

CUs can be further split into PUs and TUs. An intra predicted CU may have one of the two types of PU partitions modes: $2N \times 2N$ and $N \times N$. The first type means that the CU is not split, and the second type indicates that the CU is split into four equal-sized PUs. PUs are the blocks where Intra Prediction Modes (IPMs) are established, and each PU has its own IPM. Intra-prediction aims to remove spatial redundancies between the current block and its neighbors. Compared with H.264/AVC, the number of IPMs increases from 9 to 35 in HEVC, including planar mode numbered 0, DC mode numbered 1 and 33 angular modes defined for luma information.

In the process of intra prediction in HEVC. Firstly, Rough Mode Decision (RMD) is used to choose candidate modes from the 35 modes. The number of candidate modes is determined by the size of the PU. RMD refers to the Sum of Absolute Transformed Difference (SATD) and the length of bits used for expressing the coding information of each mode. Secondly, three Most Probable Modes (MPMs) are added into candidate set. If current IPM is one of the MPMs, only its index in the MPMs is encoded. Otherwise, its index in remaining 32 modes is encoded by using a code of 5-bit fixed length. MPMs are decided by the IPMs of the upper and left encoded PUs. If the upper and left PUs are unavailable, they will be set DC mode for calculating MPMs. Concrete calculation rule can be learned from Sullivan et al. [1]. Finally, Rate Distortion Optimization (RDO) is adopted to calculate the RD cost of candidate modes. The mode with the minimum RD cost is the optimal mode of the PU.

2.2 Modelling of IPM-Based HEVC Steganography

As already mentioned, though there is the algorithm using IPMs in multi-sized PBs as covers to improve the capacity, such as Dong et al. [9], texture rich regions are more suitable for steganography and most of IPM-based steganography algorithms only choose 4×4 PBs as covers. Therefore, the proposed steganalysis only extracts the feature based on 4×4 PBs, which is also effective against the steganography using multi-sized PBs as covers, and the following IPMs specially refer to 4×4 IPMs. Figure 1 describes a general embedding process of IPM-based HEVC steganography.

Firstly, compress the frames read from original video stream using HEVC encoder. Then, obtain embedding blocks as well as their IPMs according to the cover selection rule. Two number-adjacent blocks have similar prediction directions, and the principle of modifying IPMs is replacing them with the modes that are similar in prediction direction. In different algorithms, one prediction mode has one or several candidate IPMs. To reduce the influence on coding efficiency, concrete coding methods of secret message are mainly based on the Syndrome-Trellis Code (STC) [13]. By calculating Rate Distortion (RD) cost of the candidate and original modes for each embedding block, the cost of IPM modifying is obtained, and the sum of total cost is the final distortion function. In addition, in original videos, the IPM yielding the minimum RD cost is chosen as the optimal one to predict and encode current PU. Finally, use the modified IPMs that minimize the final distortion function to re-encode current frame.

As illustrated above, IPM-based HEVC steganography usually replaces original optimal IPMs with the modes that yield the minimum cost for IPMs changing. It may divide 35 modified IPMs into two groups, representing secret data 0 and 1 respectively. Steganography operation can be generally expressed as follows:

$$\tilde{m}_k = m_k + \beta_k \cdot \omega_k, \tag{1}$$

where the modified and the original IPMs of block k are represented by $\tilde{m}_k \in [0, 34]$ and $m_k \in [0, 34]$ respectively. $\omega_k \in [-34, 34]$ indicates the change introduced by steganography. Above parameters are all integers. $\beta_k \in \{0, 1\}$ determines whether block k is used to embed information.

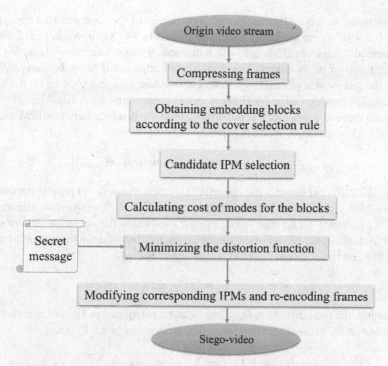

Fig. 1. General embedding process of IPM-based HEVC steganography

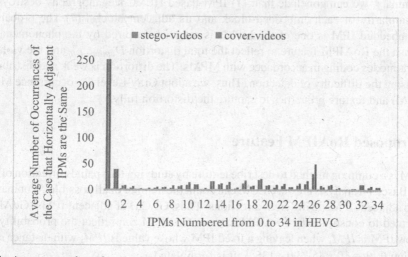

Fig. 2. Average number of occurrences of the case that horizontally adjacent IPMs are the same

Furthermore, we count the number of occurrences of the case that two horizontally adjacent 4×4 IPMs are the same, which are from 0 to 34. As shown in Fig. 2, the case that horizontally adjacent IPMs are both 8 happens 9 times in cover-videos, but it just happens 4 times in stego-videos. The similarity of adjacent IPMs is broken obviously. Through the theory analysis and experiment above, the idea that focuses on the change of relationships between adjacent IPMs to detect steganography is feasible.

For each current 4×4 block k, the distortion in the distance between IPM-numbers of it and the adjacent upper block is expressed as follow:

$$\varphi_{k-upper} = \left| dist\left(\tilde{m}_k, m_{upper}\right) - dist\left(m_k, m_{upper}\right) \right|, \tag{2}$$

where $m_{upper} \in [0, 34]$ denotes the upper IPM. Function $dist(x, y)$ represents the absolute value of the difference between number x and y. In cover-videos, the value of $dist\left(m_k, m_{upper}\right)$ may be smaller. Thus, $\varphi_{k-upper}$ indicates the deviation degree of current IPM from the upper IPM. For the same reason, the distortion in the distance between current IPM and the adjacent left IPM is defined as follow:

$$\varphi_{k-left} = \left| dist\left(\tilde{m}_k, m_{left}\right) - dist\left(m_k, m_{left}\right) \right|. \tag{3}$$

Consequently, the total distortion $D_{upper-left}$ can be calculated as Eq. (4). n indicates the total number of PUs that are embedded secret message in one I-frame.

$$D_{upper-left} = D_{upper} + D_{left} = \sum_{k=1}^{n} \varphi_{k-upper} + \sum_{k=1}^{n} \varphi_{k-left}. \tag{4}$$

In summary, we can conclude that: (1) IPM-based HEVC steganography destroys the IPM-similarity of each embedded block and its adjacent blocks. (2) The probability that embedded IPM is one of the MPMs is reduced. Inspired by the phenomena, we establish the RoAIPM feature to reflect the total distortion $D_{upper-left}$ and the violation of intra-modes coding in accordance with MPMs. The distortion is weak and distributed, increasing the difficulty of detection. Thus, we adopt Gray-Level Co-occurrence Matrix (GLCM) and texture properties to capture the distortion fully.

3   Proposed RoAIPM Feature

GLCM is a common method to describe texture by studying the spatial correction of gray level. Based on analysis above, GLCM can count the number of all possible combinations of two adjacent IPMs in different directions. Thus, GLCM of adjacent IPMs (GoAIPM) is adopted to constitute the RoAIPM feature. GoAIPM can reflect the probability that the new IPM is IPM_j when leaving a fixed IPM whose value is IPM_i with distance d and direction θ. $\theta \in \left\{0°, 45°, 90°, 135°\right\}$. It is formulated as:

$$\text{GoAIPM}\left(IPM_i, IPM_j\right) = \{|C_1, C_2| | C_1 = C(x_1, y_1) = IPM_i, C_2 = C(x_2, y_2) = IPM_j\}, \tag{5}$$

where C is original IPM-matrix with grayscale N_g, and $GoAIPM$ of size $N_g \times N_g$ represents the feature matrix of C. $|C_1, C_2|$ is the number of ordinal combination

(IPM_i, IPM_j), which denotes the coordinate of $GoAIPM$. The distance and direction between coordinate (x_1, y_1) and (x_2, y_2) are d and θ respectively. That is, the number of all possible combinations of previous and after IPMs can be expressed in the form of a matrix. In practice, the size of C is decided by the video resolution, and the element IPM is range from 0 to 34. Thus, N_g is 35. Take $d = 1$ and $\theta = 0°$ for example, as illustrated in Fig. 3, C with IPMs ranging from 1 to 8 is chosen as the original IPM-matrix, and the generation process of the GoAIPM feature of C is depicted in red.

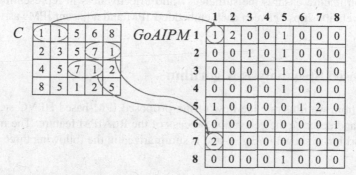

Fig. 3. GoAIPM feature generation process of matrix C (Color figure online)

Moreover, three novel texture characteristics are also proposed to characterize the textures of GoAIPM. Here we introduce three scalars: Angular Second Moment (ASM), correlation and homogeneity. ASM is the summation of squared elements in the GLCM, and ASM of Adjacent IPMs (ASMoAIPM) is defined as Eq. (6),

$$\text{ASMoAIPM} = \sum_{IPM_i=1}^{N_g} \sum_{IPM_j=1}^{N_g} \left(GoAIPM\left(IPM_i, IPM_j\right)\right)^2. \tag{6}$$

Correlation reflects the consistency of texture, and Correlation of Adjacent IPMs (CORoAIPM) is calculated as:

$$\text{CORoAIPM} = \sum_{IPM_i=1}^{N_g} \sum_{IPM_j=1}^{N_g} \frac{\left(IPM_i IPM_j\right)GoAIPM\left(IPM_i, IPM_j\right) - u_{IPM_i}u_{IPM_j}}{s_{IPM_i}s_{IPM_j}}, \tag{7}$$

$$u_{IPM_{i(j)}} = \sum_{IPM_i=1}^{N_g} \sum_{IPM_j=1}^{N_g} IPM_{i(j)} \cdot GoAIPM\left(IPM_i, IPM_j\right), \tag{8}$$

$$s_{IPM_{i(j)}}^2 = \sum_{IPM_i=1}^{N_g} \sum_{IPM_j=1}^{N_g} GoAIPM\left(IPM_i, IPM_j\right)\left(IPM_{i(j)} - u_{IPM_{i(j)}}\right)^2. \tag{9}$$

Homogeneity indicates the closeness of elements to diagonal ones, and Homogeneity of Adjacent IPMs (HOMoAIPM) is formulated as Eq. (10),

$$\text{HOMoAIPM} = \sum_{IPM_i=1}^{N_g} \sum_{IPM_j=1}^{N_g} \frac{GoAIPM\left(IPM_i, IPM_j\right)}{1 + \left|IPM_i - IPM_j\right|}. \tag{10}$$

Consequently, ASMoAIPM accurately captures the change of energy after steganography. CORoAIPM and HOMoAIPM indicate the distortion on the similarity of adjacent IPMs.

In conclusion, the proposed RoAIPM feature includes the GoAIPM feature and three novel texture characteristics, as following formula:

$$\text{RoAIPM} = \{\text{GoAIPM, ASMoAIPM, CORoAIPM, HOMoAIPM}\}. \quad (11)$$

Such fusion feature ensures the sufficiency and effectiveness in representing the distortion on relationships between each embedded IPM and adjacent IPMs as well as its MPMs.

4 Proposed Steganalysis Algorithm

In this section, we illustrate the flow of the proposed IPM-based HEVC steganalysis algorithm and describe the generation process of the RoAIPM feature. The framework of the algorithm is shown in Fig. 4, and is summarized in the following three steps:

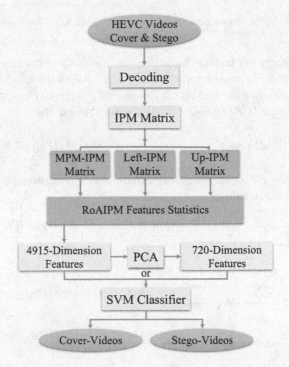

Fig. 4. Framework of the proposed steganalysis algorithm

Firstly, decode input videos to produce an IPM-matrix for each I-frame by taking 4×4 blocks as units. The coordinate of every matrix element corresponds to the position

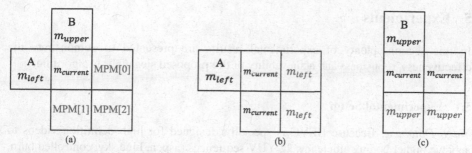

Fig. 5. Filling rules of (a) MPM-IPM, (b) Left-IPM, (c) Up-IPM matrices for uniform 4 × 4 PUs (Color figure online)

of each IPM in the image one by one. However, the IPMs in a CU are probably the same, which will weaken the expression of changes of relationships between adjacent IPMs, and the MPMs of each block need fill in adjacent positions, which is convenient for GoAIPM to reflect relationships of the IPM and its MPMs. To strengthen the statistics of embedding impact, according to Sect. 3, three refilled matrices are derived from the IPM matrix: MPM-IPM matrix, Left-IPM matrix and Up-IPM matrix. In these refilled matrices, if there are four 4 × 4 PUs with different IPMs in one 8 × 8 CU, which are classified as non-uniform 4 × 4 PUs, the IPMs remain unchanged, or else the IPM of current PU is reset according to three matrix filling rules. As depicted in Fig. 5, a small square represents a 4 × 4 block. Taking uniform 4 × 4 PUs as example, which have the same IPM named $m_{current}$. m_{left} and m_{upper} are the IPMs of block A and B respectively. MPM[0], MPM[1] and MPM[2] are MPMs of $m_{current}$, which are set according to m_{left} and m_{upper}. The reset IPMs are in blue.

Secondly, the RoAIPM feature is extracted only from 4 × 4 PUs by altering IPMs that are not in 4 × 4 PUs of the three matrices to a non-existing value and deleting the row and column of this value in the GoAIPM. Specifically, according to the characteristic of the refilled matrix, generate the GoAIPMs of MPM-IPM matrix with direction $\theta = 0°$ and $90°$ respectively, and obtain the three texture characteristics of GoAIPM with $\theta = 0°$, $90°$ and $135°$. In the same way, generate the GoAIPMs of Left-IPM matrix and Up-IPM matrix with $\theta = 0°$ and $90°$ respectively, and produce the three texture characteristics of GoAIPM from Left-IPM matrix and Up-IPM matrix with $\theta = 0°$ and $90°$ respectively. d is 1. Therefore, each GoAIPM has 35×35 features, and the dimension of the RoAIPM feature is 4915.

In this way, by using different parameters of direction, we take full advantage of filling methods of three matrices. IPMs distribution of neighboring blocks and MPMs of every current block are more intuitively presented in the three matrices. Hence, the changes of relationships between the IPM of every embedded block and the IPMs of its upper and left adjacent blocks as well as its MPMs are captured effectively, which contributes most to the high detection accuracy of the proposed steganalysis.

Thirdly, the RoAIPM feature can be directly sent into Support Vector Machine (SVM) for classification. Besides, Principal Component Analysis (PCA) [14] can be chosen to deal with dimension reduction. Experiments prove that the feature is both effective in these two ways.

5 Experiments

In this section, plenty of experimental results are presented to demonstrate the effectiveness, robustness and achievability of the proposed steganalysis algorithm.

5.1 Experimental Setup

Video Database. Because HEVC is specially designed for high definition videos to achieve higher coding efficiency, 22 YUV sequences (aspen, blue sky, controlled burn, crowd run, ducks take off, factory, in to tree, life, old town cross, park joy, pedestrian area, red kayak, riverbed, rush field cuts, rush hour, snow mint, speed bag, station, sunflower, touchdown pass, tractor, west wind easy) with 1920×1080 resolution are compressed to establish video database. In order to determine the length of GOP clearly and control experimental variables easily, all sequences are further divided into small sequences with 100 frames each, and 112 subsequences can be obtained. The details of experiment environment are listed in Table 1.

Table 1. Environment of experiments

Environment	Values
Encoder	X265 (ver 2.8)
Decoder	HM 16.7
Different videos number	22
Resolution of sequences	1920×1080
Total frames to be encoded	11200
GOP size	10
GOP structure	IPPPPPPPPPIPPPPPPPPP $\cdots$
QP range	$\{15, 20, 25\}$

Steganographic Methods. To evaluate the universal performance of the proposed steganalysis, three latest IPM-based HEVC steganography: Dong et al. [8] (denoted as Tar1 [8]), Dong et al. [9] (denoted as Tar2 [9]) and Wang et al. [11] (denoted as Tar3 [11]), are leveraged by modifying the source code of X265 encoder to produce stegovideos. The payload is 0.5, which is the common payload. In our experiments, different QPs can change the partition of PUs and embedding capacity. Hence, the detection performance under different embedding strengths also can be analyzed.

Steganalytic Methods. To compare the proposed steganalysis with current widely-used steganalytic methods, two latest steganalysis algorithms are implemented: Zhao et al. [12], which is currently the only steganalysis against IPM-based steganography specially, and Zhai et al. [15], which is the latest universal steganalysis in both partition mode domain and MV domain. Although the embedding modification of IPMs belongs to intra-frame steganography, the change of IPMs influences the selection of MVs and coding partition modes. Thus, Zhai et al. [15] is also used for comparison.

Training and Classification. To improve the statistical stability of the steganalysis feature, in each experiment, all I-frames from cover-videos or stego-videos are randomly divided into training set and testing set with the ratio of 2:1, and to ensure the preciseness of experiments, the frames from the same video are not be separated. The final accuracy rate is the average of results of 20 random partitions. The SVM [16] is employed as classifier, and we choose polynomial kernel as the kernel function.

5.2 Performance on Accuracy Rate

The proposed steganalysis is compared with steganalysis algorithms [12, 15] described above, which are represented as Zhao et al. (2015) and Zhai et al. (2020) respectively. Accuracy rate is defined as the ratio of predicted value, which is same as actual value, to all predicted results. Optimal experimental results are shown in bold.

Firstly, QP is the short for quantization parameter, which can control video bit rates and reflect the compression of spatial details. All experiments are conducted under three general and representative QPs. As shown in Table 2, when Tar1 [8] is detected, whether QP is 15, 20 or 25, the accuracy rate of the proposed steganalysis is always the highest and above 99%. The detection effect is stable. Furthermore, according to research, 4×4 PUs are selected as covers in Tar1 [8], which signifies a low embedding capacity. So, the best accuracy rate given by Zhao et al. (2015) is just 91.25% when QP is 15, and results demonstrate a strong effect of the proposed feature captured only from 4×4 PUs. The results of Zhai et al. (2020) are around 50%. Zhai et al. (2020) is mainly based on the consistency of MVs and the experiments of it were conducted for H.264/AVC videos. Thus, it may be disabled while detecting IPM-based HEVC steganography. To the contrary, as discussed in Sect. 2.2, by capturing the fundamental distortion, the proposed steganalysis can always obtain the highest detection accuracy against the stego-videos with various embedding strengths.

Table 2. Accuracy rates comparison with the three steganalysis methods for Tar1 [8]

Steganography method	Steganalysis method	QP		
		15	20	25
Tar1 [8]	Proposed steganalysis	**99.72%**	**99.72%**	**99.31%**
	Zhao et al. (2015)	91.25%	81.25%	71.94%
	Zhai et al. (2020)	48.06%	50.97%	50.97%

Table 3 presents the performance results of three steganalysis methods against steganography Tar2 [9]. The same conclusion mentioned above can also be drawn. Whatever the value of QP, the accuracy rates of the proposed steganalysis are always the highest and about 99%. When QP is 15, the result of Zhao et al. (2015) is 91.94%.

Zhao et al. (2015) shows the better results against Tar2 [9] than the results against Tar1 [8]. One major reason is that Tar2 [9] utilizes multi-sized PBs to embed information instead of just 4×4 PBs in Tar1 [8], improving the embedding capacity, and thus Tar2 [9] is easier to detect. Besides, when QP is higher, the result of Zhao et al. (2015) has a greater improvement compared with the results against Tar1 [8]. For example, when QP is 25, the results are respectively 71.94% and 78.19%, increasing about 7%. The chief reason is that, according to the recursive procedure of the block partition in HEVC, when QP increases, the number of small blocks decreases, and the number of large-size PBs increases. So, the improvement of the capacity of Tar2 [9] is more significant compared with Tar1 [8]. The IPM calibration features of Zhao et al. (2015) are extracted from multi-sized PBs. Therefore, in contrast to the results against Tar1 [8], the accuracy rate of Zhao et al. (2015) has a more growth as QP increases, but the results of the proposed steganalysis have little change.

Table 3. Accuracy rates comparison with the three steganalysis methods for Tar2 [9]

Steganography method	Steganalysis method	QP		
		15	20	25
Tar2 [9]	Proposed steganalysis	**98.33%**	**98.89%**	**99.44%**
	Zhao et al. (2015)	91.94%	85.83%	78.19%
	Zhai et al. (2020)	48.89%	48.75%	47.36%

Finally, as shown in Table 4, although the accuracy rates of the proposed steganalysis are still the highest, performances are descended compared with the results in Table 2 and Table 3. Considering that Tar3 [11] selects only IPMs of non-uniform 4×4 PUs as covers, if current IPM is equal to one of its MPMs, it will also be excluded from the cover set while the capacity of current CU is sufficient [11]. Hence, the proposed feature, which is captured by changing the IPMs of uniform 4×4 PUs to adjacent IPM or MPMs to generate refilled matrices, may has difficulty in representing the embedding distortion of Tar3 [11]. Besides, the results of Zhao et al. (2015) are about 70% and the effect is significantly reduced. This finding is understandable because it does not consider the innovation of HEVC coding and the capacity of Tar3 [11] is lower.

Table 4. Accuracy rates comparison with the three steganalysis methods for Tar3 [11]

Steganography method	Steganalysis method	QP		
		15	20	25
Tar3 [11]	Proposed steganalysis	**92.33%**	**95.14%**	**95.97%**
	Zhao et al. (2015)	74.31%	71.11%	66.67%
	Zhai et al. (2020)	50.56%	51.11%	46.67%

Figure 6 presents the trend of accuracy rates as QP increases when detecting Tar3 [11]. It is worth noting that with the increase of QP, the accuracy rate of the proposed steganalysis has an upward trend, but the results of Zhao et al. (2015) and Zhai et al. (2020) have a downward trend. According to observations, the conclusion is also applicable for Tar1 [8] and Tar2 [9]. For instance, in Table 4, the results of the proposed steganalysis are respectively 92.33%, 95.14% and 95.97%, and the results of Zhao et al. (2015) are respectively 74.31%, 71.11% and 66.67% when QP is 15, 20 and 25. The results suggest that, in HEVC, the number of small blocks decreases as QP increases, and the main embedding cover 4 × 4 PBs decrease. Thus, Zhao et al. (2015) and Zhai et al. (2020) perform worse as QP increases and capacity decreases. In contrast, the proposed feature is extracted only from 4 × 4 PBs. Thus, the change of capacity has little influence on the performance of our algorithm. Secondly, the higher the QP is, the coarser the quantization is, and some details are lost, which leads to the degradation of video quality. The embedding distortion on the relationship between the IPM and its adjacent IPMs as well as MPMs will be more obvious. Consequently, the performance results of the proposed steganalysis may be better as QP increases.

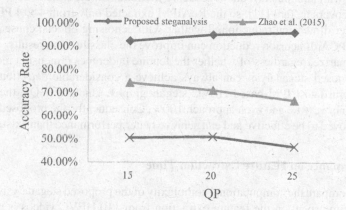

Fig. 6. Trend of accuracy rates for Tar3 [11] as QP increases

5.3 Performance with Dimension Reduction

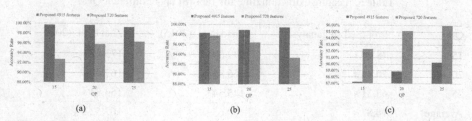

Fig. 7. Accuracy rates with the proposed feature of decreased dimension for (a) Tar1 [8], (b) Tar2 [9] and (c) Tar3 [11]

Furthermore, the proposed feature has been tested both before and after PCA dimension reduction. According to the applied conditions of PCA, considering that the sample number 720 of test set is smaller than both the sample number 1520 of training set and original dimension of 4915, we attempt to reduce the dimension of the feature to 720. As shown in Fig. 7, when detecting Tar1 [8] and Tar2 [9], the proposed feature of decreased dimension performs not as well as the original feature. Because the lower the dimension is, the less information is retained, and the training accuracy is reduced. Together with the linearity of the model may be not high, but PCA can only deal with typical linear models. Therefore, the accuracy decreases gradually. Even so, the proposed steganalysis still performs much better than other methods. For instance, when detecting Tar2 [9], the accuracy rates are respectively 97.78%, 96.39% and 93.33% under QPs of 15, 20 and 25 while the feature is reduced to 720 dimensions. In terms of Tar3 [11], when QP is 25, the result is 90.28% with the 4915-dimension feature, but the result is 95.97% with the 720-dimension feature, increasing about 6%. PCA constructs new feature set by combining original features linearly. Features are sorted according to the degree of variations in different categories. Despite the loss of little information, PCA discards the features with small contribution, reducing the redundancy, and not all 4×4 IPMs are used as covers in Tar3 [11], so the RoAIPM extracted only from 4×4 PBs is more effective after dimension reduction. Together with denoising effects, consequently, in some cases PCA dimension reduction can improve the classification results.

To summarize, regardless of whether the feature undergoes dimension reduction or not, the proposed steganalysis can always achieve a considerable detection accuracy against several latest IPM-based HEVC steganography. Under any QP, the accuracy rates are all above 90% and even approach 100%. Consequently, the proposed RoAIPM feature is proved to be effective and can achieve better performance than existing works.

5.4 Performance on Feature Extraction Time

In order to compare the computational complexity of the proposed steganalysis and other works, the time spent on the feature extraction from 110 HEVC videos is calculated. The average time for one single video is used as final feature extraction time. The experimental facility is a computer with Inter (R) Xeon (R) CPU E5-2630 v3 and 32 GB memory. Experimental results are listed in Table 5, where s is the short for second (a unit for measuring time). The optimal results are displayed in bold.

Table 5. Feature extraction time for Tar1 [8] under different QPs

QP	Proposed steganalysis	Zhao et al. (2015)	Zhai et al. (2020)
15	**78.97 s**	199.60 s	173.27 s
20	**70.42 s**	166.82 s	163.46 s
25	**63.21 s**	145.54 s	153.84 s
Average	**70.87 s**	170.65 s	163.52 s

As presented in Table 5, when QP is higher, the feature extraction time is less. Because HEVC videos codec faster as QP increases. Besides, the feature extraction time of the proposed steganalysis is always the least compared with the results of another two steganalysis methods. For a HEVC video, the extraction time is just 63.21 s when QP is 25. In Zhao et al. (2015), each video needs to be decompressed and compressed again. In Zhai et al. (2020), the feature extraction needs to use the encoding information of each P-frame. Thus, they are more time-consuming. In conclusion, the proposed steganalysis achieves the least feature extraction time compared with existing other works.

6 Conclusion

Nowadays, steganography is used frequently by spy agencies and terrorist organizations, which poses a serious threat to national interests and security. To curb the abuse of steganography, effective steganalysis has become an urgent need in most countries. In this paper, a novel IPM-based steganalysis algorithm for HEVC is proposed. The paper first models the distortion process of IPM-based HEVC steganography, concluding that such steganography destroys the IPM-similarity of each embedded block and its adjacent blocks, and the relationships of embedded IPM and the MPMs are also influenced. Accordingly, we design the RoAIPM feature, which utilizes GLCM as well as three texture properties to tackle the issue.

Experiments indicate that, when detecting several latest steganography algorithms, regardless of whether the feature undergoes dimension reduction or not, the accuracy rate of the proposed steganalysis is always the highest, demonstrating a strong effect and stability of the RoAIPM feature. Moreover, universal steganalysis has become a trend, so future research could evaluate the performance of fusion features extracted from multiple domains.

References

1. Sullivan, G.J., Ohm, J.R., Han, W.J., Wiegand, T.: Overview of the high efficiency video coding (HEVC) standard. IEEE Trans. Circuits Syst. Video Technol. **22**(12), 1649–1668 (2013)
2. Yang, J., Li, S.: An efficient information hiding method based on motion vector space encoding for HEVC. Multimedia Tools Appl. **77**(10), 11979–12001 (2017). https://doi.org/10.1007/s11 042-017-4844-1
3. Zhai, L., Wang, L., Ren, Y.: Multi-domain embedding strategies for video steganography by combining partition modes and motion vectors. In: IEEE International Conference on Multimedia and Expo (ICME), Shanghai, China, July 2019, pp. 1402–1407 (2019)
4. Rana, S., Kamra, R., Sur, A.: Motion vector based video steganography using homogeneous block selection. Multimedia Tools Appl. **79**(9–10), 5881–5896 (2019). https://doi.org/10. 1007/s11042-019-08525-w
5. Cao, Y., Wang, Y., Zhao, X., Zhu, M., Xu, Z.: Cover block decoupling for content-adaptive H. 264 steganography. In: 6th ACM Workshop Information Hiding Multimedia Security (IH and MMSec), Innsbruck, Austria, June 2018, pp. 23–30 (2018)
6. Suresh, M., Sam, I.S.: High secure video steganography based on shuffling of data on least significant DCT coefficients. In: 2nd International Conference on Intelligent Computing and Control Systems (ICICCS), Vaigai Coll Engn, Madurai, India, June 2018, pp. 877–882 (2018)

7. Zhu, Z., Zheng, N., Qiao, T., Xu, M.: Robust steganography by modifying sign of DCT coefficients. IEEE Access **7**, 168613–168628 (2019)

8. Dong, Y., Jiang, X., Sun, T., Xu, D.: Coding efficiency preserving steganography based on HEVC steganographic channel model. In: Kraetzer, C., Shi, Y.-Q., Dittmann, J., Kim, H.J. (eds.) IWDW 2017. LNCS, vol. 10431, pp. 149–162. Springer, Cham (2017). https://doi.org/10.1007/978-3-319-64185-0_12

9. Dong, Y., Sun, T., Jiang, X.: A high capacity HEVC steganographic algorithm using intra prediction modes in multi-sized prediction blocks. In: Yoo, C.D., Shi, Y.-Q., Kim, H.J., Piva, A., Kim, G. (eds.) IWDW 2018. LNCS, vol. 11378, pp. 233–247. Springer, Cham (2019). https://doi.org/10.1007/978-3-030-11389-6_18

10. Wang, Y., Cao, Y., Zhao, X., Xu, Z., Zhu, M.: Maintaining rate-distortion optimization for IPM-based video steganography by constructing isolated channels in HEVC. In: 6th ACM Workshop on Information Hiding and Multimedia Security (IH and MMSec), Innsbruck, Austria, June 2018, pp. 97–107 (2018)

11. Wang, J., Jia, X., Kang, X., Shi, Y.: A cover seletion HEVC video steganography based on intra prediction mode. IEEE Access **7**, 119393–119402 (2019)

12. Zhao, Y., Zhang, H., Cao, Y., Wang, P., Zhao, X.: Video steganalysis based on intra prediction mode calibration. In: Shi, Y.-Q., Kim, H.J., Pérez-González, F., Echizen, I. (eds.) IWDW 2015. LNCS, vol. 9569, pp. 119–133. Springer, Cham (2016). https://doi.org/10.1007/978-3-319-31960-5_11

13. Filler, T., Judas, J., Fridrich, J.: Minimizing additive distortion in steganography using syndrome-trellis codes. IEEE Trans. Inf. Forensics Secur. **6**(3), 920–935 (2011)

14. Stone, J.V.: Principal component analysis and factor analysis. In: Independent Component Analysis: A Tutorial Introduction, pp. 129–135. MIT Press (2004)

15. Zhai, L., Wang, L., Ren, Y.: Universal detection of video steganography in multiple domains based on the consistency of motion vectors. IEEE Trans. Inf. Forensics Secur. **15**, 1762–1777 (2020)

16. Chang, C., Lin, C.: LIBSVM: a library for support vector machines. ACM Trans. Intell. Syst. Technol. (TIST) **2**(3), 1–27 (2011)

Data Hiding Based on Redundant Space of WeChat Mini Program Codes

Jia Chen[1,2] ⓘ, Jiayu Wang[1,2] ⓘ, Yongjie Wang[1,2] ⓘ, and Xuehu Yan[1,2](✉) ⓘ

[1] National University of Defense Technology, Hefei 230037, China
[2] Anhui Key Laboratory of Cyberspace Security Situation Awareness
and Evaluation, Hefei 230037, China

Abstract. With the widespread use of mini program codes, research on data hiding based on mini program codes is necessary for protecting the copyright and security of the code. However, in the existing researches, the secret payload is low, which limits the practical application. In this paper, a data hiding scheme based on the redundant space of mini program codes is proposed, which embeds secret information into the uncoded redundant space. The redundant space includes adding extended modules outside each ray (also called rays extension) and adding fake rays (also called rays forgery). The proposed scheme has the advantages of large embedded capacity, good imperceptibility, and strong applicability. For the version v, and the number of modules expanded on the ray n_e, the maximum embedding capacity is $112(4 - v/18) + 13(4 - v/18) + 56n_e$. Theoretical analysis and experiments show the feasibility and effectiveness of the proposed scheme.

Keywords: WeChat mini program codes · Data hiding · Redundant space · Subjective evaluation

1 Introduction

WeChat Mini Program codes come with the WeChat Mini Program App [1]. The WeChat mini program is a lightweight App based on the WeChat platform. Unlike traditional Apps, they load instantly, do not occupy memory, and are easy to use. Relying on WeChat, a super App with over one billion users, it has attracted attention since its release on January 9, 2017, until June 2021. The number of WeChat mini programs has exceeded 4.3 million, daily active users have exceeded 410 million, the average daily usage time per capita has reached 1350 s [2].

Meanwhile, with the widespread use of mini programs, there are more and more application scenarios for mini program codes. After the release of WeChat mini programs, Alipay and Baidu have also invested in developing of mini programs. In this paper, the mini program code refers explicitly to the WeChat mini program code for the convenience of description.

X. Zhao et al. (Eds.): IWDW 2021, LNCS 13180, pp. 243–257, 2022.
https://doi.org/10.1007/978-3-030-95398-0_17

Steganography is a data protection technology that hides secret information into a cover object. Image steganography means that the cover object is an image. Generally speaking, image steganography is divided into two categories. The first is steganography based on the spatial domain. The most typical is based on Least Significant Bit (LSB) [8,11]. The other category is based on the frequency domain. The secret information is embedded into the transform coefficients, such as Discrete Cosine Transform (DCT) [3], Discrete Wavelet Transform (DWT) [9], Fresnelet transform (FT), and so on.

With the extensive use of mini program codes, its security has attracted much attention. To protect the copyright of mini program codes and prevent saboteurs from maliciously tampering with the code, it is necessary to study data hiding schemes based on mini program codes. Chen et al. [7] first proposed a data hiding scheme based on mini program codes. The secret messages are embedded into the encoding region and edge patch using the module replacement method. The process of this scheme is simple and easy to implement. However, the embedding capacity of secret information is low, which limits practical applications. In addition, they modified the module of the cover code to embed the secret. Due to rounding in the process of determining the center, there may be slight errors in the parameters, resulting in traces during the modification.

The research motivation of this paper is to protect the safety of the use of mini program codes. The copyright of the mini program code is protected by embedding private information in it. In addition, the research is also to increase the embedding capacity and the applicability of data hiding schemes based on mini program codes.

Inspired by the research on data hiding based on the padding area of QR codes [6,10,12], we consider expanding the redundant space in the unencoded area of mini program codes to embed secret information. This paper proposes a data hiding scheme based on the redundant space of mini program codes. The secret information is embedded into the redundant space, which includes adding extended modules outside each ray (also called rays extension) and adding fake rays (also called rays forgery). Moreover, when generating the stego code, we create a new canvas and redraw all modules, which can effectively solve the problem of modification traces.

The contributions of this work are summarized as follows.

1. We proposed a new modification method, directly redrawing all the modules, which effectively solved the problem of modification traces and improved the scheme's applicability.
2. A data hiding scheme based on the redundant space of the WeChat mini program code is proposed, which increases the embedding capacity and improves the practicability of the scheme.
3. We verified the effectiveness of rays extension and rays forgery, and evaluated the quality of stego code, which can effectively guide the embedding process.

The organization of this paper is given as follows. Section 2 introduces the relevant background of the mini program code. The proposed scheme is described in Sect. 3. Section 4 gives experiment and evaluation. Finally, conclusions are drawn in Sect. 5.

2 Preliminaries

The mini program code symbol is composed of black and white modules evenly distributed on each ray [4]. A module is a solid circle, and consecutive modules are connected to form a thick solid line. A module is the smallest unit, representing 1 bit, a codeword is equal to 8 bits, where the black module represents '1', and the white module represents '0'. According to the number of rays, mini program codes are divided into three versions, namely V-36, V-54, and V-72. The schematic diagram of the three versions is shown in Fig. 1.

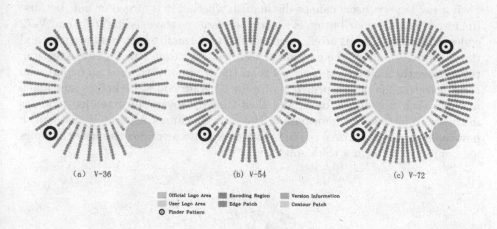

(a) V-36   (b) V-54   (c) V-72

	Official Logo Area		Encoding Region		Version Information
	User Logo Area		Edge Patch		Contour Patch
⊙	Finder Pattern				

Fig. 1. Three versions of mini program codes.

The structure of mini program codes is also shown in Fig. 1. Three finder patterns are mainly used for the positioning and detection of the mini program code and contain the ray's serial number. The version information pattern records the version, error correction level, and mask of the mini program code. The modules in the contour patch are all black, used to separate the user logo area from the encoding region. The official logo area not only indicates the owner of the WeChat platform, but also assists in detection. The user logo area is a pattern chosen by the developer. The edge patch is used to outline the mini program code and does not carry meaningful information. The encoding region contains data and error correction modules [5].

When encoding the mini program code, the Reed-Solomon code is used. The input data is first converted into a bitstream, and error correction codewords are added. Then put the final bitstream into the encoding region one by one. Next, choose one of the 32 mask patterns to balance the module of mini program code. Finally, place modules in the version information pattern, which contains the encoded version, error correction, and mask information. When decoding, remove the mask to get the bitstream according to the version information pattern.

Analyzing the version, structure, and encoding and decoding principles of the mini program code can determine the redundant space. For a V-36 mini program code, the redundant space is shown in Fig. 2, including two areas:

1. Ray extension. Extending each ray and adding extension modules marked in solid red circles to embed secret information.
2. Ray forgery. Adding fake rays marked in blue modules to embed secret information.

For ray forgery, users cannot distinguish whether it is forged or not, because the forged module distribution is exactly the same as the existing V-54 and V-72 codes. Therefore, there is no effective method to normalize such redundancies and thus effectively remove the embedded secret information. But for ray extension, there are extra modules on each ray than the original. If there is an expert who is proficient in the design principle of mini program codes, he knows how many modules each ray should have, and then directly covers all extended modules in theory to filter secret information. However, he cannot accurately distinguish how many modules are on a ray in practice, because several consecutive modules are connected to form a thick solid line.

Fig. 2. The redundant space of the V-36 mini program code.

3   The Proposed Scheme

3.1   Overall Design

The data hiding scheme based on the redundant space of the mini program code is to embed secret information in the uncoded area. In order to optimize the embedding process and overcome the problem of embedding traces, a new modification method was designed, which is to redraw the code. Read all the mini program code modules, create a new blank canvas, and redraw all the modules. In the process of redrawing, secret information is embedded in the redundant space. The flowchart of the proposed scheme is shown in Fig. 3.

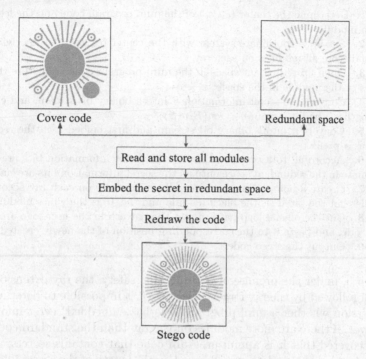

Fig. 3. The flowchart of the proposed scheme.

3.2   Embedding Process

The proposed scheme is divided into two processes, namely the embedding process and the extraction process. In the embedding process, a cover code and secret information are given. The embedding process is shown in Algorithm 1.

For Algorithm 1, there are a few points that need to be explained:

1. In steps 1 and 2, the method of determining the center and the length of the module, and establishing the coordinate system follows the processes in [7].
2. In step 3, to comply with the mini program code standard specification, we add $1(2, 3...n)$ modules on the outermost of each ray, or add 18(36) rays to become the 54(72) version at a time. To mark the embedded area, a prefix is first added during embedding to indicate the length of the secret information, and the remaining space beyond the embedding area is randomly filled with '0' or '1' bits.

Algorithm 1 The embedding process of data hiding scheme based on redundant space of mini program code.

Input: A cover code and secret information S.
Output: A stego code.

Step 1. Determine the center (c_x, c_y) of the mini program code and the length l_{cw} of each module.
Step 2. Set up a coordinate system with the center (c_x, c_y) as the origin. Then read and store all modules on each ray.
Step 3. Open up redundant space in the mini program code, and store the coordinates of the module in the space.
Step 4. Convert the secret information S into a binary bit stream, and calculate the length of the bit stream $n = len(Bin(S))$
Step 5. Convert n into a binary bit stream and first embed it in the redundant space as a prefix.
Step 6. According to a certain sequence, the secret information bits are given a coordinate in the redundant space until all the secret information bits are embedded.
Step 7. Create a new canvas and draw all the modules on each ray according to the rule that the bit '1' is the black module and the '0' is the white module.
Step 8. Cut the official logo pattern and the pattern in the user logo area in the cover code, and paste it to the corresponding position of the newly created canvas.
Step 9. Output the stego code.

---

3. In step 5, under the premise of not affecting safety, the ray extension is preferred, followed by the ray forgery. Because it is impossible to determine from the version whether a mini program code has embedded secret information. However, if there are more modules on the ray than the standard code, it can be discovered that it is a mini program code that contains secrets, and then the embedded area is determined based on the length of the secret information in the prefix.

4. In step 7, to get closer to the real mini program code, when redrawing a mini program code, a '1' is drawn as an independent solid circle, and continuous '1' is drown as a thick solid line.

3.3 Extraction Process

The extraction process is the inverse process of the embedding process. Given a mini program code, first determine whether there is an extension module on each ray. If so, judge the length of the secret information based on the prefix, and then determine the location of the redundant space. The specific extraction process is shown in Algorithm 2.

Algorithm 2 The extraction process of data hiding scheme based on redundant space of mini program code

Input: A stego code.
Output: The secret information S.
Step 1. Determine the center (c_x, c_y) of the mini program code and the length l_{cw} of each module.
Step 2. Find the redundant space of the mini program code and read the modules in it.
Step 3. Extract the embedded prefix, and further extract the secret information according to the length of the secret information.
Step 4. Convert the binary bit stream into secret information S.
Step 5. Output the secret information.

3.4 Theoretical Analysis

Feasibility. After the secret information is embedded into the redundant space of a mini program code, the stego code can still be decoded successfully. Redundant space will not affect the decoding process of mini program code. It is similar to adding codewords in the edge patch for ray extension and has no specific meaning. No module changed in the version information pattern for ray forgery, so the recorded information is still V-36 code. When decoding, the module read by the standard decoder is also the real V-36 code. Therefore, the data hiding scheme based on the redundant space of mini program codes is feasible.

Security. Steganography is to embed secret information into the carrier. Its essence is to ensure that the embedded secret is not easy to be analyzed by steganalysis. The security of the data hiding scheme based on the redundant space of mini program code is mainly reflected in the visual invisibility. In proposed scheme, the embedding method is optimized. Instead of modifying the original mini program code, all modules including secret information are redrawn, which solves the problem of embedding traces, so that the appearance of the stego code is exactly the same as that of the standard mini program code. As a result, ordinary users can not detect the abnormality of the code and the existence of secret information. Even users who know the mini program code cannot easily see the embedded secret information. Because the forged mini program code is exactly the same as the existing mini program code in the module distribution.

Robustness. The robustness of the steganography scheme is reflected in the anti-interference ability and error correction ability of embedding secret information. The data hiding scheme based on mini program code space embeds secret information by adding additional modules. One module represents one bit secret. This method can resist the change of a pixel and the interference of general Gaussian, salt and pepper noise, etc. However, it can not deal with interference such as dirt, cropping, and fouling. In addition, to increase the robustness of secret information, we can consider encoding the secret using error-correcting code before embedding.

Embedding Capacity. The data hiding scheme based on the redundant space of mini program code embeds secret information in the redundant space, including ray extension and ray forgery. When embedding, we can choose one of the two ways, or a combination of the two ways. The latter can reach the maximum embedding capacity. The maximum embedding capacity for the V-36 mini program code is to turn it into a fake V-72 and then add some extension modules outside. For V-72 mini program code, we can only add extension modules on the outside.

Analyze the difference in the number of modules of different versions of mini program codes to obtain the maximum embedding capacity. The results are shown in the Table 1. Where v represents the version, that is, the number of rays. n_e indicates the number of modules in ray extension. The maximum embedded capacity is $112(4 - v/18) + 1(4 - v/18) + 56n_e$, where $112(4 - v/18)$ represents the number of extra modules in the encoding region, $13(4 - v/18)$ represents the number of extra modules in the edge patch, and $56n_e$ indicates the number of modules in the ray extension.

Table 1. Maximum embedded capacity of different versions of mini program codes.

Version	Number of modules in the encoding region	Number of modules in the edge patch	Maximum embedded capacity
V-36	304	30	$224 + 26 + 56n_e$
V-54	416	43	$112 + 13 + 56n_e$
V-72	528	56	$56n_e$

4 Experiment and Evaluation

4.1 Experiments

In this section, several examples are given through experiments to demonstrate the feasibility of the scheme. The cover image is a V-36 mini program code with the size of 512×512. The secret information is a randomly generated binary bitstream with the length of the maximum embedded capacity. Then we test the embedding effects of ray extension, ray forgery, and the combination of the two methods, respectively. Further, we give the RS steganalysis results to verify the security of the scheme.

Ray Extension. Figure 4 shows the effect of redundant space data hiding based on ray extension, in which Fig. 4(a) shows the V-36 cover code, and Fig. 4(b), 4(d), 4(f), 4(h), and 4(j) show the stego code with the cases of $n_e = 1, 2, 3, 4, 5$. Figure 4(c), 4(e), 4(g), 4(i), and 4(k) respectively show where the secret information is embedded. As n_e increases, the size of the redrawn mini program code will also increase. For example, the size of the Fig. 4(h) is 550×550, and the size of Fig. 4(j) is 570×570.

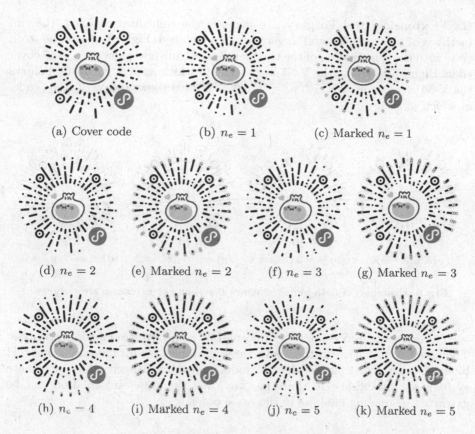

(a) Cover code   (b) $n_e = 1$ (c) Marked $n_e = 1$

(d) $n_e = 2$ (e) Marked $n_e = 2$ (f) $n_e = 3$ (g) Marked $n_e = 3$

(h) $n_e - 4$ (i) Marked $n_e = 4$ (j) $n_c = 5$ (k) Marked $n_e = 5$

Fig. 4. Examples of data hiding schemes based on ray extension.

Ray Forgery. Figure 5 shows the effect of redundant space data hiding based on ray forgery. Figure 5(a) shows the V-36 cover code. Figure 5(b) is the forged V-54 mini program code for embedding secret information. Figure 5(c) is the forged V-72 code. The decoding results of these three mini program codes are the same App.

(a) Cover code   (b) $v = 54$ (c) $v = 72$

Fig. 5. Examples of data hiding schemes based on ray forgery.

Ray Extension and Forgery. To increase the embedded capacity, the two methods of ray extension and forgery can be combined. Figure 6 shows the stego code with the combination of the two methods. Figure 6(a) shows the V-36 cover code. Figure 6(b) shows the V-54 stego code, of which $n_e = 1$. Figure 6(c) shows the V-54 stego code, of which $n_e = 2$. And Fig. 6(d) shows the V-72 stego code, of which $n_e = 3$.

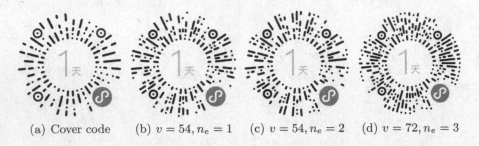

(a) Cover code   (b) $v = 54, n_e = 1$ (c) $v = 54, n_e = 2$ (d) $v = 72, n_e = 3$

Fig. 6. Examples of data hiding schemes based on ray extension and forgery.

The extraction process of secret information is the inverse embedding process. The secret information in the above three examples is all randomly generated bitstreams with the length of the maximum embedding capacity. The coordinate systems are established in the same way, and the secret information can be extracted by reading modules in the same order.

Steganalysis. To evaluate the security of the proposed scheme, we apply RS steganalysis to evaluate the cover and stego code, because the idea of our proposed scheme is similar to LSB embedding. The RS steganalysis is to detect LSB-based steganography and is widely used in data hiding. We conduct RS steganalysis for each type of stego code. Figure 7 shows the result of the $n_e = 2$ in ray extension. The results of other types are consistent with Fig. 7. As the mini program code is special, its texture is simple, and the black and white modules are strictly distributed. The RS steganalysis result of the cover code is different from the pure standard picture, but the RS steganalysis curve of the stego code is consistent with the cover code. Therefore, the results of the RS steganalysis indicate that the proposed scheme can withstand RS steganalysis.

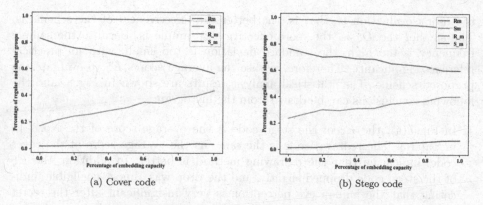

(a) Cover code   (b) Stego code

Fig. 7. The RS analysis of the cover and stego code.

4.2 Subjective Evaluation

Considering the purpose of mini program code, the user accesses the mini program by scanning the code. We can evaluate the quality of a mini program code through subjective evaluation. Even though sometimes the evaluation result may be one-sided, it can accurately reflect the real feelings of users. At the same time, the user's feelings can indicate the imperceptibility of the embedded information, further verifying the security of the scheme.

The subjective evaluation is realized by issuing questionnaires. A questionnaire survey is made online, which contains 45 mini program codes of 15 types. Based on the user's habits, we design criteria to evaluate the user experience, including whether it can be correctly decoded and the speed of recognition, whether the modification trace can be seen, etc. After viewing the mini program code, each survey participant marks a score following Table 2. In the scoring system, 1–4 points correspond to four intuitive perceptions of the human eye: disastrous, poor, moderate, and comfortable.

Sending questionnaires online to a group of students and teachers with ages between 18 and 45, and no knowledge of the mini program code. Finally, 27 valid questionnaires were collected. The results of questionnaires are shown in Table 3. In subjective evaluation, the average $E\xi$ and standard deviation $D\xi$ are two commonly used evaluation indicators [13]. The larger the $E\xi$ is, the better

Table 2. Scoring system in the subjective evaluation

Scores	Descriptions
4	Comfortable
3	Moderate
2	Poor
1	Disastrous

the user's evaluation is, that is, the better the effectiveness of the scheme is. The smaller the $D\xi$ is, the more effective the sample is. Because the sample frequency is too high, the standard deviation is too small, with no practical reference significance. Therefore, we use the average scores $E\xi$ to evaluate the proposed scheme. The statistical analysis results are shown in Fig. 8, and the following conclusions can be drawn from the histogram.

1. In Fig. 8(a), the $E\xi$ of the stego code is the average score of the No. 3–15 in Table 3. The redrawn code is the same as the average score of the cover code, indicating that the redrawing method is better. In addition, the $E\xi$ of the stego code dropped slightly, and the drop was almost negligible, indicating that the human eye perception is very insignificant after the secret information is embedded.
2. In Fig. 8(b), $v - 36$, $v - 54$, and $v - 72$ correspond to the average score of the No. 3–7, No. 8–11, and No. 12–15 in Table 3, respectively. The $E\xi$ of $v - 36$ is higher than $v - 54$, and $v - 72$, indicating the embedding effect of the ray extension is better than the ray forgery and the combination of the two methods.
3. In Fig. 8(c), n_e represents the number of modules expanded on each ray. The histogram result shows that the embedding effect has no direct relationship with the number of extension modules on each ray in ray extension.
4. Figure 8(d) shows the average score of the mini program code with different n_e in ray forgery. The embedding effect of the V-54 forged code is better than V-72. Meanwhile, the stego code quality decreases in the same forged version as the number of modules expanded on each ray increases.

4.3   Comparison

Chen *et al.* [7] first proposed a data hiding scheme based on mini program codes. The secret information is embedded into the encoding region or edge patch. Figure 9 shows an examples of the scheme proposed by Chen *et al.* The cover code with the size of 512×512 is shown in Fig. 9(a). Figure 9(b) shows the module in which the secret information is embedded. The stego code is shown in Fig. 9(c). Look carefully for modification traces, which are marked as red circles in Fig. 9(d).

Table 4 shows the attribute comparison between our scheme and Chen *et al.'* scheme. Our scheme is an improvement based on Chen *et al.* In Chen *et al.'* scheme, the secret information is embedded into the encoding region or edge patch. And they modify modules on the original mini program code to embed secret, so there are likely to be modification traces. Our proposed scheme embeds the secret information into the unencoded redundant space of mini program

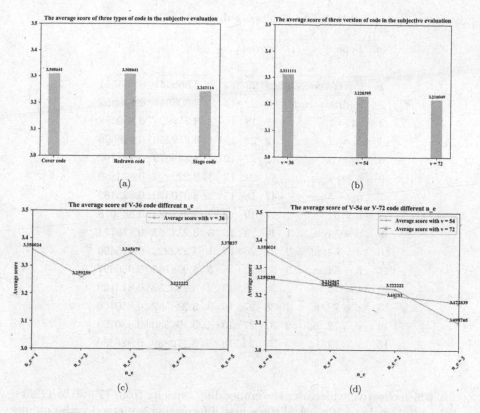

Fig. 8. The statistical analysis results of subjective evaluation.

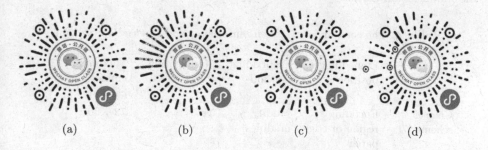

Fig. 9. An example of the scheme proposed by Chen *et al.*

Table 3. The results of subjective evaluation.

No.	Type	Scores				$E\xi$	$D\xi$
		4	3	2	1		
1	Cover code	43	23	12	3	3.308641	0.855511
2	Redrawn code	43	22	14	2	3.308641	0.840957
3	$n_e = 1$	47	18	14	2	3.358024	0.850688
4	$n_e = 2$	42	22	13	4	3.259259	0.899626
5	$n_e = 3$	42	27	10	2	3.345679	0.788192
6	$n_e = 4$	39	24	15	3	3.222222	0.874889
7	$n_e = 5$	47	18	15	1	3.370370	0.823189
8	$v = 54$	47	19	12	3	3.358024	0.865078
9	$v = 54, n_e = 1$	40	23	15	3	3.234567	0.878714
10	$v = 54, n_e = 2$	37	26	17	1	3.222222	0.816496
11	$v = 54, n_e = 3$	36	22	18	5	3.098765	0.950697
12	$v = 72$	38	28	13	2	3.259259	0.813129
13	$v = 72, n_e = 1$	38	27	13	3	3.234567	0.850150
14	$v = 72, n_e = 2$	37	27	13	4	3.197530	0.880793
15	$v = 72, n_e = 3$	38	24	14	5	3.172839	0.926830

codes, which effectively increases the embedding capacity from $72 + 30$ to $112(4 - v/18) + 13(4 - v/18) + 56n_e$. And the secret information is merged with modules of the cover code, then all modules are redrawn in our scheme, which overcomes the modification traces.

Table 4. The comparison between our scheme and Chen *et al.*' scheme

	Embedding position	Embedding method	Modification traces	Maximum embedding capacity
Chen *et al.*' scheme [7]	Encoding region or edge patch	Modify modules	Yes	$72 + 30$
Our scheme	Unencoded redundant space	Redraw modules	No	$112(4 - v/18) + 13(4 - v/18) + 56n_e$

5   Conclusion

After further research on the version, structure, and encoding and decoding principles of mini program codes, this paper proposes a data hiding scheme based on the redundant space of mini program codes, which effectively improves the embedded capacity. We opened up the redundant space (ray extension and ray forgery) in the mini program code, and then embedded the secret information into the uncoded redundant space. In addition, the method of fusing the secret information with cover modules and redrawing all the modules effectively solves the problem of modifying traces, which improves the imperceptibility of embedded information. In future work, we will continue to study new data hiding schemes based on mini program codes to increase embedded capacity, such as syndrome-based data hiding. Further, with the development of steganography schemes, we will study steganalysis based on mini program codes to enhance its security.

References

1. MiniApp standardization white paper W3C first public working draft 12 September 2019, September 2019. https://www.w3.org/TR/mini-app-white-paper/
2. Aladdin: White paper on mini program internet development in the first half of 2021 (2021)
3. Chang, C.C., Lin, C.C., Tseng, C.S., Tai, W.L.: Reversible hiding in DCT-based compressed images. Inf. Sci. Int. J. **177**(13), 2768–2786 (2007)
4. Chen, J.: How does the mini program bloom, September 2017. https://www.ifanr.com/minapp/904702
5. Chen, S.: WeChat mini program code private coding protocol analysis, October 2019. https://zhuanlan.zhihu.com/p/85164898
6. Fu, Z., Cheng, Y., Yu, B.: Visual cryptography scheme with meaningful shares based on QR codes. IEEE Access **6**, 59567–59574 (2018)
7. Chen, J., Qi, Q., Wang, Y., Yan, X., Li, L.: Data hiding based on mini program code. Secur. Commun. Netw. **2021** (2021). https://doi.org/10.1155/2021/5546344
8. Johnson, N.F., Duric, Z., Jajodia, S., Memon, N.: Information hiding: steganography and watermarking-attacks and countermeasures. J. Electron. Imaging **10**(3), 825 (2001)
9. Ramanjaneyulu, K., Rajarajeswari, K.: Wavelet-based oblivious image watermarking scheme using genetic algorithm. IET Image Proc. **6**(4), 364–373 (2012)
10. Tan, L., Lu, Y., Yan, X., Liu, L., Chen, J.: (2, 2) threshold robust visual secret sharing scheme for QR code based on pad codewords. In: Yang, C.-N., Peng, S.-L., Jain, L.C. (eds.) SICBS 2018. AISC, vol. 895, pp. 619–628. Springer, Cham (2020). https://doi.org/10.1007/978-3-030-16946-6_50
11. Luo, W., Huang, F., Huang, J.: Edge adaptive image steganography based on LSB matching revisited. IEEE Trans. Inform. Forensics Secur. **5**(2), 201–214 (2010)
12. Yan, X., Lu, Y., Liu, L., Song, X.: Reversible image secret sharing. IEEE Trans. Inf. Forensics Secur. **15**, 3848–3858 (2020). https://doi.org/10.1109/TIFS.2020.3001735
13. Yan, X., Lu, Y., Yang, C.N., Zhang, X., Wang, S.: A common method of share authentication in image secret sharing. IEEE Trans. Circ. Syst. Video Technol. Early Access **31**(7), 2896–2908 (2020)

Image Block Regression Based on Feature Fusion for CNN-Based Spatial Steganalysis

Ziqing Chen[iD], Xiangyu Yu[✉][iD], and Runze Chen[iD]

School of Electronic and Information Engineering, South China University
of Technology, Guangzhou, China
`201921012373@mail.scut.edu.cn`, `yuxy@scut.edu.cn`

Abstract. The research on image steganalysis has taken a great step forward thanks to the development of convolutional neural network (CNN). However, most existing CNN steganalyzers require deep network architecture and a long training time to obtain good performance. Besides, most methods input a cover image and the corresponding stego image as a pair during the training stage. In this case, not only the label, but also the texture difference between the cover and the stego can be used. In this paper, we propose a novel method for spatial domain steganalysis to boost the detection performance through a secondary task. First, a concise and efficient CNN is used to distinguish stego images from cover images. Second, an up-sampling module via transposed convolution and feature fusion is used to predict the number of modified pixels in different blocks of the image, which is called block regression. The loss functions of these two parts above are optimized simultaneously. Experimental results show that the proposed method can obtain a better performance in detection error rate compared to previous works and a good trade-off between training time and detection accuracy.

Keywords: Image steganalysis · Convolutional Neural Network · Block regression

1 Introduction

Steganalysis, the opposite of steganography, has received lots of attention in recent years. Image steganography [1] achieves the purpose of covert communication by hiding secret message within the specific cover image in an imperceptible manner. On the contrary, steganalysis aims at revealing whether the embedded data exists in the image or not. Modern image steganalysis are mainly divided into hand-crafted features based methods and deep learning methods.

Hand-crafted features based steganalyzers usually consist of three stages: residual computation, feature extraction and classification. Higher-order statistical features capturing complex texture patterns of neighboring samples of image were put into use, which greatly improved the detection accuracy.

X. Zhao et al. (Eds.): IWDW 2021, LNCS 13180, pp. 258–272, 2022.
https://doi.org/10.1007/978-3-030-95398-0_18

One of the typical staganalyzers in spatial domain is Spatial Rich Model (SRM) [9]. It employs a set of high-pass filters (HPF) to extract the noise residual among neighboring pixels, and calculates the fourth-order co-occurrence matrices of the truncated residual. To better cope with the adaptive steganography algorithms, a few methods incorporating selection channel, like maxSRM [7], were proposed. However, the success of these machine learning methods requires tens of thousands of hand-crafted features, which need professional domain knowledge and lots of time to construct.

In recent years, the rapid development of Convolutional Neural Network (CNN) [14] has paved the way for the researchers in the field of image steganalysis [6]. With the help of CNN, feature extraction and classification can be integrated into a framework for training and optimization. Tan and Li [20] proposed an CNN based on stacked convolutional auto-encoders with pre-training. Qian et al. [18] presented Gaussian-Neuron Convolutional Neural Network (GNCNN), which equipped with fixed KV kernel in the SRM, Gaussian function and average pooling. Soon after, Xu et al. [21] took the domain knowledge into account and designed a CNN architecture called Xu-Net. The results showed that it was the first CNN with competitive performance to the SRM. Ye et al. [22] proposed Ye-Net, which used 30 filters of the SRM as the preprocessing layer and Truncated Linear Unit (TLU). The work achieved superior performance to previous methods and proved that incorporating the selection channel in the training can further boost the performance of CNN steganalyzer. Yedroudj et al. [23] proposed Yedroudj-Net, which fuses the beneficial practice of previous propositions, converges well and is able to learn on a small dataset. Boroumand et al. [5] proposed SRNet, which replaced the preprocessing HPFs with 7 convolutional layers without pooling and employed residual shortcut connections. It outperformed previous works in both spatial domain and JPEG domain. Deng et al. [8] proposed a network with the global covariance pooling which exploit the second-order statistic of high-level features. Zhang et al. [26] proposed Zhu-Net, which introduced separable convolution and spatial pyramid pooling (SPP) into steganalysis CNN. You et al. [24] proposed a siamese CNN-based architecture which captured the relationships between different sub-regions in the same image to distinguish the existence of stego signal.

Since the widely use of CNN in steganalysis, the detection performance against content-adaptive steganographic algorithms has made great progress. It becomes more difficult to further improve the network architecture efficiently without larger amount of parameters, long training time and extra help of domain knowledge. For instance, SRNet builts a 12-layer CNN with shortcut connections. Meanwhile, in order to preserve the noise-like stego signals as much as possible, the front 7 layers in SRNet use no pooling operations. However, it is time-consuming to train a network with such huge parameters. In addition, the above-mentioned selection channel does work to improve the performance. But it is also required to compute the selection channel from the stego images with the knowledge of specific steganographic algorithm.

In this paper, we proposed a CNN-based, multi-task learning method, which can further boost the performance of steganalysis. More precisely, the number of embedded pixels in a certain size block, e.g. 4×4 block, of the image, is predicted via deconvolution and feature fusion. The error between the predict map and the cover map is combined with the cross-entropy loss of steganalysis to form a total loss. Experimental results prove the effectiveness of the proposed method. Better detection performance compared to existing methods is obtained without introducing large number of parameters and the time consumption of training is acceptable.

The rest of the paper is organized as follows. In Sect. 2, our method is presented and described. In Sect. 3, the experimental results, relevant discussions and analyses are given. Finally, the conclusions are drawn in Sect. 4.

2   Proposed Method

As shown in Fig. 1, our proposed network consists of two parts: a common steganalysis CNN backbone, and a block regression module for estimating the number of modified pixels in image blocks. On one hand, the backbone network is used for extracting hierarchical features, and finally classifying the features into cover or stego. On the other hand, the block regression module utilizes several feature maps of various size obtained from the upper layers and transforms them into features associated with modified pixels in image block via transpose convolution and concatenation, which will be described in detail.

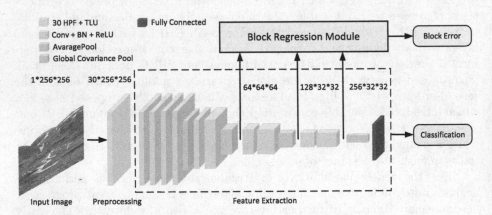

Fig. 1. The architecture of our network which is composed of a backbone network and a block regression module.

2.1   Backbone Network

Preprocessing. As previous works have shown [18,22], random initialized parameters in pre-processing layer bring the problem of slow convergence. Hence, most researchers initialize the first layer with HPFs for transforming the raw image into noise residuals since modeling the residuals can extract more robust features. Therefore, we initialize the preprocessing layer with 30 5×5 HPFs in SRM and keep it trainable during training. It largely suppresses the image content and increases the signal-to-noise ratio between the stego signals and the image signals. The experimental results prove the effectiveness of this scheme compared to fixed kernels, which will be described in detail in Sect. 3.

After the HPFs, Truncated Linear Unit (TLU) [22] is applied for adapting to the distribution of the noise residuals. The TLU is essential to steganalysis since the embedding signals are quite subtle (usually in the range of $[-1, 1]$) and the values of the residuals which are too large or too small should be removed. Hence, the TLU can accelerate the convergence of CNN.

Feature Extraction. In the backbone CNN, 3×3 kernels were used, since small kernels can reduce the number of parameters and two stacked 3×3 convolutional layers achieve the same receptive field as one 5×5 convolutional layer. Two types of convolutional layers marked as Layer T1-C and Layer T2-C shown in Fig. 2(a) are employed, where C denotes the number of channels. The difference between T1 and T2 lies in the abs layer [21] for discarding the signs of the elements in the feature maps and force the model to learn the sign symmetry automatically. Besides, the use of convolutions, batch normalization (BN) [13] and ReLU is generally the same.

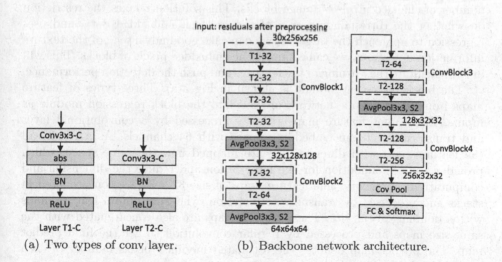

(a) Two types of conv layer.   (b) Backbone network architecture.

Fig. 2. The backbone network architecture and detail designs.

The architecture of feature extraction stage is shown in Fig. 2(b). Convolutional blocks marked as ConvBlock1 through ConvBlock4 extract spatial correlation between feature maps. Average pooling layers are used to down-sample feature maps and extract high-order features. ConvBlock1 contains one Layer

T1-32 and three Layer T2-32, while the rest of the convolutional blocks contains two Layer T2 and the channel numbers are depending on the computational complexity and network performance.

Subsequently, a global covariance pooling [16] is used to capture second-order statistics of the last layer feature maps from ConvBlock4. The global covariance pooling replaces global average pooling. It computes the covariance matrix of the feature vectors and repeats Newton-Schulz iteration to estimate the matrix square root. The output of covariance pooling is fed into the FC layer and binary classification is performed to distinguish covers from stegos.

2.2 Block Regression Module

Research on steganalysis based on CNN has made great progress, but most works focus on the design of backbone network. In this paper, we further explore how to take full advantage of the features extracted by convolutions.

Yu et al. [25] proposed a multi-task learning CNN, which learns the pixel label of an input image as an assistant. They referred from the FCN [17] in semantic segmentation and see the pixels as classifiable objects. However, the number of unchanged pixels is too large compared with the modified ones. Moreover, the embedded data is mostly in $[-1, 1]$, which makes it hard to predict whether the pixel is changed or not. Therefore, we shift the target to block steganalysis and proposed the carefully designed block regression module, which depends on the number of changed pixels of image blocks. This solution relaxes the restriction on whether the corresponding area of the image is embedded data, and uses regression to approach the target. If we can take good advantage of the texture information in features, we can estimate the embedded pixels of blocks. This will in turn facilitate the learning of the features and push the detection performance.

The block regression module is shown in Fig. 3(a). Three types of feature maps from the backbone network are fed into the block regression module as inputs. Each input feature map is firstly processed by a convolutional layer and transformed into an embedding space with 64 channels. As a result, all the feature maps with different size are mapped into the same space, which provides a good foundation for the later fusion and reduce the dimension and computation complexity. The feature maps of size 32×32 are concatenated in stacks and processed by transpose convolution, where we obtain feature maps with a doubling of the size. These feature maps are also concatenated with the same-size maps and processed by regular convolution to get the final predict map. The predict map denotes the estimated modified pixels number of each 4×4 block in the image.

Eventually, the known ground truth map is used as a target to calculate the loss of mean square error (MSE). The process of calculating the ground truth map is shown in Fig. 4. To construct the map, the difference map between the covers and their corresponding stegos is required. To better comprehend the situation, we represent unchanged pixels with label 0, and embedded pixels with label 1. Then, the ground truth map can be obtained by counting the difference

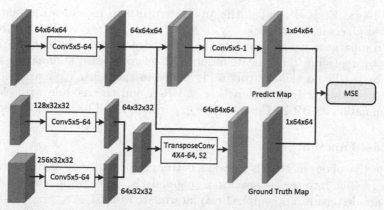

(a) Block regression module with feature maps concatenation.

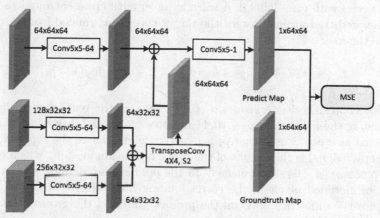

(b) Block regression module with element-wise summation.

Fig. 3. The block regression module using for feature fusion and auxiliary task.

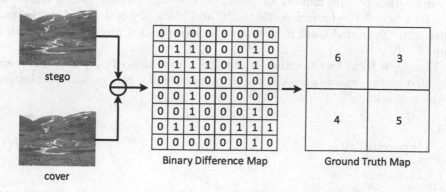

Fig. 4. The process of obtaining ground truth map from a cover and a stego.

map by block. Each element in the ground truth map indicates the number of embedded pixels in 4×4 block.

For comparison, we also explore the other structure of the block regression module by replacing the concatenation with element-wise summation on the feature maps. The detailed structure is shown in Fig. 3(b). We mark the block regression module with concatenation as BR-A and the module with element-wise summation as BR-B. Comparative experiments will be shown in Sect. 3.

2.3   Loss Function

The objective of our method is to gain a better performance by incorporating the block regression into the framework of steganalysis. To this end, two supervised signals are designed to accomplish two interrelated tasks.

One signal is used for classification. We denote the stegos with class label 1 and the covers with class label 0. A softmax layer with cross-entropy loss is used to get the predicted probability for the target class label ranged from 0 to 1 and calculate the loss:

$$L_{CLS} = -\frac{1}{N} \sum_{i=1}^{N} [y_i \times log(p_i) + (1 - y_i) \times log(1 - p_i)] \tag{1}$$

where N denotes the batch size, $y_i \in \{0, 1\}$ denotes the real label of the input image among the batch, and $p_i \in \{0, 1\}$ denotes the probability which the input is predicted as stego. Noted that p_i is exactly the output of the softmax.

The other signal is the output of the block regression module, which is a predict map of size 64×64. Each element in the predict map denotes the estimated number of modified pixels in the corresponding block. Here, MSE loss is used to measure the difference between the predict map and the ground truth map. Hence, the loss of block regression is:

$$L_{BR} = \frac{1}{N \times M} \sum_{i=1}^{N} \sum_{j=1}^{M} (\hat{z}_j - z_j)^2 \tag{2}$$

where M denotes the number of blocks in the input image, which equals to 64×64 when the input size is 256×256 and block size is 4×4. $\hat{z}_j$ is the real number in the ground truth map, and z_j is the estimated number in the predict map.

Finally, a total loss function is obtained from these two parts. They are weighted by hyperparameter λ in the total loss used for the overall optimization of the network:

$$L = L_{CLS} + \lambda \times L_{BR} \tag{3}$$

3   Experiments

3.1   Datasets

In our experiments, we consider three state-of-the-art content-adaptive steganographic algorithms: WOW [11], S-UNIWARD [12] and HILL [15]. Two datasets,

BOSSBase 1.01 [2] and BOWS2 [3] are used to test the performance of the proposed method. Each of the datasets contains 10,000 greyscale images with an original size of 512×512. Considering the training time limitation and computation capacity, we use "imresize" with default settings in MATLAB to resize them into 256×256. We randomly divided BOSSBase dataset into 3 independent parts in the ratio of 4:1:5. The training set includes all 10,000 pairs from BOWS2 dataset and 4,000 pairs randomly selected from BOSSBase dataset. The validation set and the test set respectively contain the remaining 1,000 and 5,000 pairs from BOSSBase dataset. Besides, we randomly split the BOSSBase dataset 3 times to construct three different datasets and performed the experiments on the same steganographic algorithm and payload 3 times on different training sets. In each training, we choose the best performing model on the validation set as the final model for testing. The average results of three training/validation/test sets will be reported in the following experiments.

3.2 Training Settings

Our experiments are carried out on a Nvidia RTX 2080 Ti GPU and the proposed CNN-based method is implemented on the Pytorch framework. Mini-batch stochastic gradient descent (SGD) are employed with momentum 0.9 and weight decay 5×10^{-4}. In the training phase, a batch size of 32 (16 pairs of cover-stego) is used. Data augmentation is performed on the training set, which is randomly rotated by $90°$, $180°$ and $270°$ and flipped horizontally. For the preprocessing layer, the 30 kernels are initialized with spam high-pass filters in SRM and their weights are updated during training. The truncated hyperparameter T in the TLU is set to 3. For the convolutional layers and transpose convolutions, the filter weights are initialized with Kaiming initializer [10] and the bias are disable. L2 regularization is used on the convolutions. For the fully-connected layer, a zero mean Gaussian distribution with standard deviation 0.01 is applied for initialization. For the loss function, we adjust the value of λ experimentally and find out that $\lambda = 0.2$ is an appropriate setting.

We construct the strategy of curriculum learning [4,19] for various payloads similar with previous works [5,22], which can be described symbolically as $0.5 \rightarrow 0.4 \rightarrow 0.3 \rightarrow 0.2 \rightarrow 0.1$. Firstly, the detector for payload 0.5 bit per pixel (bpp) is trained from scratch with an initial learning rate of 1×10^{-2}. The learning rate is divided by 10 at epoch 75, 125, 165 and the model is trained for 200 epochs. For instance, Fig. 5 shows the accuracy and loss(including image loss and block regression loss) convergence plots of our network when training and validating using embedding algorithm HILL at 0.5 bpp. We can observe that the accuracy value reaches stability at around 200th epoch. From Fig. 5(c), we observe that the block regression loss decreases during the training phase and converges with the image loss. This is a strong proof of the effectiveness of our method. Then, the detector for payload 0.4 bpp is fine-tuned with the pretrained model for payload 0.5 bpp and is trained for 100 epochs. The learning rate is set to 1×10^{-3} and is divided by 10 at epoch 50, 75. Similar approaches are used for payload 0.3 bpp, 0.2 bpp and 0.1 bpp.

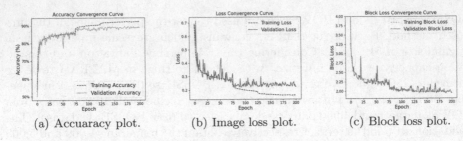

(a) Accuaracy plot.　　　(b) Image loss plot.　　　(c) Block loss plot.

Fig. 5. The accuracy, loss and block regression loss convergence plots of our method when training and validating using the HILL at 0.5 bpp.

3.3 Evaluation Metric

The performance of a steganalyzer was measured by the classification detection error rate on the test set, which is

$$P_E = min_{P_{FA}} \frac{1}{2} (P_{FA} + P_{MD}) \tag{4}$$

where P_{FA} and P_{MD} are the false-alarm and missed-detection probabilities.

3.4 Results

Ablation Study. As mentioned above, the kernels of the preprocessing layer are unfixed and optimizable in the training stage. To verify the selection of this setting, we perform experiments to compare the performance with fixed and unfixed kernels respectively. Fixed kernels of the preprocessing layer are also initialized with SRM filter sets, but they are not updated during training. The detection results on error rate are shown in Table 1 and the best results are underlined. From Table 1, we can observe that unfixed preprocessing layer has better performance than the fixed one.

Table 1. Detection error rates of different settings on the preprocessing layer against WOW, S-UNIWARD and HILL at 0.5 bpp.

Various settings	WOW	S-UNIWARD	HILL
Fixed kernels w/Abs	0.0695	0.0787	0.1204
Unfixed kernels w/o Abs	0.0647	0.0752	0.1152
Unfixed kernels w/Abs	**0.0635**	**0.0732**	**0.1104**

The use of abs layer in the first ConvBlock affects the detection error rate. In this experiment, we compare the network with abs layer to the network without abs layer. Noted that the layer T2 is the same as the layer T1 discarding the abs layer. The detection results are shown in Table 1. From Table 1, it is observed that the abs layer brings slight gain in performance of the network.

The training loss convergence curves of three different settings against HILL at 0.5 bpp are shown in Fig. 6. The performance of our network with three settings is compared as illustrated in the legend. It is observed that using abs layer in the first convolutional block and updating the kernels in the preprocessing layer can both decrease the training loss, accerlerate the convergence and improve the detection accuracy.

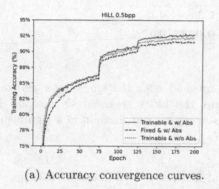
(a) Accuracy convergence curves.

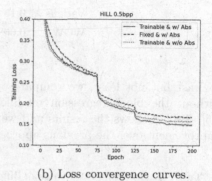
(b) Loss convergence curves.

Fig. 6. The training accuracy and loss convergence curves of different network settings on the preprocessing layer against HILL at 0.5 bpp.

To investigate the impact of different block sizes on network performance, we conducted experiments on block size 2×2, 4×4 and 8×8 respectively. Here, the structure of the block regression module needs to be fine-tuned to suit the output size. For instance, for 8×8 block, up-sampling operation is not required. The predict map is outputted from the concatenation of 32×32 feature maps. For 2×2 block, it is necessary to draw another branch from the backbone network and correspondingly modify the block regression module. The experiment results are shown in Table 2. Noted that the underlined data represent the best results. From Table 2, 4×4 block has the lowest error rate of detection. We attribute this to the appropriate and balance ratio between positive and negative samples in the 4×4 image block. Hence, we choose 4×4 as the block size of our method.

Table 2. Detection error rates of various block size against WOW, S-UNIWARD and HILL at 0.5 bpp.

Various block size	WOW	S-UNIWARD	HILL
2×2	0.0776	0.0851	0.1330
4×4	**0.0635**	**0.0732**	**0.1104**
8×8	0.0688	0.0780	0.1180

We also performed experiments to choose a suitable weight parameter λ for the block regression loss. Due to the auxiliary property of the block regression module task compared to the main task of image steganalysis, the λ should be small for a good result. Table 3 shows the results for different λ. We can observe that 0.2 is the best option for the weight parameter in our work. So we choose it for the continuous experiments.

Table 3. Detection error rates of different λ selected values against WOW at 0.5 bpp.

Various λ	0.15	0.2	0.25
WOW	0.0685	**0.0635**	0.0792

Last but not least, we compare our method with the single-task network without the block regression module and the block steganalysis method in [25]. Table 4 shows the results and we observe that our method is a significant improvement over the previous approaches.

Table 4. Detection error rates of different methods related to ours at 0.5 bpp.

Algorithms	Single-task network	Block steganalysis [25]	Our method
WOW	0.0750	0.0725	**0.0635**
S-UNIWARD	0.0847	0.0827	**0.0732**
HILL	0.1269	0.1235	**0.1104**

Comparison with Other Methods. To evaluate the effectiveness of our method, we compare it with some state-of-the-art steganalyzers, i.e. SRNet [5], Zhu-Net [26] and Cov-pool Net [8]. Noted that our backbone network is referenced from Cov-pool Net, so the comparison makes a lot of sense. We report the results at five payloads for WOW, S-UNIWARD and HILL. The detection error rates P_E of different CNN-based networks are shown in Table 4 and Fig. 7. Noted that the underlined data represent the best results for a particular embedding algorithm at a specific payload. We can observe that both structures of our methods (BR-A and BR-B) achieve better performance than other networks against various embedding algorithms and payloads.

Compared with the Cov-pool Net, our methods can boost the detection error rates by over 1% on average. For instance, for WOW at payload 0.4 bpp and 0.2 bpp, our method can obtain accuracies by 1.64% and 1.22% higher than Cov-pool Net. For HILL at payload 0.5 bpp and 0.2 bpp, the detection accuracy of ours is 2.10% and 1.57% better than Cov-pool Net. The corresponding training

Table 5. Detection error rates comparison using SRNet, Zhu-Net, Cov-pool Net and our method against WOW, S-UNIWARD and at different payloads.

Algorithms	Payload (bpp)	SRNet [5]	Zhu-Net [26]	Cov-pool net [8]	BR-A (Ours)	BR-B (Ours)
WOW	0.1	0.2707	0.2961	0.2654	**0.2515**	0.2528
	0.2	0.1824	0.2080	0.1753	**0.1631**	0.1647
	0.3	0.1368	0.1573	0.1273	**0.1148**	0.1207
	0.4	0.1095	0.1227	0.1011	**0.0847**	0.0870
	0.5	0.0772	0.0956	0.0750	**0.0635**	0.0645
S-UNIWARD	0.1	0.3218	0.3442	0.3076	**0.3004**	0.3016
	0.2	0.2258	0.2438	0.2090	**0.2031**	0.2054
	0.3	0.1620	0.1900	0.1458	**0.1379**	0.1398
	0.4	0.1195	0.1557	0.1104	**0.1000**	0.1007
	0.5	0.0877	0.1379	0.0847	**0.0732**	0.0746
HILL	0.1	0.3467	0.3744	0.3265	**0.3197**	0.3209
	0.2	0.2709	0.2925	0.2486	**0.2329**	0.2403
	0.3	0.2017	0.2424	0.1926	**0.1812**	0.1818
	0.4	0.1688	0.2054	0.1526	**0.1426**	0.1430
	0.5	0.1381	0.1783	0.1314	**0.1104**	0.1112

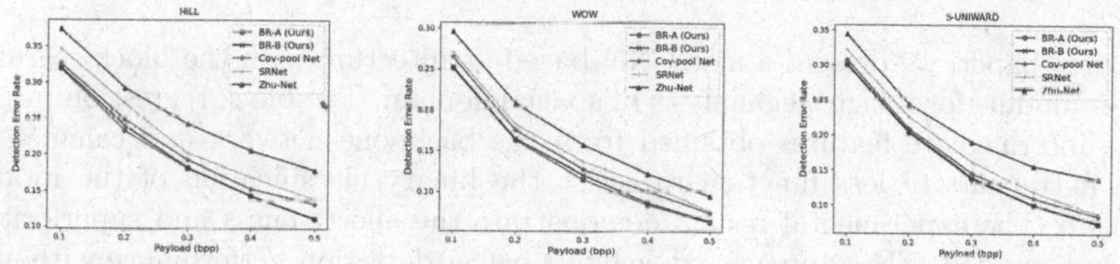

(a) HILL   (b) WOW   (c) S-UNIWARD

Fig. 7. Detection error rates comparison of different methods presented as line charts.

loss and accuracy curves are shown in Fig. 8. These results demonstrate that the proposed block regression module and the schemes of two-task learning can take good advantage of the features to improve the detection performance, which proves the effectiveness of our method (Table 5).

In terms of the different structures of the block regression module, we observe that BR-A is slightly better than BR-B. For instance, BR-A is 0.6% better than BR-B against WOW at 0.3 bpp and 0.74% better than BR-B against HILL at 0.2 bpp. Although the gap is not so obvious at other payloads and embedding algorithms, BR-A is better than BR-B overall. Moreover, both of these two structures outperform other existing methods, which verifies the effectiveness of block regression approach in image steganalysis.

3.5 Time Performance Comparison

We compare the training and testing time of the three networks: SRNet, Cov-pool Net and our network. Noted that the runtime environment for different networks is the same and has been introduced in training settings above. The results are shown in Table 4. We note that with the addition of a small quantity of parameters, our method takes 24 s longer than Cov-pool Net to train an epoch. This is within the acceptable range considering the improvement in detection accuracy. In addition, our network takes a lot less time for convergence than SRNet (Table 6).

Table 6. Time performance comparison of different methods.

Network	Training time/epoch	Testing time	Execution time to convergence
SRNet	252 s	50 s	15 h
Cov-pool net	155 s	41 s	9 h
Ours	179 s	43 s	10.5 h

4   Conclusion

In this paper, we present a new CNN-based architecture with the block regression module for image steganalysis in spatial domain. The block regression fuses the intermediate features obtained from the backbone network and calculates an extra part of loss function to assist the binary classification of the input image. The experimental results demonstrate the effectiveness and superiority of our method. The approach can achieve better detection performance without too much loss in time performance. Although the results are pretty good, some improvements are still considerable for the method. For instance, different payloads correspond to different modified pixel numbers, so the optimal block size and weight in the loss function should also vary for various payloads. Hence, we believe that our method still has potential to go further.

References

1. Artz, D.: Digital steganography: hiding data within data. IEEE Internet Comput. **5**(3), 75–80 (2001)
2. Bas, P., Filler, T., Pevný, T.: "Break our steganographic system": the ins and outs of organizing BOSS. In: Filler, T., Pevný, T., Craver, S., Ker, A. (eds.) IH 2011. LNCS, vol. 6958, pp. 59–70. Springer, Heidelberg (2011). https://doi.org/10.1007/978-3-642-24178-9_5
3. Bas, P., Furon, T.: Bows-2 (2007)
4. Bengio, Y., Louradour, J., Collobert, R., Weston, J.: Curriculum learning. In: Proceedings of the 26th Annual International Conference on Machine Learning, pp. 41–48 (2009)
5. Boroumand, M., Chen, M., Fridrich, J.: Deep residual network for steganalysis of digital images. IEEE Trans. Inf. Forensics Secur. **14**(5), 1181–1193 (2018)
6. Chaumont, M.: Deep learning in steganography and steganalysis. In: Digital Media Steganography, pp. 321–349. Elsevier (2020)

7. Denemark, T., Sedighi, V., Holub, V., Cogranne, R., Fridrich, J.: Selection-channel-aware rich model for steganalysis of digital images. In: 2014 IEEE International Workshop on Information Forensics and Security (WIFS), pp. 48–53. IEEE (2014)
8. Deng, X., Chen, B., Luo, W., Luo, D.: Fast and effective global covariance pooling network for image steganalysis. In: Proceedings of the ACM Workshop on Information Hiding and Multimedia Security, pp. 230–234 (2019)
9. Fridrich, J., Kodovsky, J.: Rich models for steganalysis of digital images. IEEE Trans. Inf. Forensics Secur. **7**(3), 868–882 (2012)
10. He, K., Zhang, X., Ren, S., Sun, J.: Delving deep into rectifiers: surpassing human-level performance on ImageNet classification. In: Proceedings of the IEEE International Conference on Computer Vision, pp. 1026–1034 (2015)
11. Holub, V., Fridrich, J.: Designing steganographic distortion using directional filters. In: 2012 IEEE International Workshop on Information Forensics and Security (WIFS), pp. 234–239. IEEE (2012)
12. Holub, V., Fridrich, J., Denemark, T.: Universal distortion function for steganography in an arbitrary domain. EURASIP J. Inf. Secur. **2014**(1), 1–13 (2014). https://doi.org/10.1186/1687-417X-2014-1
13. Ioffe, S., Szegedy, C.: Batch normalization: accelerating deep network training by reducing internal covariate shift. arXiv preprint arXiv:1502.03167 (2015)
14. LeCun, Y., Bottou, L., Bengio, Y., Haffner, P., et al.: Gradient-based learning applied to document recognition. Proc. IEEE **86**(11), 2278–2324 (1998)
15. Li, B., Wang, M., Huang, J., Li, X.: A new cost function for spatial image steganography. In: 2014 IEEE International Conference on Image Processing (ICIP), pp. 4206–4210. IEEE (2014)
16. Li, P., Xie, J., Wang, Q., Gao, Z.: Towards faster training of global covariance pooling networks by iterative matrix square root normalization. In: Proceedings of the IEEE Conference on Computer Vision and Pattern Recognition, pp. 947–955 (2018)
17. Long, J., Shelhamer, E., Darrell, T.: Fully convolutional networks for semantic segmentation. In: Proceedings of the IEEE Conference on Computer Vision and Pattern Recognition, pp. 3431–3440 (2015)
18. Qian, Y., Dong, J., Wang, W., Tan, T.: Deep learning for steganalysis via convolutional neural networks. In: Media Watermarking, Security, and Forensics 2015, vol. 9409, p. 94090J. International Society for Optics and Photonics (2015)
19. Qian, Y., Dong, J., Wang, W., Tan, T.: Learning and transferring representations for image steganalysis using convolutional neural network. In: 2016 IEEE International Conference on Image Processing (ICIP), pp. 2752–2756. IEEE (2016)
20. Tan, S., Li, B.: Stacked convolutional auto-encoders for steganalysis of digital images. In: 2014 Asia-Pacific Signal and Information Processing Association Annual Summit and Conference (APSIPA), pp. 1–4. IEEE (2014)
21. Xu, G., Wu, H.Z., Shi, Y.Q.: Structural design of convolutional neural networks for steganalysis. IEEE Signal Process. Lett. **23**(5), 708–712 (2016)
22. Ye, J., Ni, J., Yi, Y.: Deep learning hierarchical representations for image steganalysis. IEEE Trans. Inf. Forensics Secur. **12**(11), 2545–2557 (2017)
23. Yedroudj, M., Comby, F., Chaumont, M.: Yedroudj-Net: an efficient CNN for spatial steganalysis. In: 2018 IEEE International Conference on Acoustics, Speech and Signal Processing (ICASSP), pp. 2092–2096. IEEE (2018)
24. You, W., Zhang, H., Zhao, X.: A Siamese CNN for image steganalysis. IEEE Trans. Inf. Forensics Secur. **16**, 291–306 (2020)

25. Yu, X., Tan, H., Liang, H., Li, C.T., Liao, G.: A multi-task learning CNN for image steganalysis. In: 2018 IEEE International Workshop on Information Forensics and Security (WIFS), pp. 1–7. IEEE (2018)
26. Zhang, R., Zhu, F., Liu, J., Liu, G.: Depth-wise separable convolutions and multi-level pooling for an efficient spatial CNN-based steganalysis. IEEE Trans. Inf. Forensics Secur. **15**, 1138–1150 (2019)

Author Index

Printed in the United States
by Baker & Taylor Publisher Services